THE GREEN LANTERN GREEN ARROW

COLLECTION

DENNIS O'NEIL
WRITER

NEAL ADAMS
PENCILLER

NEAL ADAMS / DICK GIORDANO
FRANK GIACOIA / DAN ADKINS
BERNI WRIGHTSON
INKERS

CORY ADAMS / JACK ADLER
COLORISTS

JOHN C...
LETT...

D1294053

GREEN LANTERN/GREEN ARROW VOLUME ONE

DC Comics, 1700 Broadway, New York, NY 10019
A Warner Bros. Entertainment Company
Printed in Canada. First Printing.
ISBN: 1-4012-0224-1

Cover illustration by Neal Adams.

TABLE OF CONTENTS

INTRODUCTION BY

DENNIS O'NEIL

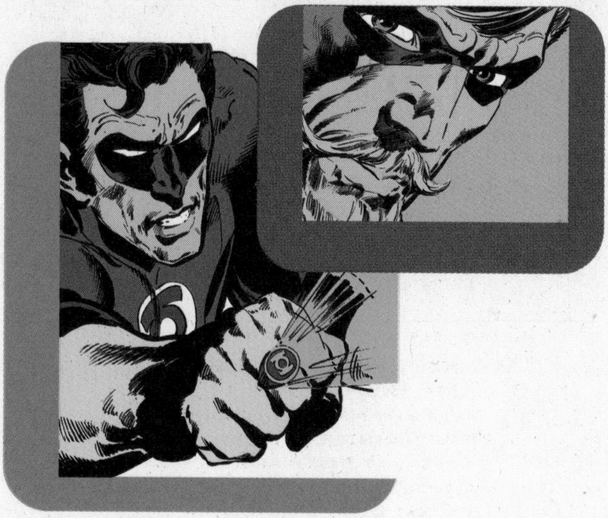

The temptation, here, is to cheat—to grin and shuffle and vamp until a respectable interval has passed, then quick bow and exit stage left without ever really saying anything. The reason is, I'm not sure these stories, or any stories, should be discussed; I think perhaps that stories should simply be enjoyed or not enjoyed, absorbed or forgotten. Archibald MacLeish said it: "A poem should not mean, but be."

But I guess that honoring a publisher's request for a hasty reminiscence won't do any harm—that is, it won't impair your reaction to the stories themselves. I won't presume to judge quality, something I'm obviously not qualified to do anyway. But I can comment on what the GREEN LANTERN/GREEN ARROW series meant to one of its creators—me—and how It came to be.

Of course, the question of how it came to be has two sets of answers, the first a large, historical, sociological, and a trifle cosmic. It has to do with those years marked indelibly, in Day Glo, on the soul of anyone who experienced them, the praised and damned Sixties. Although GREEN LANTERN/GREEN ARROW was published in 1970 and 1971, the stories belong to the previous decade as surely as do Owsley Acid, the Fillmore, protest marches, draft-card burning, the Johnson Presidency and those innocent, arrogant naifs, the Flower Children.

While they flourished, the Sixties were a period charged with exhilaration. The arts benefited from the gestalt of optimism and possibility, particularly the popular arts. Creativity, the flower children would say, is good, and so manifestations of creativity are good, too. But anything tainted with the Establishment—the University—was suspect: all these ponderous mainstream novels about middle-class mommies and daddies and their dready hang-ups, and music performed by a brigade of faceless penguins and allusion-ridden poetry full of foreign phrases, T.S. Eliot here and Ezra Pound there... draggy, dead, who needed it? Only professorial graybloods, livers of by-the-numbers lives who wouldn't recognize a sunbeam if it bit them, who knew only what they were supposed to know, not what they *did* know. For the rest of us, there was rock, the animal throb of Led Zeppelin and the angelic Beatles, singers of poems that could be danced to. And the science fiction writers, rediscovering mythology and that science and technology could be used exactly as bards once used magic, to excite mystery and wonder. And even the journalists, Tom Wolfe and the younger Village Voice contributors and patriarchal Norman Mailer, jettisoning the who-what-where-when-why straight jackets and lending fact the dazzle and insight once the exclusive property of fiction.

Oh, and comic books. I didn't mention the comics, did I? Well, the Sixties provided the comics with an audience: not anonymous children bribed to decorum with a copy of SUPERMAN, but a cadre of knowledgeable, enthusiastic readers. Some were ordinary adults rediscovering the joys of childhood and some were anti-establishment rebels. More anti-establishment than the comics you couldn't get. For 20 years the graybloods employed the term "comic book" as a synonym for "functional illiterate" and a few saw them as worse than trashy debasers of youthful sensibilities, corrupters of morals. With enemies like these, comics had to have a friend in the anti-establishment counterculture. But I think their appeal was deeper than the cultural mutiny. Comics offered color, flamboyance, legend, fantasy, humor, the highest of high adventure—things missing from the lives of kids whose usual amusement was a slice-of-life sitcom on a 17-inch monochromatic screen and, for that matter, from the lives of adults who had just lived through the leaden Eisenhower era. The national mood of playfulness and the graybloods' disdain made it socially acceptable to like what the comics had to offer.

Meanwhile, the comics and their staple characters, the super-heroes, had changed from their crudely energetic beginnings. The form, which has been termed "comic strip," "sequential art," "panel art"—this had existed since 1895 as a newspaper feature and as a newsstand commodity since the mid-1930s. It had evolved rules, conventions, formats, a rough aesthetic—a special language which melded image and word into a single unit of information. By trial and error, mostly, the early practitioners had learned to use that language and a generation had grown up learning from their successes and mistakes. The content of that language had been inspired by or borrowed from the pulp magazines, the American blue collar literature that eased the workingman's lot with stories of crime, cowboys, adventure (frequently in erotic climes) and fantasy masquerading as science fiction, all flavored with the tall tale tradition of the frontier. That hadn't altered much; that was still what people bought when they bought comics. But characterizations had gotten perhaps a bit more subtle, plots a bit more sophisticated. I suggest that writers and artists were becoming aware of their medium's potential, a potential already realized by such diverse talents as Will Eisner, Milton Caniff, and George Herriman. They may also have started to become aware of a genuinely appreciative readership, and decided these people were worth some effort.

That is what I consider the state of the comics to have been in 1970. I'd been working as a freelance writer for five years, the previous 18 months for DC Comics, when my favorite editor, Julius Schwartz—

But wait. I've sketched the era and the comic-book industry—the background—and we've arrived. It's the place where I must describe how a particular series, GREEN LANTERN/GREEN ARROW, came to be. I've got to tender the second set of answers I mentioned earlier. So I must enter a hesitant disclaimer. At the time, I wasn't taking notes, or keeping a diary or even paying a lot of attention. Like most young men, I was ad-libbing my life. Consequently, others may remember details differently. There are my memories, and they're not pure, either, because I've recounted them at parties, conventions, interviews—and, on headier afternoons, radio talk shows—and I've edited them to fit the audience on each of those hundreds of occasions. Who knows what I may have omitted so frequently as to lose it entirely? I feel like a physicist tracking a single electron; I can promise only a very sincere approximation of the truth. With that in mind—

Julius Schwartz asked me to do something with GREEN LANTERN. Sales of the title were slipping, apparently, and there were reasons not to cancel it. I'm not guessing what those reasons may have been. The business of comic-book publishing was unusually chaotic at the time, and sometimes decisions seemed to be made by consulting a drunken gypsy fortune teller. (One editor resigned after his boss justified a position by citing three different sales figures for the same magazine within 45 minutes.) For me, the assignment was unusually interesting and potentially exciting: I had an idea. For a while, I'd been wondering if it might be possible to combine my various professional and personal concerns. Before migrating to New York, I'd worked on a Midwestern daily and before that I'd edited a Navy newspaper, in 1967 I'd produced a short book on presidential elections and I was regularly contributing political and social reportage to a news magazine. I suppose I considered myself as much journalist as fiction writer. And there, in the reporter-fabulist combination, was a glimmer: the "new journalists"—Wolfe, Mailer, Jimmy Breslin, Pete Hamill, Gene Marine, Hunter S. Thompson, these men I admired tremendously—weren't they combining fiction techniques with reporting? Could a comic-book equivalent of the new journalism be possible? Probably not. But something—? Not fact, not current events, presented in panel art rooted in the issues of the day? Now *there* was a possibility.

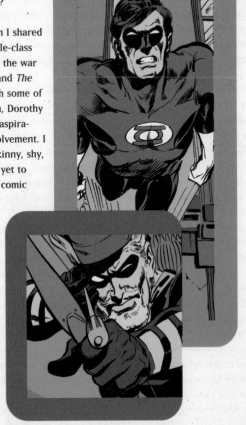

I was peripherally involved in those issues, a nondistinction I shared with millions of liberal, vaguely well-meaning people of middle-class origin. I signed petitions. I went on marches. I argued against the war and supported Martin Luther King. I subscribed to *Ramparts* and *The Catholic Worker*. I lived in the East Village and consorted with some of the headline makers—David Miller, Daniel and Philip Berrigan, Dorothy Day, Paul Krasner—and, I would have insisted, I shared their aspirations. But I was not like them. I lacked their capacity for involvement. I was not a leader. I had the charisma of library paste. I was skinny, shy, self-effacing, with some killer shark personal problems I had yet to recognize. However, I was getting published, every month, in comic books. And suddenly, I was being asked to revamp *Green Lantern*. It was an opportunity to stop lurking at the edges of the social movements I admired and participate by dramatizing their concerns.

The question was, how?

Okay, try this: What would happen if we put a super-hero in a real-life setting dealing with a real-life problem?

Begin with the character. Green Lantern was, in effect, a cop. An incorruptible cop, to be sure, with noble intentions but still a cop, a crypto-fascist; he took orders, he committed violence at the behest of commanders whose authority he did not question. If you showed him a law being broken, his instinct would be to strike at the lawbreaker without ever asking any *whys*. Wasn't this the mentality that sent American troops into Korea and Vietnam? That brought

Federal marshals' clubs down on the heads of lunch-counter protestors? Wasn't this the cowboy authoritarianism responsible for the mess we were in? Not that Green Lantern was evil, he or any of the other heroes who championed Nineteenth-Century American at the expense of Twentieth-Century justice—and at the expense of the environment and perhaps the survival of the planet. No, nor were their flesh-and-blood counterparts evil. They just never had cause to doubt their assumptions. All right, there was a place to begin: I'd give them doubts.

As I mulled possible plots, I realized that Green Lantern needed a foil, someone to argue with. Green Arrow was the logical choice, and not because of their first names, either. Green Arrow—GA for short—was the utility infielder of DC's heroes. He'd been in existence since 1941, but he'd never been considered popular enough to warrant being given his own title. For the past several years he'd been in THE JUSTICE LEAGUE OF AMERICA, which was functioning in part as a sort of holding company for characters who had lost their own magazines during a marketing recession: has-beens, like Hawkman, and never-quite-wases like GA. I'd taken advantage of fluid status in a Justice League story—had him lose his fortune and in so doing precipitate his friends into a crisis. I'd been given permission to do this because none of the editors at DC seemed to care about him; nobody had a vested interest in GA's status quo. Coincidentally, Neal Adams had altered GA's appearance, redesigned his costume and given him a beard while illustrating a story Bob Haney wrote for BRAVE & BOLD. So Green Arrow had a new wardrobe and a new life style already. Why not give him a new characterization, particularly since the old one was so undefined that nobody really knew what it was? He could be a lusty, hot-tempered anarchist to contrast with the cerebral, sedate model citizen who was Green Lantern. They would form the halves of a dialogue on the issues we chose to dramatize.

We would dramatize issues. We would not resolve them. We were not in the polemic business. I was smart enough to know enormously complex problems couldn't be dissected within the limitations of a 25-page comic book and humble enough to know that I didn't have solutions anyway. Still, I cherished the notion that the stories might be socially useful: I could hope they might awaken youngsters, eight- or nine-year-olds, to the world's dilemmas and these children, given such an early start, might be able to find solutions in their maturity. My generation, and my father's, had grown up ignorant; my son's didn't have to. Maybe I could help, a little.

It's necessary to guess at exactly what happened after we decided that Green Arrow was to be Green Lantern's co-star. Probably, I submitted a plot outline to Julie Schwartz, then listened to his suggestions and improvements; that was how we usually operated. (Later, the outline became unnecessary. We established such a rapport that I could tell him briefly what I wanted to do and he would trust me to produce printable material, as I would trust him to correct my mistakes.)

Then I wrote "No Evil Shall Escape My Sight." I must have felt giddy with liberation. It was as though the Angel Gabriel appeared and said the commandments didn't apply to me any longer. I was being *told* to break the rules. I didn't have to worry about writing stuff that couldn't possibly offend anyone, anywhere, at any time, a stricture which had handicapped comic-book writers terribly since the early 1950s. And, though I didn't realize it, I was to be given another liberty implicitly forbidden to comic-book writers: my characters could change—*would* change, all of them; the alteration of Green Arrow from playboy to anarchist was only the beginning. Events would transform their perceptions and personalities. I was, in short, being allowed drama, and a rich gift it was. These liberties would confer on me a final and splendid gift: I would be able to put into Green Arrow's speeches some of my own feelings, some of the pain and bewilderment recent events had caused. The comic-book form could be, for the duration of the assignment, a means of self-expression, as well as a means of amusing strangers. How wonderful. It would be like writing those first short stories when I was a teenager: the excitement of making a narrative from raw material the soul provides which is, to the fledgling writer, its own incomparable reward. Of course, rules can protect as well as restrict; without them, I would be dancing naked, I would have few excuses for failure. But I wasn't considering risks. I was satisfied that I had done a worthy script, and I was reasonably certain Gil Kane's drawings would complement my prose. I expected him to do an especially nice job with the rooftop scene in which the ancient black man introduces Green Lantern to ghetto-bitterness.

The three panels concluding that scene are among the most reproduced panels in comic-book history. But Gil didn't draw them. Instead, "No Evil Shall Escape My Sight" went to a relative newcomer, Neal Adams. Again, I don't know why. But Neal did get the assignment instead of Gil, the regular GREEN LANTERN artist, and that was an extension of what was, to me, a gloriously satisfying collaboration, begun about a year earlier with some Batman stories. Neal was wonderful. He consistently equaled or exceeded the pictures my mind formed while I was writing the stories. Every time, he did it. Every one of the 150 images in that story would be better than I'd imagined it. To see my descriptions so totally realized was a spooky and stunning experience and I think it inspired me to innovate, to improve. I felt confident that Neal would be there for me. Neal would deliver. And Neal did, on GREEN LANTERN/GREEN ARROW as well as the Ra's al Ghul and Talia saga we did for the BATMAN and DETECTIVE titles. He is an immensely gifted individual, with his own approach to comic art, basically a realist whose imagination can stretch the parameters of things-as-they-are to include the extravagant, the fantastic. "If super-heroes existed," he once told me, "they'd have to look the way I draw them."

We are vastly different people, Neal Adams and I. A few years ago we were together in Chicago on a public relations junket, and after a full day in Neal's company I began to realize we agreed on nothing, zero, zip, from which movies to watch on the hotel's closed circuit television to the merits of the paintings hanging in the Art Institute to which of the pretty women strolling on Michigan Avenue we would most enjoy discussing Schopenhauer with. While we were actually collaborating, though, we hummed in unison like tuning forks, our psyches were twins. Only the best marriages approximate the closeness of such an artistic pairing. As marriages have an alarming tendency to culminate in divorce, close collaborations generate jealousy, rivalry and pettiness. Neal and I never became actively hostile, but the relationship did get strained and edgy toward the end. It might have gotten worse had we continued working exclusively with each other.

We didn't. GREEN LANTERN/GREEN ARROW was cancelled after a run of 13 issues, not counting a reprint—number 88—that Julie had to include because of a deadline problem. We had every reason to believe the series was a huge success: it was mentioned in hundreds of newspapers and magazines, it got us invited to universities and television shows, it brought in heaps of mail. The response was overwhelmingly favorable. We received a few hate letters and veiled threats, but even these were perversely flattering; I'll always welcome bigots as enemies. As Joseph Conrad said, "You shall judge a man by his foes as well as his friends."

Despite all the attention, however, the series was abruptly discontinued. Bad sales were given for the reason. Bad sales were always given as the reason, for everything. Perhaps the drunken gypsy had gazed into her crystal and frowned. Or perhaps the sales *were* bad. I doubt that I'll ever know, any more than I'll ever know the true origin of the universe, the mermaid's song, or what it's like to actually read Marcel Proust.

The series wasn't quite finished. Julie decided to ease it into limbo by doing a final story to run three months in the back pages of THE FLASH. For our farewell, we decided to depart from our usual modus operandi and concentrate on our heroes' personalities instead of their relationship with society. The eight pages per month we were restricted to forced technical limitations on us, resulting in a certain awkwardness in pacing and storytelling. Still, I think this three-parter is one of the most interesting things we did: the conflict in it arises mostly from contradictions in Green Arrow's character, the same contradictions that prompted him into his cherished role as costumed rebel. For once, we were turning inward instead of outward and perhaps unintentionally commenting on the failure of the dream of the Sixties. Would we have continued in that vein—exploring our heroes' souls—if we'd been given the opportunity? I can't say. Probably not. I think we would have returned to social drama and since we'd already done stories on every current problem I was genuinely concerned about, soon I would have been scouring the back pages of *The New York Times* for ideas. Eventually, we'd have degenerated into self-parody. Cause-of-the-Month Comics. As it was, we took the lessons we'd learned and moved on, a bit the better for wear. For over a year we'd involved ourselves in a project that had engaged all the craft we had, and doing that had demonstrated to us exactly what our skills were and how they could be bettered. We'd done work that was both personally and professionally meaningful. We'd had our moment of fame. We'd influenced others of our kind. We had fun.

I don't like to think of these stories often. They are a relic of a person I'll never again be, of a time as spiritually remote as the Pleistocene. To gaze at them would be to look in the wrong direction. But I'm glad they exist, and I hope you enjoy them.

—Dennis O'Neil
1983

POSTSCRIPT

As I reread the words above, I am me looking back at another version of myself who was, in turn, looking back at another version of *himself.* I feel a little like the hero of one of those time-travel stories in which the hero is sucked back through his history to meet himself-as-he-was *then.* I also feel just a bit like Methuselah. The introduction that precedes this postscript was written 17 years ago and described events that occurred more than a decade earlier. I'm not sure I remember much about the Dennis O'Neil who typed that essay; a lot has happened on the way to him becoming me and, as he observes, he/I do not keep journals, nor even always pay attention. He had more hair than me, of that I'm sure. But was he living in Soho? Greenwich Village? Or was that the year of the ill-fated sojourn in Brooklyn? Was he editing for Marvel yet? Or was he still freelancing? Had he discovered computers or was he still pounding the ancient Olympia portable? Without doing some research, I'm not sure.

But I'll trust him. He was closer, both temporally and psychologically, to the genesis of the GREEN LANTERN/GREEN ARROW series reprinted in this book than I, and I know of no reason why he might have lied. Let's accept that he told the truth as he knew it and thank him for the effort.

Having lived through those 17 years since he existed, I could tell him things he might find interesting. He'd want to know what happened to comics, for example. I'd be happy to inform him that, not only are they still around, they're more or less what he was familiar with and they're even populated by many of the characters that had occupied his professional attention. But they've mutated a bit, comics have. Graphic novels, miniseries, maxiseries, Prestige

Format publications—most of these existed embryonically, if at all, in 1983 and today the shops are full of them, as well as the slim, magazine-format publications he and others of his era thought "comic books" had to be. And here's a fact that would astonish him: some comics creators have become millionaires—not many, but some. For a while, there were more comics *buyers* than comics *readers*. Tens of thousands of people bought comics, particularly if they had a *#1* on the cover, and immediately stashed them in plastic bags because of the vastly erroneous assumption that comics were not a vehicle for stories, but an *investment*. They weren't—at least, they weren't a very *good* investment, and they weren't *any* kind of investment for long. Still, the comics-as-capitalism delusion lasted long years for some writers, pencillers and inkers, as well as a few shrewd businessmen, to become quite prosperous.

The Dennis O'Neil of 1983 might be further surprised to hear that some observers consider comics' brief explosion of fiduciary glory to have been harmful to comics as an art form. These observers, who *may* be cynics, skeptics or plain old crybabies and are probably *not* among the millionaires mentioned earlier, say that young talent got too rich too fast and weren't ever motivated to learn the storytellers' craft; nor did they have a chance to serve an apprenticeship with an experienced mentor. The result is comics in which narrative is sacrificed to gaudy graphics by creators who may not know exactly what narrative *is*.

But there's a counterargument the younger O'Neil might want to heed. It's this: comics have made considerable artistic advances in the last decade and a half. Art Spiegelman's *Maus* is so commanding and important that the Pulitzer Committee had to award it their coveted Prize. Howard Cruse's *Stuck Rubber Baby* tells a coming-of-age story that's as compelling and unmistakably honest as any I know of. These are comic books. Admittedly, they're extraordinary comic books which have, deservedly, gotten noticed by non-comics audiences. (Most comics aren't this good, true, but neither is most of anything else.) But *Maus* and *Stuck Rubber Baby* and several dozen lesser-recognized works of great merit are, at the end of the day, *comics,* and they demonstrate that the form is capable of much more than low-common-denominator action yarns. And even those action yarns, most often featuring costumed super-heroes like our friends Green Arrow and Green Lantern, are just occasionally executed with a precision of theme and, especially, character, that artists and writers working in other forms might learn from.

So, I might say to my younger self, comics are both better and worse artistically. Financially? As a business? Well, at the moment, that aspect is pretty grim; we haven't recovered from the implosion following the mass realization that comics are not even Krugerrands, much less Microsoft stock. But doomsayers have predicted comics' demise before, wrongly. Wait and see. Certainly, the way comics are produced and sold will have to change, but everything is changing all the time. (When that's no longer true, we may be in *cosmic* trouble.)

And finally—

The youngish me would be curious about the GREEN LANTERN/GREEN ARROW series. Not *too* curious: he never allowed his conscious self to worry much about his status or the reputation of past work. As he wrote, referring to the GL/GA stories, "To gaze at them would be to look in the wrong direction." Amen, I say to him—*shout* to him— from a distance of 17 years. But I think he would be interested to know that the series is sometimes credited with introducing serious themes and characterization to super-hero comics, and with helping them on their slow, torturous journey to the decent amount of recognition they're beginning to have. And he would be absolutely delighted to learn that he achieved his most revered goal "...I cherished the notion that the stories might be socially useful," he wrote, "I could hope they might awaken youngsters, eight- or nine-year-olds, to the world's dilemmas..." People have approached me at conventions, signings and lectures to say that, yes, these stories stimulated them to question and think. The earlier Dennis would relish that, but he might be even more pleased to hear, at those public events, readers talking about how much they *enjoyed* the series.

I imagine him holding this fine, utterly gorgeous volume, surprised that the stories are still remembered, amazed that they're considered worthy of such a handsome reprinting, and smiling as he wonders whether a few more of his fellow humans might find something to enjoy here.

Dennis O'Neil, the Elder
June, 2000

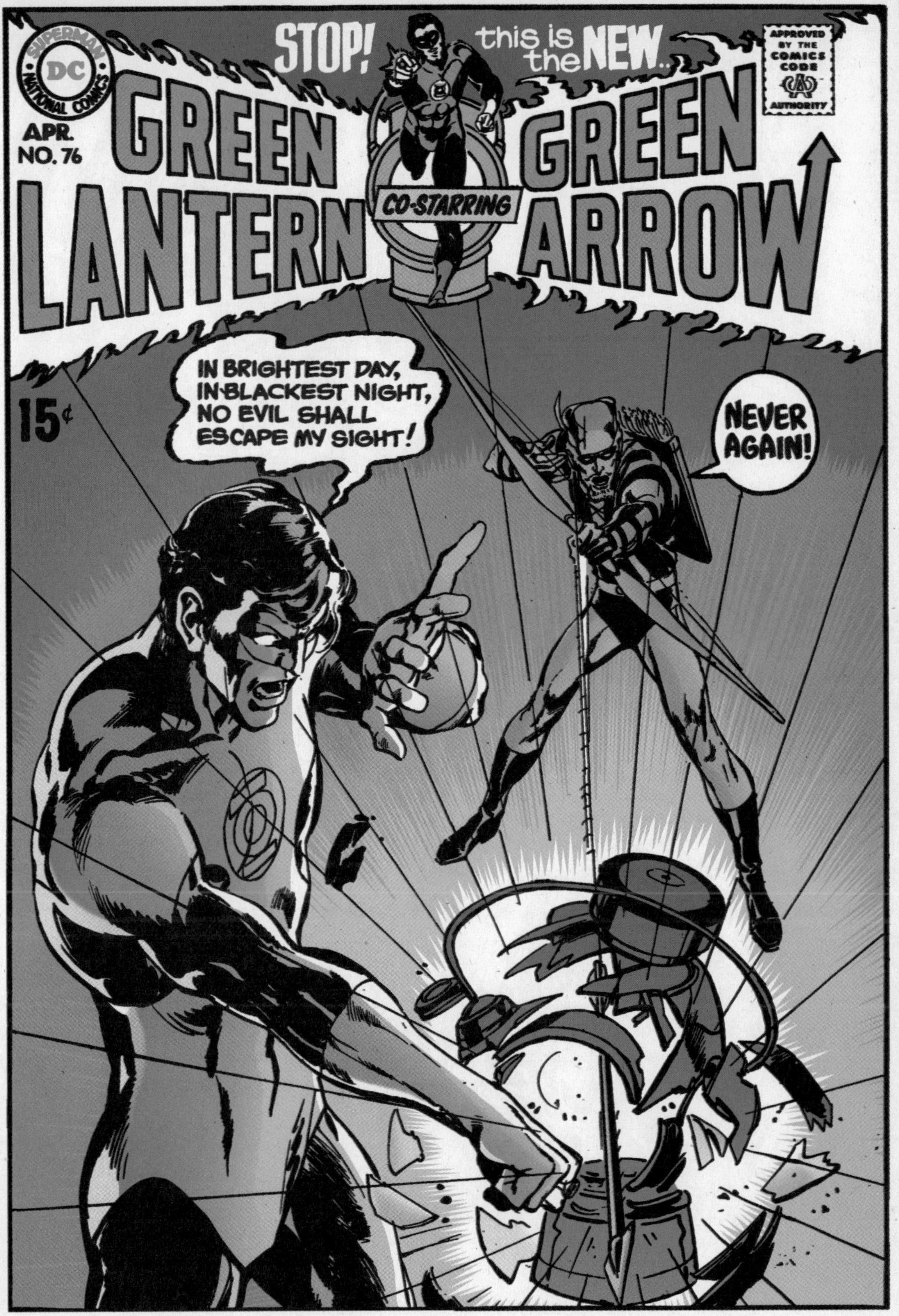
STOP! this is the NEW..
APPROVED BY THE COMICS CODE AUTHORITY
SUPERMAN DC NATIONAL COMICS
APR. NO. 76
GREEN LANTERN CO-STARRING GREEN ARROW
15¢
IN BRIGHTEST DAY, IN BLACKEST NIGHT, NO EVIL SHALL ESCAPE MY SIGHT!
NEVER AGAIN!

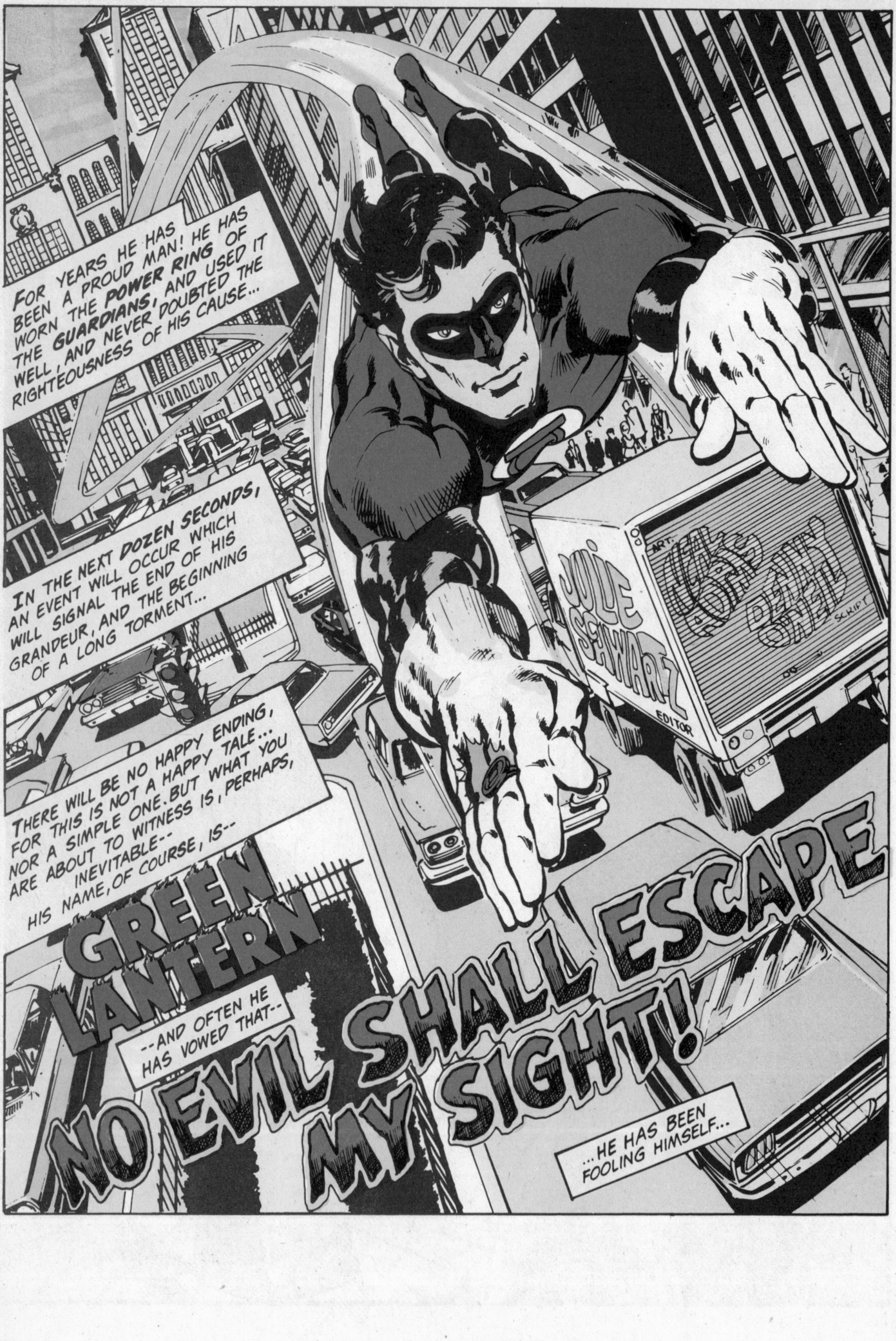
FOR YEARS HE HAS BEEN A PROUD MAN! HE HAS WORN THE **POWER RING** OF THE **GUARDIANS**, AND USED IT WELL, AND NEVER DOUBTED THE RIGHTEOUSNESS OF HIS CAUSE...
IN THE NEXT **DOZEN SECONDS**, AN EVENT WILL OCCUR WHICH WILL SIGNAL THE END OF HIS GRANDEUR, AND THE BEGINNING OF A LONG TORMENT...
THERE WILL BE NO HAPPY ENDING, FOR THIS IS NOT A HAPPY TALE... NOR A SIMPLE ONE. BUT WHAT YOU ARE ABOUT TO WITNESS IS, PERHAPS, INEVITABLE--
HIS NAME, OF COURSE, IS--
GREEN LANTERN
--AND OFTEN HE HAS VOWED THAT--
NO EVIL SHALL ESCAPE MY SIGHT!
...HE HAS BEEN FOOLING HIMSELF...
JULIE SCHWARTZ
EDITOR
ART
SCRIPT

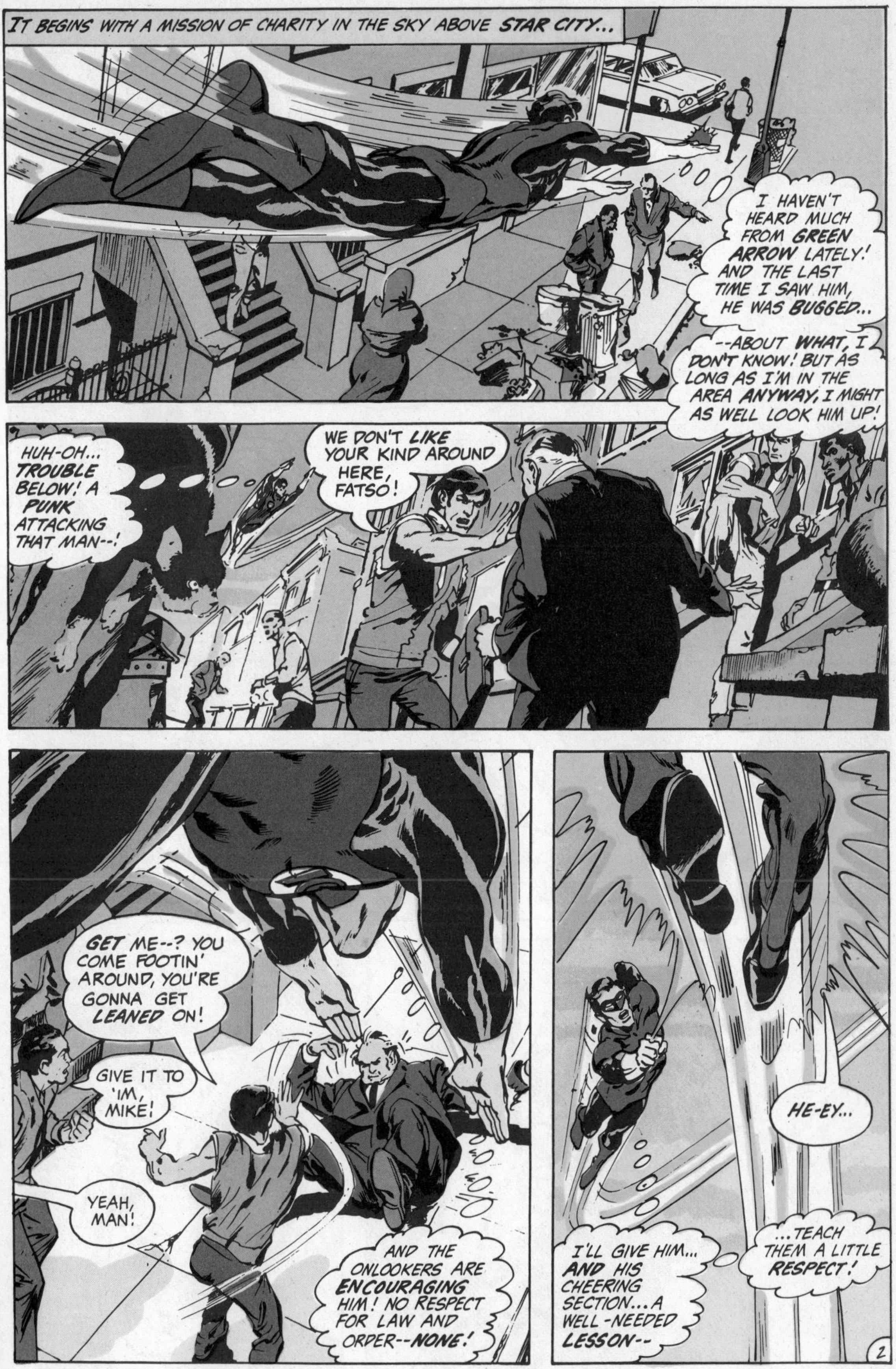

IT BEGINS WITH A MISSION OF CHARITY IN THE SKY ABOVE STAR CITY...
I HAVEN'T HEARD MUCH FROM GREEN ARROW LATELY! AND THE LAST TIME I SAW HIM, HE WAS BUGGED...
--ABOUT WHAT, I DON'T KNOW! BUT AS LONG AS I'M IN THE AREA ANYWAY, I MIGHT AS WELL LOOK HIM UP!
HUH-OH... TROUBLE BELOW! A PUNK ATTACKING THAT MAN--!
WE DON'T LIKE YOUR KIND AROUND HERE, FATSO!
GET ME--? YOU COME FOOTIN' AROUND, YOU'RE GONNA GET LEANED ON!
GIVE IT TO 'IM, MIKE!
YEAH, MAN!
AND THE ONLOOKERS ARE ENCOURAGING HIM! NO RESPECT FOR LAW AND ORDER--NONE!
HE-EY...
I'LL GIVE HIM... AND HIS CHEERING SECTION... A WELL-NEEDED LESSON--
...TEACH THEM A LITTLE RESPECT!
2

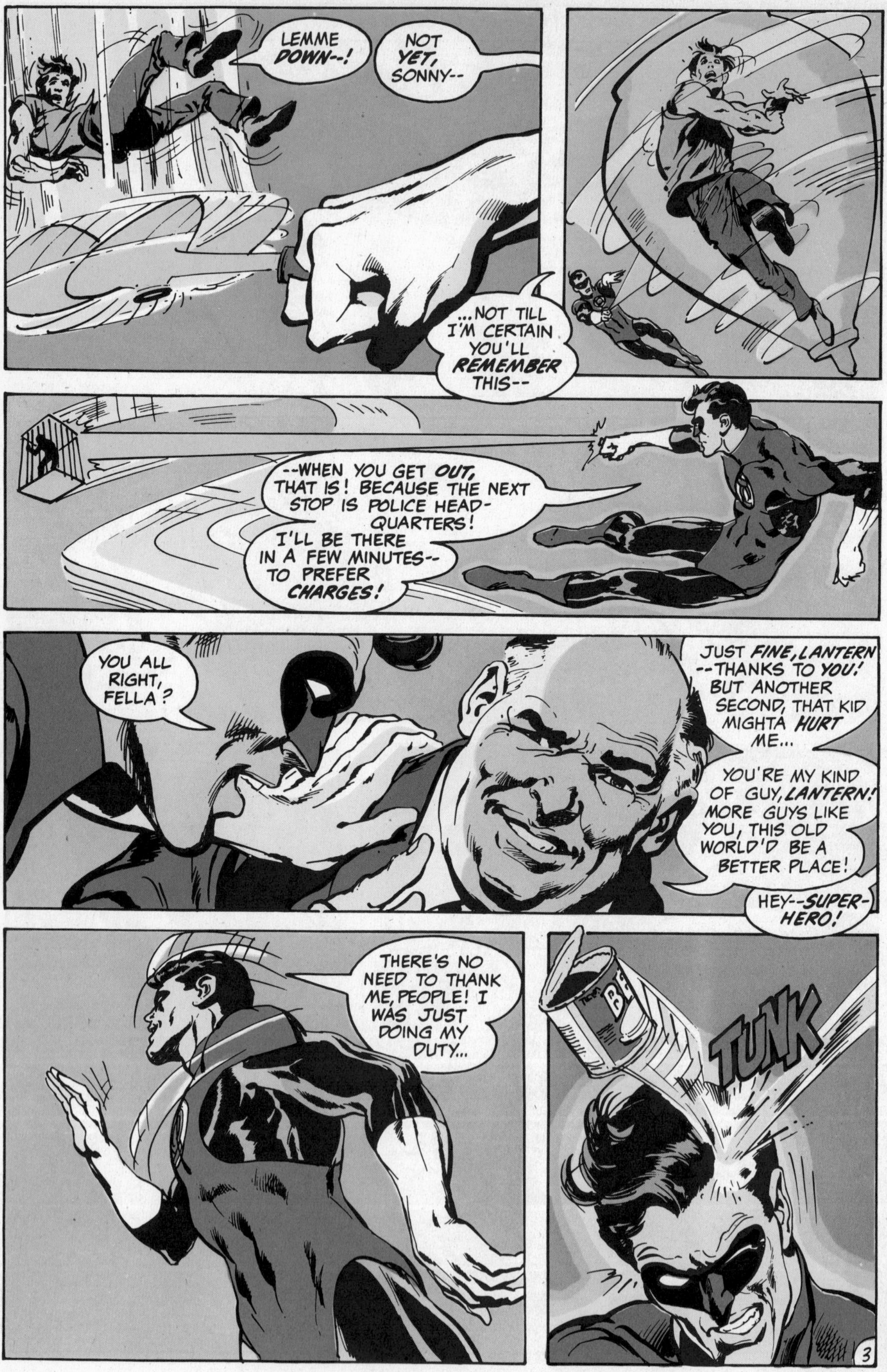
LEMME DOWN--!
NOT YET, SONNY--
...NOT TILL I'M CERTAIN YOU'LL REMEMBER THIS--
--WHEN YOU GET OUT, THAT IS! BECAUSE THE NEXT STOP IS POLICE HEAD-QUARTERS!
I'LL BE THERE IN A FEW MINUTES--TO PREFER CHARGES!
YOU ALL RIGHT, FELLA?
JUST FINE, LANTERN --THANKS TO YOU! BUT ANOTHER SECOND, THAT KID MIGHTA HURT ME...
YOU'RE MY KIND OF GUY, LANTERN! MORE GUYS LIKE YOU, THIS OLD WORLD'D BE A BETTER PLACE!
HEY--SUPER-HERO!
THERE'S NO NEED TO THANK ME, PEOPLE! I WAS JUST DOING MY DUTY...
TUNK
3

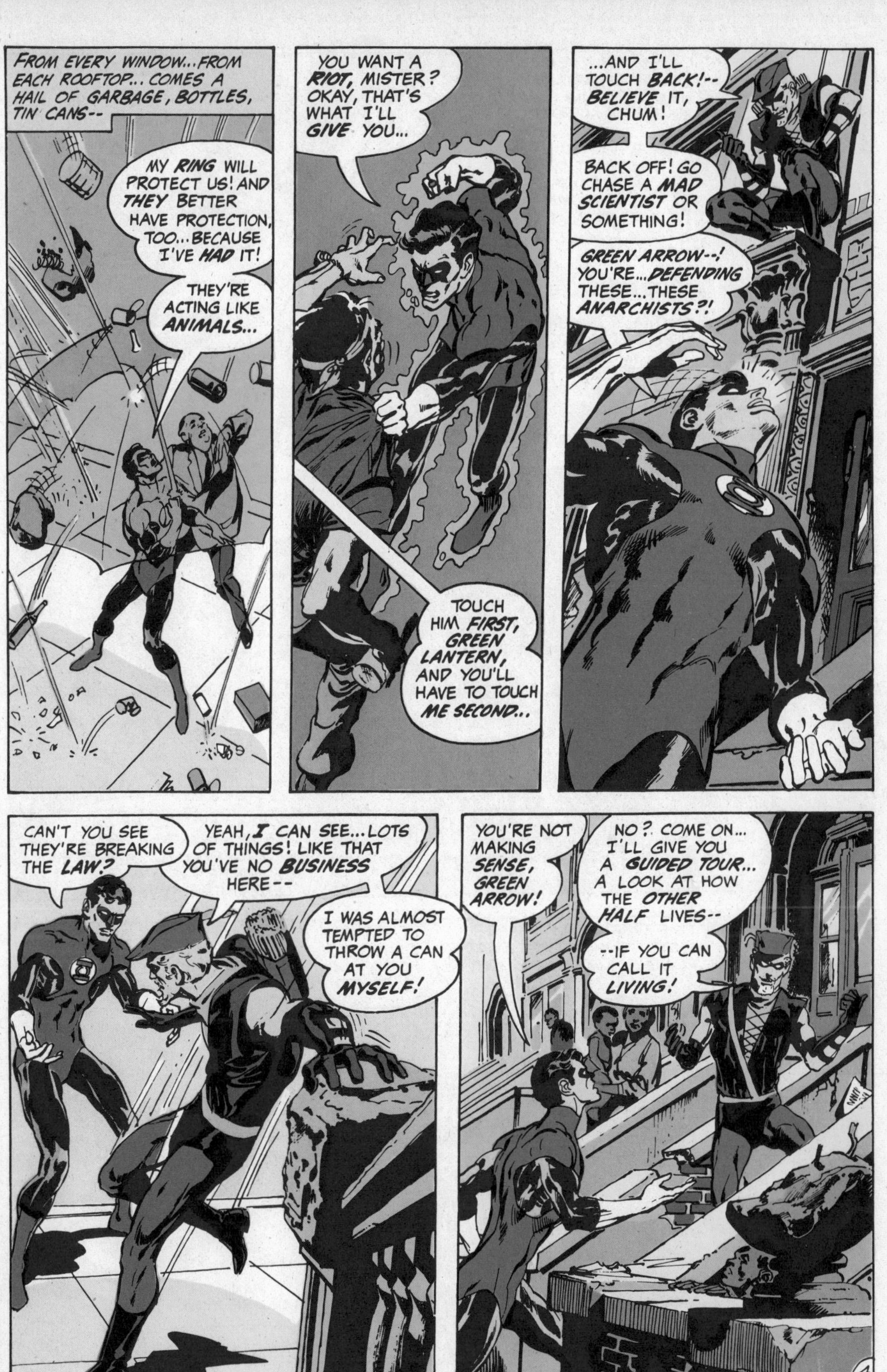
FROM EVERY WINDOW... FROM EACH ROOFTOP... COMES A HAIL OF GARBAGE, BOTTLES, TIN CANS--
MY RING WILL PROTECT US! AND THEY BETTER HAVE PROTECTION, TOO... BECAUSE I'VE HAD IT!
THEY'RE ACTING LIKE ANIMALS...
YOU WANT A RIOT, MISTER? OKAY, THAT'S WHAT I'LL GIVE YOU...
TOUCH HIM FIRST, GREEN LANTERN, AND YOU'LL HAVE TO TOUCH ME SECOND...
...AND I'LL TOUCH BACK!-- BELIEVE IT, CHUM!
BACK OFF! GO CHASE A MAD SCIENTIST OR SOMETHING!
GREEN ARROW--! YOU'RE... DEFENDING THESE... THESE ANARCHISTS?!
CAN'T YOU SEE THEY'RE BREAKING THE LAW?
YEAH, I CAN SEE... LOTS OF THINGS! LIKE THAT YOU'VE NO BUSINESS HERE--
I WAS ALMOST TEMPTED TO THROW A CAN AT YOU MYSELF!
YOU'RE NOT MAKING SENSE, GREEN ARROW!
NO? COME ON... I'LL GIVE YOU A GUIDED TOUR... A LOOK AT HOW THE OTHER HALF LIVES--
--IF YOU CAN CALL IT LIVING!
4

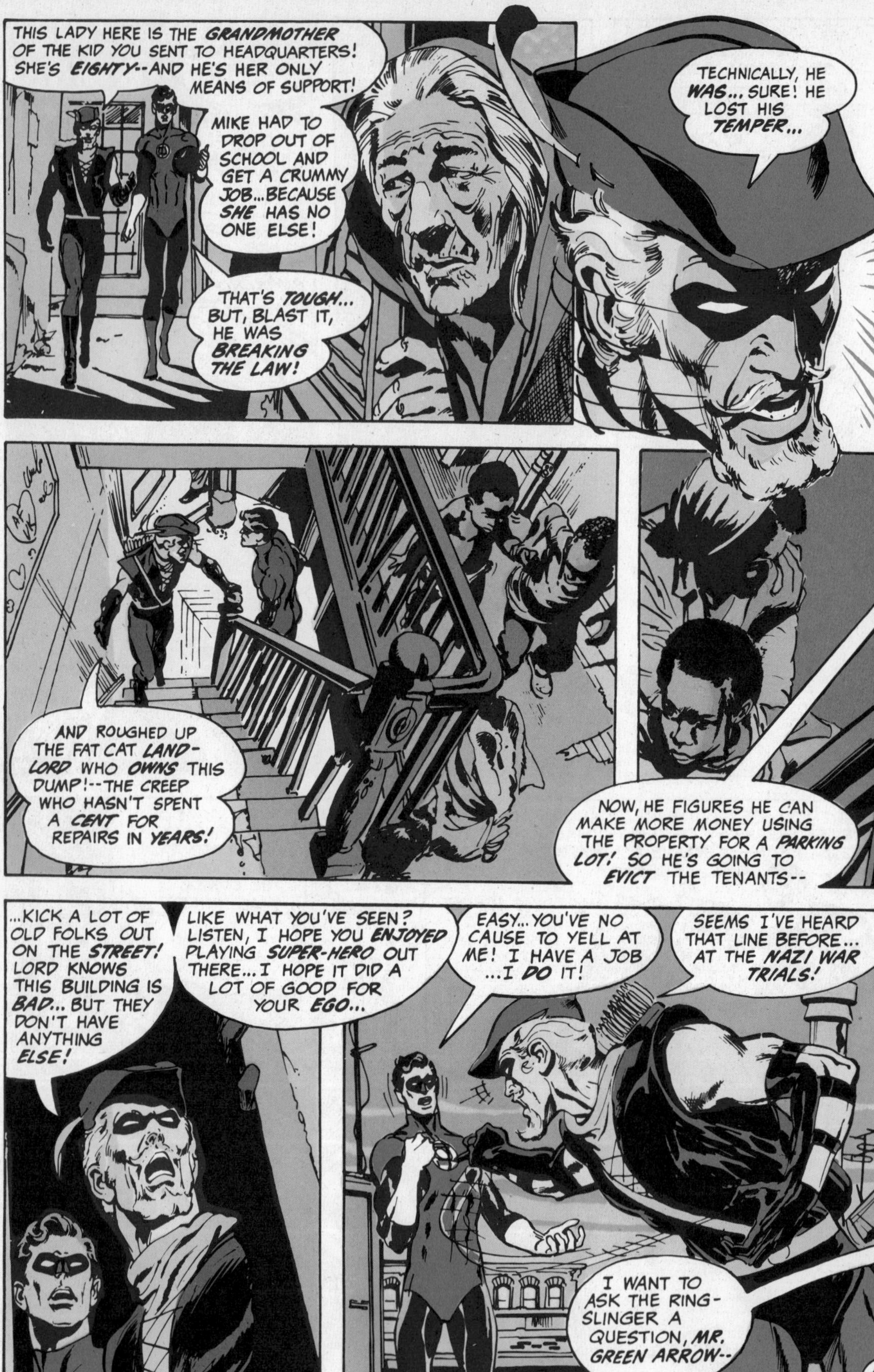
THIS LADY HERE IS THE GRANDMOTHER OF THE KID YOU SENT TO HEADQUARTERS! SHE'S EIGHTY--AND HE'S HER ONLY MEANS OF SUPPORT!
MIKE HAD TO DROP OUT OF SCHOOL AND GET A CRUMMY JOB...BECAUSE SHE HAS NO ONE ELSE!
THAT'S TOUGH... BUT, BLAST IT, HE WAS BREAKING THE LAW!
TECHNICALLY, HE WAS... SURE! HE LOST HIS TEMPER...
AND ROUGHED UP THE FAT CAT LANDLORD WHO OWNS THIS DUMP!--THE CREEP WHO HASN'T SPENT A CENT FOR REPAIRS IN YEARS!
NOW, HE FIGURES HE CAN MAKE MORE MONEY USING THE PROPERTY FOR A PARKING LOT! SO HE'S GOING TO EVICT THE TENANTS--
...KICK A LOT OF OLD FOLKS OUT ON THE STREET! LORD KNOWS THIS BUILDING IS BAD... BUT THEY DON'T HAVE ANYTHING ELSE!
LIKE WHAT YOU'VE SEEN? LISTEN, I HOPE YOU ENJOYED PLAYING SUPER-HERO OUT THERE...I HOPE IT DID A LOT OF GOOD FOR YOUR EGO...
EASY...YOU'VE NO CAUSE TO YELL AT ME! I HAVE A JOB ...I DO IT!
SEEMS I'VE HEARD THAT LINE BEFORE... AT THE NAZI WAR TRIALS!
I WANT TO ASK THE RING-SLINGER A QUESTION, MR. GREEN ARROW--
5

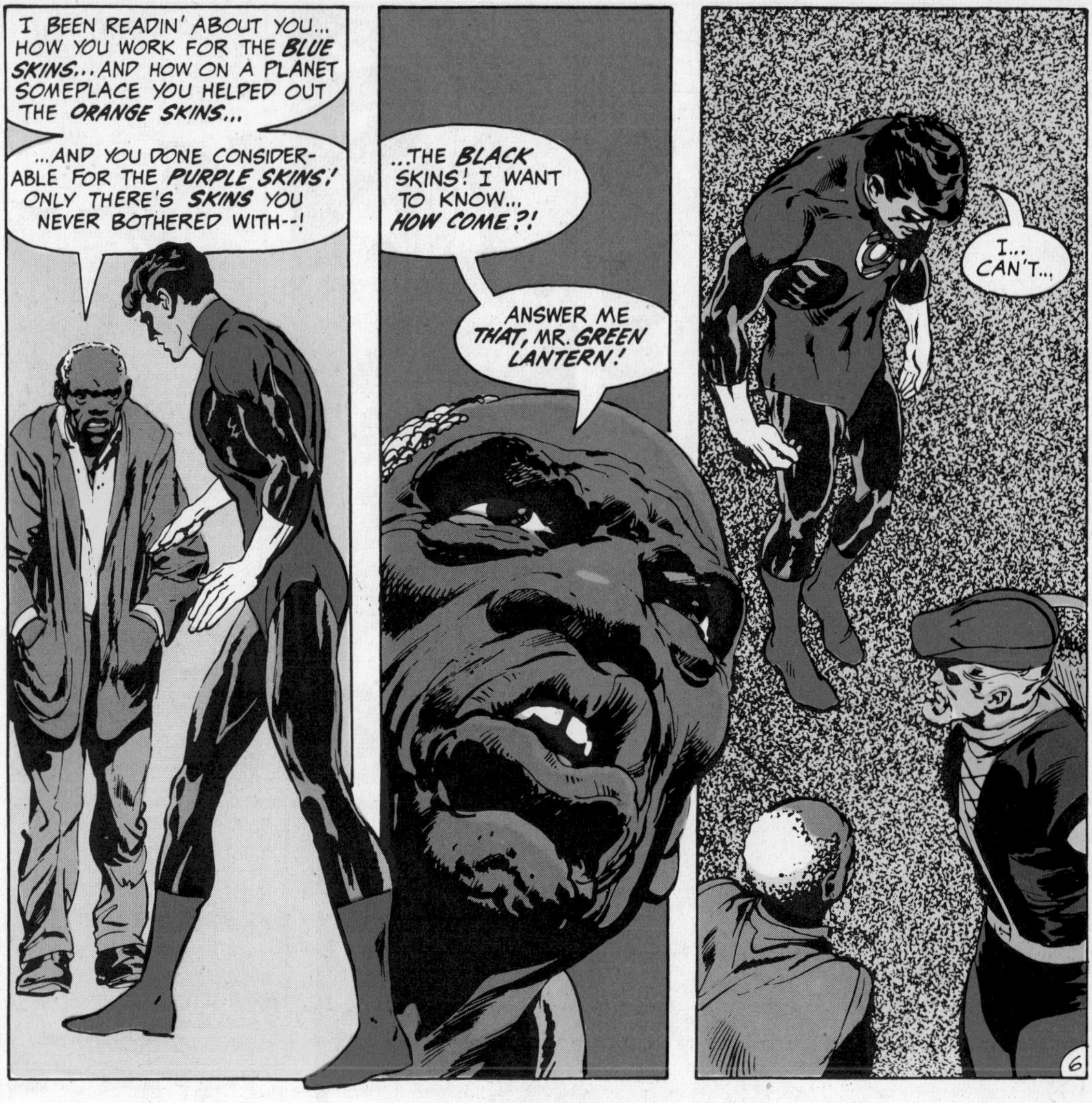
I BEEN READIN' ABOUT YOU... HOW YOU WORK FOR THE BLUE SKINS... AND HOW ON A PLANET SOMEPLACE YOU HELPED OUT THE ORANGE SKINS...
...AND YOU DONE CONSIDER-ABLE FOR THE PURPLE SKINS! ONLY THERE'S SKINS YOU NEVER BOTHERED WITH--!
...THE BLACK SKINS! I WANT TO KNOW... HOW COME?!
ANSWER ME THAT, MR. GREEN LANTERN!
I... CAN'T...
6

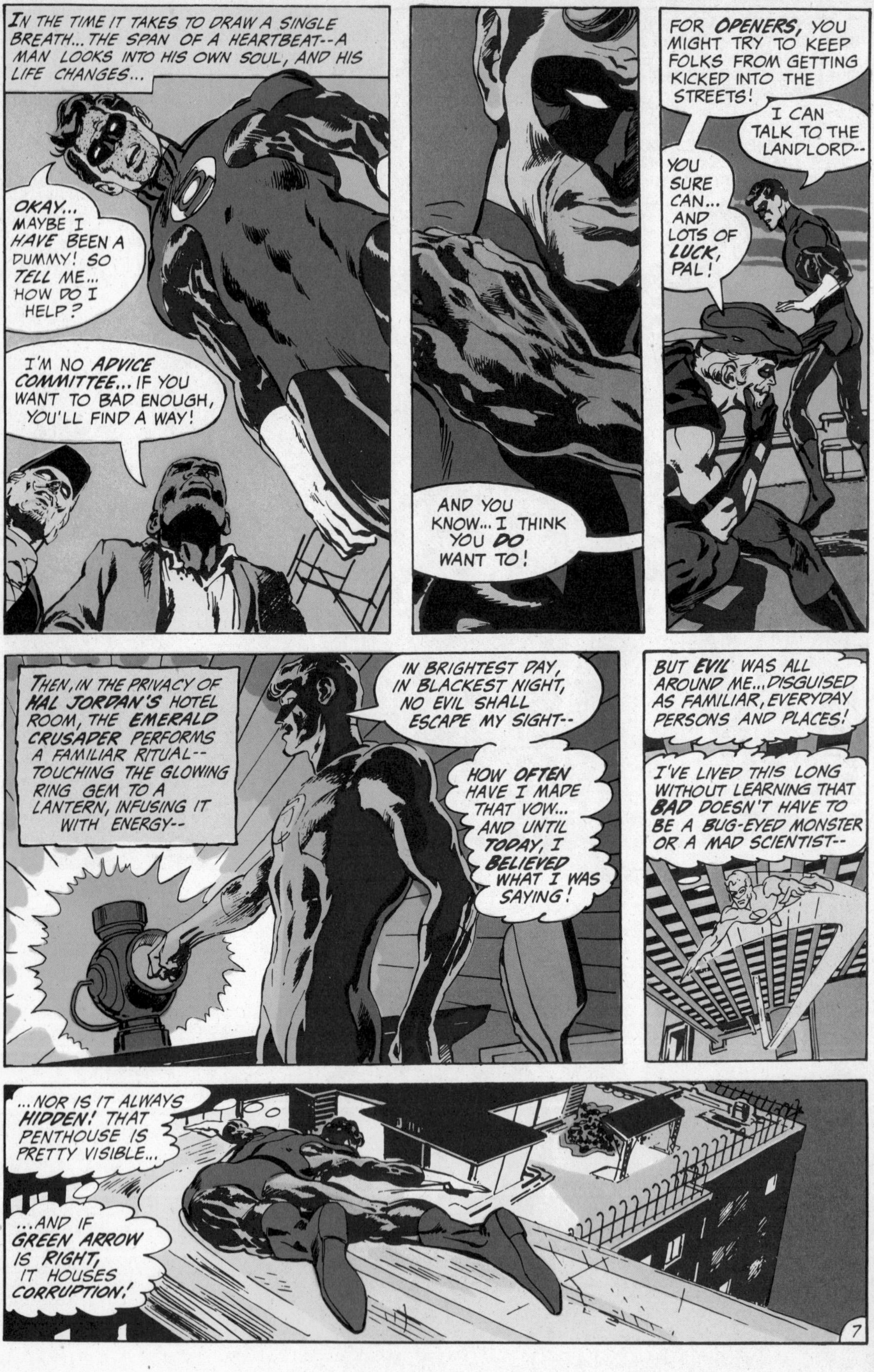
IN THE TIME IT TAKES TO DRAW A SINGLE BREATH... THE SPAN OF A HEARTBEAT--A MAN LOOKS INTO HIS OWN SOUL, AND HIS LIFE CHANGES...
OKAY... MAYBE I HAVE BEEN A DUMMY! SO TELL ME... HOW DO I HELP?
I'M NO ADVICE COMMITTEE... IF YOU WANT TO BAD ENOUGH, YOU'LL FIND A WAY!
AND YOU KNOW... I THINK YOU DO WANT TO!
FOR OPENERS, YOU MIGHT TRY TO KEEP FOLKS FROM GETTING KICKED INTO THE STREETS!
I CAN TALK TO THE LANDLORD--
YOU SURE CAN... AND LOTS OF LUCK, PAL!
THEN, IN THE PRIVACY OF HAL JORDAN'S HOTEL ROOM, THE EMERALD CRUSADER PERFORMS A FAMILIAR RITUAL-- TOUCHING THE GLOWING RING GEM TO A LANTERN, INFUSING IT WITH ENERGY--
IN BRIGHTEST DAY, IN BLACKEST NIGHT, NO EVIL SHALL ESCAPE MY SIGHT--
HOW OFTEN HAVE I MADE THAT VOW... AND UNTIL TODAY, I BELIEVED WHAT I WAS SAYING!
BUT EVIL WAS ALL AROUND ME... DISGUISED AS FAMILIAR, EVERYDAY PERSONS AND PLACES!
I'VE LIVED THIS LONG WITHOUT LEARNING THAT BAD DOESN'T HAVE TO BE A BUG-EYED MONSTER OR A MAD SCIENTIST--
...NOR IS IT ALWAYS HIDDEN! THAT PENTHOUSE IS PRETTY VISIBLE...
...AND IF GREEN ARROW IS RIGHT, IT HOUSES CORRUPTION!
7

JUBAL SLADE...

WHY, YA-AS! TO WHAT DO I OWE THE...AH...*PLEASURE*, GREEN LANTERN?

For a long hour, the EMERALD CRUSADER argues, insists, and finally pleads...

...TO NO AVAIL!

HEH, HEH...I MEAN YOU REALLY BREAK ME UP, *LANTERN!* YOU AND YOUR *BLEEDING HEART*--

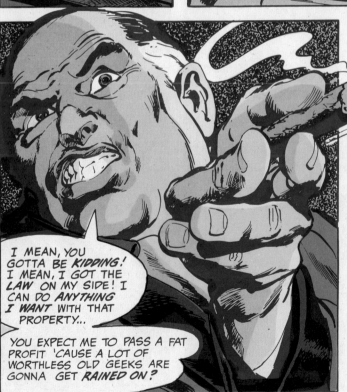

I MEAN, YOU GOTTA BE *KIDDING!* I MEAN, I GOT THE *LAW* ON MY SIDE! I CAN DO *ANYTHING I WANT* WITH THAT PROPERTY...

YOU EXPECT ME TO PASS A FAT PROFIT 'CAUSE A LOT OF WORTHLESS OLD GEEKS ARE GONNA GET *RAINED ON?*

DON'T *TOUCH* ME...

WHY NOT, TOUGHY? YOU AFRAID YOU'LL *BRUISE?*

BOYS, ESCORT THE CRUSADER-- *OUT!*

8

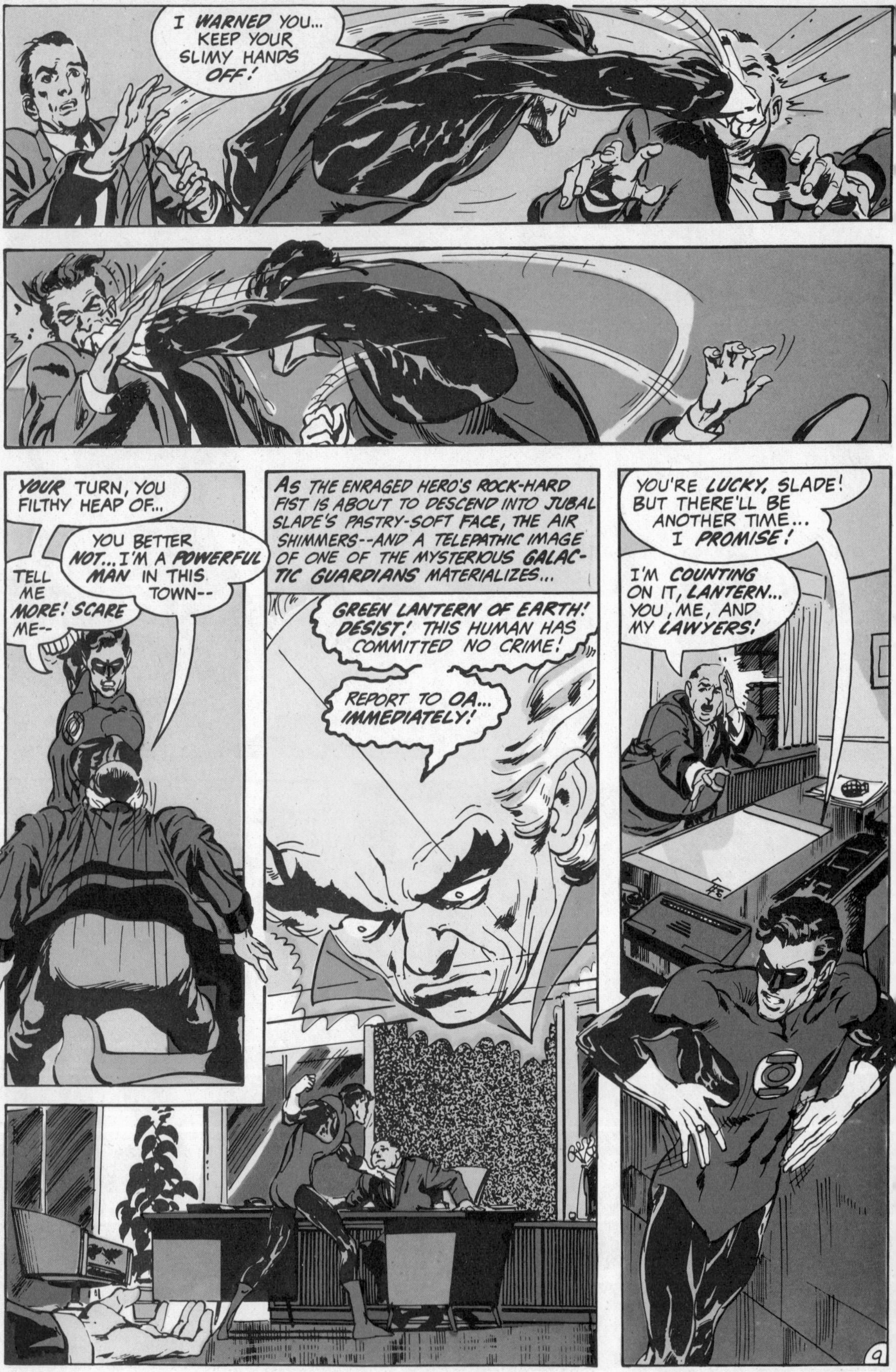

I WARNED YOU... KEEP YOUR SLIMY HANDS OFF!
YOUR TURN, YOU FILTHY HEAP OF...
YOU BETTER NOT... I'M A POWERFUL MAN IN THIS TOWN--
TELL ME MORE! SCARE ME--
AS THE ENRAGED HERO'S ROCK-HARD FIST IS ABOUT TO DESCEND INTO JUBAL SLADE'S PASTRY-SOFT FACE, THE AIR SHIMMERS--AND A TELEPATHIC IMAGE OF ONE OF THE MYSTERIOUS GALACTIC GUARDIANS MATERIALIZES...
GREEN LANTERN OF EARTH! DESIST! THIS HUMAN HAS COMMITTED NO CRIME!
REPORT TO OA... IMMEDIATELY!
YOU'RE LUCKY, SLADE! BUT THERE'LL BE ANOTHER TIME... I PROMISE!
I'M COUNTING ON IT, LANTERN... YOU, ME, AND MY LAWYERS!
9

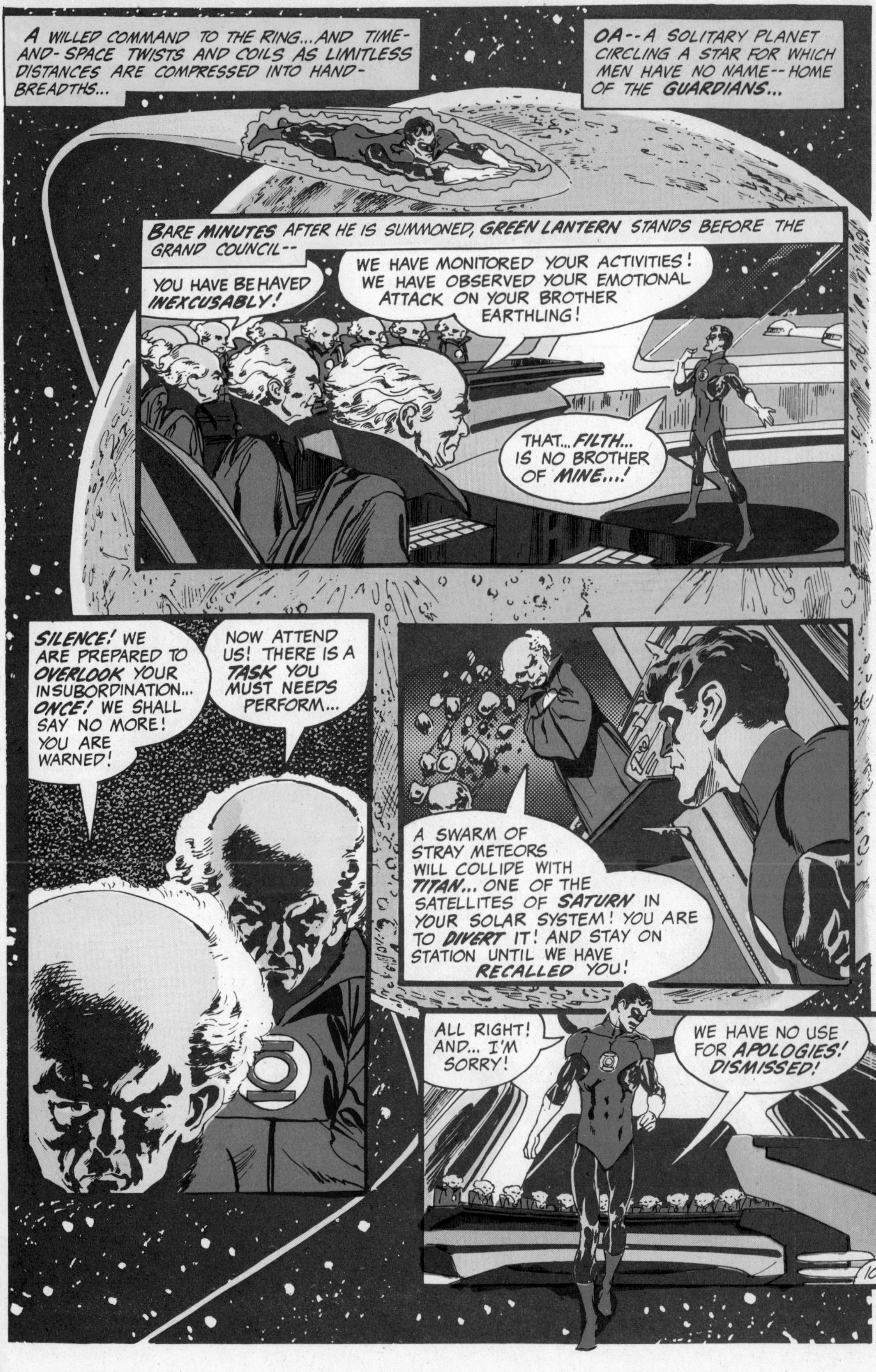
A WILLED COMMAND TO THE RING... AND TIME-AND-SPACE TWISTS AND COILS AS LIMITLESS DISTANCES ARE COMPRESSED INTO HAND-BREADTHS...
OA--A SOLITARY PLANET CIRCLING A STAR FOR WHICH MEN HAVE NO NAME--HOME OF THE GUARDIANS...
BARE MINUTES AFTER HE IS SUMMONED, GREEN LANTERN STANDS BEFORE THE GRAND COUNCIL--
YOU HAVE BEHAVED INEXCUSABLY!
WE HAVE MONITORED YOUR ACTIVITIES! WE HAVE OBSERVED YOUR EMOTIONAL ATTACK ON YOUR BROTHER EARTHLING!
THAT... FILTH... IS NO BROTHER OF MINE...!
SILENCE! WE ARE PREPARED TO OVERLOOK YOUR INSUBORDINATION... ONCE! WE SHALL SAY NO MORE! YOU ARE WARNED!
NOW ATTEND US! THERE IS A TASK YOU MUST NEEDS PERFORM...
A SWARM OF STRAY METEORS WILL COLLIDE WITH TITAN... ONE OF THE SATELLITES OF SATURN IN YOUR SOLAR SYSTEM! YOU ARE TO DIVERT IT! AND STAY ON STATION UNTIL WE HAVE RECALLED YOU!
ALL RIGHT! AND... I'M SORRY!
WE HAVE NO USE FOR APOLOGIES! DISMISSED!
10

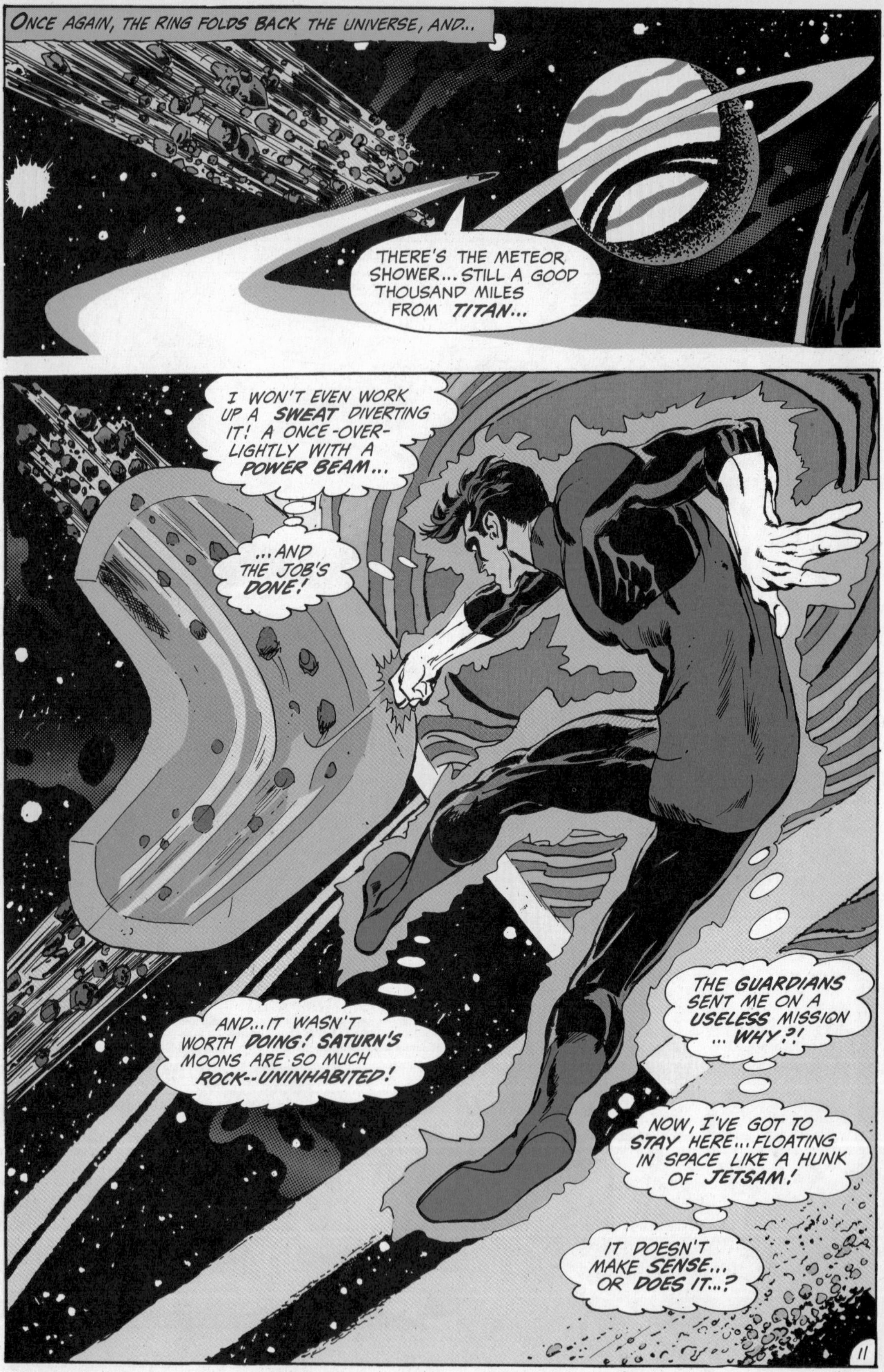
ONCE AGAIN, THE RING FOLDS BACK THE UNIVERSE, AND...
THERE'S THE METEOR SHOWER... STILL A GOOD THOUSAND MILES FROM TITAN...
I WON'T EVEN WORK UP A SWEAT DIVERTING IT! A ONCE-OVER-LIGHTLY WITH A POWER BEAM...
...AND THE JOB'S DONE!
AND...IT WASN'T WORTH DOING! SATURN'S MOONS ARE SO MUCH ROCK--UNINHABITED!
THE GUARDIANS SENT ME ON A USELESS MISSION ... WHY?!
NOW, I'VE GOT TO STAY HERE...FLOATING IN SPACE LIKE A HUNK OF JETSAM!
IT DOESN'T MAKE SENSE... OR DOES IT...?
11

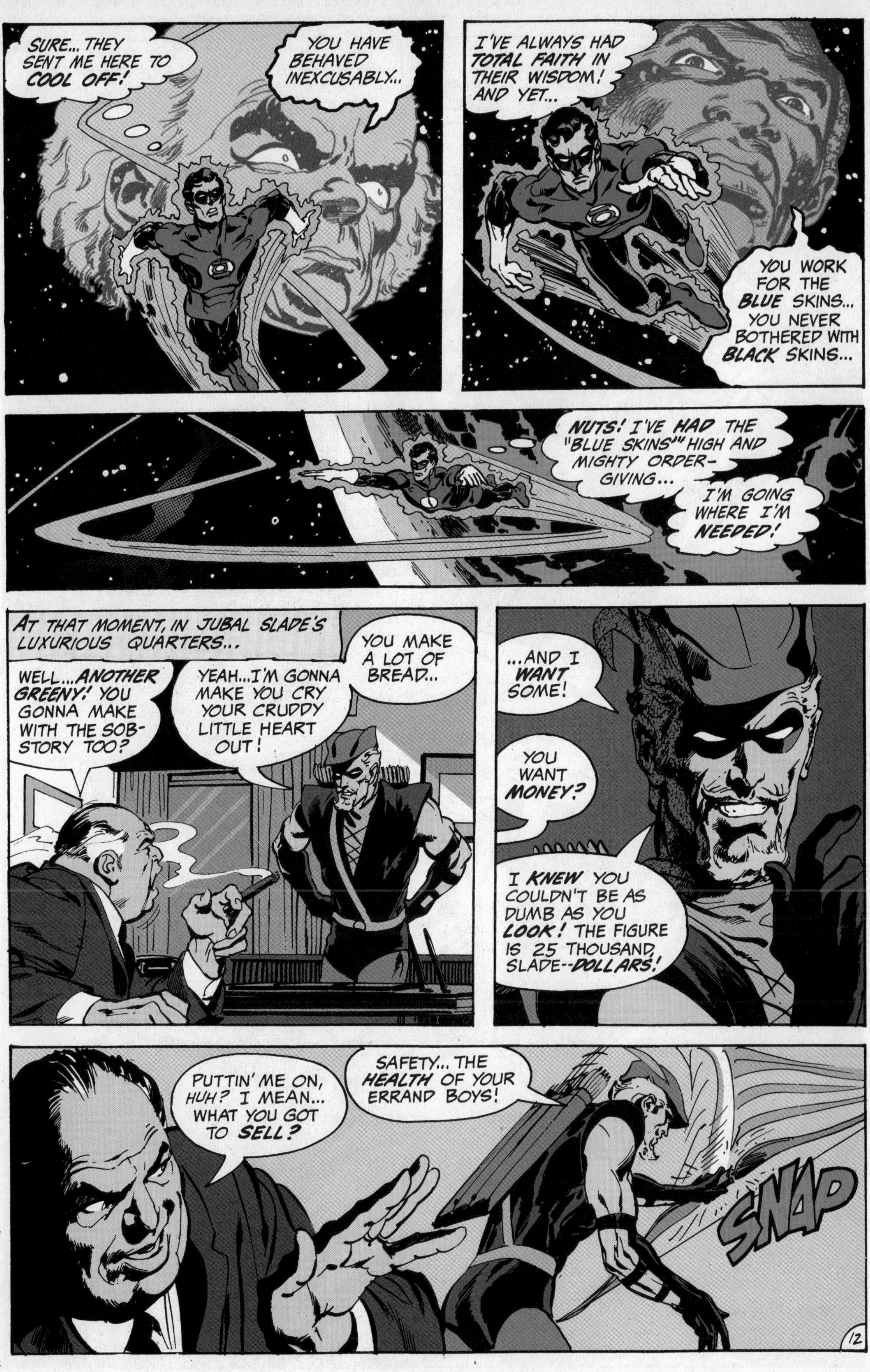
SURE... THEY SENT ME HERE TO COOL OFF!
YOU HAVE BEHAVED INEXCUSABLY...
I'VE ALWAYS HAD TOTAL FAITH IN THEIR WISDOM! AND YET...
YOU WORK FOR THE BLUE SKINS... YOU NEVER BOTHERED WITH BLACK SKINS...
NUTS! I'VE HAD THE "BLUE SKINS'" HIGH AND MIGHTY ORDER-GIVING...
I'M GOING WHERE I'M NEEDED!
AT THAT MOMENT, IN JUBAL SLADE'S LUXURIOUS QUARTERS...
WELL... ANOTHER GREENY! YOU GONNA MAKE WITH THE SOB-STORY TOO?
YEAH... I'M GONNA MAKE YOU CRY YOUR CRUDDY LITTLE HEART OUT!
YOU MAKE A LOT OF BREAD...
...AND I WANT SOME!
YOU WANT MONEY?
I KNEW YOU COULDN'T BE AS DUMB AS YOU LOOK! THE FIGURE IS 25 THOUSAND, SLADE--DOLLARS!
PUTTIN' ME ON, HUH? I MEAN... WHAT YOU GOT TO SELL?
SAFETY... THE HEALTH OF YOUR ERRAND BOYS!
SNAP
12

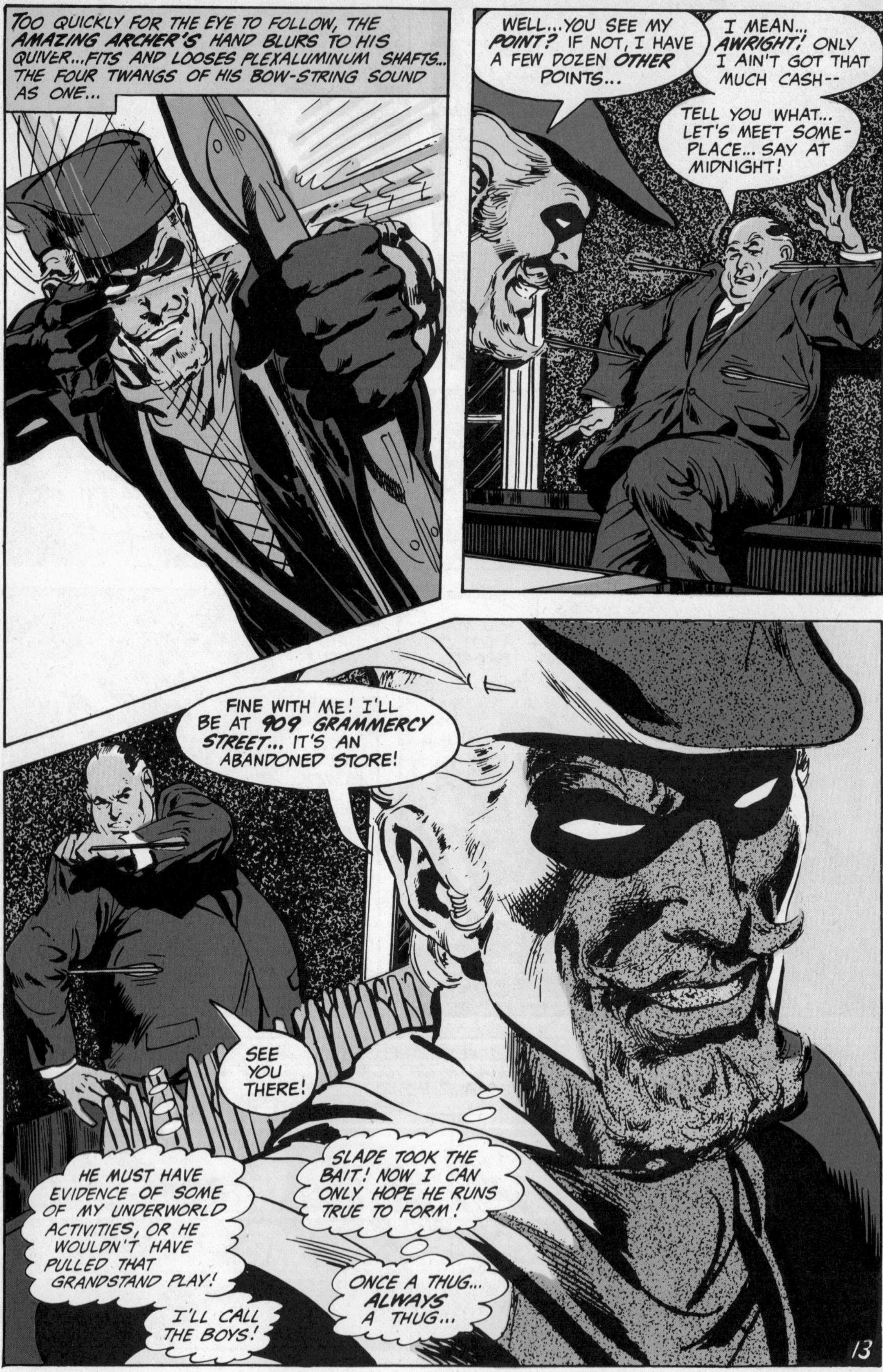
TOO QUICKLY FOR THE EYE TO FOLLOW, THE AMAZING ARCHER'S HAND BLURS TO HIS QUIVER...FITS AND LOOSES PLEXALUMINUM SHAFTS... THE FOUR TWANGS OF HIS BOW-STRING SOUND AS ONE...
WELL...YOU SEE MY POINT? IF NOT, I HAVE A FEW DOZEN OTHER POINTS...
I MEAN... AWRIGHT! ONLY I AIN'T GOT THAT MUCH CASH--
TELL YOU WHAT... LET'S MEET SOME-PLACE... SAY AT MIDNIGHT!
FINE WITH ME! I'LL BE AT 909 GRAMMERCY STREET... IT'S AN ABANDONED STORE!
SEE YOU THERE!
HE MUST HAVE EVIDENCE OF SOME OF MY UNDERWORLD ACTIVITIES, OR HE WOULDN'T HAVE PULLED THAT GRANDSTAND PLAY!
I'LL CALL THE BOYS!
SLADE TOOK THE BAIT! NOW I CAN ONLY HOPE HE RUNS TRUE TO FORM!
ONCE A THUG... ALWAYS A THUG...
13

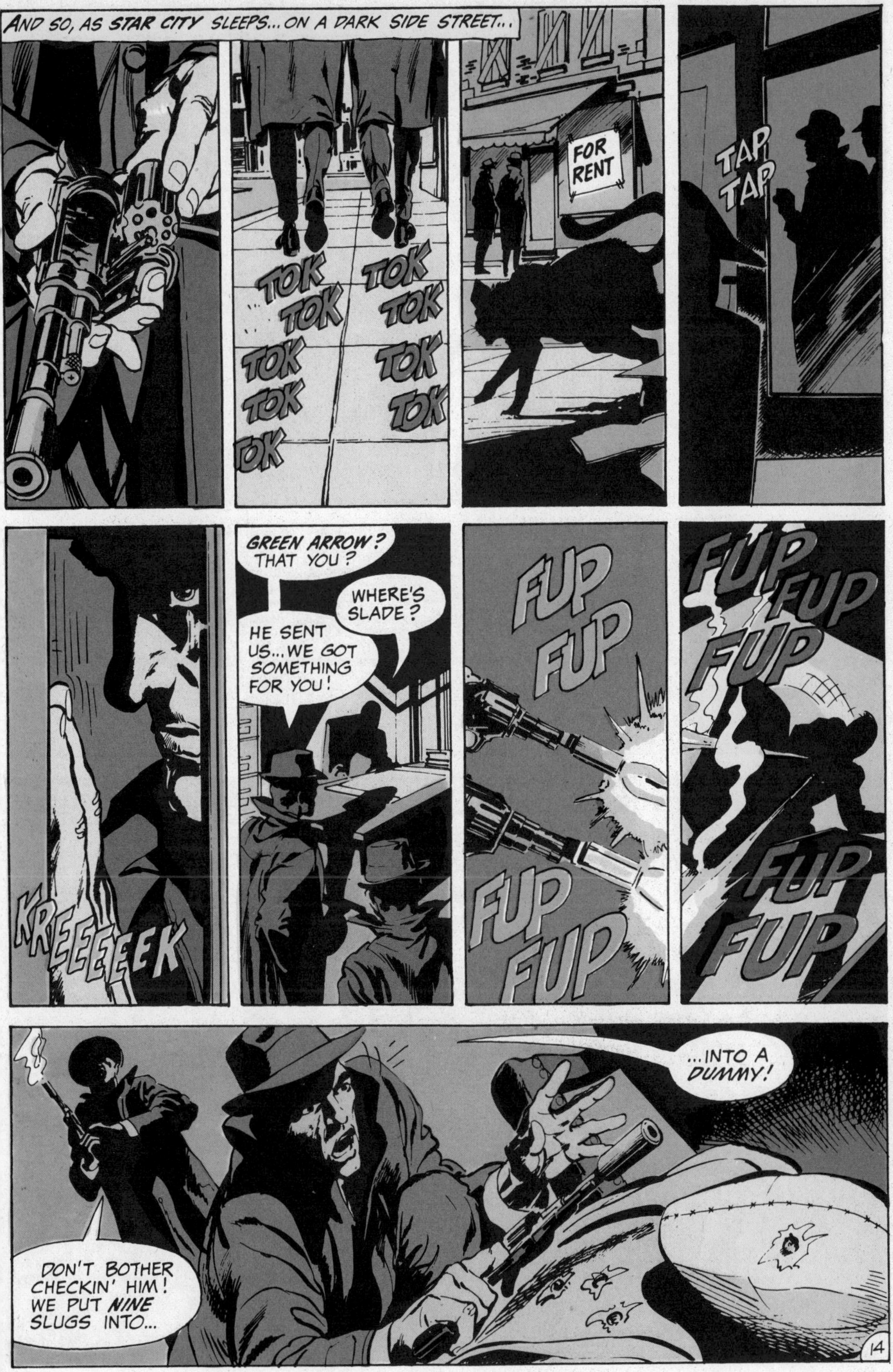
AND SO, AS STAR CITY SLEEPS... ON A DARK SIDE STREET...
TOK TOK TOK TOK TOK TOK TOK TOK TOK
FOR RENT
TAP TAP
KREEEEEEK
GREEN ARROW? THAT YOU?
WHERE'S SLADE?
HE SENT US... WE GOT SOMETHING FOR YOU!
FUP FUP
FUP FUP
FUP FUP FUP
FUP FUP
DON'T BOTHER CHECKIN' HIM! WE PUT NINE SLUGS INTO...
...INTO A DUMMY!
14

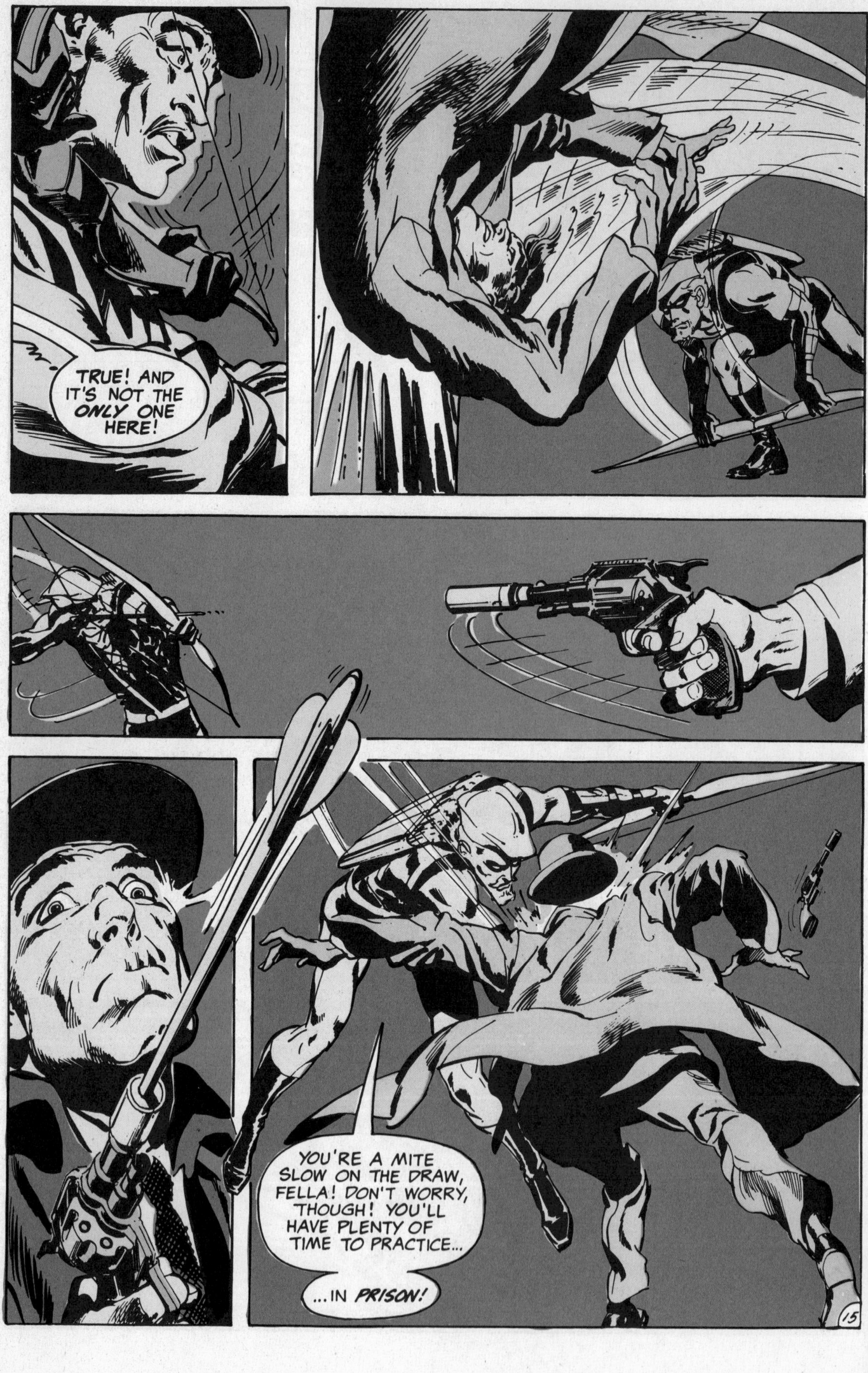
TRUE! AND IT'S NOT THE *ONLY* ONE HERE!
YOU'RE A MITE SLOW ON THE DRAW, FELLA! DON'T WORRY, THOUGH! YOU'LL HAVE PLENTY OF TIME TO PRACTICE...
...IN *PRISON!*
15

NOW, TO COLLECT THE EVIDENCE... THE TAPE-RECORDING OF OUR LITTLE TALK ABOUT SLADE--
OH... NO!
ONE OF THE BULLETS HIT IT... THE TAPE IS RUINED!
WHY THE DEVIL COULDN'T THEY SHOOT STRAIGHT?
I'M BACK WHERE I STARTED... WITH A COUPLE OF LITTLE FISH NETTED...
...WHILE THE BIG BOSS SHARK GOES HIS WAY!
16

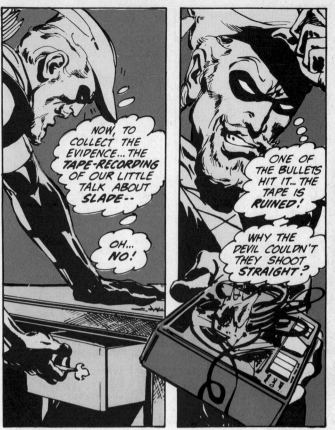

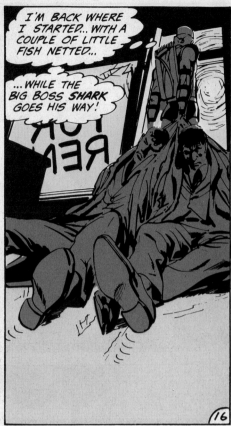

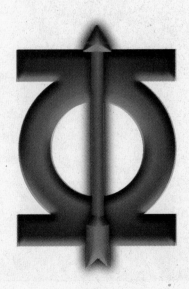

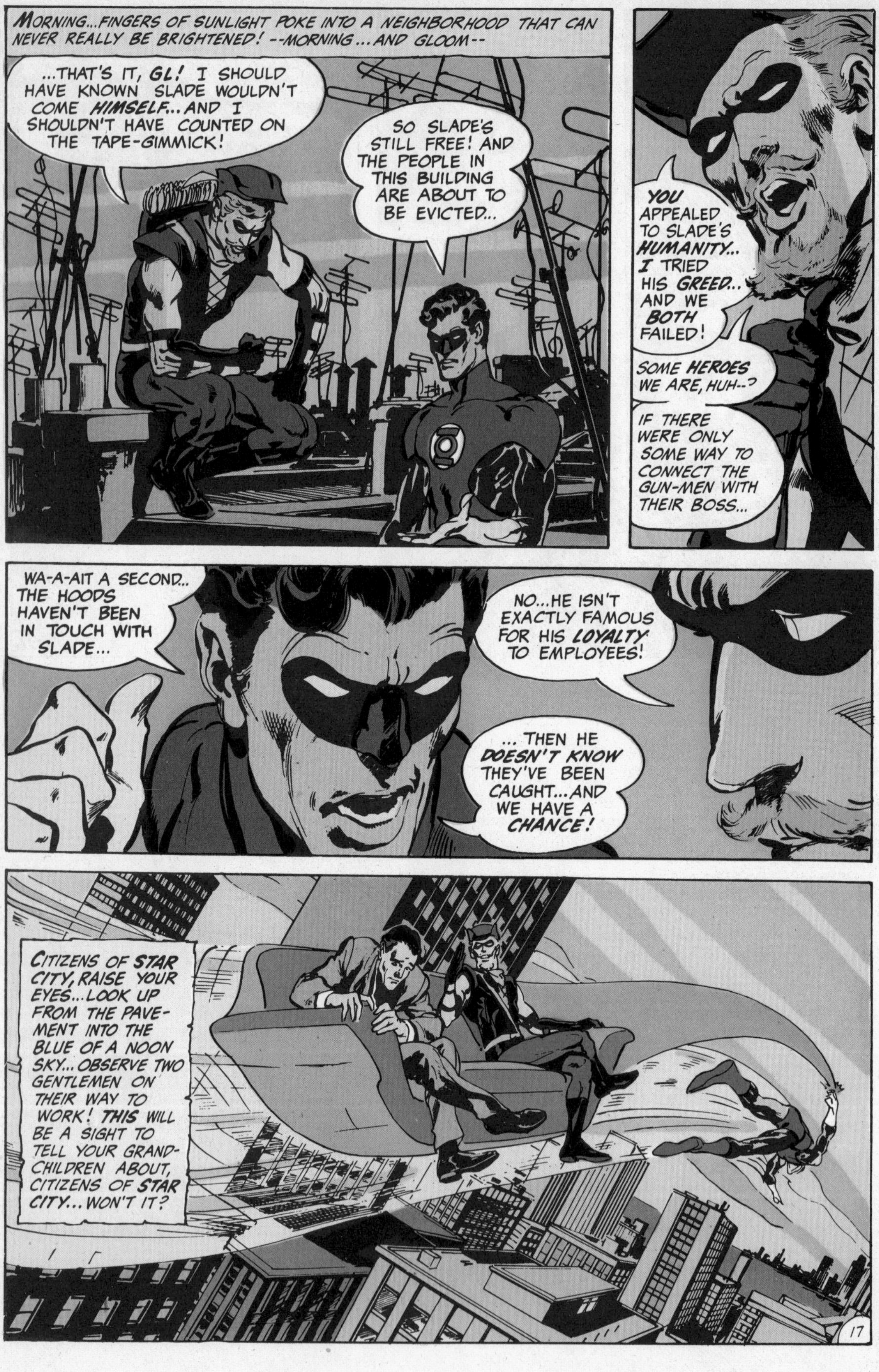
MORNING...FINGERS OF SUNLIGHT POKE INTO A NEIGHBORHOOD THAT CAN NEVER REALLY BE BRIGHTENED! --MORNING... AND GLOOM--
...THAT'S IT, GL! I SHOULD HAVE KNOWN SLADE WOULDN'T COME HIMSELF... AND I SHOULDN'T HAVE COUNTED ON THE TAPE-GIMMICK!
SO SLADE'S STILL FREE! AND THE PEOPLE IN THIS BUILDING ARE ABOUT TO BE EVICTED...
YOU APPEALED TO SLADE'S HUMANITY... I TRIED HIS GREED... AND WE BOTH FAILED!
SOME HEROES WE ARE, HUH--?
IF THERE WERE ONLY SOME WAY TO CONNECT THE GUN-MEN WITH THEIR BOSS...
WA-A-AIT A SECOND.. THE HOODS HAVEN'T BEEN IN TOUCH WITH SLADE...
NO... HE ISN'T EXACTLY FAMOUS FOR HIS LOYALTY TO EMPLOYEES!
... THEN HE DOESN'T KNOW THEY'VE BEEN CAUGHT... AND WE HAVE A CHANCE!
CITIZENS OF STAR CITY, RAISE YOUR EYES... LOOK UP FROM THE PAVE-MENT INTO THE BLUE OF A NOON SKY... OBSERVE TWO GENTLEMEN ON THEIR WAY TO WORK! THIS WILL BE A SIGHT TO TELL YOUR GRAND-CHILDREN ABOUT, CITIZENS OF STAR CITY... WON'T IT?
17

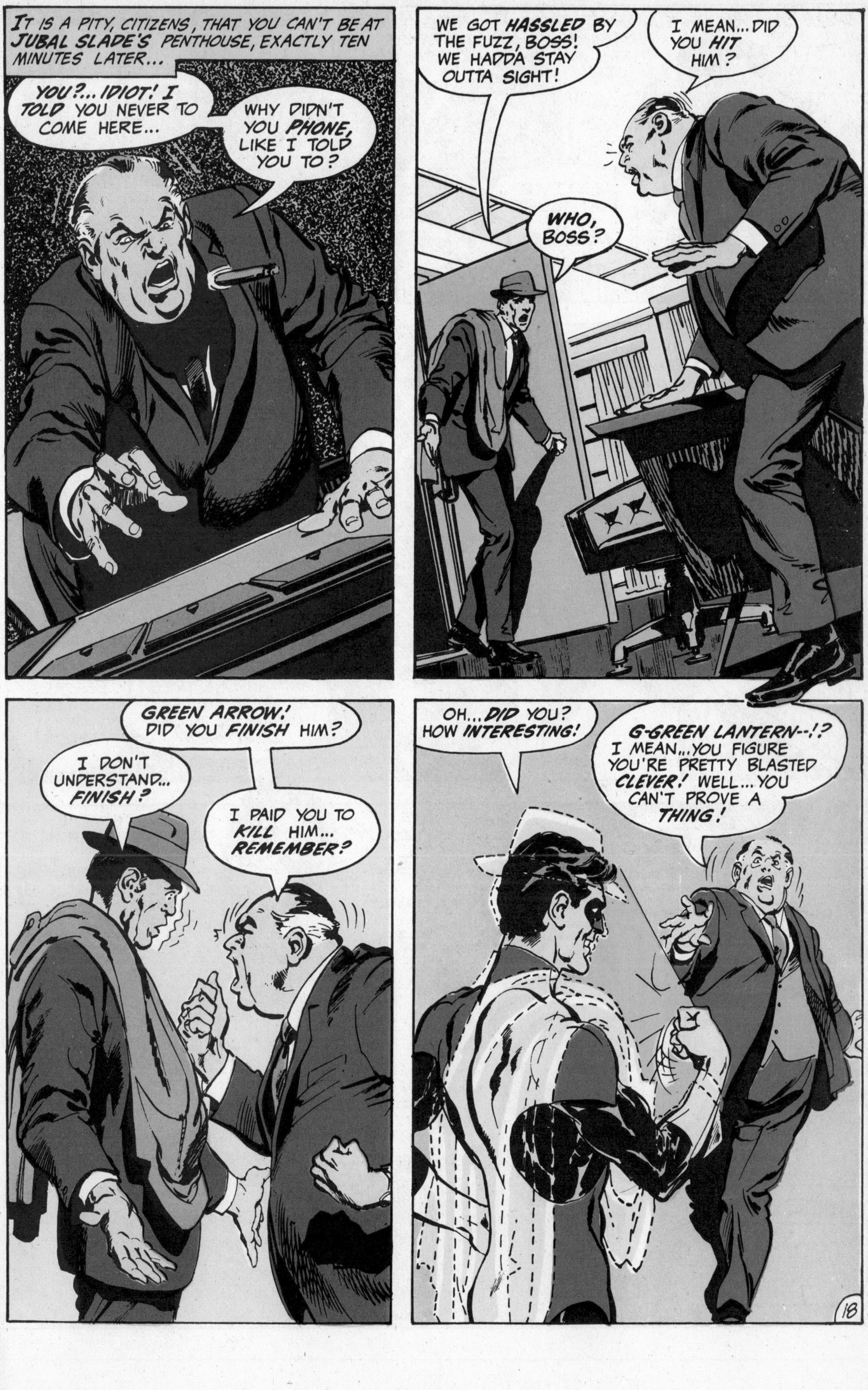

IT IS A PITY, CITIZENS, THAT YOU CAN'T BE AT JUBAL SLADE'S PENTHOUSE, EXACTLY TEN MINUTES LATER...
YOU?... IDIOT! I TOLD YOU NEVER TO COME HERE...
WHY DIDN'T YOU PHONE, LIKE I TOLD YOU TO?
WE GOT HASSLED BY THE FUZZ, BOSS! WE HADDA STAY OUTTA SIGHT!
I MEAN... DID YOU HIT HIM?
WHO, BOSS?
GREEN ARROW! DID YOU FINISH HIM?
I DON'T UNDERSTAND... FINISH?
I PAID YOU TO KILL HIM... REMEMBER?
OH... DID YOU? HOW INTERESTING!
G-GREEN LANTERN--!? I MEAN... YOU FIGURE YOU'RE PRETTY BLASTED CLEVER! WELL... YOU CAN'T PROVE A THING!
18

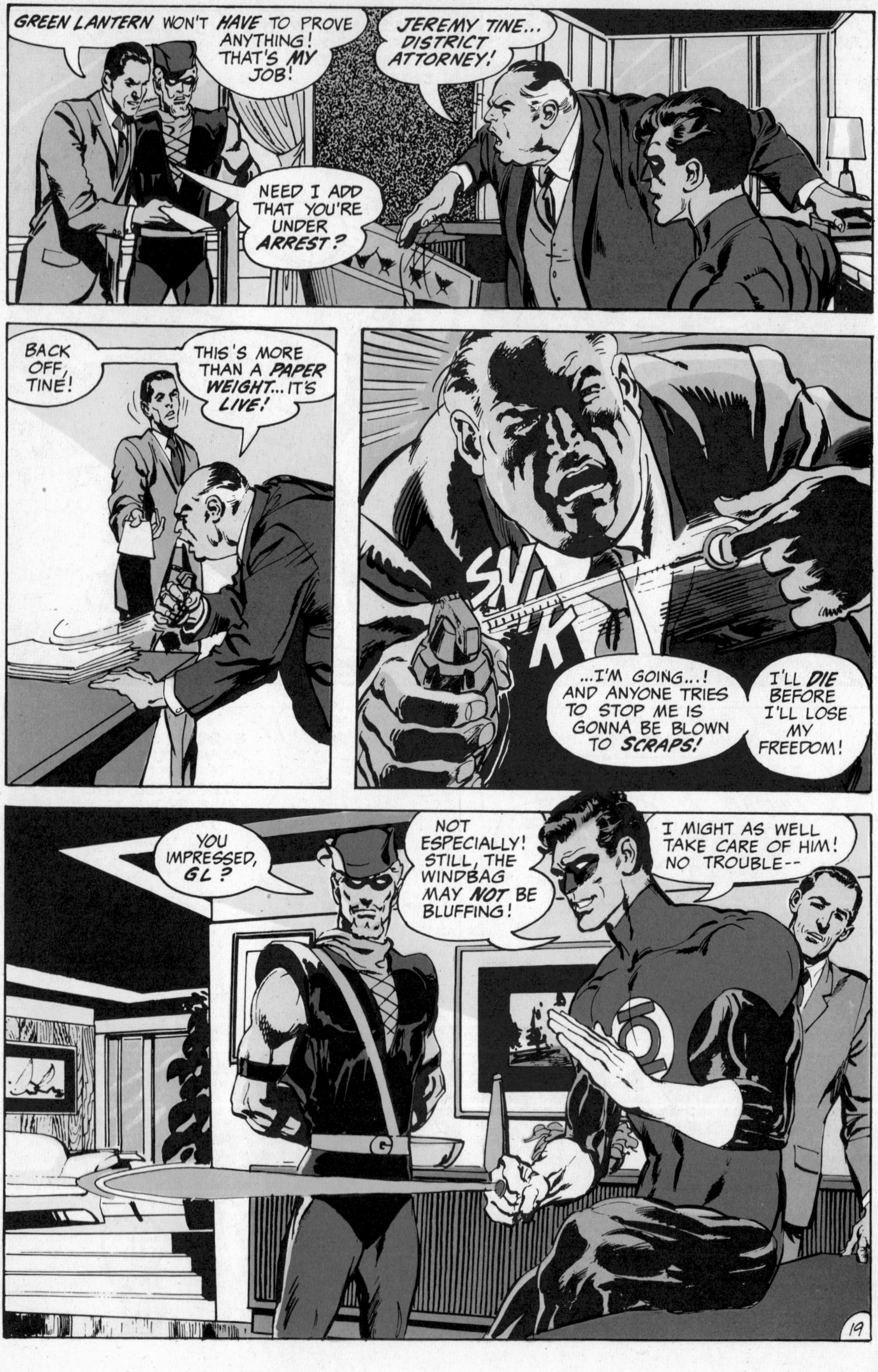

GREEN LANTERN WON'T HAVE TO PROVE ANYTHING! THAT'S MY JOB!
JEREMY TINE... DISTRICT ATTORNEY!
NEED I ADD THAT YOU'RE UNDER ARREST?
BACK OFF, TINE!
THIS'S MORE THAN A PAPER WEIGHT... IT'S LIVE!
SNIK
...I'M GOING...! AND ANYONE TRIES TO STOP ME IS GONNA BE BLOWN TO SCRAPS!
I'LL DIE BEFORE I'LL LOSE MY FREEDOM!
YOU IMPRESSED, GL?
NOT ESPECIALLY! STILL, THE WINDBAG MAY NOT BE BLUFFING!
I MIGHT AS WELL TAKE CARE OF HIM! NO TROUBLE--
19

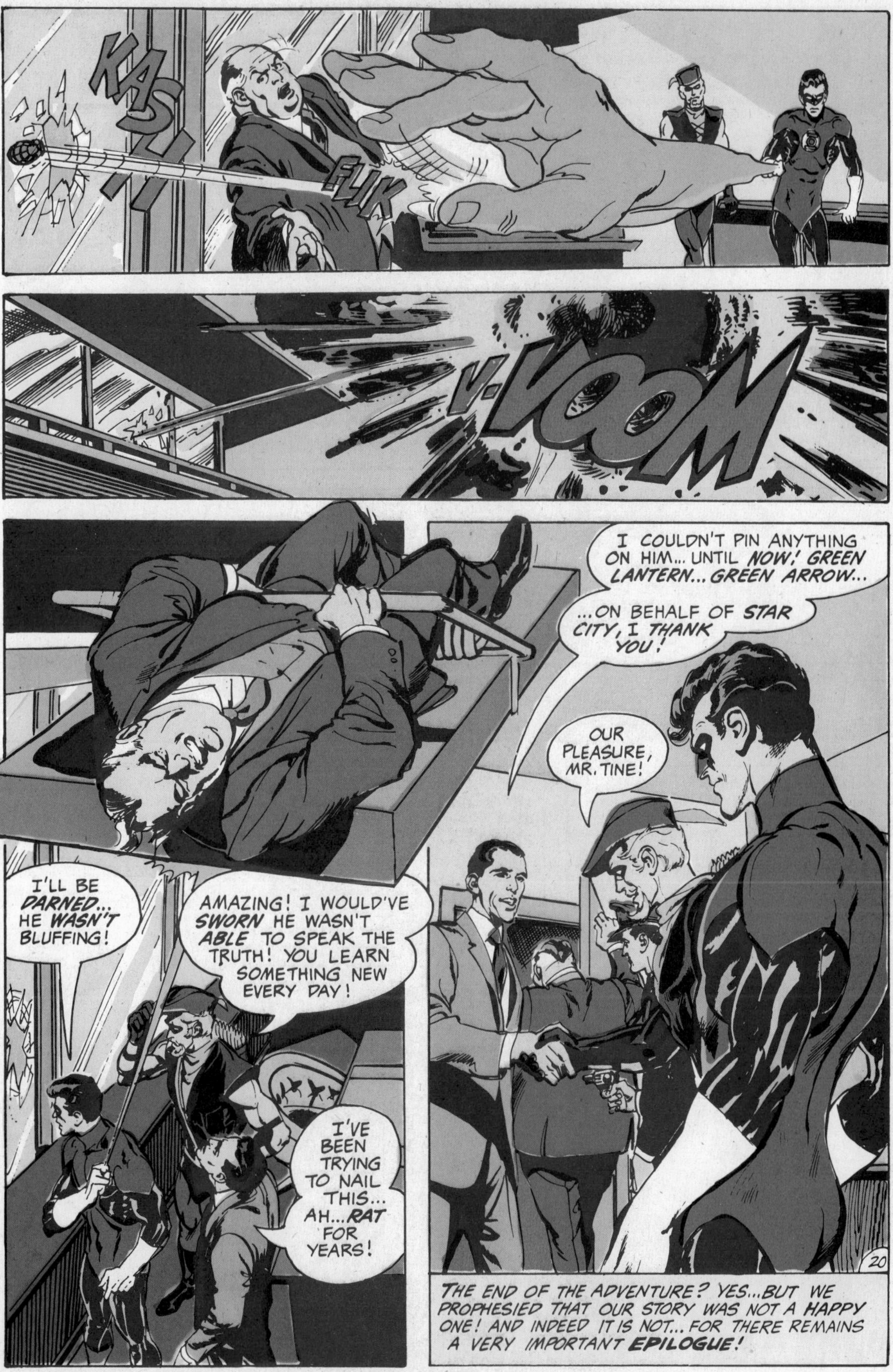
KASLIT
FLIK
V-VOOM
I COULDN'T PIN ANYTHING ON HIM... UNTIL NOW! GREEN LANTERN... GREEN ARROW...
...ON BEHALF OF STAR CITY, I THANK YOU!
OUR PLEASURE, MR. TINE!
I'LL BE DARNED... HE WASN'T BLUFFING!
AMAZING! I WOULD'VE SWORN HE WASN'T ABLE TO SPEAK THE TRUTH! YOU LEARN SOMETHING NEW EVERY DAY!
I'VE BEEN TRYING TO NAIL THIS... AH... RAT FOR YEARS!
20
THE END OF THE ADVENTURE? YES... BUT WE PROPHESIED THAT OUR STORY WAS NOT A HAPPY ONE! AND INDEED IT IS NOT... FOR THERE REMAINS A VERY IMPORTANT EPILOGUE!

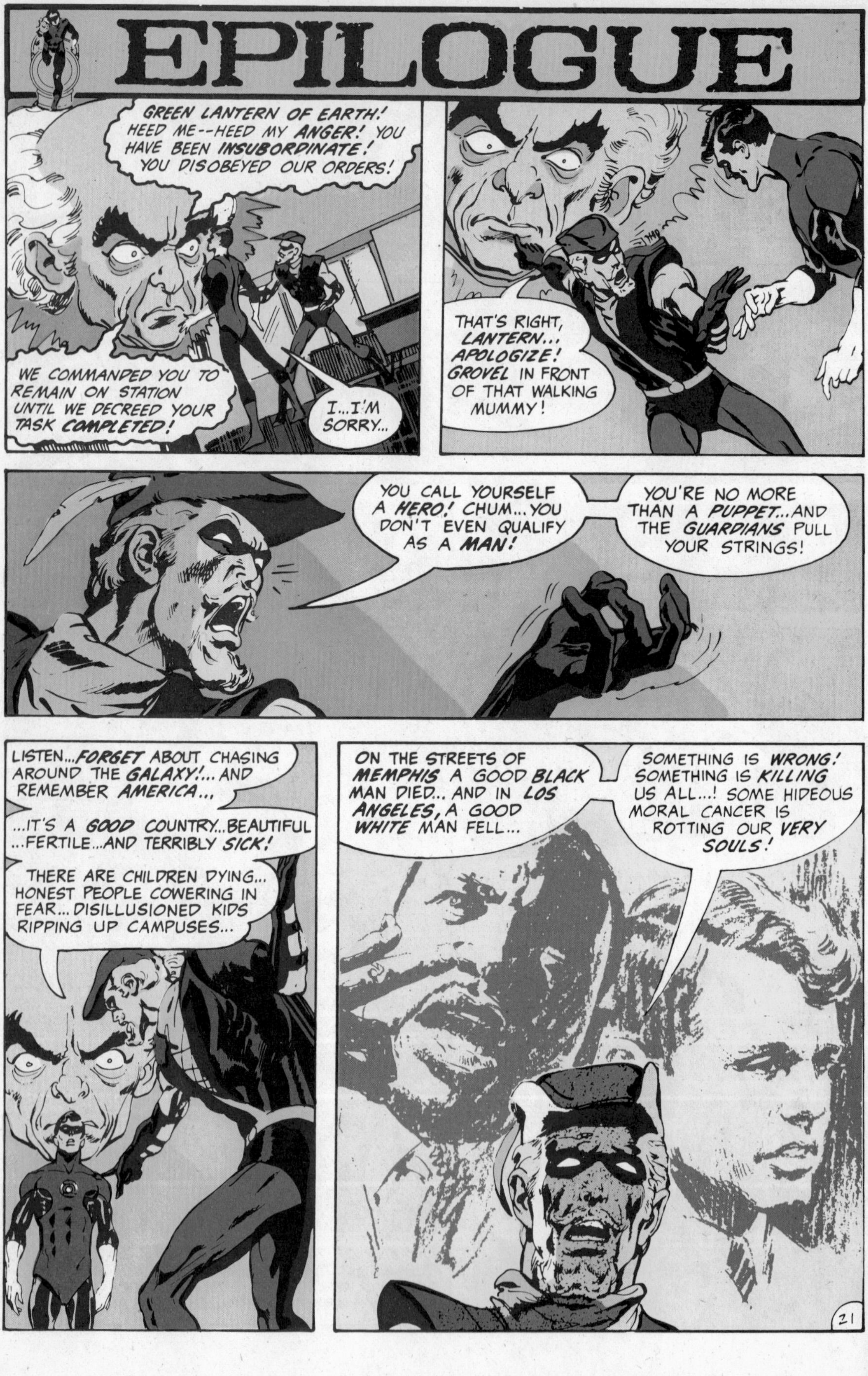

EPILOGUE
GREEN LANTERN OF EARTH! HEED ME--HEED MY ANGER! YOU HAVE BEEN INSUBORDINATE! YOU DISOBEYED OUR ORDERS!
WE COMMANDED YOU TO REMAIN ON STATION UNTIL WE DECREED YOUR TASK COMPLETED!
I...I'M SORRY...
THAT'S RIGHT, LANTERN... APOLOGIZE! GROVEL IN FRONT OF THAT WALKING MUMMY!
YOU CALL YOURSELF A HERO! CHUM...YOU DON'T EVEN QUALIFY AS A MAN!
YOU'RE NO MORE THAN A PUPPET...AND THE GUARDIANS PULL YOUR STRINGS!
LISTEN...FORGET ABOUT CHASING AROUND THE GALAXY!...AND REMEMBER AMERICA...,
...IT'S A GOOD COUNTRY...BEAUTIFUL ...FERTILE...AND TERRIBLY SICK!
THERE ARE CHILDREN DYING... HONEST PEOPLE COWERING IN FEAR...DISILLUSIONED KIDS RIPPING UP CAMPUSES...
ON THE STREETS OF MEMPHIS A GOOD BLACK MAN DIED...AND IN LOS ANGELES, A GOOD WHITE MAN FELL...
SOMETHING IS WRONG! SOMETHING IS KILLING US ALL...! SOME HIDEOUS MORAL CANCER IS ROTTING OUR VERY SOULS!
21

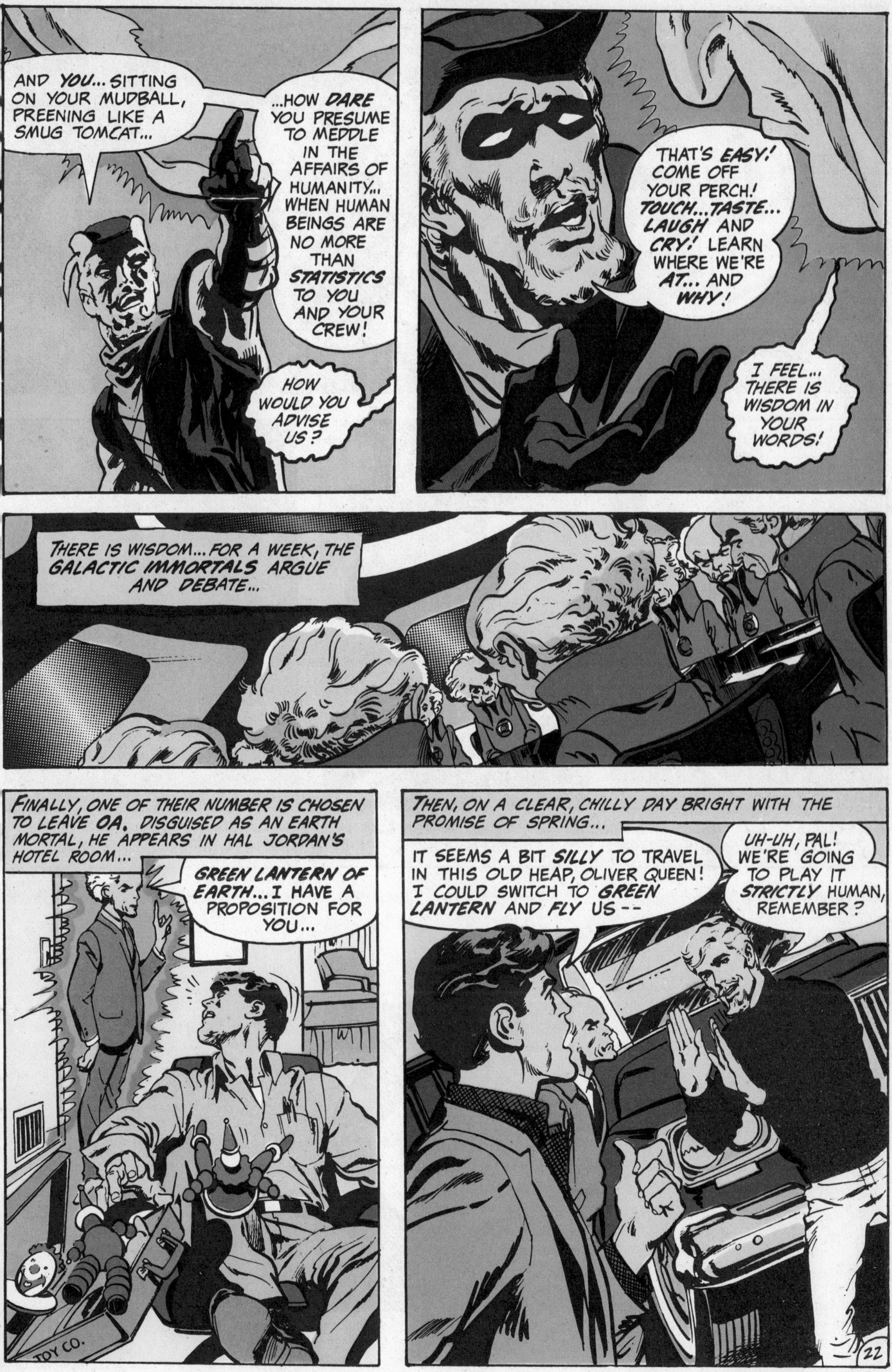

AND YOU... SITTING ON YOUR MUDBALL, PREENING LIKE A SMUG TOMCAT...
...HOW DARE YOU PRESUME TO MEDDLE IN THE AFFAIRS OF HUMANITY... WHEN HUMAN BEINGS ARE NO MORE THAN STATISTICS TO YOU AND YOUR CREW!
HOW WOULD YOU ADVISE US?
THAT'S EASY! COME OFF YOUR PERCH! TOUCH...TASTE... LAUGH AND CRY! LEARN WHERE WE'RE AT... AND WHY!
I FEEL... THERE IS WISDOM IN YOUR WORDS!
THERE IS WISDOM... FOR A WEEK, THE GALACTIC IMMORTALS ARGUE AND DEBATE...
FINALLY, ONE OF THEIR NUMBER IS CHOSEN TO LEAVE OA. DISGUISED AS AN EARTH MORTAL, HE APPEARS IN HAL JORDAN'S HOTEL ROOM...
GREEN LANTERN OF EARTH... I HAVE A PROPOSITION FOR YOU...
TOY CO.
THEN, ON A CLEAR, CHILLY DAY BRIGHT WITH THE PROMISE OF SPRING...
IT SEEMS A BIT SILLY TO TRAVEL IN THIS OLD HEAP, OLIVER QUEEN! I COULD SWITCH TO GREEN LANTERN AND FLY US --
UH-UH, PAL! WE'RE GOING TO PLAY IT STRICTLY HUMAN, REMEMBER?
22

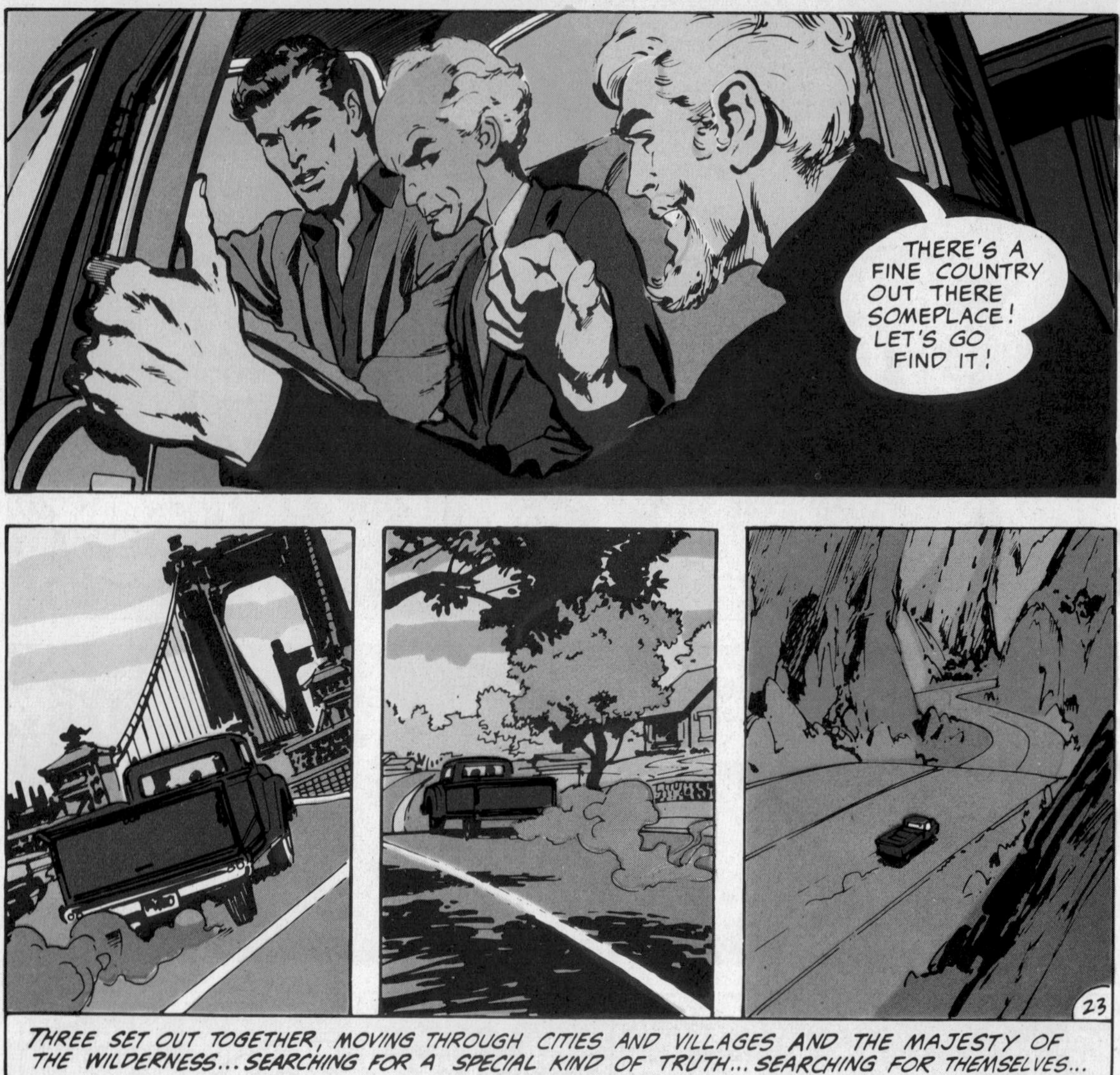
THERE'S A FINE COUNTRY OUT THERE SOMEPLACE! LET'S GO FIND IT!
23
THREE SET OUT TOGETHER, MOVING THROUGH CITIES AND VILLAGES AND THE MAJESTY OF THE WILDERNESS... SEARCHING FOR A SPECIAL KIND OF TRUTH... SEARCHING FOR THEMSELVES...

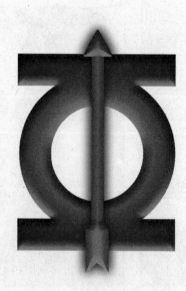

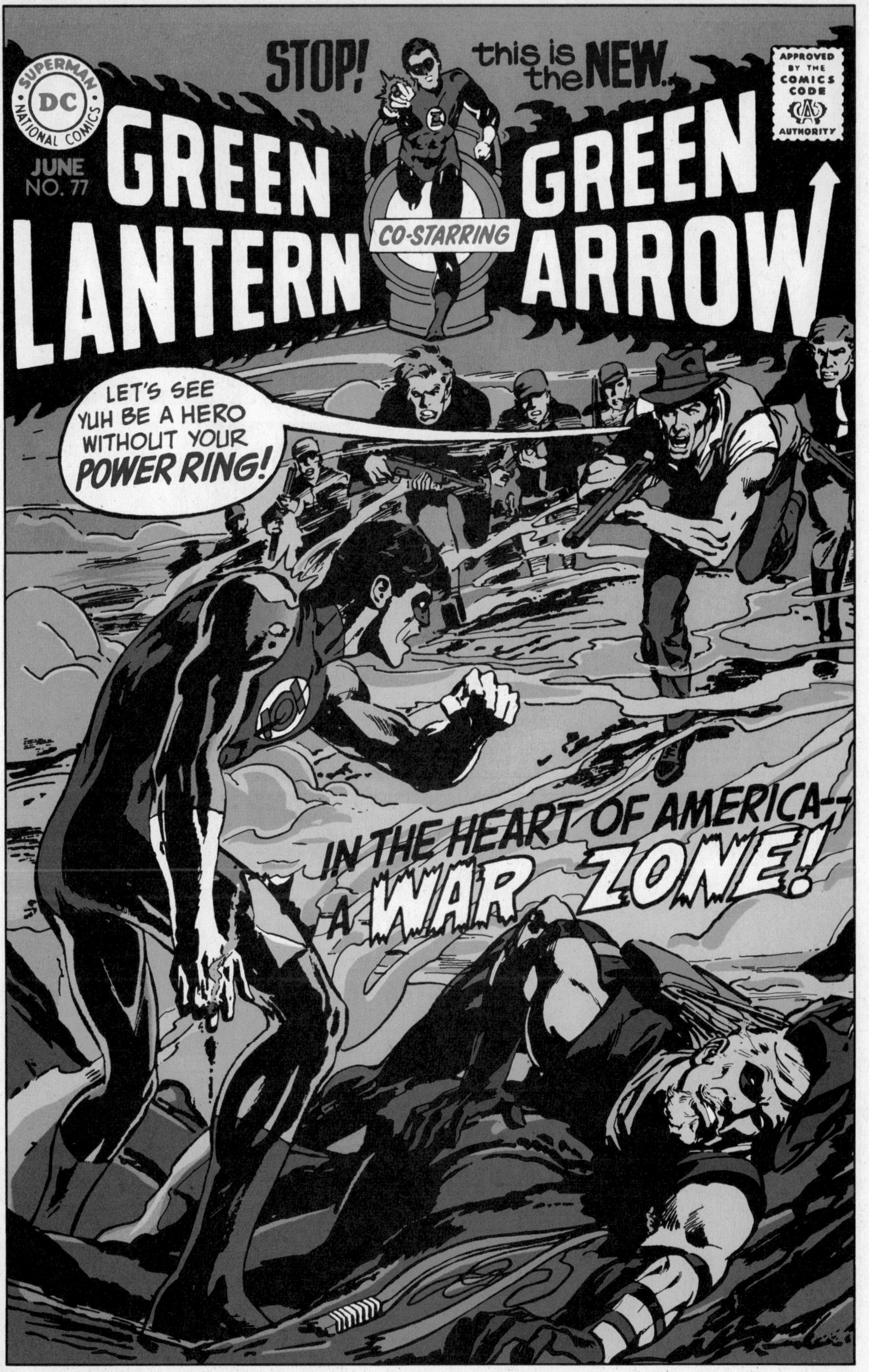

SUPERMAN
DC
NATIONAL COMICS
STOP! this is the NEW...
APPROVED BY THE COMICS CODE AUTHORITY
JUNE
NO. 77
GREEN LANTERN
CO-STARRING
GREEN ARROW
LET'S SEE YUH BE A HERO WITHOUT YOUR POWER RING!
IN THE HEART OF AMERICA--A WAR ZONE!

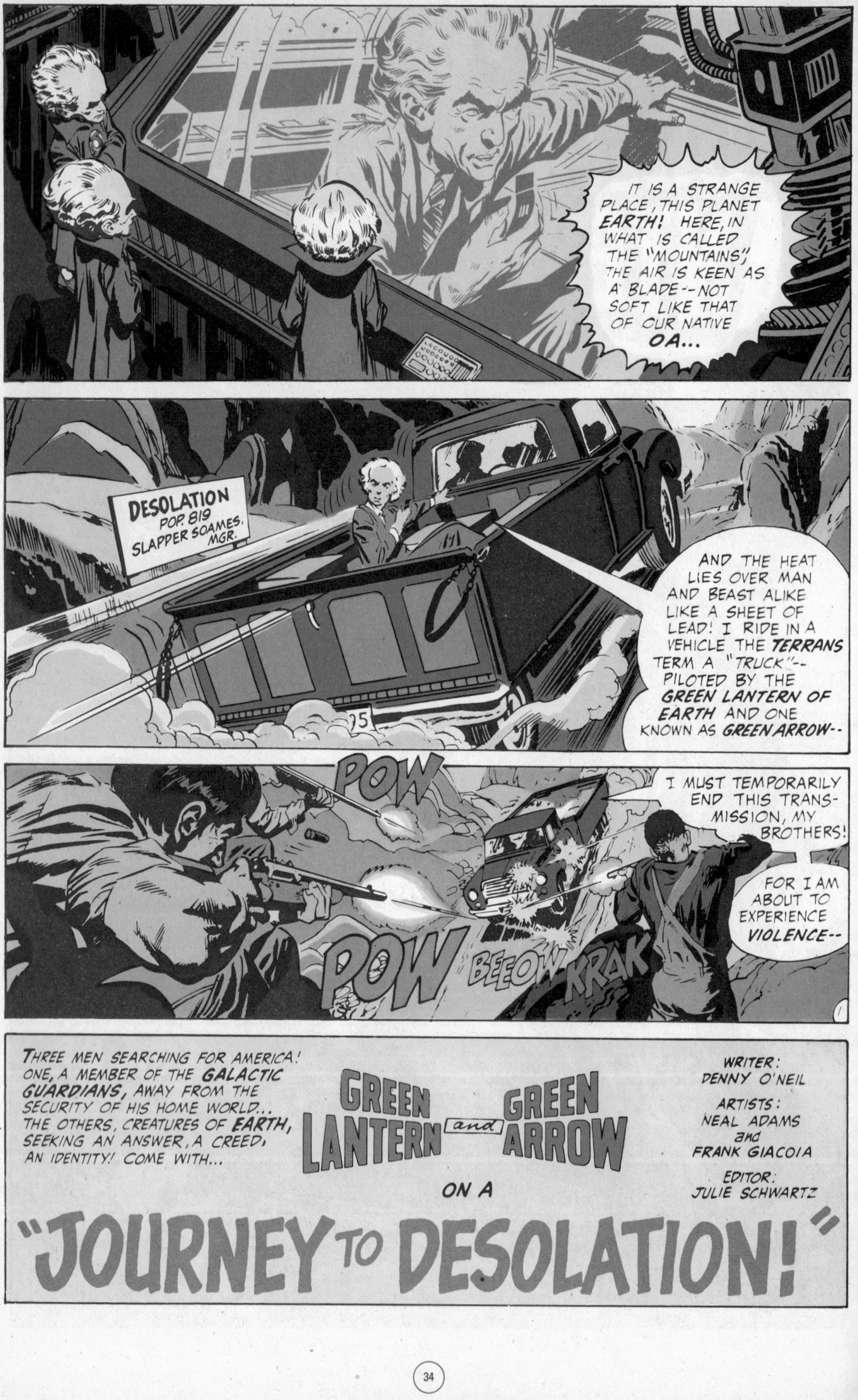
IT IS A STRANGE PLACE, THIS PLANET EARTH! HERE, IN WHAT IS CALLED THE "MOUNTAINS," THE AIR IS KEEN AS A BLADE--NOT SOFT LIKE THAT OF OUR NATIVE OA...
DESOLATION
POP. 819
SLAPPER SOAMES, MGR.
AND THE HEAT LIES OVER MAN AND BEAST ALIKE LIKE A SHEET OF LEAD! I RIDE IN A VEHICLE THE TERRANS TERM A "TRUCK"-- PILOTED BY THE GREEN LANTERN OF EARTH AND ONE KNOWN AS GREEN ARROW--
POW
I MUST TEMPORARILY END THIS TRANS-MISSION, MY BROTHERS!
FOR I AM ABOUT TO EXPERIENCE VIOLENCE--
POW
BEEOW
KRAK
THREE MEN SEARCHING FOR AMERICA! ONE, A MEMBER OF THE GALACTIC GUARDIANS, AWAY FROM THE SECURITY OF HIS HOME WORLD... THE OTHERS, CREATURES OF EARTH, SEEKING AN ANSWER, A CREED, AN IDENTITY! COME WITH...
GREEN LANTERN and GREEN ARROW
ON A
WRITER: DENNY O'NEIL
ARTISTS: NEAL ADAMS and FRANK GIACOIA
EDITOR: JULIE SCHWARTZ
"JOURNEY TO DESOLATION!"

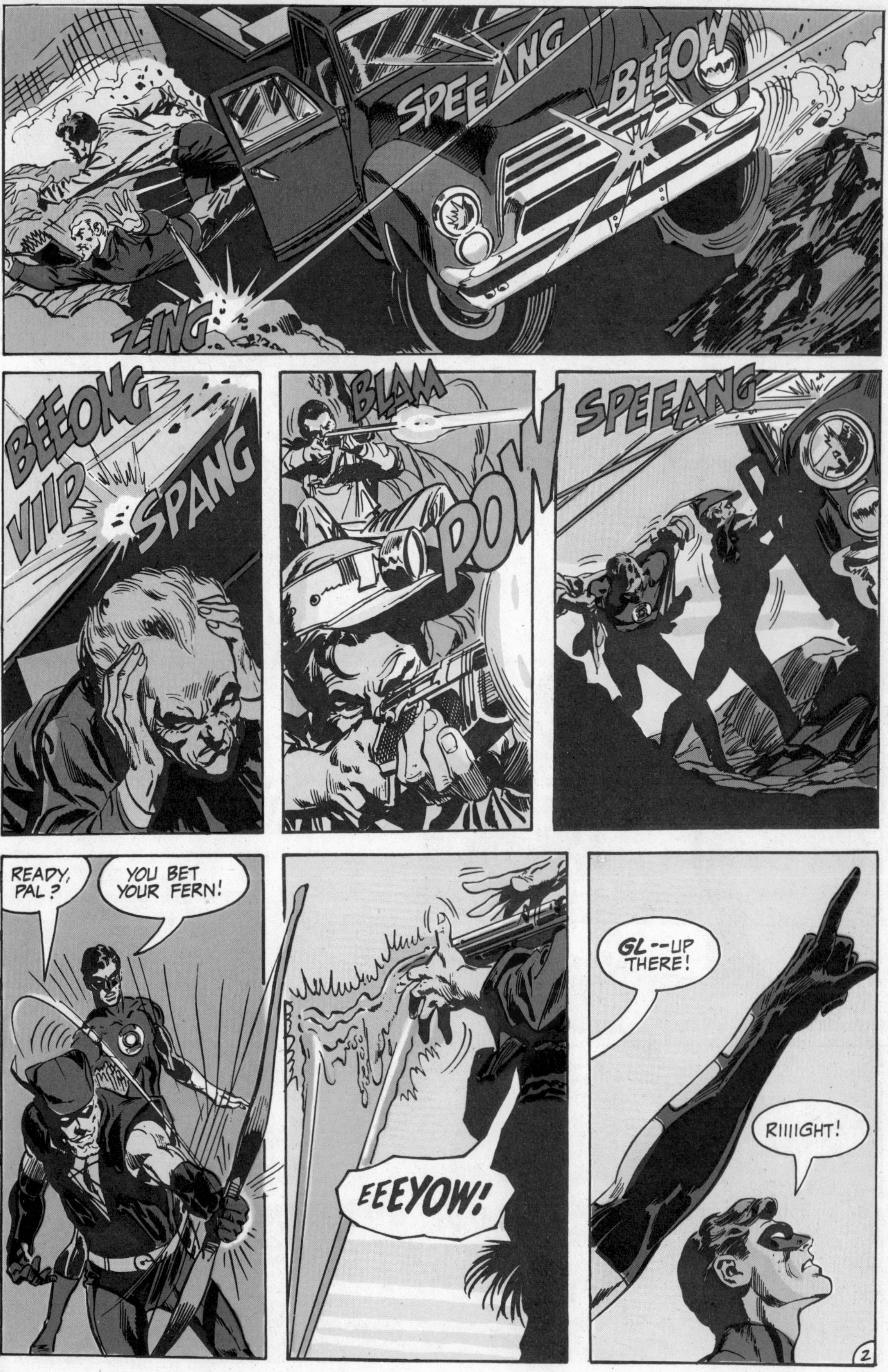
SPEEANG
BEEOW
ZING
BEEONG
VIIP
SPANG
BLAM
POW
SPEEANG
READY, PAL?
YOU BET YOUR FERN!
EEEYOW!
GL--UP THERE!
RIIIGHT!
2

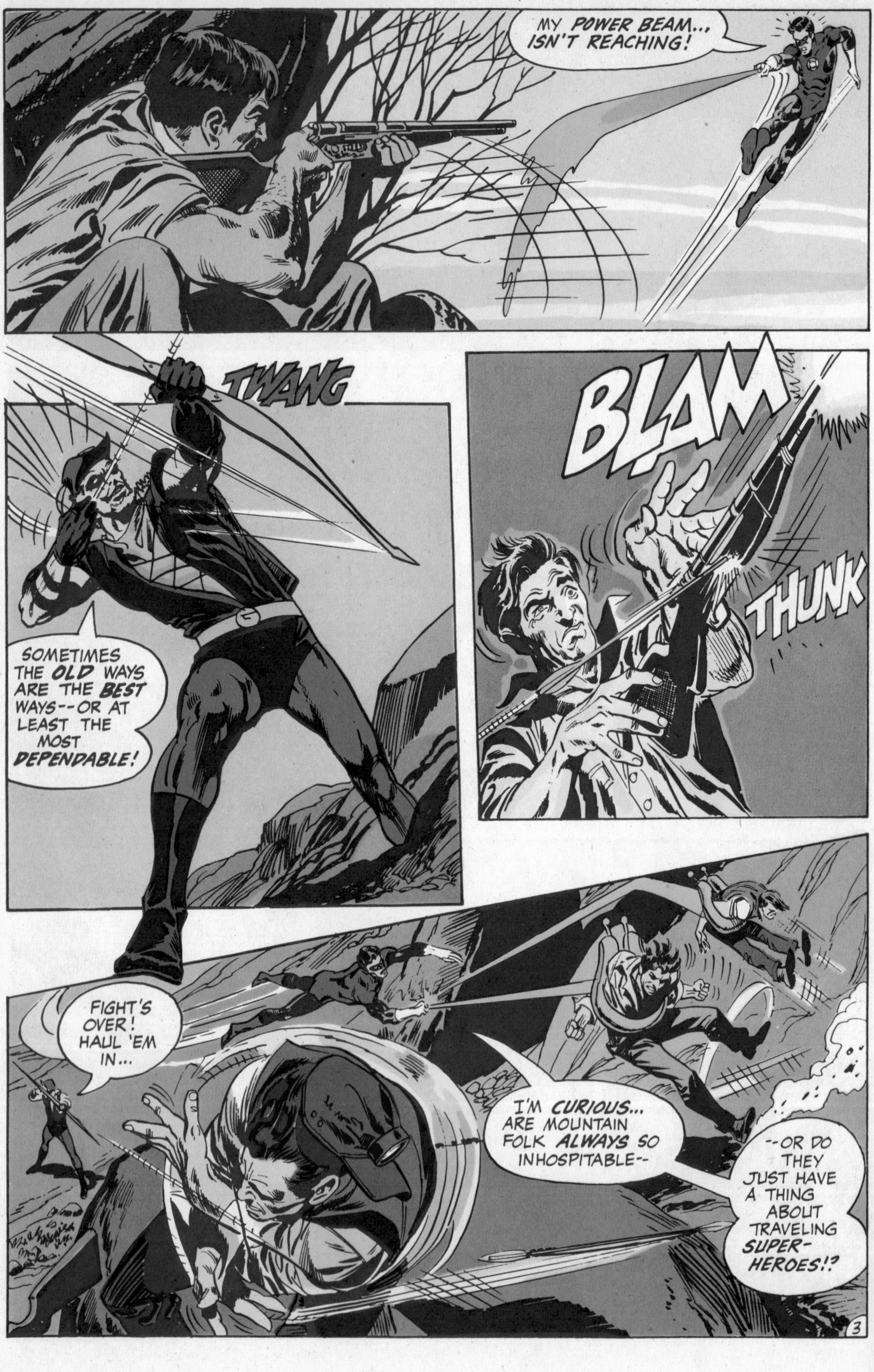
MY POWER BEAM... ISN'T REACHING!
TWANG
BLAM
THUNK
SOMETIMES THE OLD WAYS ARE THE BEST WAYS--OR AT LEAST THE MOST DEPENDABLE!
FIGHT'S OVER! HAUL 'EM IN...
I'M CURIOUS... ARE MOUNTAIN FOLK ALWAYS SO INHOSPITABLE--
--OR DO THEY JUST HAVE A THING ABOUT TRAVELING SUPER-HEROES!?
3

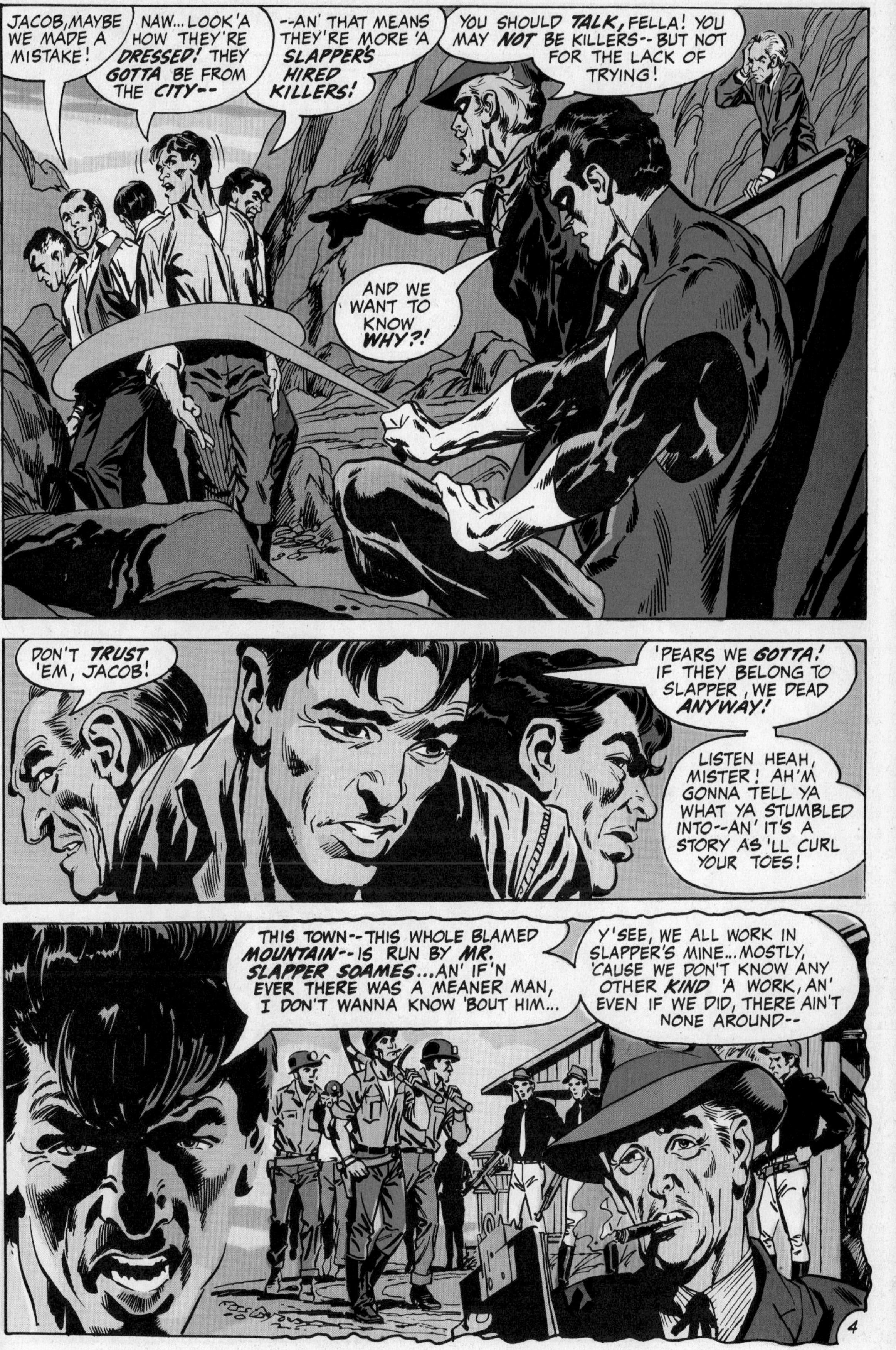
JACOB, MAYBE WE MADE A MISTAKE!
NAW... LOOK'A HOW THEY'RE DRESSED! THEY GOTTA BE FROM THE CITY--
--AN' THAT MEANS THEY'RE MORE 'A SLAPPER'S HIRED KILLERS!
YOU SHOULD TALK, FELLA! YOU MAY NOT BE KILLERS-- BUT NOT FOR THE LACK OF TRYING!
AND WE WANT TO KNOW WHY?!
DON'T TRUST 'EM, JACOB!
'PEARS WE GOTTA! IF THEY BELONG TO SLAPPER, WE DEAD ANYWAY!
LISTEN HEAH, MISTER! AH'M GONNA TELL YA WHAT YA STUMBLED INTO--AN' IT'S A STORY AS 'LL CURL YOUR TOES!
THIS TOWN--THIS WHOLE BLAMED MOUNTAIN--IS RUN BY MR. SLAPPER SOAMES... AN' IF'N EVER THERE WAS A MEANER MAN, I DON'T WANNA KNOW 'BOUT HIM...
Y'SEE, WE ALL WORK IN SLAPPER'S MINE... MOSTLY, 'CAUSE WE DON'T KNOW ANY OTHER KIND 'A WORK, AN' EVEN IF WE DID, THERE AIN'T NONE AROUND--
4

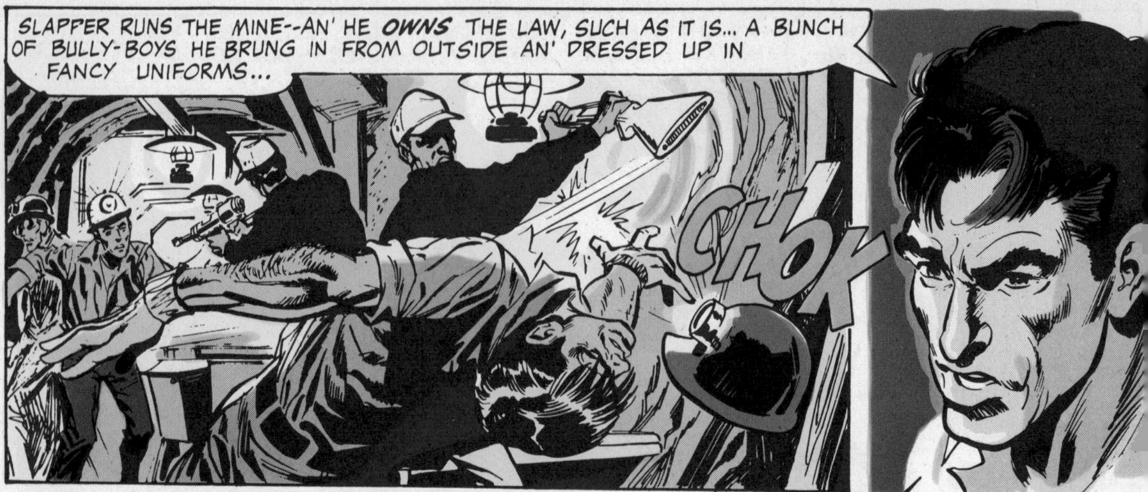

SLAPPER RUNS THE MINE--AN' HE **OWNS** THE LAW, SUCH AS IT IS... A BUNCH OF BULLY-BOYS HE BRUNG IN FROM OUTSIDE AN' DRESSED UP IN FANCY UNIFORMS...
CHOK

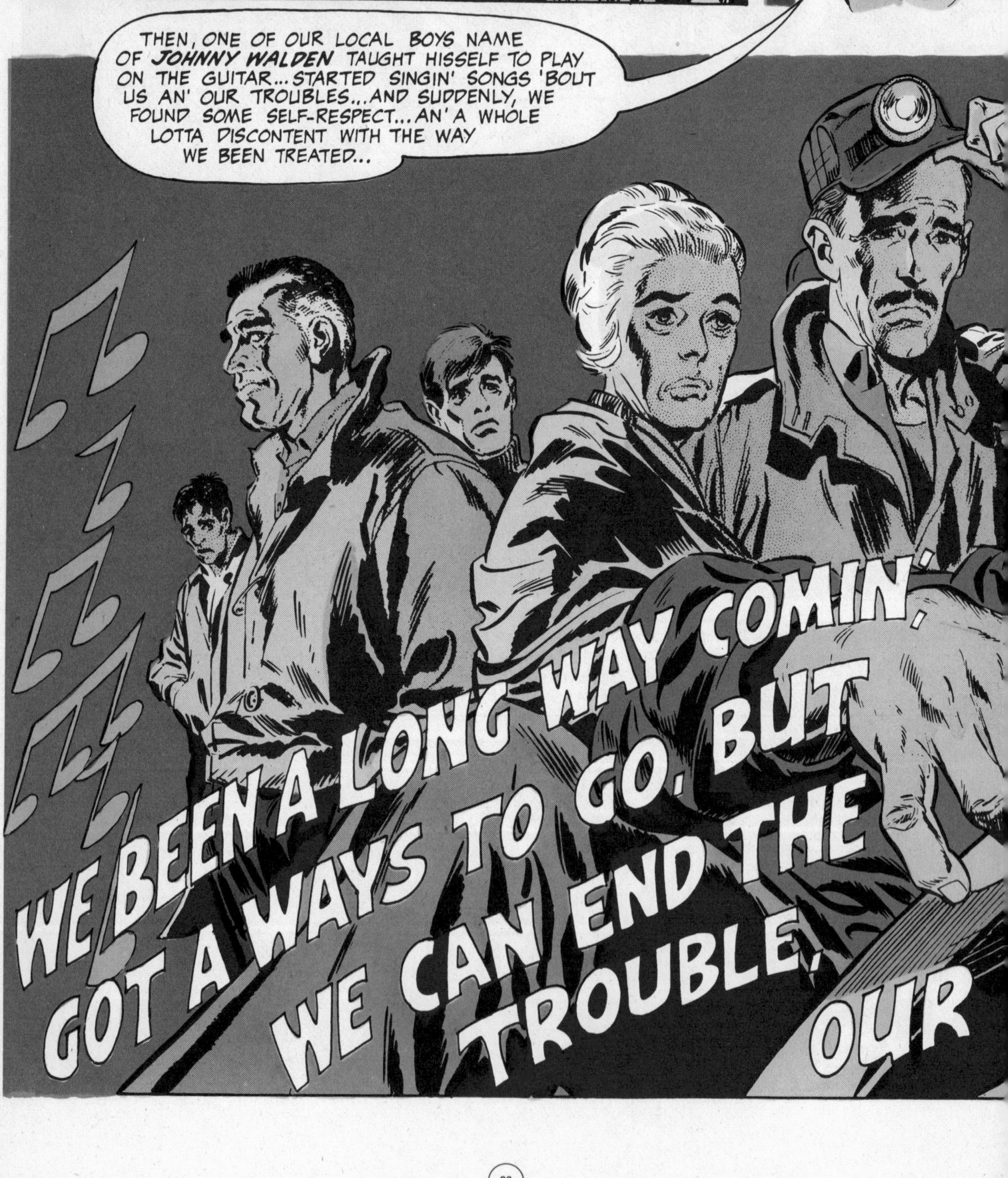

THEN, ONE OF OUR LOCAL BOYS NAME OF **JOHNNY WALDEN** TAUGHT HISSELF TO PLAY ON THE GUITAR... STARTED SINGIN' SONGS 'BOUT US AN' OUR TROUBLES...AND SUDDENLY, WE FOUND SOME SELF-RESPECT... AN' A WHOLE LOTTA DISCONTENT WITH THE WAY WE BEEN TREATED...
WE BEEN A LONG WAY COMIN',
GOT A WAYS TO GO. BUT
WE CAN END THE
TROUBLE,
OUR

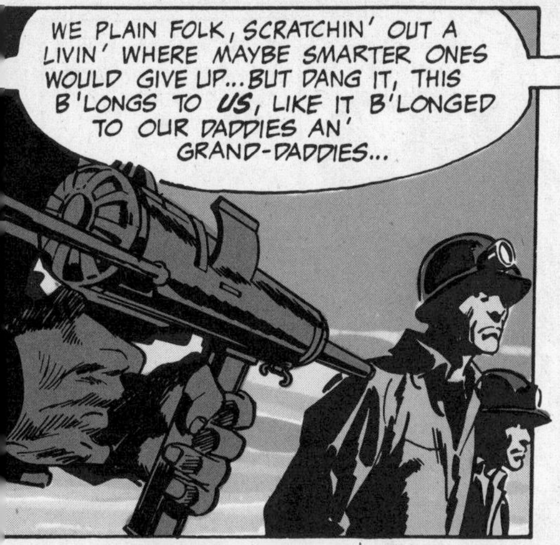
WE PLAIN FOLK, SCRATCHIN' OUT A LIVIN' WHERE MAYBE SMARTER ONES WOULD GIVE UP...BUT DANG IT, THIS B'LONGS TO *US*, LIKE IT B'LONGED TO OUR DADDIES AN' GRAND-DADDIES...

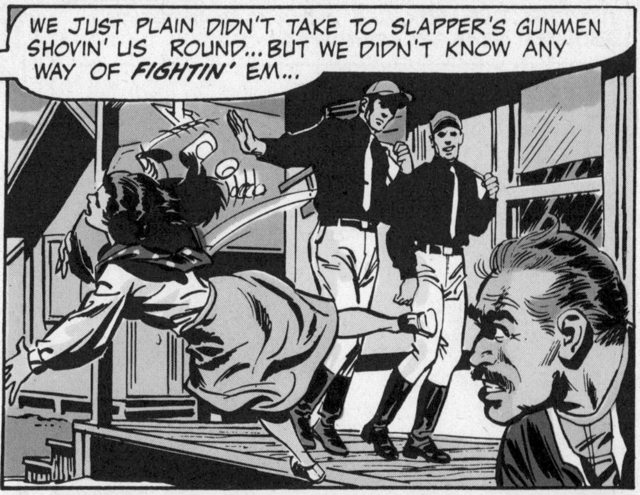
WE JUST PLAIN DIDN'T TAKE TO SLAPPER'S GUNMEN SHOVIN' US ROUND...BUT WE DIDN'T KNOW ANY WAY OF *FIGHTIN'* EM...

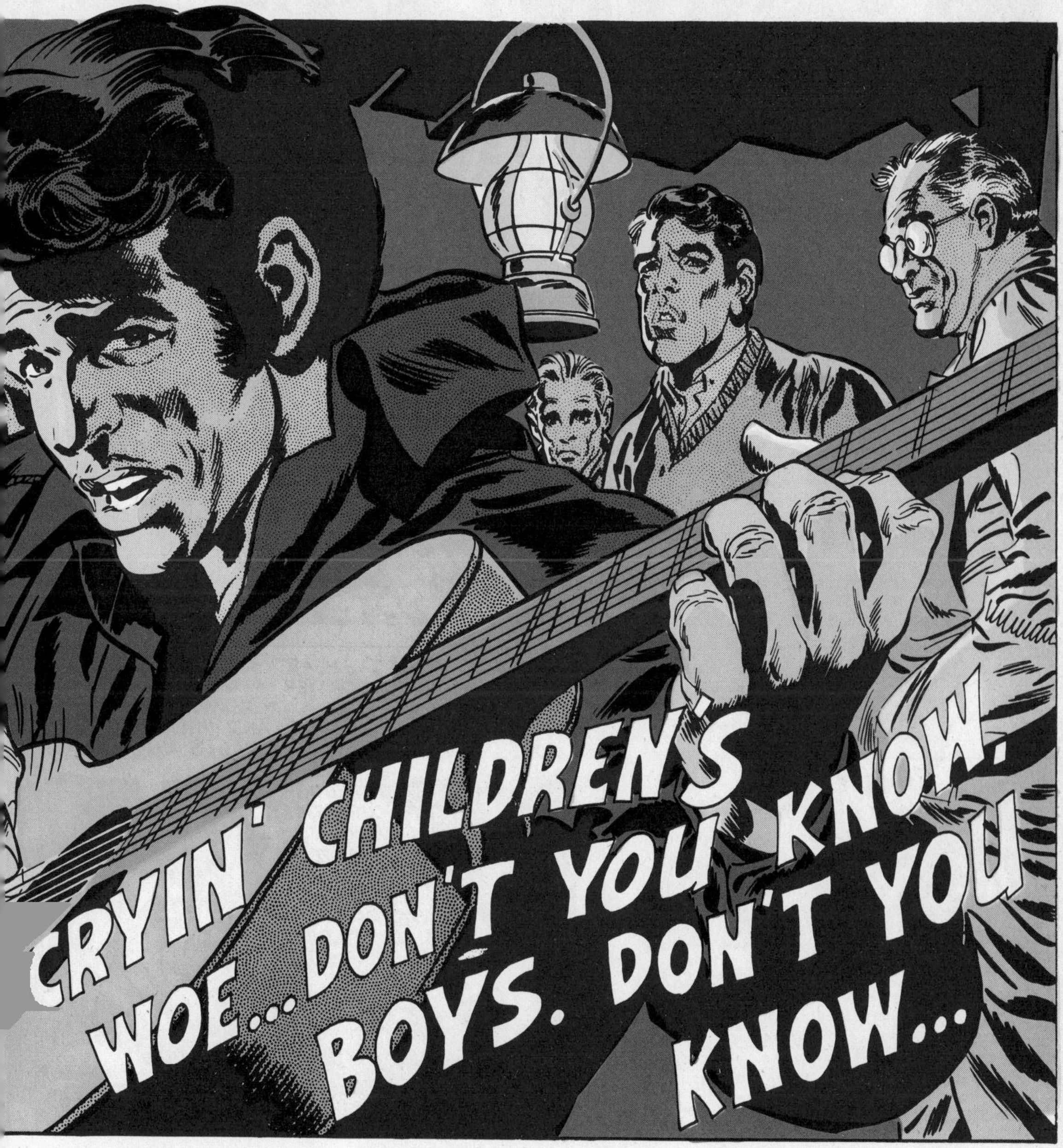
CRYIN' CHILDREN'S WOE... DON'T YOU KNOW. BOYS. DON'T YOU KNOW...

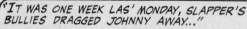

"IT WAS ONE WEEK LAS' MONDAY, SLAPPER'S BULLIES DRAGGED JOHNNY AWAY..."

"THEY RIGGED A KANGAROO COURT... AND SLAPPER, *PERSONAL*, SENTENCED JOHNNY TO... *HANG!*"

THAT'S GONNA HAPPEN *TOMORROW*-- AT *DAWN*... 'LESS WE *STOP* IT! AN' WE'RE *GONNA*--

WE'RE GONNA *JUMP* SLAPPER'S PLACE *TONIGHT!*

YOU BLASTED AT *US* BECAUSE YOU MISTOOK US FOR MORE *HOODS*, HUH?

WELL, MISTER, YOU WERE *WRONG!*

YOU'RE ABOUT TO GET SOME FIRST-CLASS *HELP!*-- EXPERIENCE *GUARANTEED!*

HOLD *ON*, GREEN ARROW! THIS IS NONE OF OUR *BUSINESS*... IF THIS SOAMES *IS REALLY* IN CHARGE--

OH, BOY! NOW I'VE HEARD IT ALL...BECAUSE SOAMES MUSCLED HIS WAY INTO *AUTHORITY*, HE'S A *GOOD* GUY, HUH?

PAL, *HITLER* WAS THE "BOSS" OF *GERMANY*, REMEMBER? AND THERE WAS *GENGHIS KHAN, NERO*...

THROUGH-OUT *HISTORY*, CHEAP PUNKS HAVE MADE THEMSELVES LEADERS! *REGARDLESS* OF THEIR TITLES, THEY WERE *STILL* CHEAP PUNKS!

7

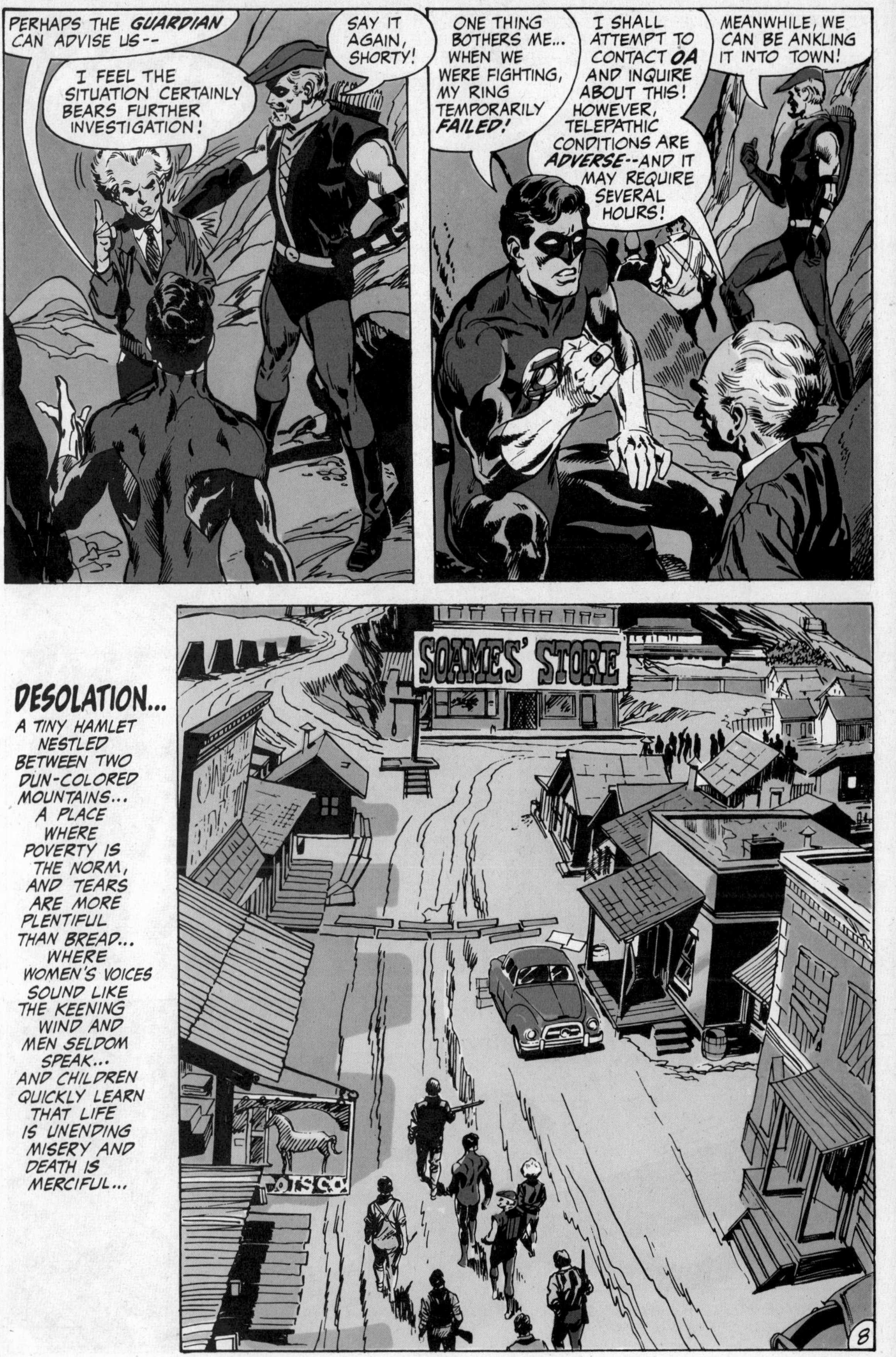

PERHAPS THE GUARDIAN CAN ADVISE US--
I FEEL THE SITUATION CERTAINLY BEARS FURTHER INVESTIGATION!
SAY IT AGAIN, SHORTY!
ONE THING BOTHERS ME... WHEN WE WERE FIGHTING, MY RING TEMPORARILY FAILED!
I SHALL ATTEMPT TO CONTACT OA AND INQUIRE ABOUT THIS! HOWEVER, TELEPATHIC CONDITIONS ARE ADVERSE--AND IT MAY REQUIRE SEVERAL HOURS!
MEANWHILE, WE CAN BE ANKLING IT INTO TOWN!
DESOLATION... A TINY HAMLET NESTLED BETWEEN TWO DUN-COLORED MOUNTAINS... A PLACE WHERE POVERTY IS THE NORM, AND TEARS ARE MORE PLENTIFUL THAN BREAD... WHERE WOMEN'S VOICES SOUND LIKE THE KEENING WIND AND MEN SELDOM SPEAK... AND CHILDREN QUICKLY LEARN THAT LIFE IS UNENDING MISERY AND DEATH IS MERCIFUL...
SOAMES' STORE
8

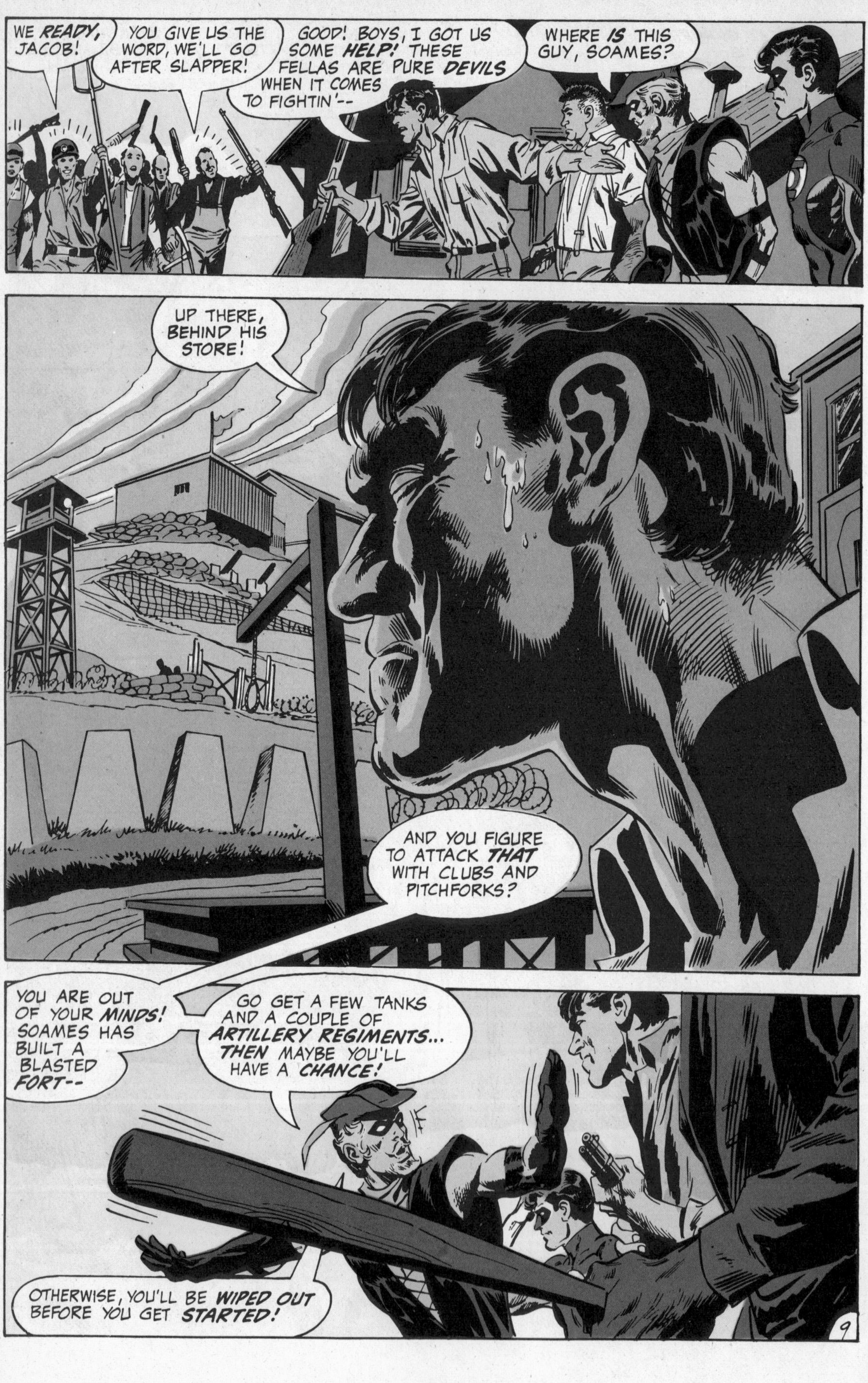

WE READY, JACOB!
YOU GIVE US THE WORD, WE'LL GO AFTER SLAPPER!
GOOD! BOYS, I GOT US SOME HELP! THESE FELLAS ARE PURE DEVILS WHEN IT COMES TO FIGHTIN'--
WHERE IS THIS GUY, SOAMES?
UP THERE, BEHIND HIS STORE!
AND YOU FIGURE TO ATTACK THAT WITH CLUBS AND PITCHFORKS?
YOU ARE OUT OF YOUR MINDS! SOAMES HAS BUILT A BLASTED FORT--
GO GET A FEW TANKS AND A COUPLE OF ARTILLERY REGIMENTS... THEN MAYBE YOU'LL HAVE A CHANCE!
OTHERWISE, YOU'LL BE WIPED OUT BEFORE YOU GET STARTED!
9

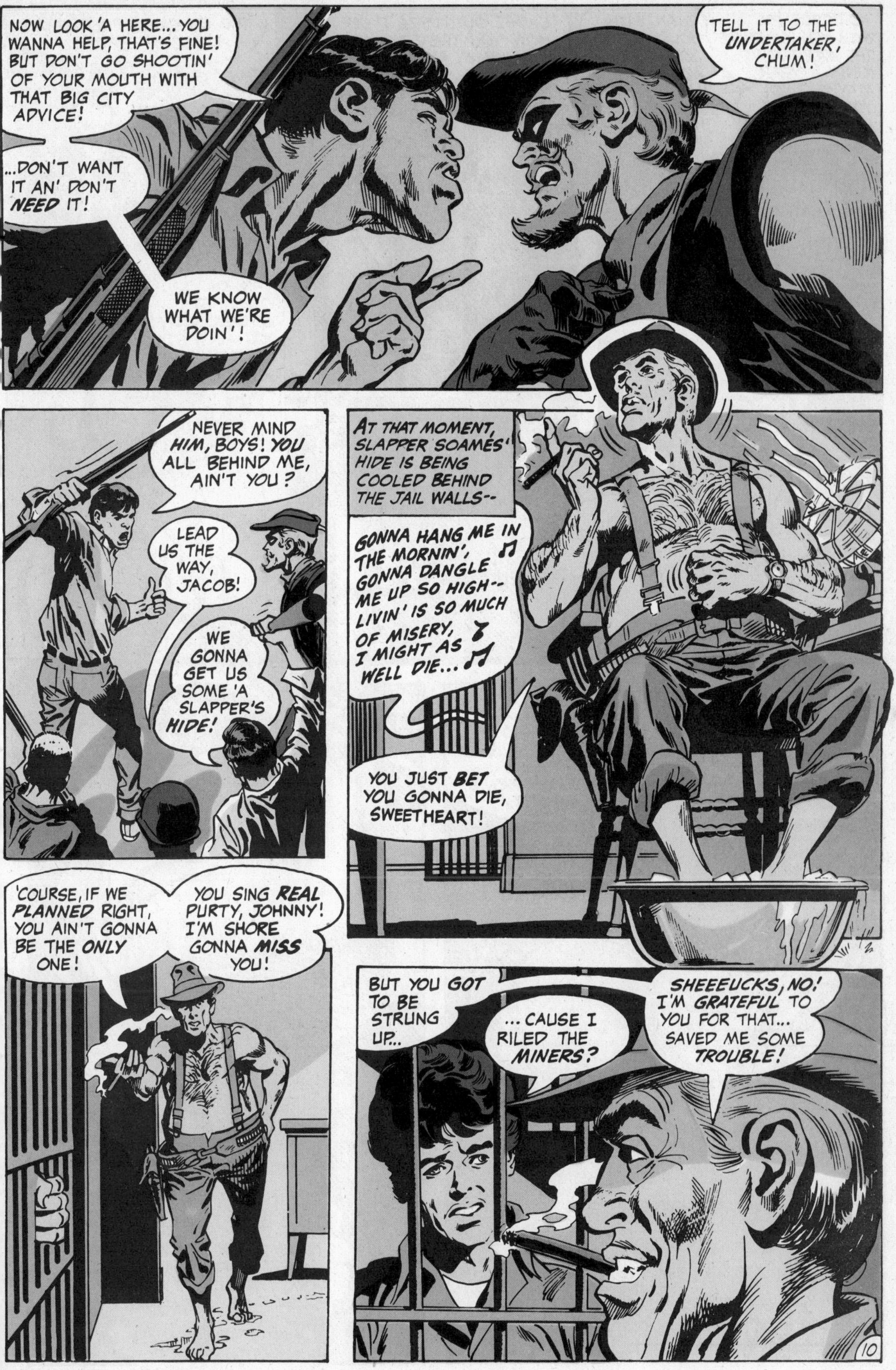

NOW LOOK 'A HERE... YOU WANNA HELP, THAT'S FINE! BUT DON'T GO SHOOTIN' OF YOUR MOUTH WITH THAT BIG CITY ADVICE!
...DON'T WANT IT AN' DON'T NEED IT!
WE KNOW WHAT WE'RE DOIN'!
TELL IT TO THE UNDERTAKER, CHUM!
NEVER MIND HIM, BOYS! YOU ALL BEHIND ME, AIN'T YOU?
LEAD US THE WAY, JACOB!
WE GONNA GET US SOME 'A SLAPPER'S HIDE!
AT THAT MOMENT, SLAPPER SOAMES' HIDE IS BEING COOLED BEHIND THE JAIL WALLS--
GONNA HANG ME IN THE MORNIN', GONNA DANGLE ME UP SO HIGH-- LIVIN' IS SO MUCH OF MISERY, I MIGHT AS WELL DIE...
YOU JUST BET YOU GONNA DIE, SWEETHEART!
'COURSE, IF WE PLANNED RIGHT, YOU AIN'T GONNA BE THE ONLY ONE!
YOU SING REAL PURTY, JOHNNY! I'M SHORE GONNA MISS YOU!
BUT YOU GOT TO BE STRUNG UP..
... CAUSE I RILED THE MINERS?
SHEEEUCKS, NO! I'M GRATEFUL TO YOU FOR THAT... SAVED ME SOME TROUBLE!
10

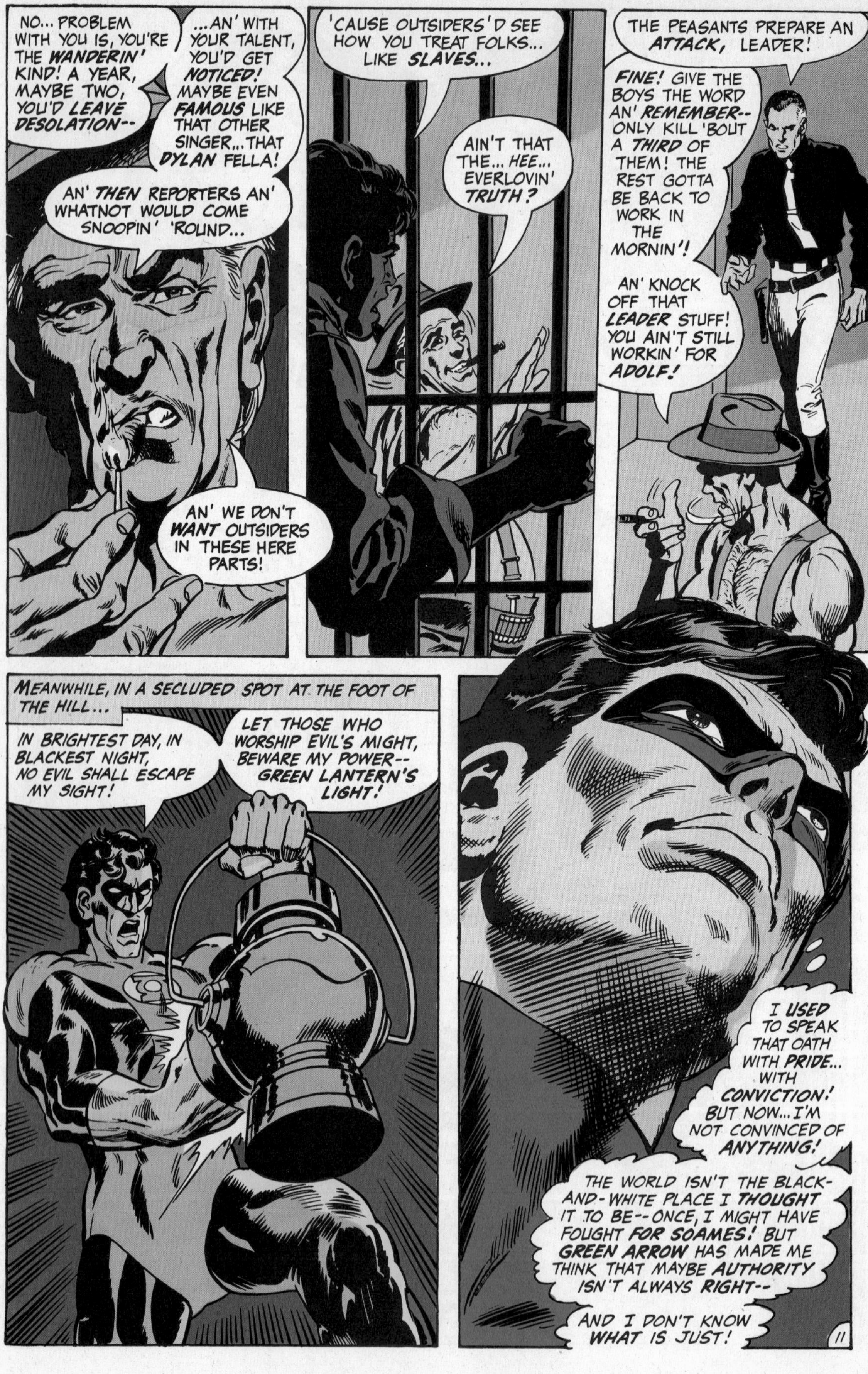
NO... PROBLEM WITH YOU IS, YOU'RE THE WANDERIN' KIND! A YEAR, MAYBE TWO, YOU'D LEAVE DESOLATION--
...AN' WITH YOUR TALENT, YOU'D GET NOTICED! MAYBE EVEN FAMOUS LIKE THAT OTHER SINGER... THAT DYLAN FELLA!
AN' THEN REPORTERS AN' WHATNOT WOULD COME SNOOPIN' 'ROUND...
AN' WE DON'T WANT OUTSIDERS IN THESE HERE PARTS!
'CAUSE OUTSIDERS'D SEE HOW YOU TREAT FOLKS... LIKE SLAVES...
AIN'T THAT THE... HEE... EVERLOVIN' TRUTH?
THE PEASANTS PREPARE AN ATTACK, LEADER!
FINE! GIVE THE BOYS THE WORD AN' REMEMBER-- ONLY KILL 'BOUT A THIRD OF THEM! THE REST GOTTA BE BACK TO WORK IN THE MORNIN'!
AN' KNOCK OFF THAT LEADER STUFF! YOU AIN'T STILL WORKIN' FOR ADOLF!
MEANWHILE, IN A SECLUDED SPOT AT THE FOOT OF THE HILL...
IN BRIGHTEST DAY, IN BLACKEST NIGHT, NO EVIL SHALL ESCAPE MY SIGHT!
LET THOSE WHO WORSHIP EVIL'S MIGHT, BEWARE MY POWER-- GREEN LANTERN'S LIGHT!
I USED TO SPEAK THAT OATH WITH PRIDE... WITH CONVICTION! BUT NOW... I'M NOT CONVINCED OF ANYTHING!
THE WORLD ISN'T THE BLACK-AND-WHITE PLACE I THOUGHT IT TO BE--ONCE, I MIGHT HAVE FOUGHT FOR SOAMES! BUT GREEN ARROW HAS MADE ME THINK THAT MAYBE AUTHORITY ISN'T ALWAYS RIGHT--
AND I DON'T KNOW WHAT IS JUST!
11

ARE WE GOING TO **HELP** THEM... OR **NOT**?

HELP THEM COMMIT **SUICIDE**? NOT **THIS** ARCHER!

ALL SET, BOYS? THEN-- **CHARGE!**

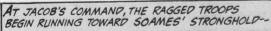

At Jacob's command, the ragged troops begin running toward Soames' stronghold--

--Across a field seeded with deadly land mines! Some die immediately...

BLAM

...Others live to face a withering storm of heavy caliber machine-gun fire--

CHUCKETA CHUCKETA

BEEOW ZING

BEEOW

THAT DIRTY... DIRTY... DIRTY...

12

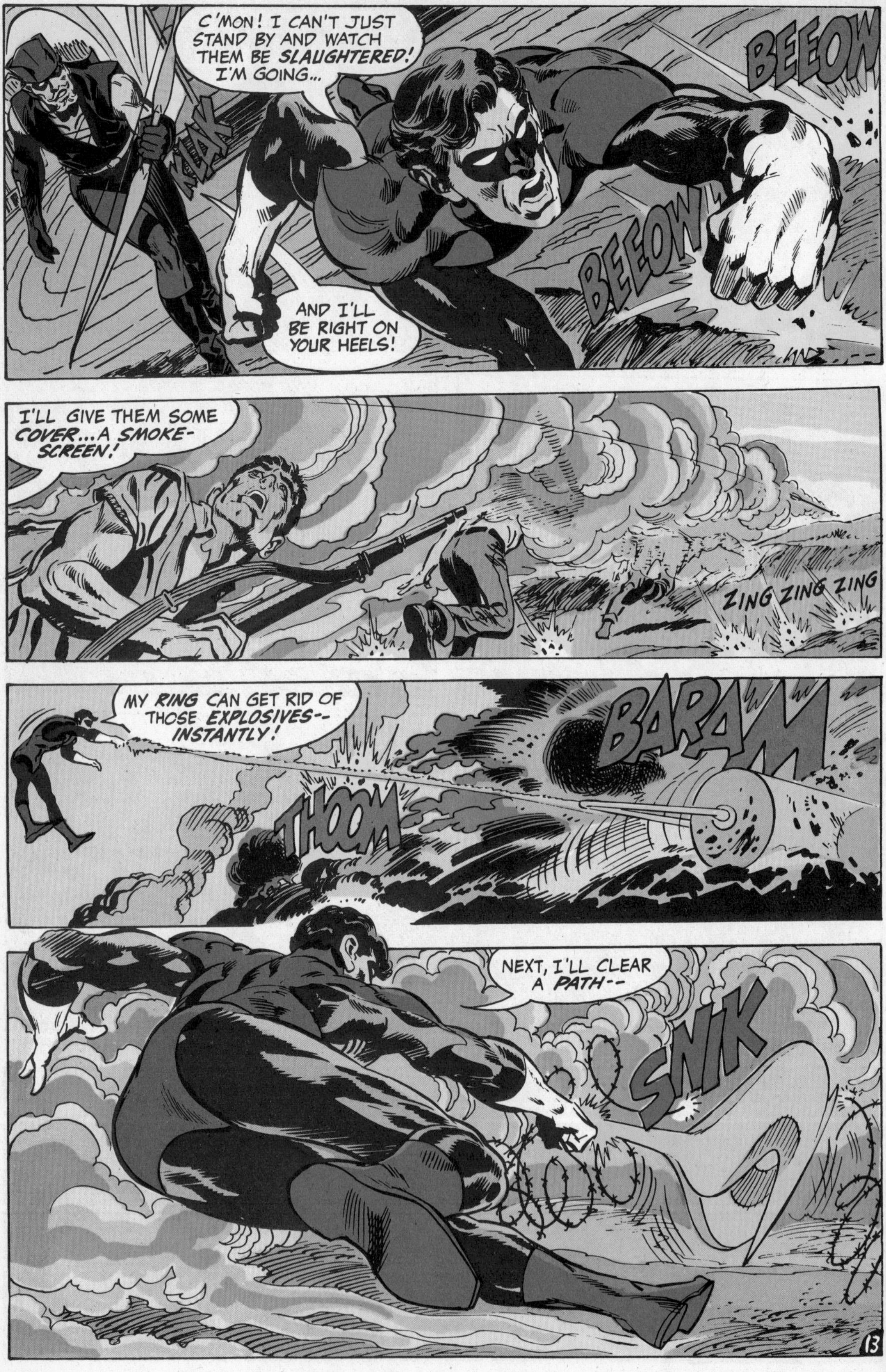
C'MON! I CAN'T JUST STAND BY AND WATCH THEM BE SLAUGHTERED! I'M GOING...
KLAK
BEEOW
BEEOW
AND I'LL BE RIGHT ON YOUR HEELS!
I'LL GIVE THEM SOME COVER...A SMOKE-SCREEN!
ZING ZING ZING
MY RING CAN GET RID OF THOSE EXPLOSIVES--INSTANTLY!
BARAM
THOOM
NEXT, I'LL CLEAR A PATH--
SNIK
13

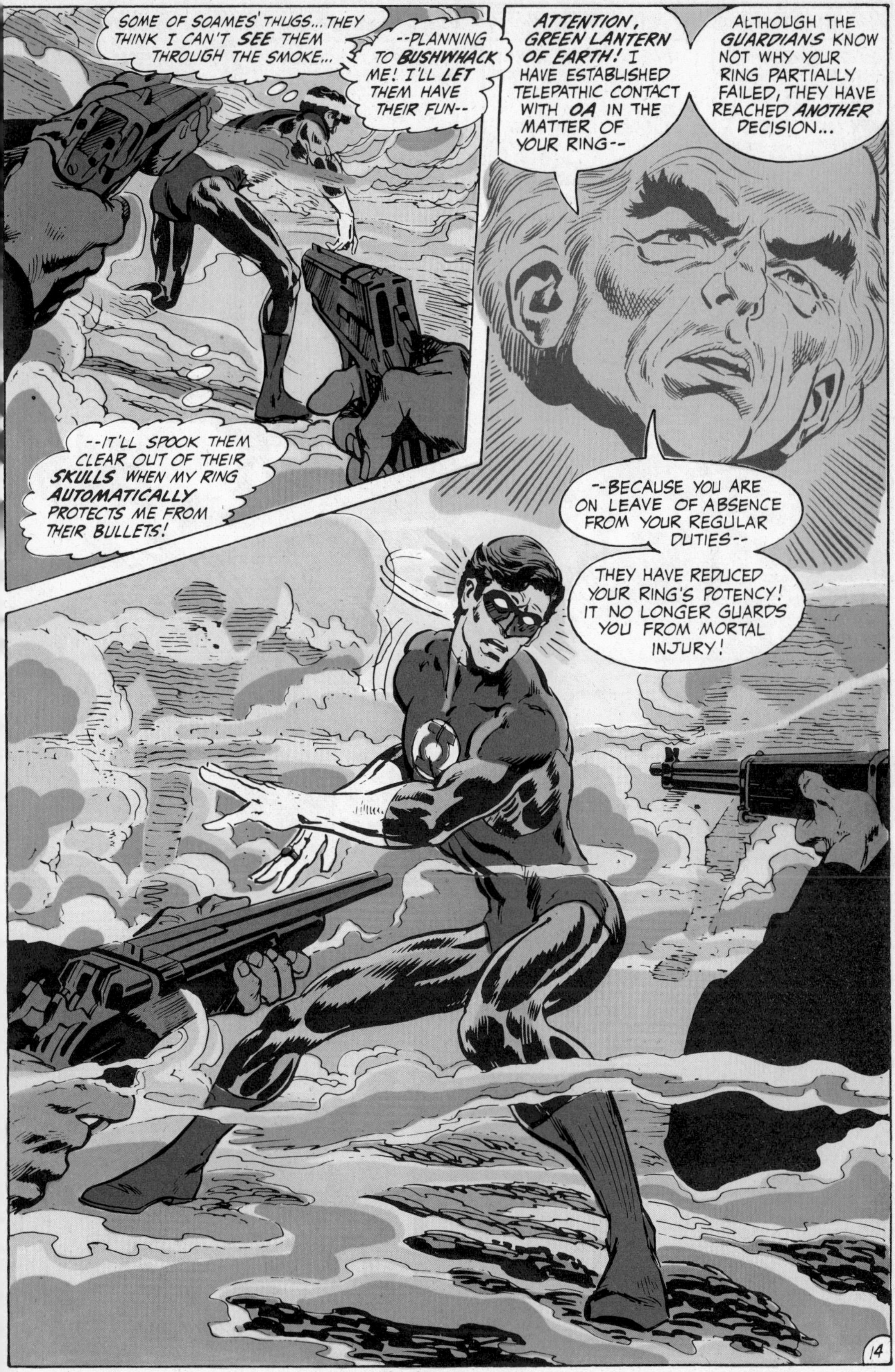
SOME OF SOAMES' THUGS... THEY THINK I CAN'T SEE THEM THROUGH THE SMOKE...
--PLANNING TO BUSHWHACK ME! I'LL LET THEM HAVE THEIR FUN--
--IT'LL SPOOK THEM CLEAR OUT OF THEIR SKULLS WHEN MY RING AUTOMATICALLY PROTECTS ME FROM THEIR BULLETS!
ATTENTION, GREEN LANTERN OF EARTH! I HAVE ESTABLISHED TELEPATHIC CONTACT WITH OA IN THE MATTER OF YOUR RING--
ALTHOUGH THE GUARDIANS KNOW NOT WHY YOUR RING PARTIALLY FAILED, THEY HAVE REACHED ANOTHER DECISION...
--BECAUSE YOU ARE ON LEAVE OF ABSENCE FROM YOUR REGULAR DUTIES--
THEY HAVE REDUCED YOUR RING'S POTENCY! IT NO LONGER GUARDS YOU FROM MORTAL INJURY!
14

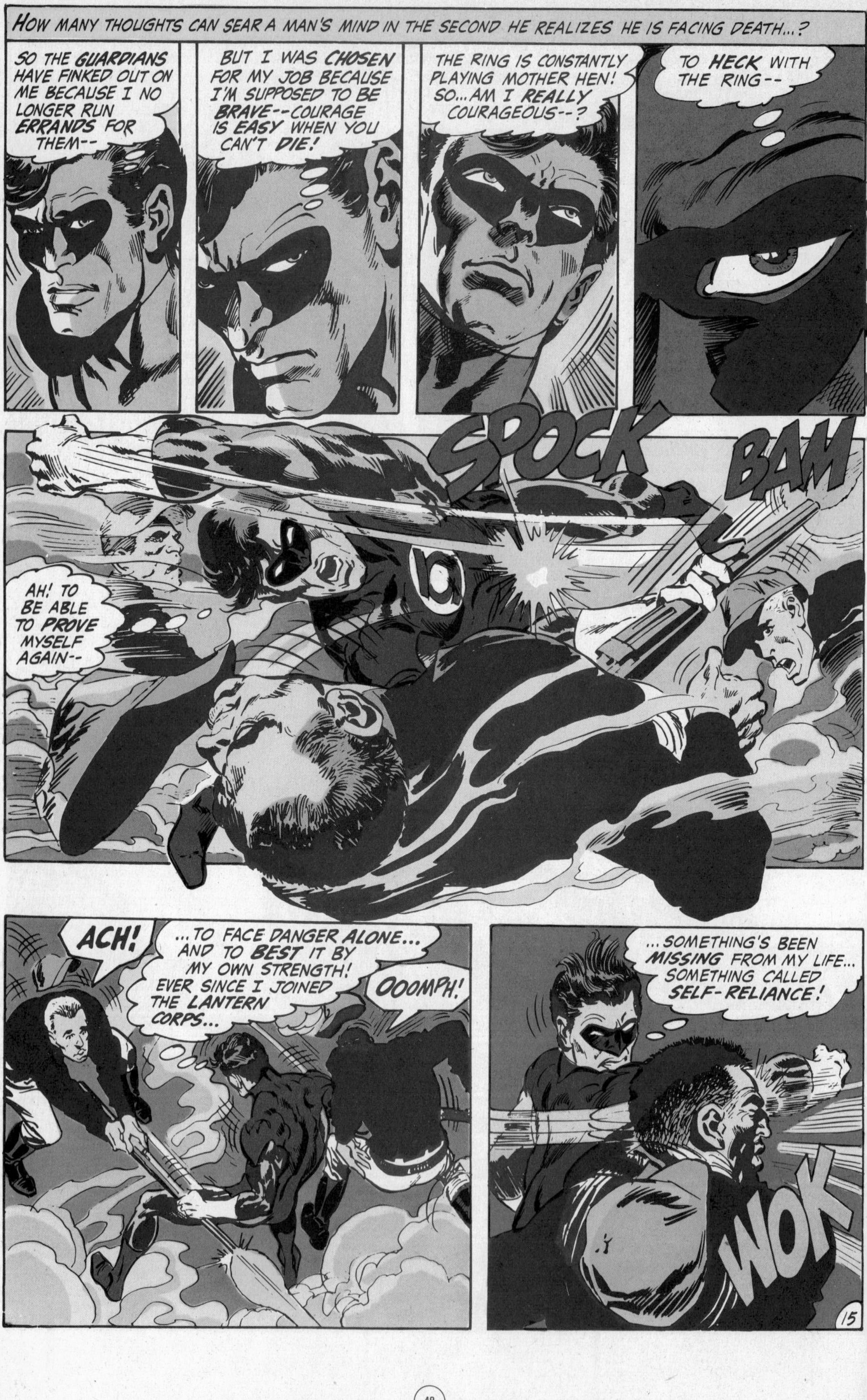
HOW MANY THOUGHTS CAN SEAR A MAN'S MIND IN THE SECOND HE REALIZES HE IS FACING DEATH...?
SO THE GUARDIANS HAVE FINKED OUT ON ME BECAUSE I NO LONGER RUN ERRANDS FOR THEM--
BUT I WAS CHOSEN FOR MY JOB BECAUSE I'M SUPPOSED TO BE BRAVE--COURAGE IS EASY WHEN YOU CAN'T DIE!
THE RING IS CONSTANTLY PLAYING MOTHER HEN! SO...AM I REALLY COURAGEOUS--?
TO HECK WITH THE RING--
SPOCK
BAM
AH! TO BE ABLE TO PROVE MYSELF AGAIN--
ACH!
...TO FACE DANGER ALONE... AND TO BEST IT BY MY OWN STRENGTH! EVER SINCE I JOINED THE LANTERN CORPS...
OOOMPH!
...SOMETHING'S BEEN MISSING FROM MY LIFE... SOMETHING CALLED SELF-RELIANCE!
WOK
15

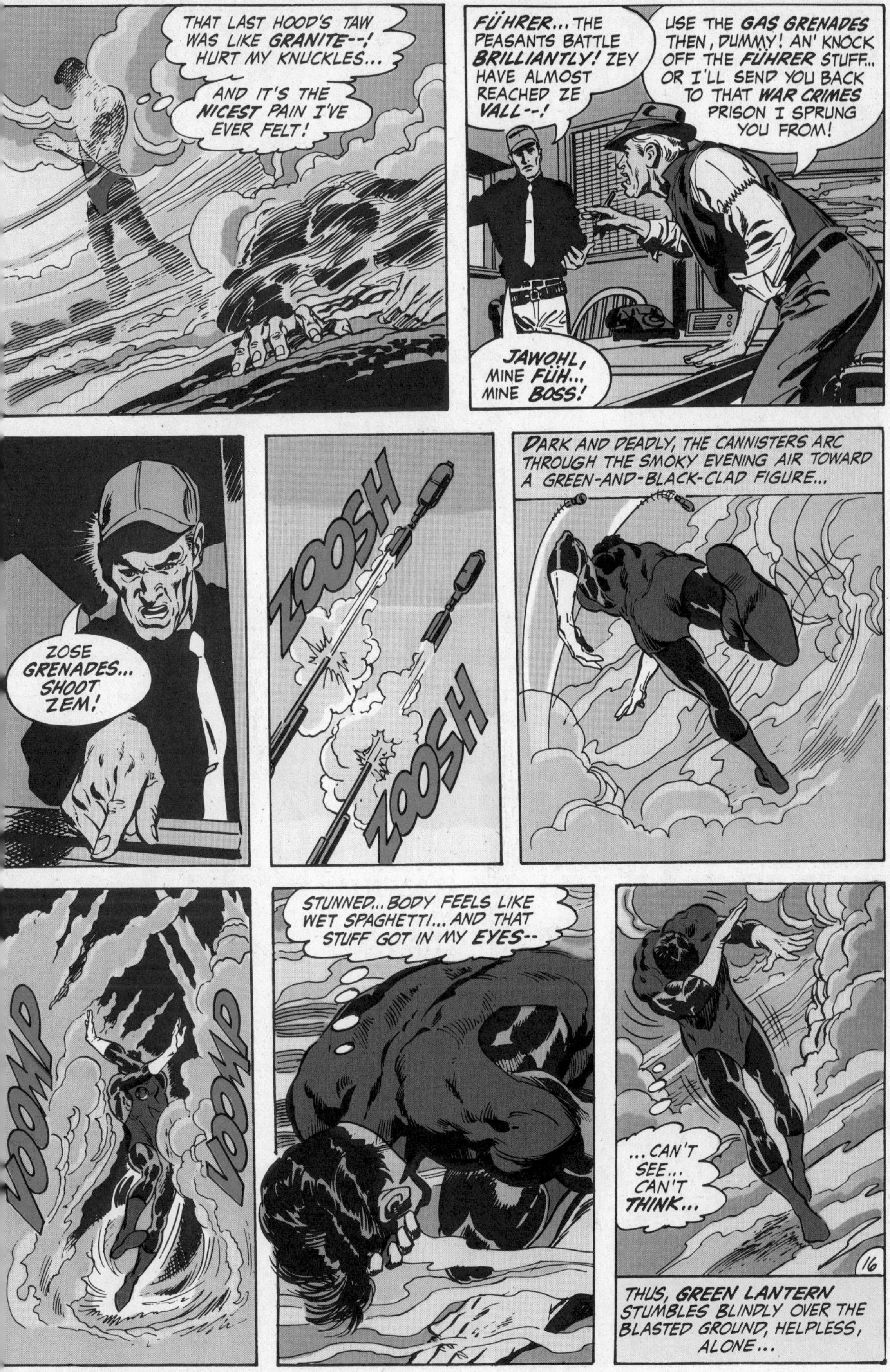
THAT LAST HOOD'S TAW WAS LIKE GRANITE--! HURT MY KNUCKLES...
AND IT'S THE NICEST PAIN I'VE EVER FELT!
FÜHRER... THE PEASANTS BATTLE BRILLIANTLY! ZEY HAVE ALMOST REACHED ZE VALL--!
USE THE GAS GRENADES THEN, DUMMY! AN' KNOCK OFF THE FÜHRER STUFF... OR I'LL SEND YOU BACK TO THAT WAR CRIMES PRISON I SPRUNG YOU FROM!
JAWOHL, MINE FÜH... MINE BOSS!
ZOSE GRENADES... SHOOT ZEM!
ZOOSH
ZOOSH
DARK AND DEADLY, THE CANNISTERS ARC THROUGH THE SMOKY EVENING AIR TOWARD A GREEN-AND-BLACK-CLAD FIGURE...
VOOMP
VOOMP
STUNNED... BODY FEELS LIKE WET SPAGHETTI... AND THAT STUFF GOT IN MY EYES--
...CAN'T SEE... CAN'T THINK...
16
THUS, GREEN LANTERN STUMBLES BLINDLY OVER THE BLASTED GROUND, HELPLESS, ALONE...

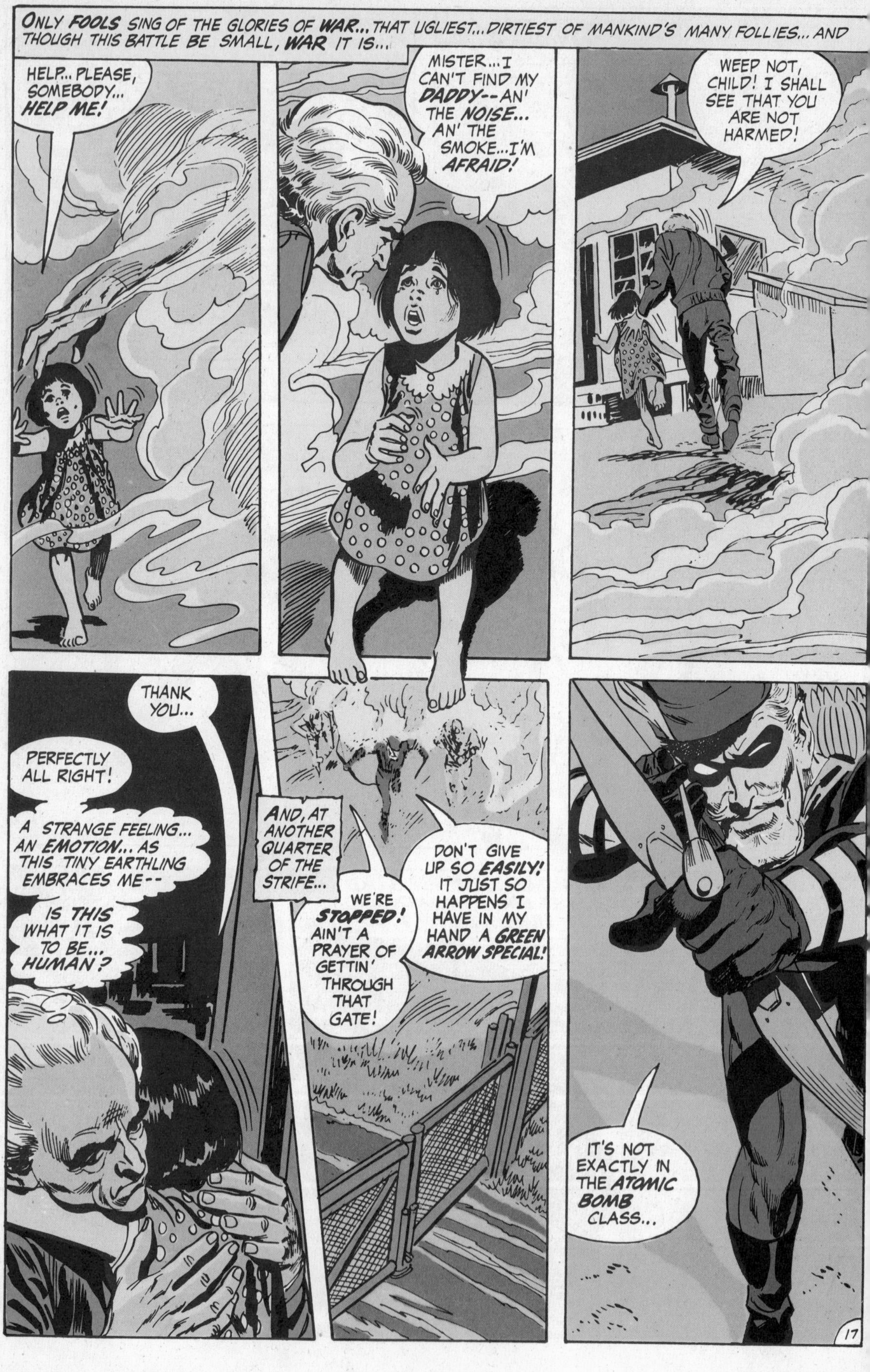

ONLY FOOLS SING OF THE GLORIES OF WAR... THAT UGLIEST... DIRTIEST OF MANKIND'S MANY FOLLIES... AND THOUGH THIS BATTLE BE SMALL, WAR IT IS...
HELP... PLEASE, SOMEBODY... HELP ME!
MISTER... I CAN'T FIND MY DADDY--AN' THE NOISE... AN' THE SMOKE... I'M AFRAID!
WEEP NOT, CHILD! I SHALL SEE THAT YOU ARE NOT HARMED!
THANK YOU...
PERFECTLY ALL RIGHT!
A STRANGE FEELING... AN EMOTION... AS THIS TINY EARTHLING EMBRACES ME--
IS THIS WHAT IT IS TO BE... HUMAN?
AND, AT ANOTHER QUARTER OF THE STRIFE...
WE'RE STOPPED! AIN'T A PRAYER OF GETTIN' THROUGH THAT GATE!
DON'T GIVE UP SO EASILY! IT JUST SO HAPPENS I HAVE IN MY HAND A GREEN ARROW SPECIAL!
IT'S NOT EXACTLY IN THE ATOMIC BOMB CLASS...
17

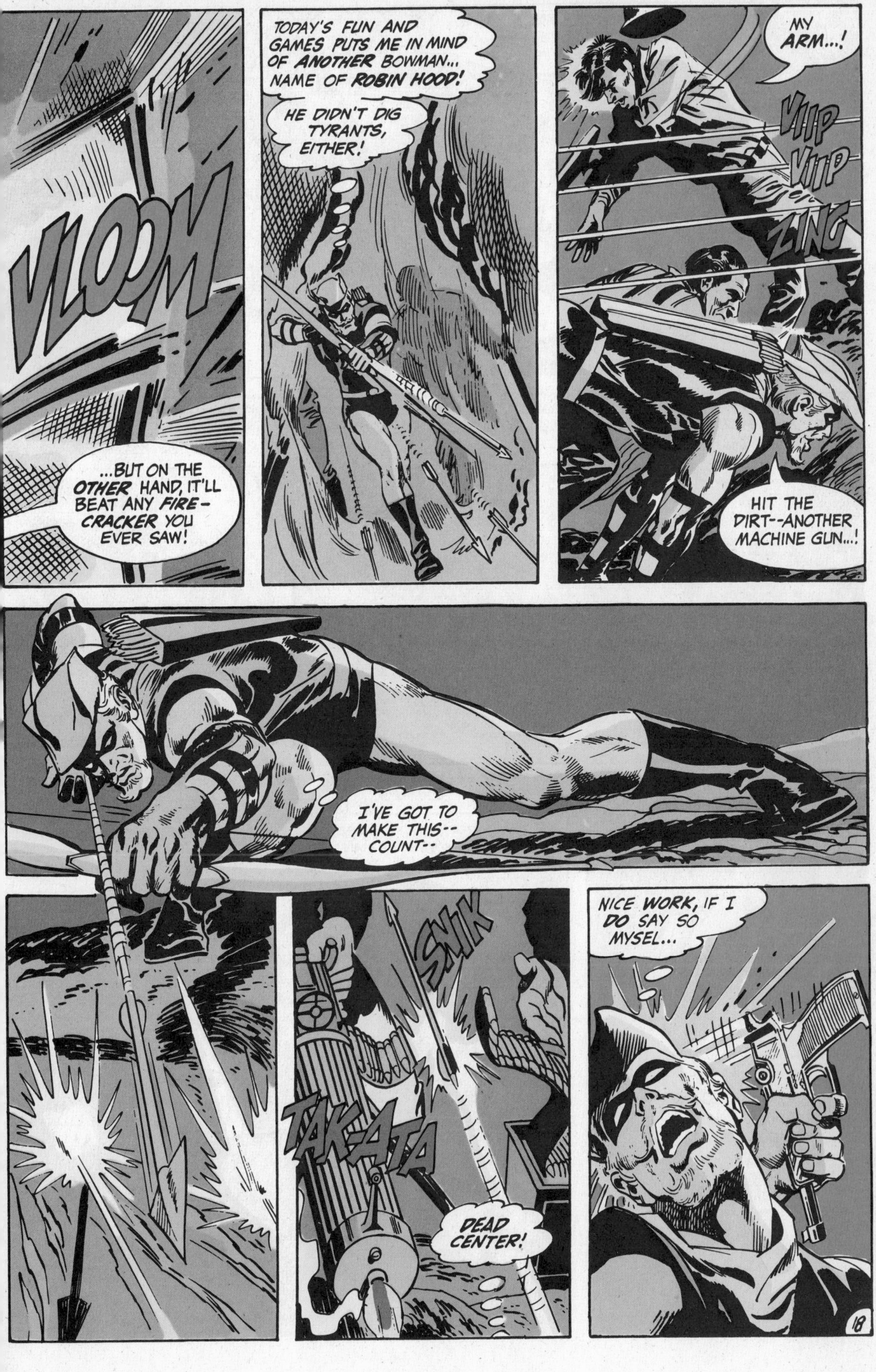

VLOOM
...BUT ON THE OTHER HAND, IT'LL BEAT ANY FIRE-CRACKER YOU EVER SAW!
TODAY'S FUN AND GAMES PUTS ME IN MIND OF ANOTHER BOWMAN... NAME OF ROBIN HOOD!
HE DIDN'T DIG TYRANTS, EITHER!
MY ARM...!
VIIP
VIIP
ZING
HIT THE DIRT--ANOTHER MACHINE GUN...!
I'VE GOT TO MAKE THIS--COUNT--
SNIK
TAKATA
DEAD CENTER!
NICE WORK, IF I DO SAY SO MYSEL...
18

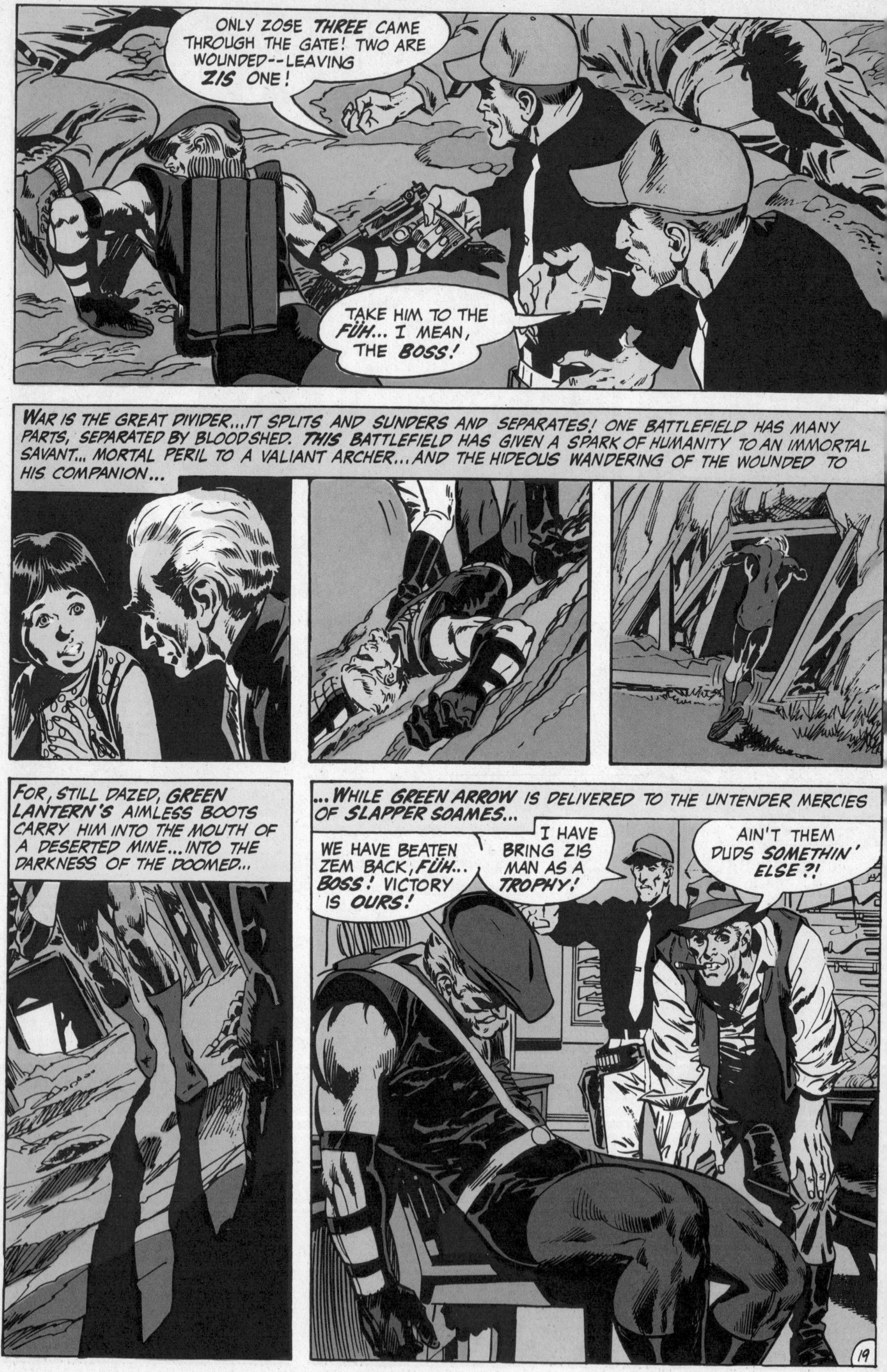
ONLY ZOSE THREE CAME THROUGH THE GATE! TWO ARE WOUNDED--LEAVING ZIS ONE!
TAKE HIM TO THE FÜH... I MEAN, THE BOSS!
WAR IS THE GREAT DIVIDER...IT SPLITS AND SUNDERS AND SEPARATES! ONE BATTLEFIELD HAS MANY PARTS, SEPARATED BY BLOODSHED. THIS BATTLEFIELD HAS GIVEN A SPARK OF HUMANITY TO AN IMMORTAL SAVANT... MORTAL PERIL TO A VALIANT ARCHER...AND THE HIDEOUS WANDERING OF THE WOUNDED TO HIS COMPANION...
FOR, STILL DAZED, GREEN LANTERN'S AIMLESS BOOTS CARRY HIM INTO THE MOUTH OF A DESERTED MINE...INTO THE DARKNESS OF THE DOOMED...
...WHILE GREEN ARROW IS DELIVERED TO THE UNTENDER MERCIES OF SLAPPER SOAMES...
WE HAVE BEATEN ZEM BACK, FÜH... BOSS! VICTORY IS OURS!
I HAVE BRING ZIS MAN AS A TROPHY!
AIN'T THEM DUDS SOMETHIN' ELSE?!
19

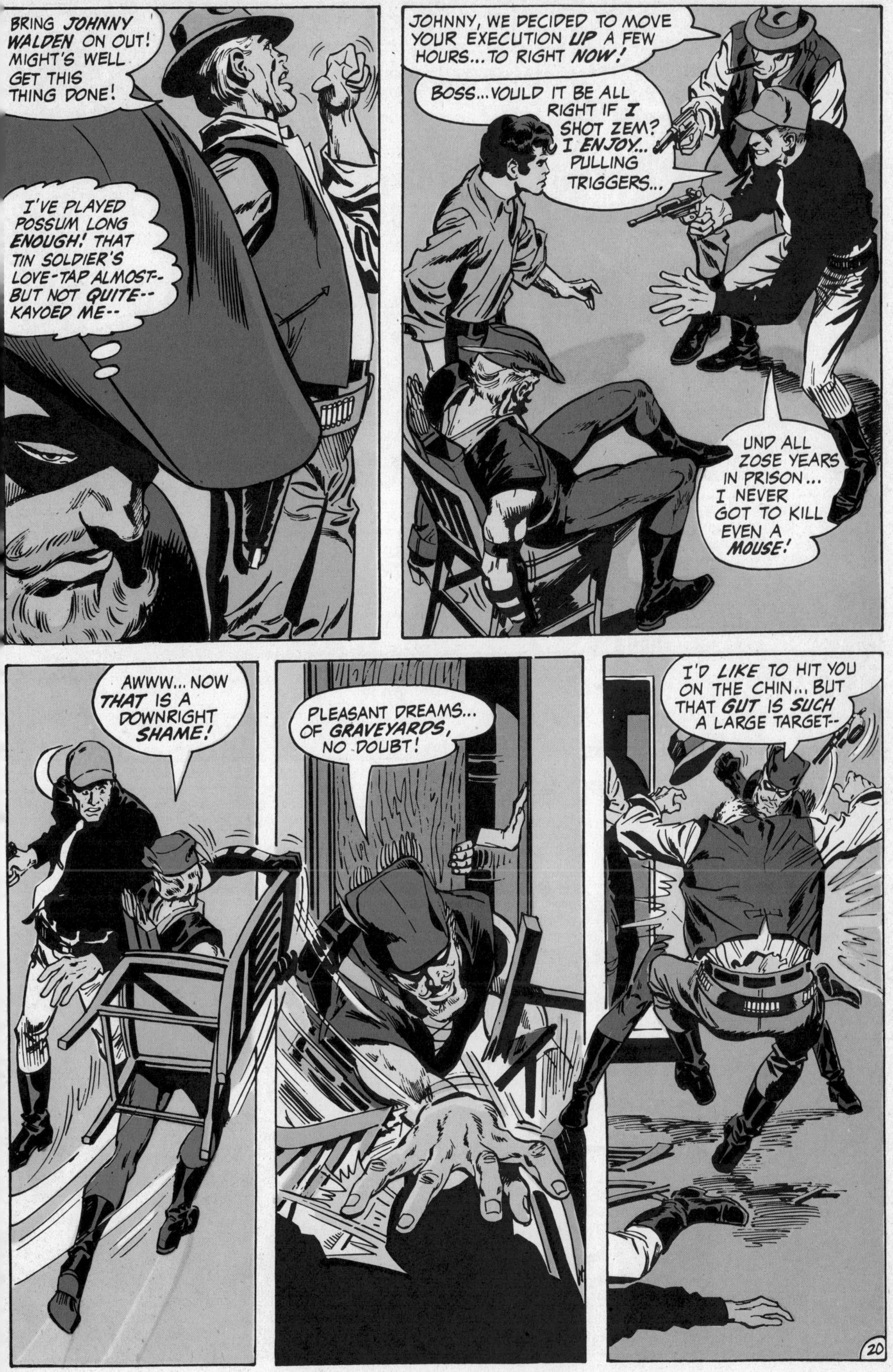
BRING JOHNNY WALDEN ON OUT! MIGHT'S WELL GET THIS THING DONE!
I'VE PLAYED POSSUM LONG ENOUGH! THAT TIN SOLDIER'S LOVE-TAP ALMOST-- BUT NOT QUITE-- KAYOED ME--
JOHNNY, WE DECIDED TO MOVE YOUR EXECUTION UP A FEW HOURS... TO RIGHT NOW!
BOSS... VOULD IT BE ALL RIGHT IF I SHOT ZEM? I ENJOY... PULLING TRIGGERS...
UND ALL ZOSE YEARS IN PRISON... I NEVER GOT TO KILL EVEN A MOUSE!
AWWW... NOW THAT IS A DOWNRIGHT SHAME!
PLEASANT DREAMS... OF GRAVEYARDS, NO DOUBT!
I'D LIKE TO HIT YOU ON THE CHIN... BUT THAT GUT IS SUCH A LARGE TARGET--
20

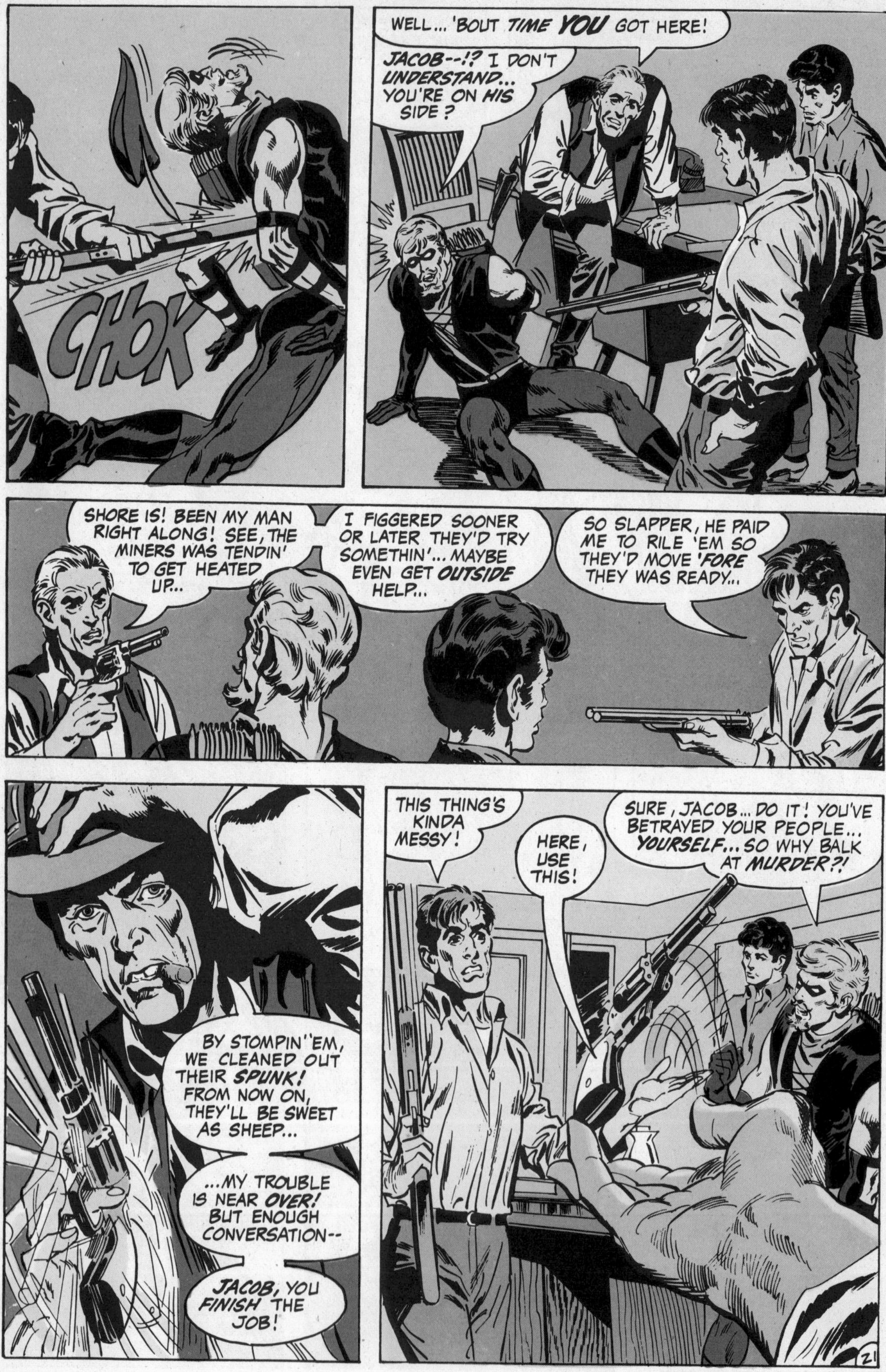
CHOK
WELL... 'BOUT TIME YOU GOT HERE!
JACOB--!? I DON'T UNDERSTAND... YOU'RE ON HIS SIDE?
SHORE IS! BEEN MY MAN RIGHT ALONG! SEE, THE MINERS WAS TENDIN' TO GET HEATED UP...
I FIGGERED SOONER OR LATER THEY'D TRY SOMETHIN'... MAYBE EVEN GET OUTSIDE HELP...
SO SLAPPER, HE PAID ME TO RILE 'EM SO THEY'D MOVE 'FORE THEY WAS READY...
BY STOMPIN' 'EM, WE CLEANED OUT THEIR SPUNK! FROM NOW ON, THEY'LL BE SWEET AS SHEEP...
...MY TROUBLE IS NEAR OVER! BUT ENOUGH CONVERSATION--
JACOB, YOU FINISH THE JOB!
THIS THING'S KINDA MESSY!
HERE, USE THIS!
SURE, JACOB... DO IT! YOU'VE BETRAYED YOUR PEOPLE... YOURSELF... SO WHY BALK AT MURDER?!
21

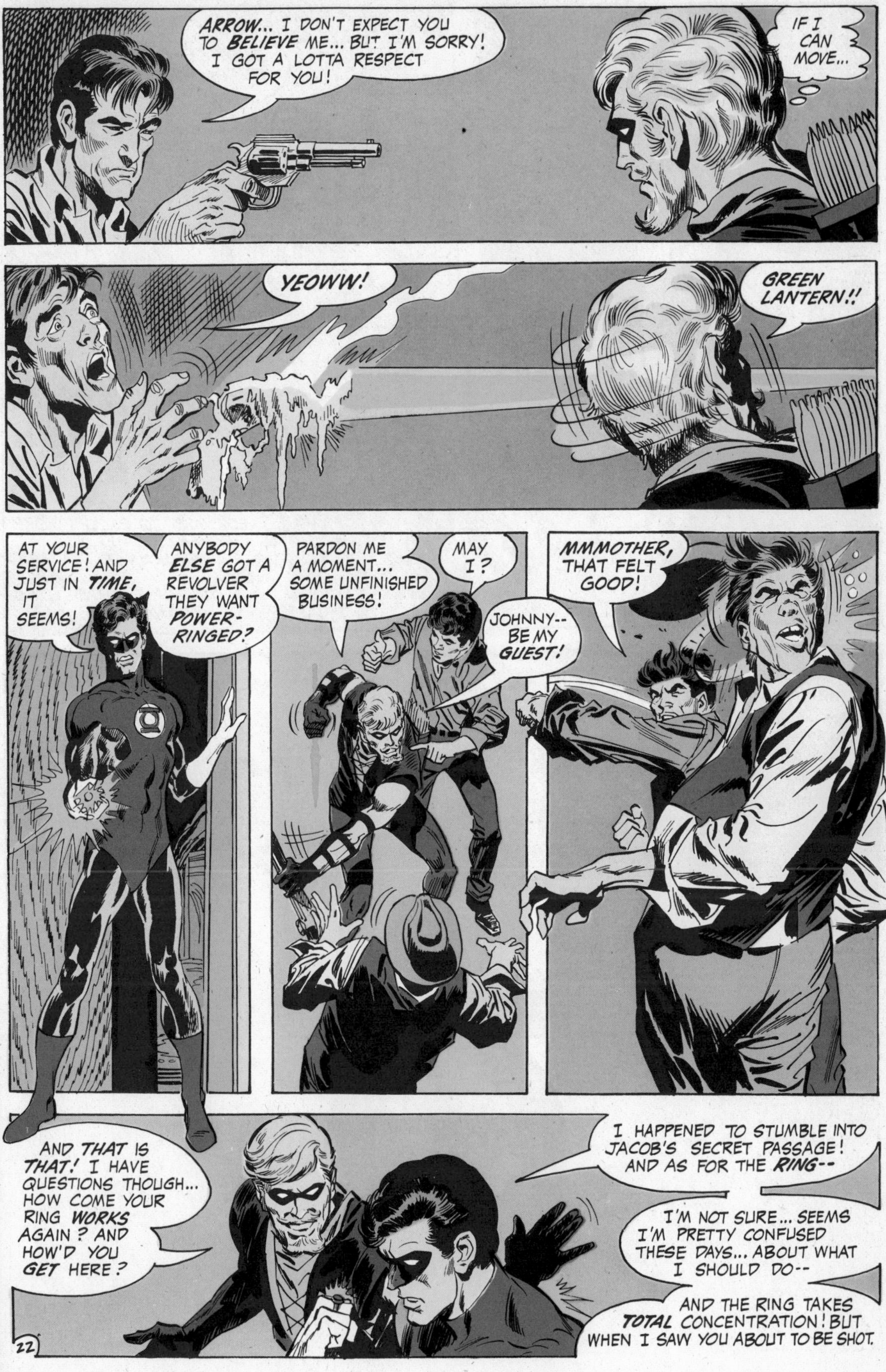
ARROW... I DON'T EXPECT YOU TO BELIEVE ME... BUT I'M SORRY! I GOT A LOTTA RESPECT FOR YOU!
IF I CAN MOVE...
YEOWW!
GREEN LANTERN!!
AT YOUR SERVICE! AND JUST IN TIME, IT SEEMS!
ANYBODY ELSE GOT A REVOLVER THEY WANT POWER-RINGED?
PARDON ME A MOMENT... SOME UNFINISHED BUSINESS!
MAY I?
JOHNNY-- BE MY GUEST!
MMMOTHER, THAT FELT GOOD!
AND THAT IS THAT! I HAVE QUESTIONS THOUGH... HOW COME YOUR RING WORKS AGAIN? AND HOW'D YOU GET HERE?
I HAPPENED TO STUMBLE INTO JACOB'S SECRET PASSAGE! AND AS FOR THE RING--
I'M NOT SURE... SEEMS I'M PRETTY CONFUSED THESE DAYS... ABOUT WHAT I SHOULD DO--
AND THE RING TAKES TOTAL CONCENTRATION! BUT WHEN I SAW YOU ABOUT TO BE SHOT.
22

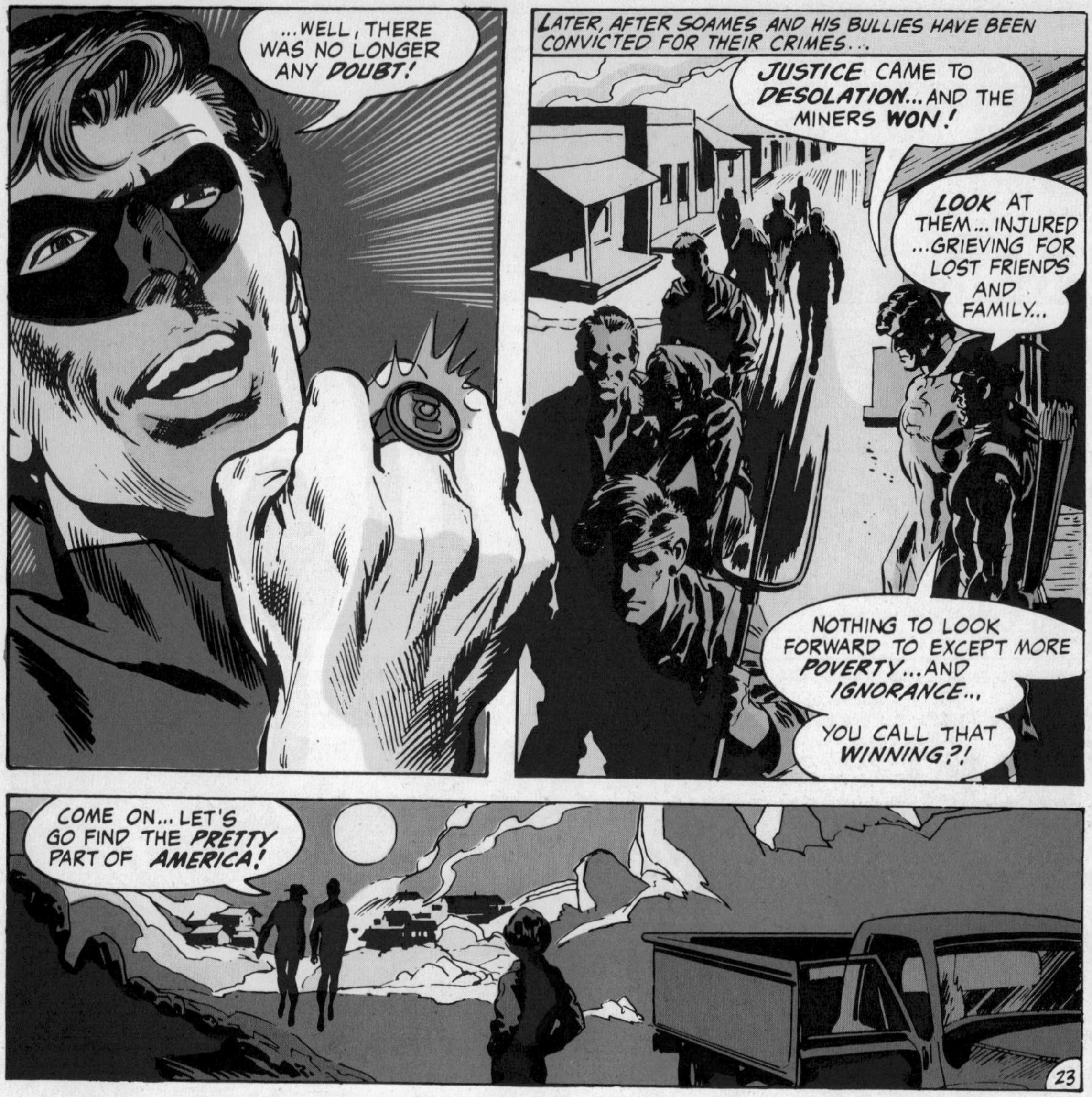
...WELL, THERE WAS NO LONGER ANY DOUBT!
LATER, AFTER SOAMES AND HIS BULLIES HAVE BEEN CONVICTED FOR THEIR CRIMES...
JUSTICE CAME TO DESOLATION...AND THE MINERS WON!
LOOK AT THEM... INJURED ...GRIEVING FOR LOST FRIENDS AND FAMILY...
NOTHING TO LOOK FORWARD TO EXCEPT MORE POVERTY...AND IGNORANCE...
YOU CALL THAT WINNING?!
COME ON... LET'S GO FIND THE PRETTY PART OF AMERICA!
23

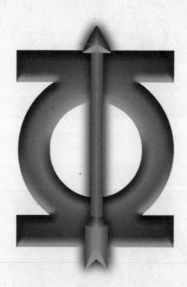

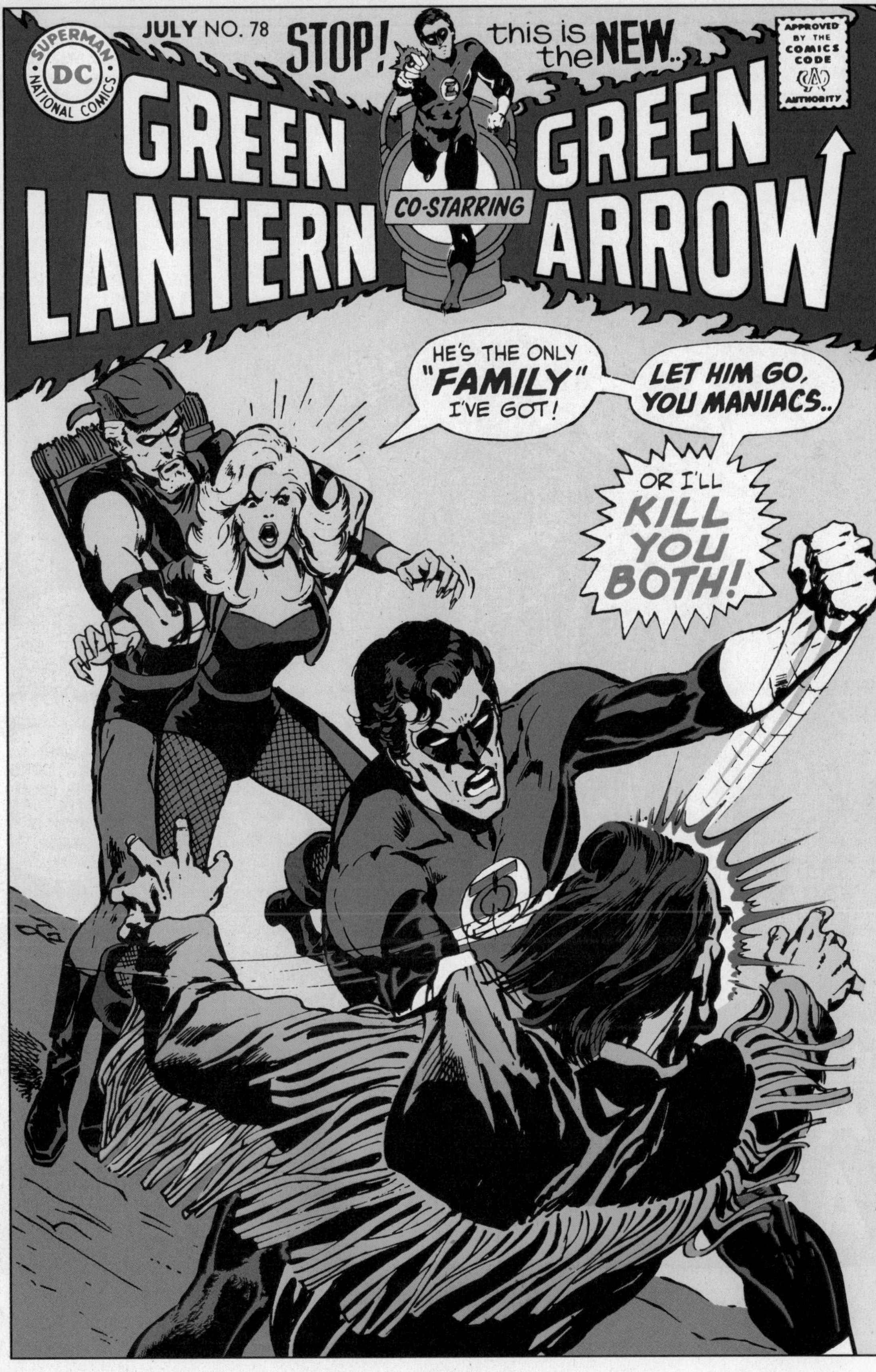
SUPERMAN DC NATIONAL COMICS
JULY NO. 78
STOP! this is the NEW..
APPROVED BY THE COMICS CODE AUTHORITY
GREEN LANTERN
CO-STARRING
GREEN ARROW
HE'S THE ONLY "FAMILY" I'VE GOT!
LET HIM GO, YOU MANIACS..
OR I'LL KILL YOU BOTH!

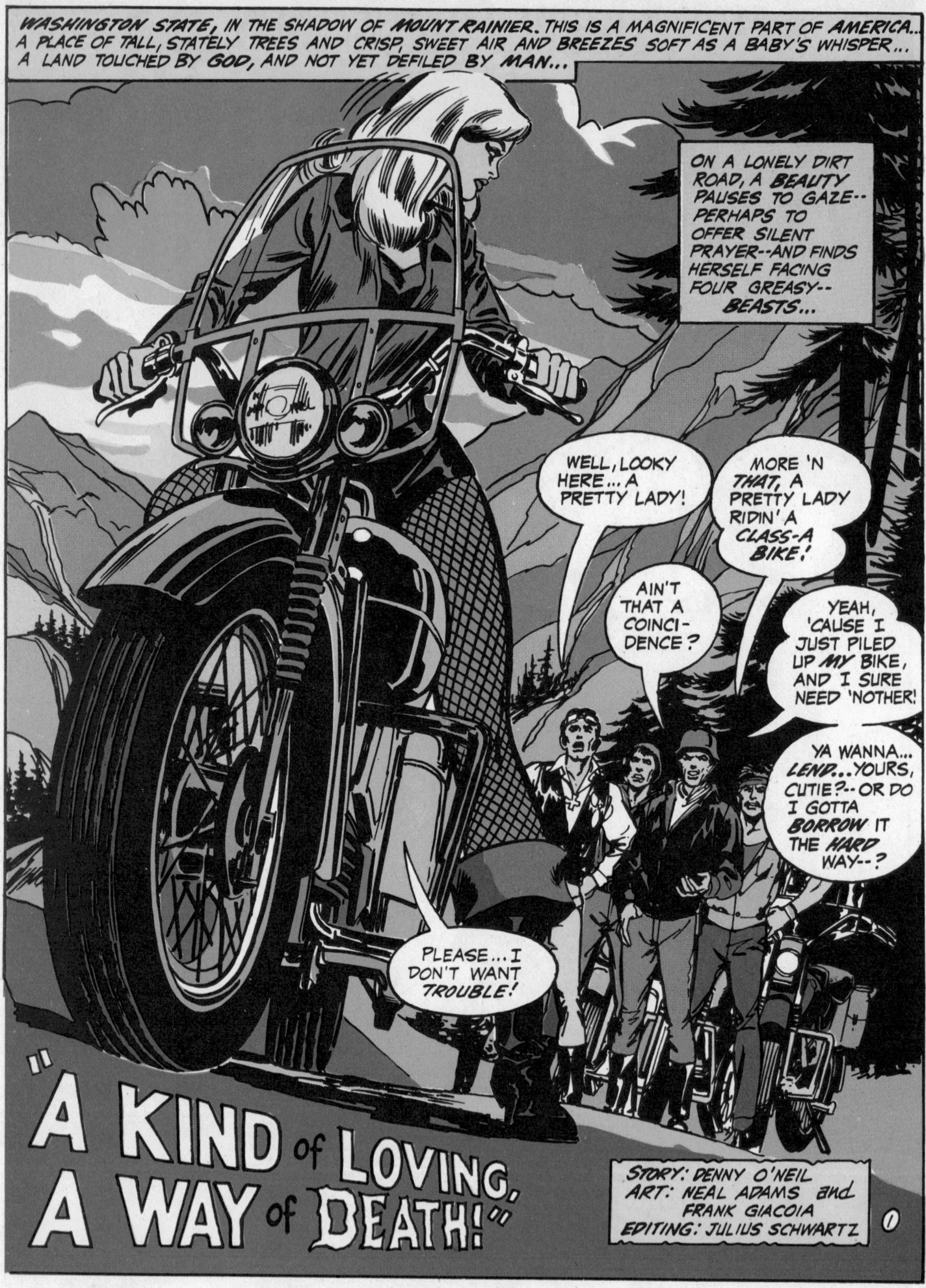
WASHINGTON STATE, IN THE SHADOW OF MOUNT RAINIER. THIS IS A MAGNIFICENT PART OF AMERICA... A PLACE OF TALL, STATELY TREES AND CRISP, SWEET AIR AND BREEZES SOFT AS A BABY'S WHISPER... A LAND TOUCHED BY GOD, AND NOT YET DEFILED BY MAN...
ON A LONELY DIRT ROAD, A BEAUTY PAUSES TO GAZE-- PERHAPS TO OFFER SILENT PRAYER--AND FINDS HERSELF FACING FOUR GREASY-- BEASTS...
WELL, LOOKY HERE... A PRETTY LADY!
MORE 'N THAT, A PRETTY LADY RIDIN' A CLASS-A BIKE!
AIN'T THAT A COINCI-DENCE?
YEAH, 'CAUSE I JUST PILED UP MY BIKE, AND I SURE NEED 'NOTHER!
YA WANNA... LEND... YOURS, CUTIE?--OR DO I GOTTA BORROW IT THE HARD WAY--?
PLEASE... I DON'T WANT TROUBLE!
"A KIND of LOVING, A WAY of DEATH!"
STORY: DENNY O'NEIL
ART: NEAL ADAMS and FRANK GIACOIA
EDITING: JULIUS SCHWARTZ
1

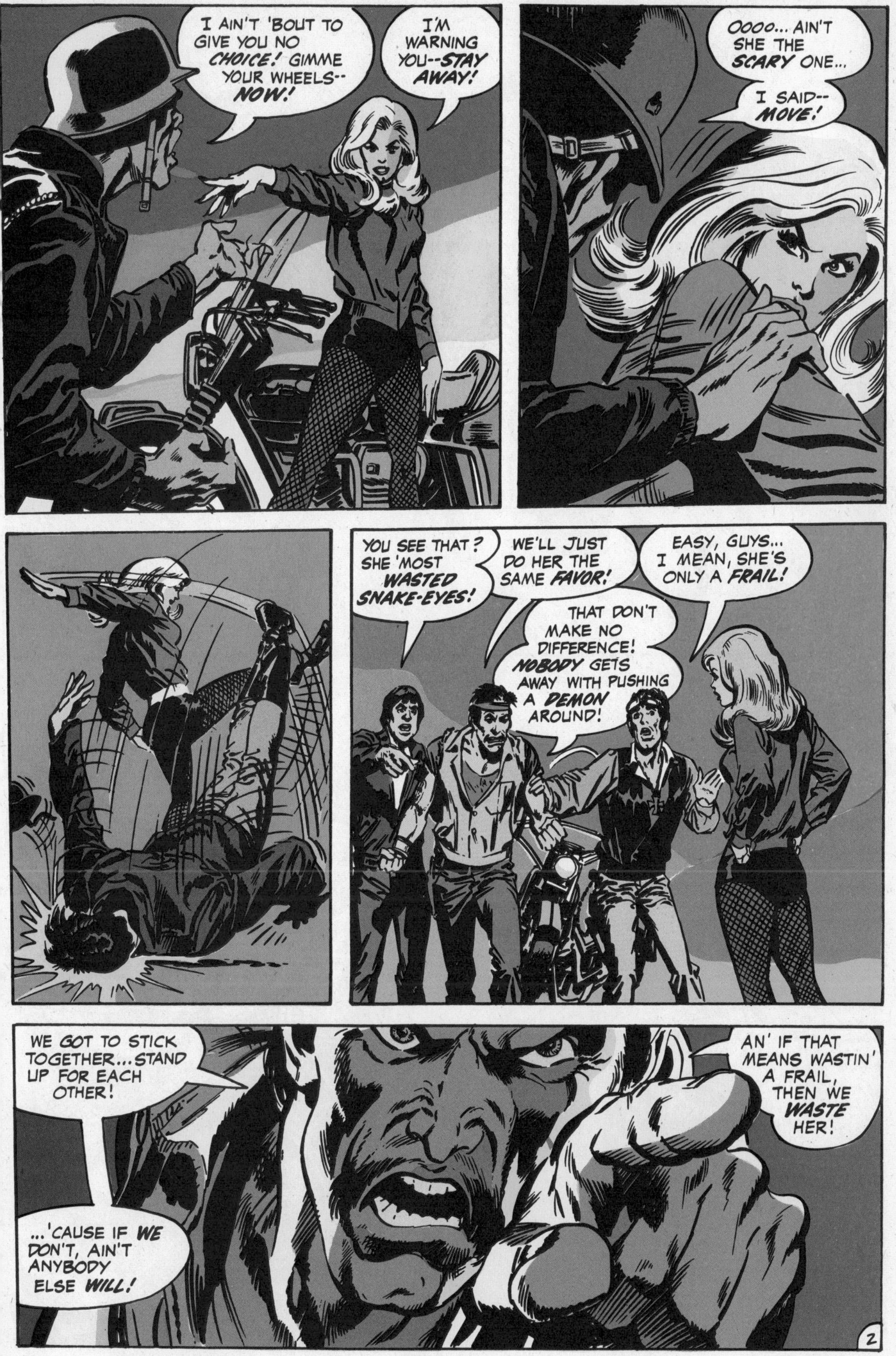

I AIN'T 'BOUT TO GIVE YOU NO CHOICE! GIMME YOUR WHEELS-- NOW!
I'M WARNING YOU--STAY AWAY!
OOOO... AIN'T SHE THE SCARY ONE...
I SAID-- MOVE!
YOU SEE THAT? SHE 'MOST WASTED SNAKE-EYES!
WE'LL JUST DO HER THE SAME FAVOR!
EASY, GUYS... I MEAN, SHE'S ONLY A FRAIL!
THAT DON'T MAKE NO DIFFERENCE! NOBODY GETS AWAY WITH PUSHING A DEMON AROUND!
WE GOT TO STICK TOGETHER... STAND UP FOR EACH OTHER!
AN' IF THAT MEANS WASTIN' A FRAIL, THEN WE WASTE HER!
...'CAUSE IF WE DON'T, AIN'T ANYBODY ELSE WILL!
2

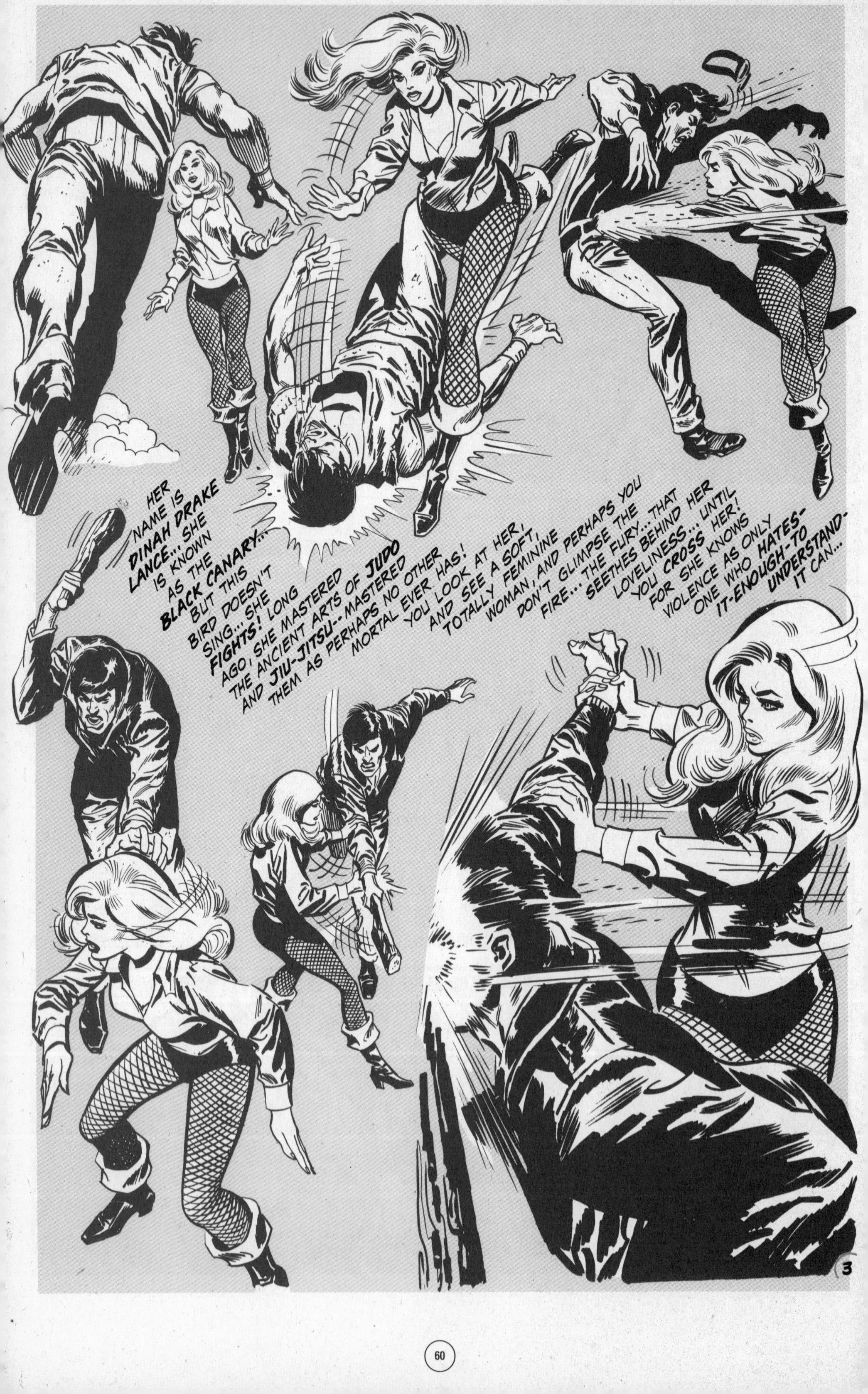
HER NAME IS DINAH DRAKE LANCE... SHE IS KNOWN AS THE BLACK CANARY... BUT THIS BIRD DOESN'T SING... SHE FIGHTS! LONG AGO, SHE MASTERED THE ANCIENT ARTS OF JUDO AND JIU-JITSU-- MASTERED THEM AS PERHAPS NO OTHER MORTAL EVER HAS! YOU LOOK AT HER, AND SEE A SOFT, TOTALLY FEMININE WOMAN, AND PERHAPS YOU DON'T GLIMPSE THE FIRE... THE FURY... THAT SEETHES BEHIND HER LOVELINESS... UNTIL YOU CROSS HER! FOR SHE KNOWS VIOLENCE AS ONLY ONE WHO HATES-IT-ENOUGH-TO UNDERSTAND-IT CAN...
3

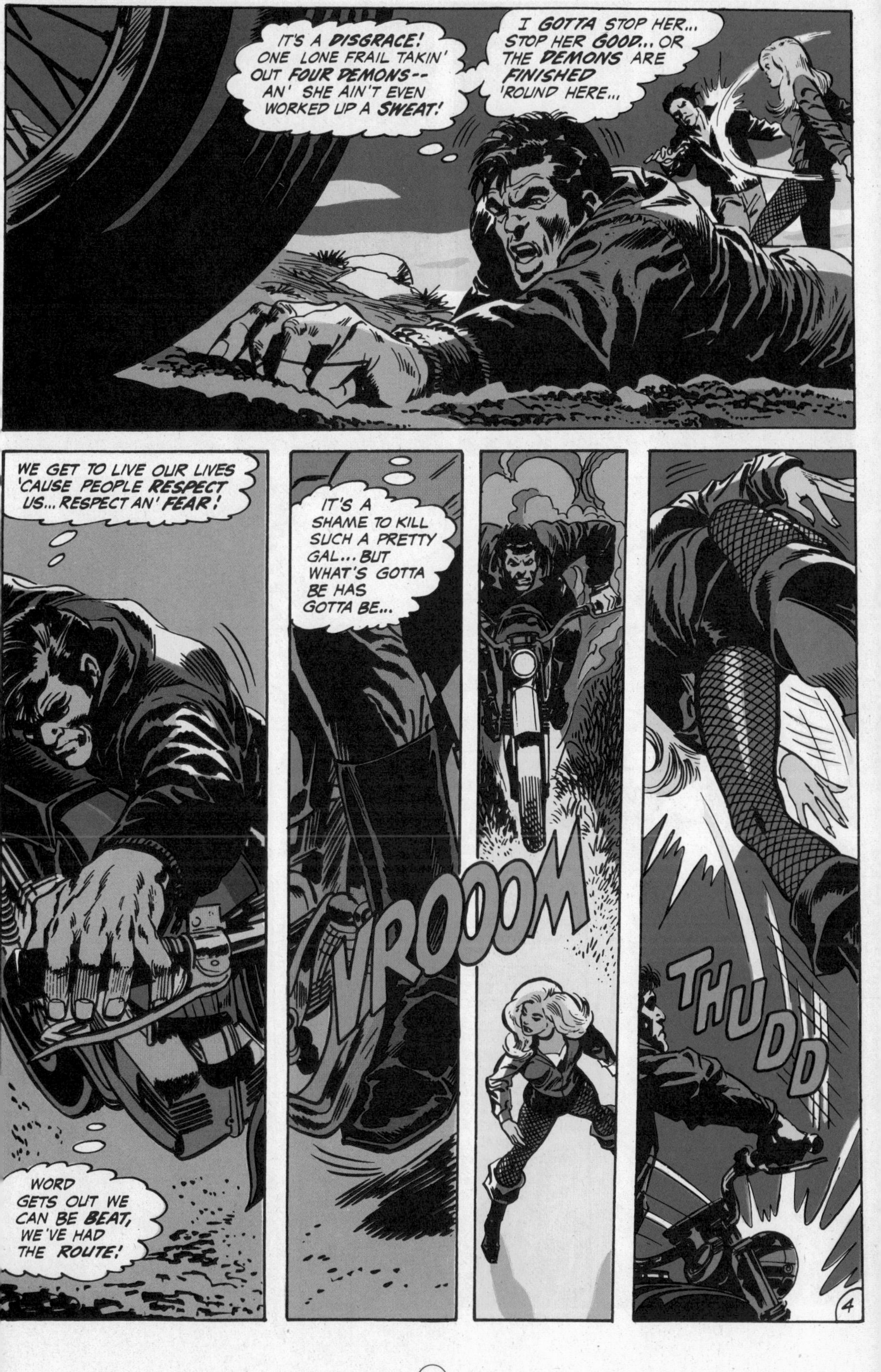
IT'S A DISGRACE! ONE LONE FRAIL TAKIN' OUT FOUR DEMONS-- AN' SHE AIN'T EVEN WORKED UP A SWEAT!
I GOTTA STOP HER... STOP HER GOOD... OR THE DEMONS ARE FINISHED 'ROUND HERE...
WE GET TO LIVE OUR LIVES 'CAUSE PEOPLE RESPECT US... RESPECT AN' FEAR!
WORD GETS OUT WE CAN BE BEAT, WE'VE HAD THE ROUTE!
IT'S A SHAME TO KILL SUCH A PRETTY GAL... BUT WHAT'S GOTTA BE HAS GOTTA BE...
VROOOM
THUDD
4

MOMENTS LATER, THE *DEMONS MOTOR-CYCLE CLUB* ROARS OFF... LEAVING THE *BLACK CANARY* LYING IN THE DIRT LIKE A BROKEN DOLL...

TWO WEEKS PASS. THE LONG FINGER OF *COINCIDENCE* NUDGES A BATTERED PICKUP TRUCK INTO THE SINGLE STREET OF A TINY HAMLET...

MAN, I'M *STARVED!*

ME TOO! MAYBE WE CAN GRAB A MEAL IN THIS TOWN!

I'VE SEEN LIVELIER BURGS ON *MODEL TRAIN* LAYOUTS!

ACCORDING TO THE MAP, THIS IS PART OF AN *INDIAN RESERVATION!*

THAT'S OKAY! INDIAN FOOD IS AS GOOD AS ANY!

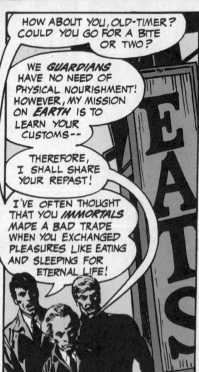

HOW ABOUT YOU, OLD-TIMER? COULD YOU GO FOR A BITE OR TWO?

WE *GUARDIANS* HAVE NO NEED OF PHYSICAL NOURISHMENT! HOWEVER, MY MISSION ON *EARTH* IS TO LEARN YOUR CUSTOMS--

THEREFORE, I SHALL SHARE YOUR REPAST!

I'VE OFTEN THOUGHT THAT YOU *IMMORTALS* MADE A BAD TRADE WHEN YOU EXCHANGED PLEASURES LIKE EATING AND SLEEPING FOR ETERNAL LIFE!

WHADDAYA SAY, PALEFACES?

WE SAY... FOOD! PRONTO!

WHAT'S ON THE MENU?

5

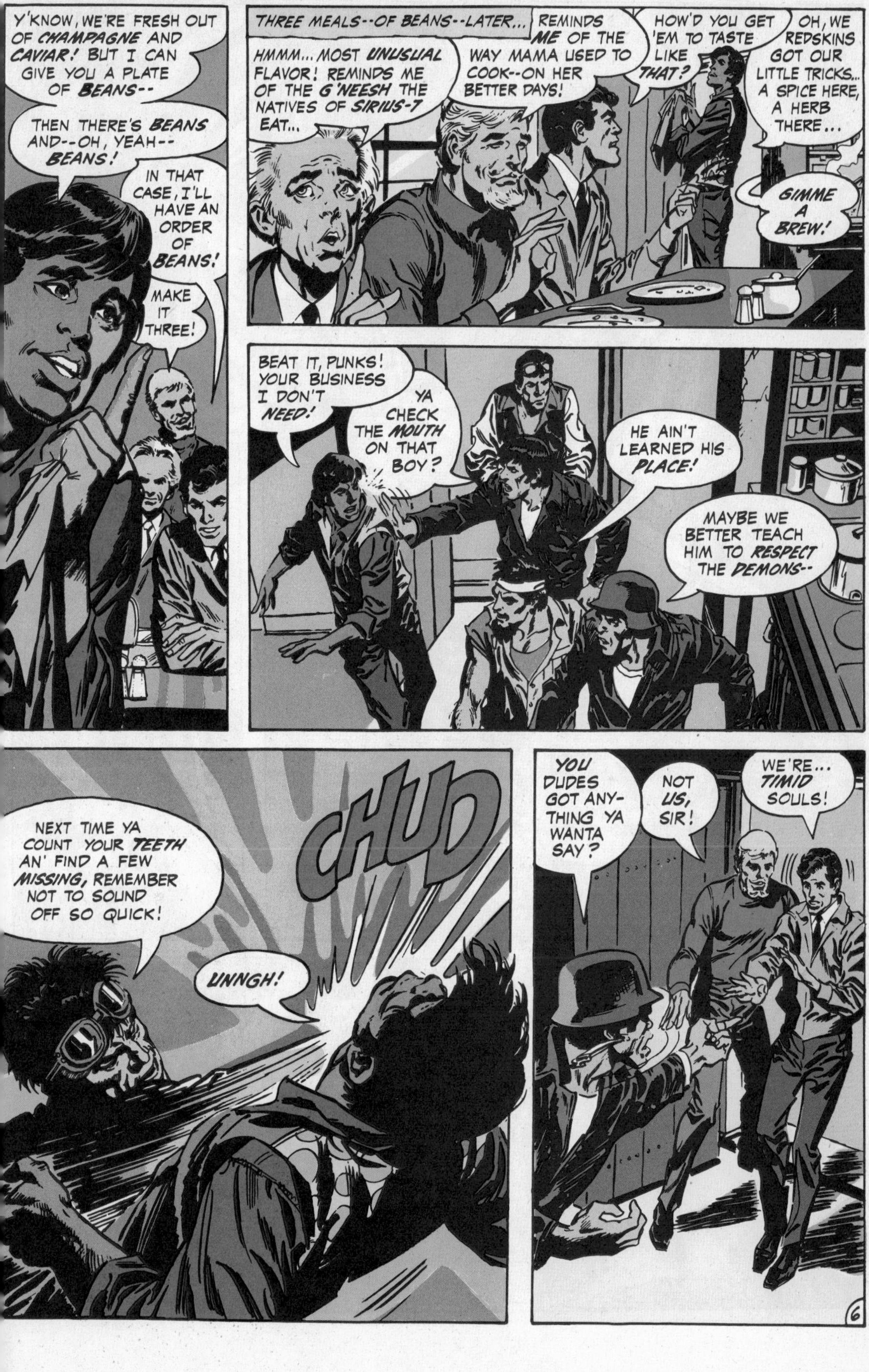
Y'KNOW, WE'RE FRESH OUT OF CHAMPAGNE AND CAVIAR! BUT I CAN GIVE YOU A PLATE OF BEANS--
THEN THERE'S BEANS AND--OH, YEAH--BEANS!
IN THAT CASE, I'LL HAVE AN ORDER OF BEANS!
MAKE IT THREE!
THREE MEALS--OF BEANS--LATER...
HMMM... MOST UNUSUAL FLAVOR! REMINDS ME OF THE G'NEESH THE NATIVES OF SIRIUS-7 EAT...
REMINDS ME OF THE WAY MAMA USED TO COOK--ON HER BETTER DAYS!
HOW'D YOU GET 'EM TO TASTE LIKE THAT?
OH, WE REDSKINS GOT OUR LITTLE TRICKS... A SPICE HERE, A HERB THERE...
GIMME A BREW!
BEAT IT, PUNKS! YOUR BUSINESS I DON'T NEED!
YA CHECK THE MOUTH ON THAT BOY?
HE AIN'T LEARNED HIS PLACE!
MAYBE WE BETTER TEACH HIM TO RESPECT THE DEMONS--
NEXT TIME YA COUNT YOUR TEETH AN' FIND A FEW MISSING, REMEMBER NOT TO SOUND OFF SO QUICK!
CHUD
UNNGH!
YOU DUDES GOT ANYTHING YA WANTA SAY?
NOT US, SIR!
WE'RE... TIMID SOULS!
6

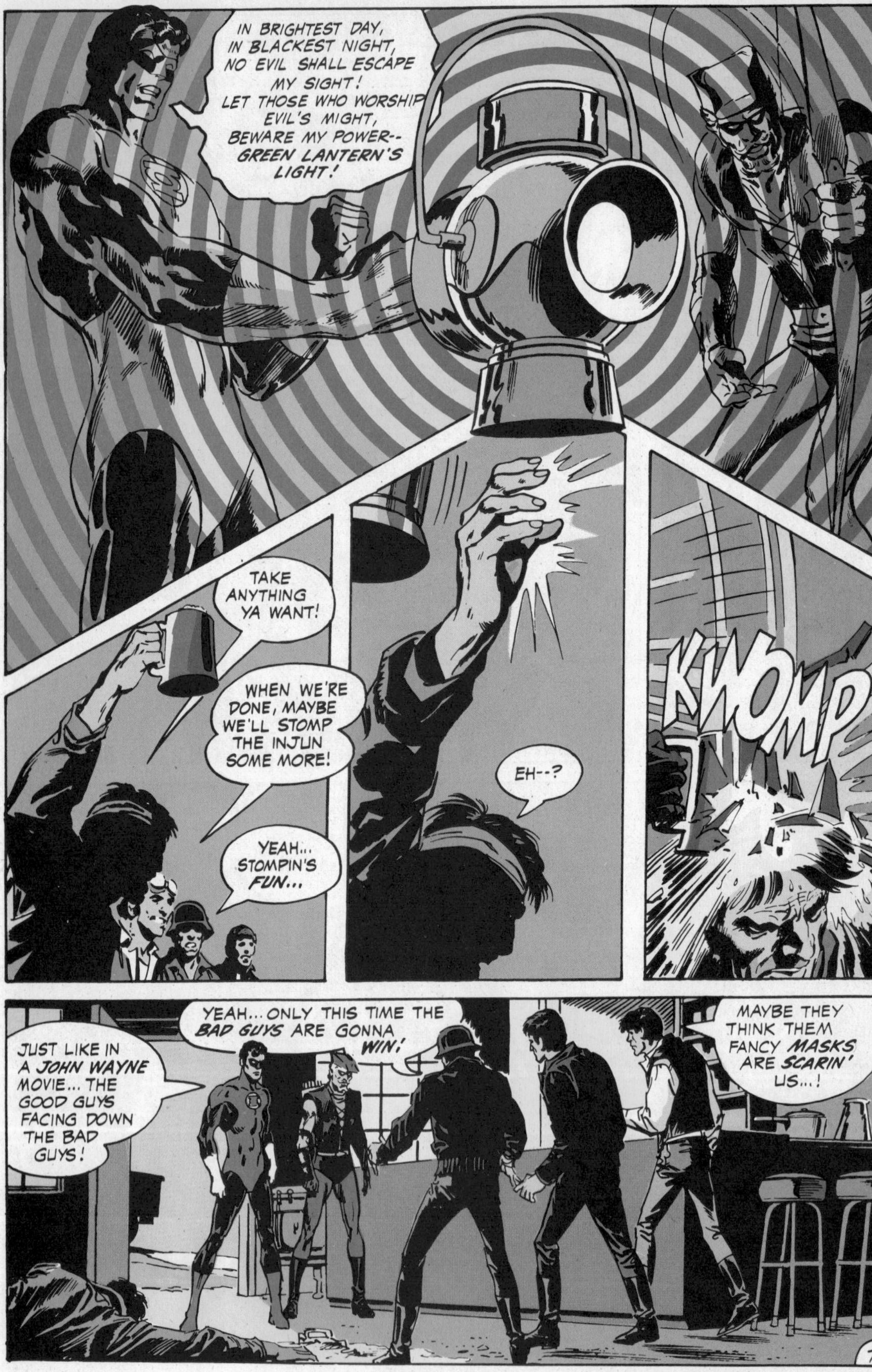

IN BRIGHTEST DAY, IN BLACKEST NIGHT, NO EVIL SHALL ESCAPE MY SIGHT! LET THOSE WHO WORSHIP EVIL'S MIGHT, BEWARE MY POWER-- GREEN LANTERN'S LIGHT!
TAKE ANYTHING YA WANT!
WHEN WE'RE DONE, MAYBE WE'LL STOMP THE INJUN SOME MORE!
YEAH... STOMPIN'S FUN...
EH--?
KWOMP
JUST LIKE IN A JOHN WAYNE MOVIE... THE GOOD GUYS FACING DOWN THE BAD GUYS!
YEAH... ONLY THIS TIME THE BAD GUYS ARE GONNA WIN!
MAYBE THEY THINK THEM FANCY MASKS ARE SCARIN' US...!
7

I'LL JUST CUT THAT MASK OFF-- AT THE COLLAR-BONE!

MAKING YOUR PLAY, HUH? OKAY...

FASTEST POWER RING IN THE WEST...!

I BELIEVE IT'S TRADITIONAL TO END WESTERN BRAWLS LIKE THIS!

WHAT MAKES YA THINK IT HAS ENDED, DUDE?

FIRST, I'M GONNA BASH YOUR PAL'S CAP DOWN 'ROUND HIS ANKLES... THEN I'LL MAKE YOU EAT THAT FREAKY RING...

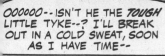

OOOOOO--ISN'T HE THE TOUGH LITTLE TYKE--? I'LL BREAK OUT IN A COLD SWEAT, SOON AS I HAVE TIME--

PROBABLY WON'T GET TO IT--

OOOMPH!

--UNTIL AFTER--

--HE BEGINS HIS SIESTA!

CHOK

8

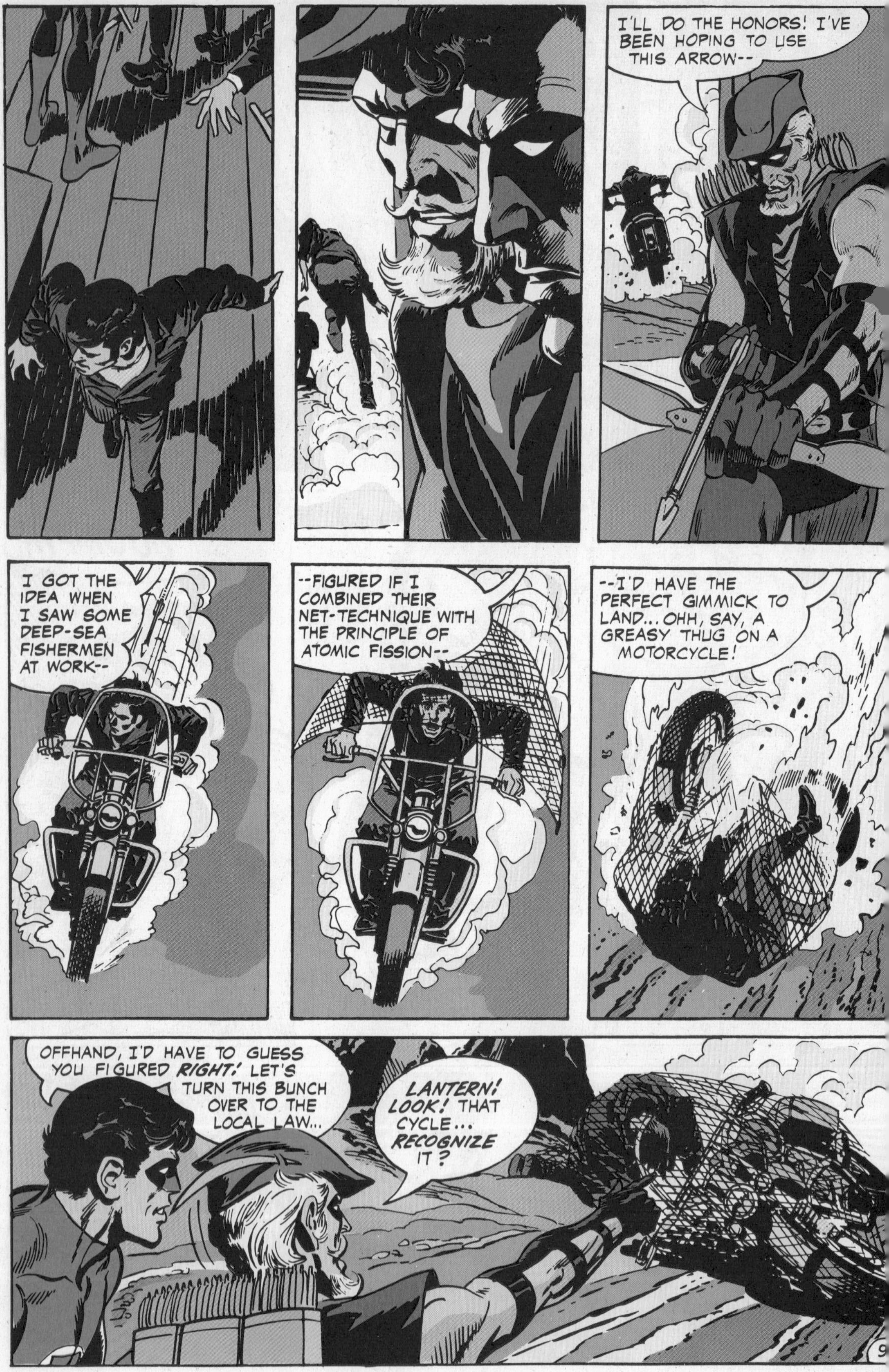
I'LL DO THE HONORS! I'VE BEEN HOPING TO USE THIS ARROW--
I GOT THE IDEA WHEN I SAW SOME DEEP-SEA FISHERMEN AT WORK--
--FIGURED IF I COMBINED THEIR NET-TECHNIQUE WITH THE PRINCIPLE OF ATOMIC FISSION--
--I'D HAVE THE PERFECT GIMMICK TO LAND... OHH, SAY, A GREASY THUG ON A MOTORCYCLE!
OFFHAND, I'D HAVE TO GUESS YOU FIGURED *RIGHT!* LET'S TURN THIS BUNCH OVER TO THE LOCAL LAW...
LANTERN! LOOK! THAT CYCLE... *RECOGNIZE* IT?
9

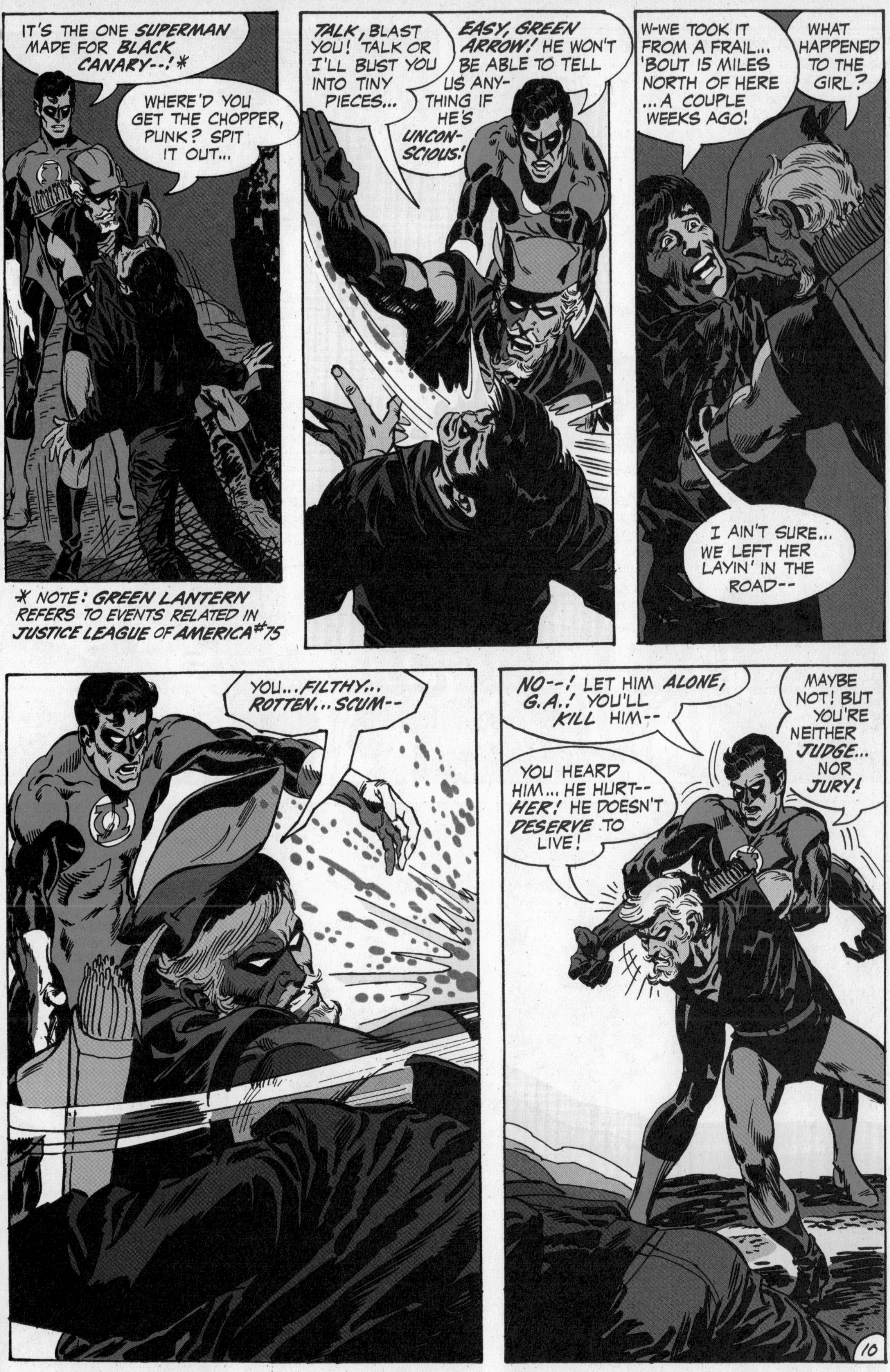
IT'S THE ONE SUPERMAN MADE FOR BLACK CANARY--! *
WHERE'D YOU GET THE CHOPPER, PUNK? SPIT IT OUT...
* NOTE: GREEN LANTERN REFERS TO EVENTS RELATED IN JUSTICE LEAGUE OF AMERICA #75
TALK, BLAST YOU! TALK OR I'LL BUST YOU INTO TINY PIECES...
EASY, GREEN ARROW! HE WON'T BE ABLE TO TELL US ANYTHING IF HE'S UNCONSCIOUS!
W-WE TOOK IT FROM A FRAIL... 'BOUT 15 MILES NORTH OF HERE ...A COUPLE WEEKS AGO!
WHAT HAPPENED TO THE GIRL?
I AIN'T SURE... WE LEFT HER LAYIN' IN THE ROAD--
YOU...FILTHY... ROTTEN...SCUM--
NO--! LET HIM ALONE, G.A.! YOU'LL KILL HIM--
YOU HEARD HIM... HE HURT-- HER! HE DOESN'T DESERVE TO LIVE!
MAYBE NOT! BUT YOU'RE NEITHER JUDGE... NOR JURY!
10

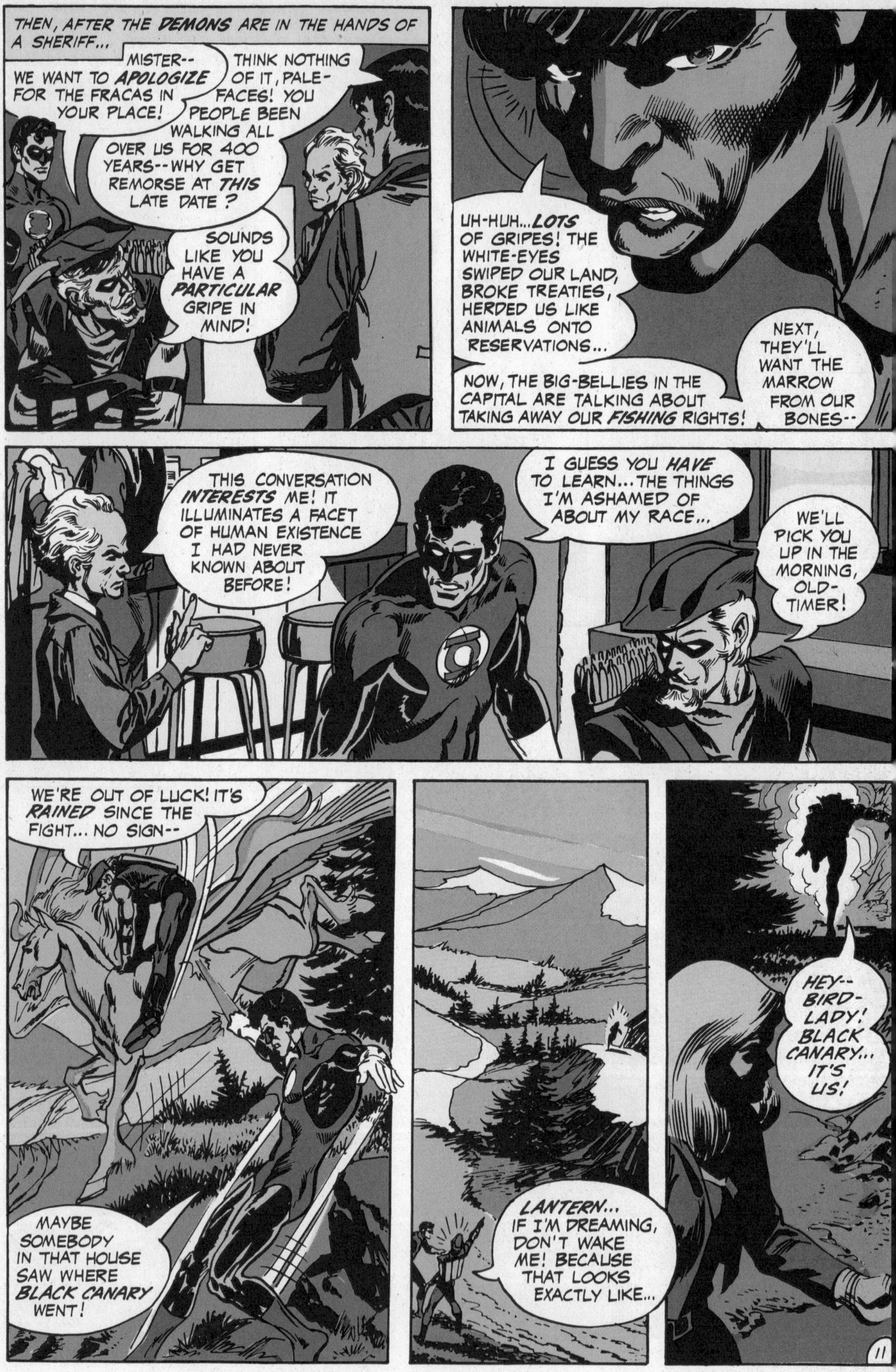
THEN, AFTER THE DEMONS ARE IN THE HANDS OF A SHERIFF...
MISTER-- WE WANT TO APOLOGIZE FOR THE FRACAS IN YOUR PLACE!
THINK NOTHING OF IT, PALE-FACES! YOU PEOPLE BEEN WALKING ALL OVER US FOR 400 YEARS--WHY GET REMORSE AT THIS LATE DATE?
SOUNDS LIKE YOU HAVE A PARTICULAR GRIPE IN MIND!
UH-HUH...LOTS OF GRIPES! THE WHITE-EYES SWIPED OUR LAND, BROKE TREATIES, HERDED US LIKE ANIMALS ONTO RESERVATIONS...
NOW, THE BIG-BELLIES IN THE CAPITAL ARE TALKING ABOUT TAKING AWAY OUR FISHING RIGHTS!
NEXT, THEY'LL WANT THE MARROW FROM OUR BONES--
THIS CONVERSATION INTERESTS ME! IT ILLUMINATES A FACET OF HUMAN EXISTENCE I HAD NEVER KNOWN ABOUT BEFORE!
I GUESS YOU HAVE TO LEARN... THE THINGS I'M ASHAMED OF ABOUT MY RACE...
WE'LL PICK YOU UP IN THE MORNING, OLD-TIMER!
WE'RE OUT OF LUCK! IT'S RAINED SINCE THE FIGHT... NO SIGN--
MAYBE SOMEBODY IN THAT HOUSE SAW WHERE BLACK CANARY WENT!
LANTERN... IF I'M DREAMING, DON'T WAKE ME! BECAUSE THAT LOOKS EXACTLY LIKE...
HEY--BIRD-LADY! BLACK CANARY... IT'S US!
11

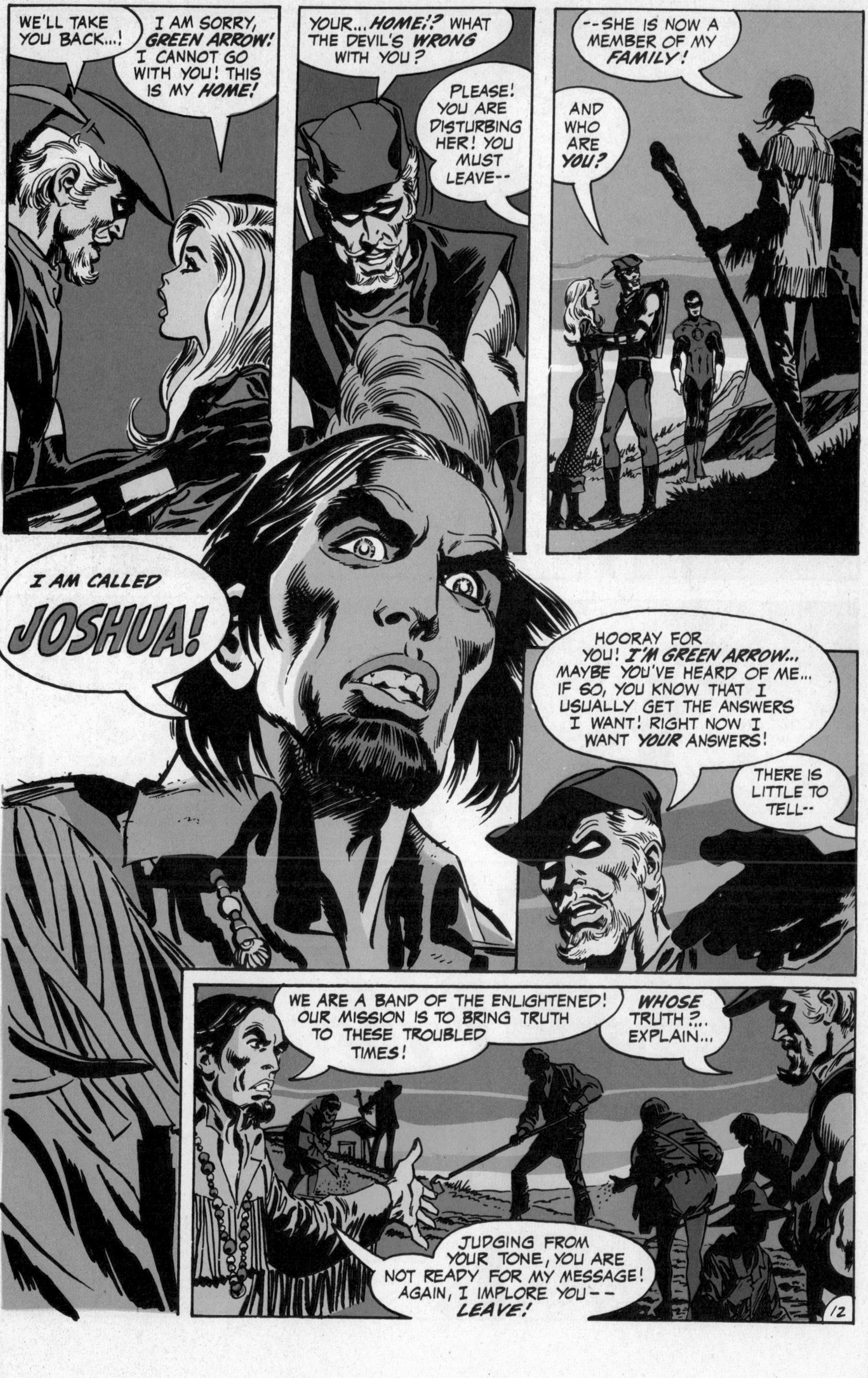
WE'LL TAKE YOU BACK...!
I AM SORRY, GREEN ARROW! I CANNOT GO WITH YOU! THIS IS MY HOME!
YOUR... HOME!? WHAT THE DEVIL'S WRONG WITH YOU?
PLEASE! YOU ARE DISTURBING HER! YOU MUST LEAVE--
--SHE IS NOW A MEMBER OF MY FAMILY!
AND WHO ARE YOU?
I AM CALLED JOSHUA!
HOORAY FOR YOU! I'M GREEN ARROW... MAYBE YOU'VE HEARD OF ME... IF SO, YOU KNOW THAT I USUALLY GET THE ANSWERS I WANT! RIGHT NOW I WANT YOUR ANSWERS!
THERE IS LITTLE TO TELL--
WE ARE A BAND OF THE ENLIGHTENED! OUR MISSION IS TO BRING TRUTH TO THESE TROUBLED TIMES!
WHOSE TRUTH?... EXPLAIN...
JUDGING FROM YOUR TONE, YOU ARE NOT READY FOR MY MESSAGE! AGAIN, I IMPLORE YOU-- LEAVE!
12

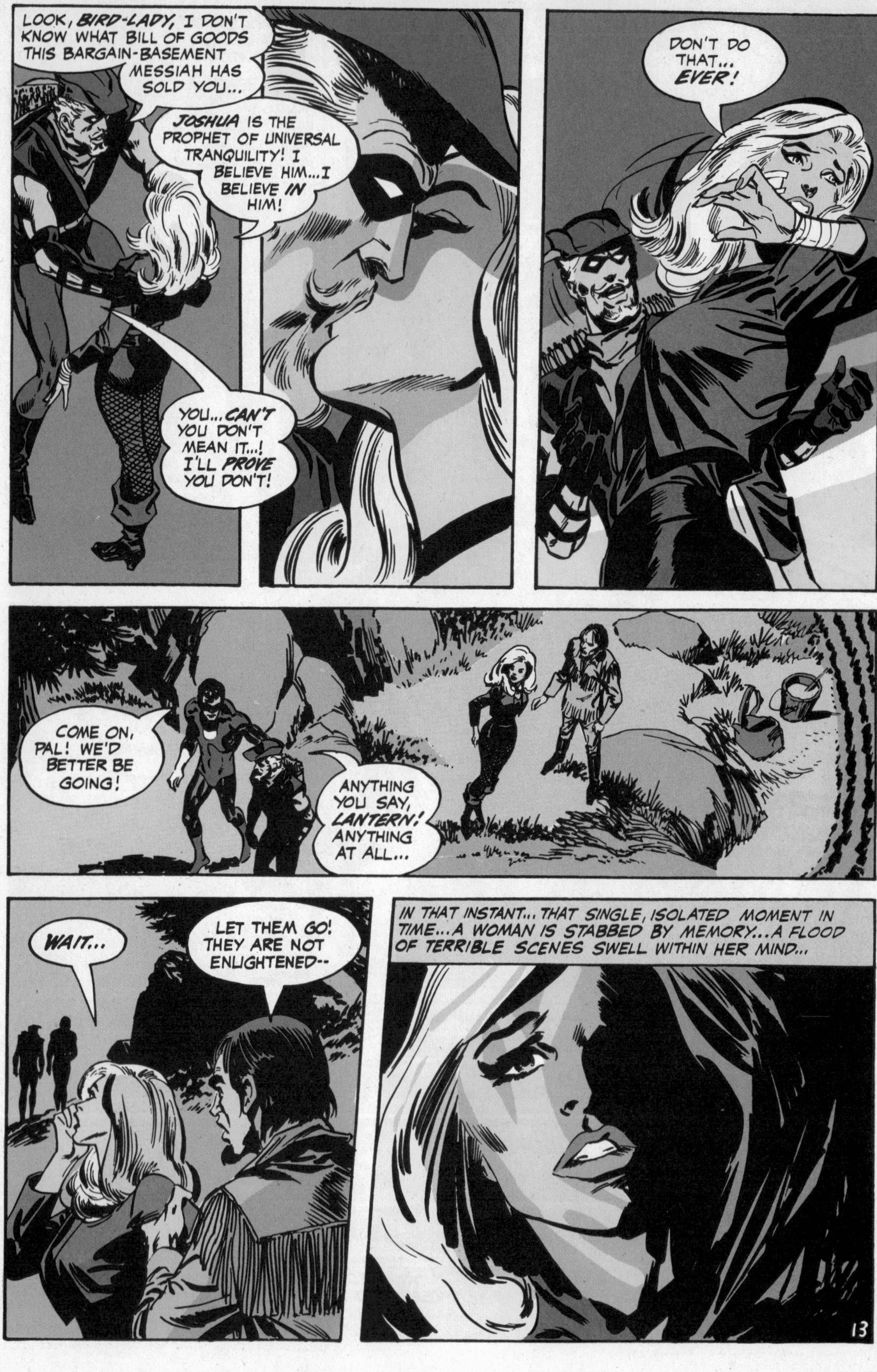
LOOK, BIRD-LADY, I DON'T KNOW WHAT BILL OF GOODS THIS BARGAIN-BASEMENT MESSIAH HAS SOLD YOU...
JOSHUA IS THE PROPHET OF UNIVERSAL TRANQUILITY! I BELIEVE HIM...I BELIEVE IN HIM!
YOU...CAN'T YOU DON'T MEAN IT...! I'LL PROVE YOU DON'T!
DON'T DO THAT... EVER!
COME ON, PAL! WE'D BETTER BE GOING!
ANYTHING YOU SAY, LANTERN! ANYTHING AT ALL...
WAIT...
LET THEM GO! THEY ARE NOT ENLIGHTENED--
IN THAT INSTANT... THAT SINGLE, ISOLATED MOMENT IN TIME...A WOMAN IS STABBED BY MEMORY...A FLOOD OF TERRIBLE SCENES SWELL WITHIN HER MIND...
13

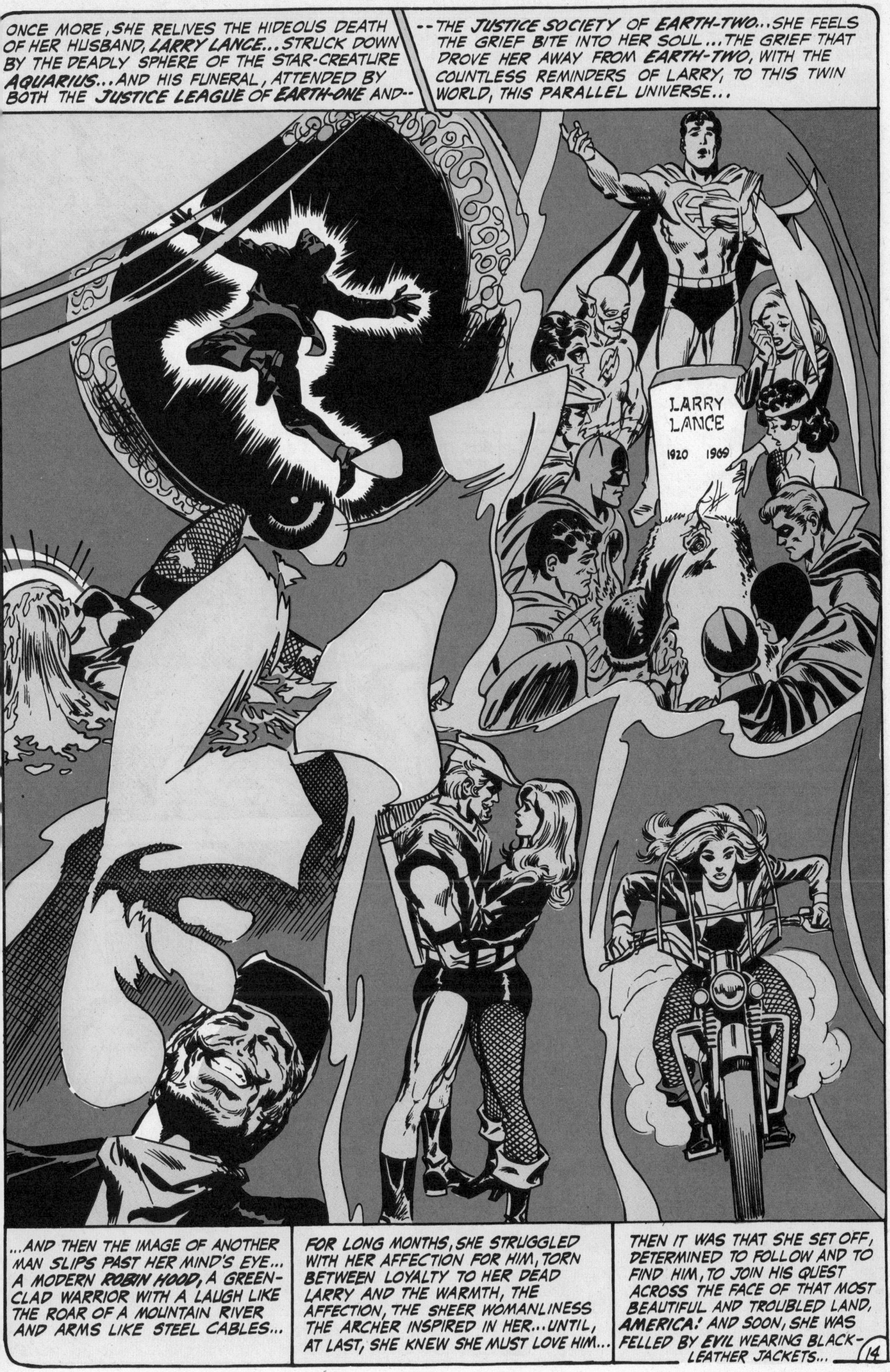
ONCE MORE, SHE RELIVES THE HIDEOUS DEATH OF HER HUSBAND, LARRY LANCE... STRUCK DOWN BY THE DEADLY SPHERE OF THE STAR-CREATURE AQUARIUS... AND HIS FUNERAL, ATTENDED BY BOTH THE JUSTICE LEAGUE OF EARTH-ONE AND--
--THE JUSTICE SOCIETY OF EARTH-TWO... SHE FEELS THE GRIEF BITE INTO HER SOUL... THE GRIEF THAT DROVE HER AWAY FROM EARTH-TWO, WITH THE COUNTLESS REMINDERS OF LARRY, TO THIS TWIN WORLD, THIS PARALLEL UNIVERSE...
LARRY LANCE
1920 1969
...AND THEN THE IMAGE OF ANOTHER MAN SLIPS PAST HER MIND'S EYE... A MODERN ROBIN HOOD, A GREEN-CLAD WARRIOR WITH A LAUGH LIKE THE ROAR OF A MOUNTAIN RIVER AND ARMS LIKE STEEL CABLES...
FOR LONG MONTHS, SHE STRUGGLED WITH HER AFFECTION FOR HIM, TORN BETWEEN LOYALTY TO HER DEAD LARRY AND THE WARMTH, THE AFFECTION, THE SHEER WOMANLINESS THE ARCHER INSPIRED IN HER... UNTIL, AT LAST, SHE KNEW SHE MUST LOVE HIM...
THEN IT WAS THAT SHE SET OFF, DETERMINED TO FOLLOW AND TO FIND HIM, TO JOIN HIS QUEST ACROSS THE FACE OF THAT MOST BEAUTIFUL AND TROUBLED LAND, AMERICA! AND SOON, SHE WAS FELLED BY EVIL WEARING BLACK-LEATHER JACKETS...
14

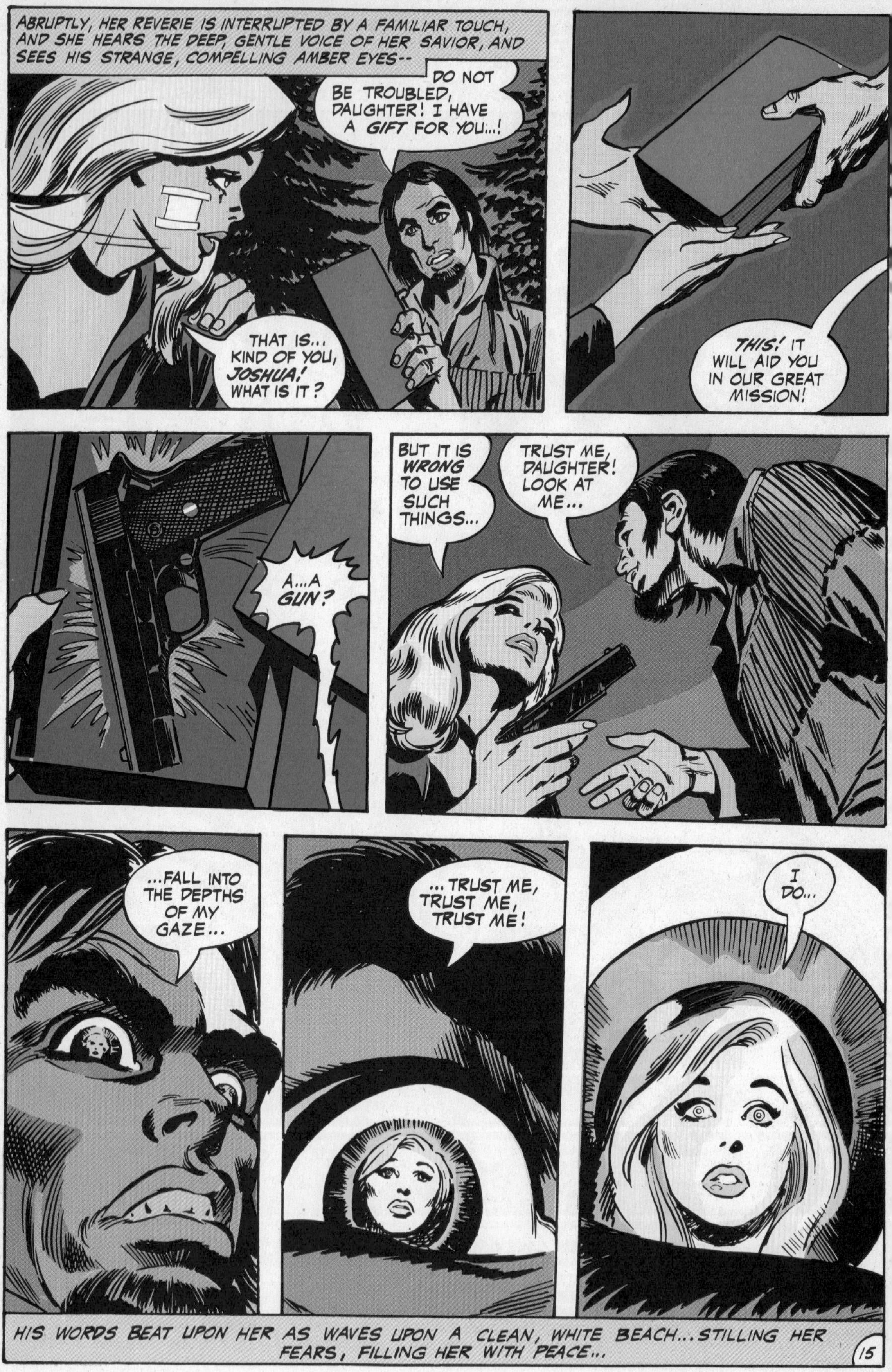
ABRUPTLY, HER REVERIE IS INTERRUPTED BY A FAMILIAR TOUCH, AND SHE HEARS THE DEEP, GENTLE VOICE OF HER SAVIOR, AND SEES HIS STRANGE, COMPELLING AMBER EYES--
DO NOT BE TROUBLED, DAUGHTER! I HAVE A GIFT FOR YOU...!
THAT IS... KIND OF YOU, JOSHUA! WHAT IS IT?
THIS! IT WILL AID YOU IN OUR GREAT MISSION!
A...A GUN?
BUT IT IS WRONG TO USE SUCH THINGS...
TRUST ME, DAUGHTER! LOOK AT ME...
...FALL INTO THE DEPTHS OF MY GAZE...
...TRUST ME, TRUST ME, TRUST ME!
I DO...
HIS WORDS BEAT UPON HER AS WAVES UPON A CLEAN, WHITE BEACH... STILLING HER FEARS, FILLING HER WITH PEACE...
15

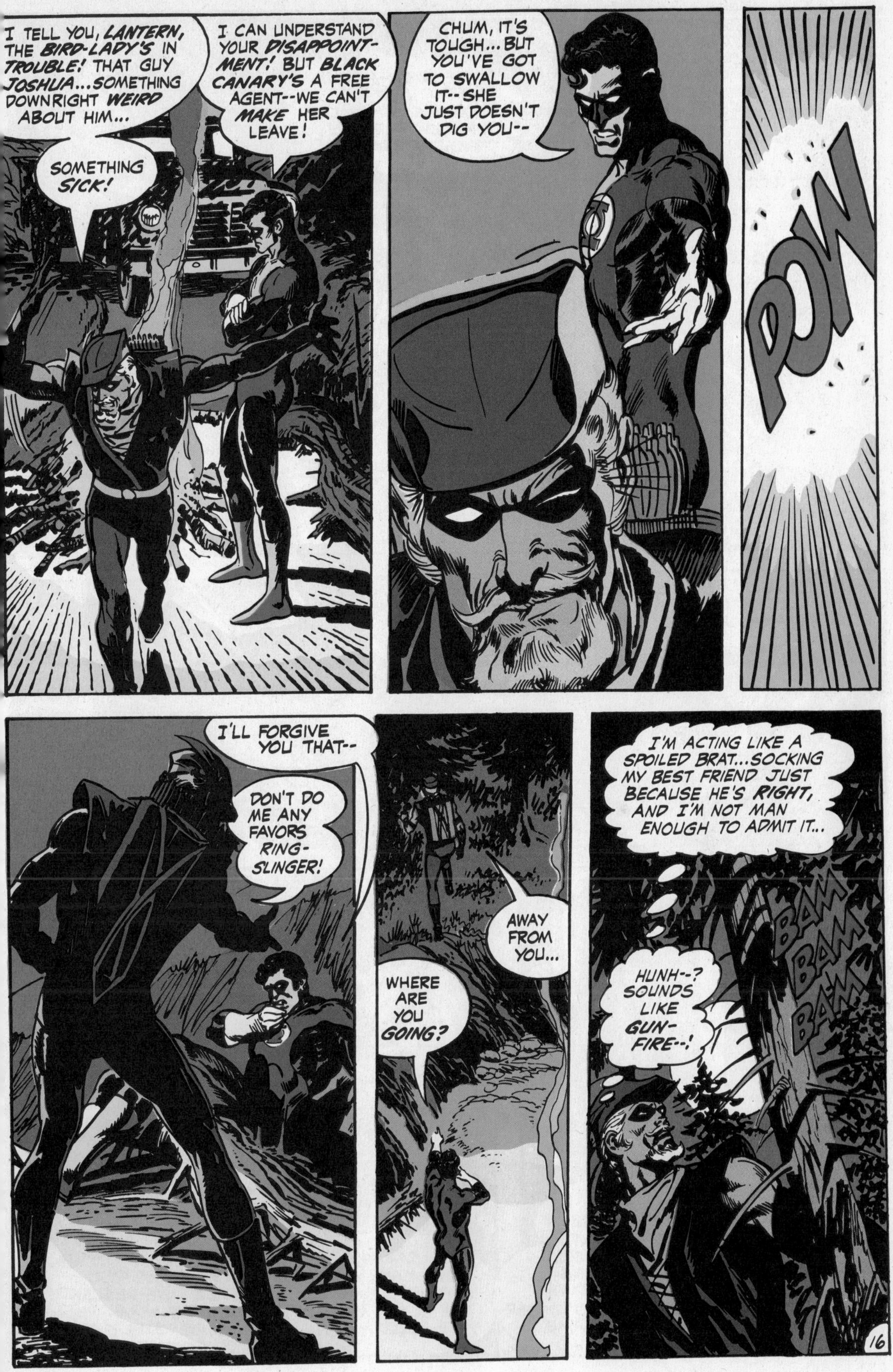
I TELL YOU, LANTERN, THE BIRD-LADY'S IN TROUBLE! THAT GUY JOSHUA...SOMETHING DOWNRIGHT WEIRD ABOUT HIM...
SOMETHING SICK!
I CAN UNDERSTAND YOUR DISAPPOINTMENT! BUT BLACK CANARY'S A FREE AGENT--WE CAN'T MAKE HER LEAVE!
CHUM, IT'S TOUGH... BUT YOU'VE GOT TO SWALLOW IT--SHE JUST DOESN'T DIG YOU--
POW
I'LL FORGIVE YOU THAT--
DON'T DO ME ANY FAVORS RING-SLINGER!
WHERE ARE YOU GOING?
AWAY FROM YOU...
I'M ACTING LIKE A SPOILED BRAT...SOCKING MY BEST FRIEND JUST BECAUSE HE'S RIGHT, AND I'M NOT MAN ENOUGH TO ADMIT IT...
BAM BAM BAM
HUNH--? SOUNDS LIKE GUN-FIRE--!
16

GRACEFUL AS A GREAT CAT, THE *EMERALD ARCHER* MOVES THROUGH THE WOODS TOWARD THE SOURCE OF THE STACCATO REPORTS...

--AND SEES--

THE *BIRD-LADY*... AND THE REST OF JOSHUA'S SO-CALLED *"FAMILY"*-- TAKING *TARGET-PRACTICE!*

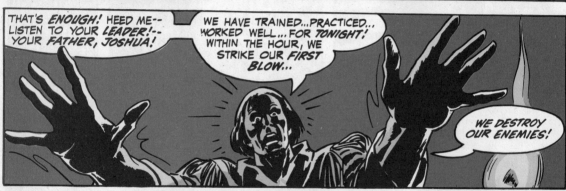

THAT'S *ENOUGH!* HEED ME-- LISTEN TO YOUR *LEADER!*-- YOUR *FATHER,* JOSHUA!

WE HAVE *TRAINED...PRACTICED...* WORKED WELL...FOR *TONIGHT!* WITHIN THE HOUR, WE STRIKE OUR *FIRST BLOW...*

WE DESTROY OUR ENEMIES!

SUCH HAS BEEN THE COURSE OF HISTORY IN THIS NATION THAT THE *WHITE* MAN AND THE *NON-WHITE MAN* ARE ENEMIES...

IT IS A *PITY* THAT WE MUST *KILL--!* BUT WE HAVE NO *CHOICE--* THOSE OF WHITE ANCESTRY AND THE *OTHERS* CAN NO LONGER SHARE THE SAME LAND...

TO *SURVIVE,* WE MUST MAKE *CORPSES* OF THE RED MAN... THE BLACK MAN... THE YELLOW MAN...

NOW IS THE TIME! WE STRIKE OUR *FIRST BLOW* FOR PEACE...WE DESCEND UPON THE INDIAN VILLAGE LIKE AVENGING GODS-- AND LEAVE *NOTHING...ALIVE!!*

17

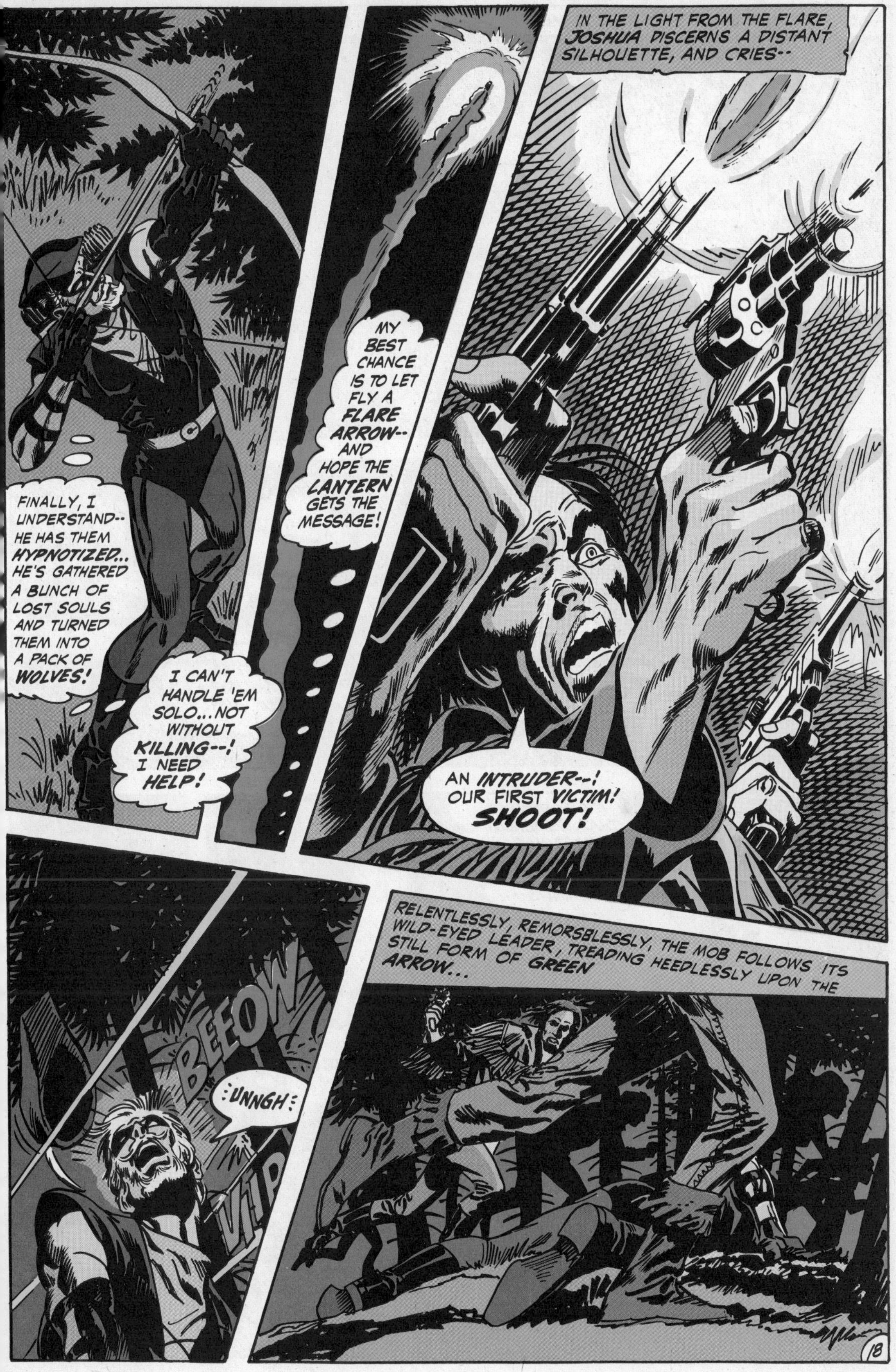
FINALLY, I UNDERSTAND-- HE HAS THEM HYPNOTIZED.. HE'S GATHERED A BUNCH OF LOST SOULS AND TURNED THEM INTO A PACK OF WOLVES!
I CAN'T HANDLE 'EM SOLO...NOT WITHOUT KILLING--! I NEED HELP!
MY BEST CHANCE IS TO LET FLY A FLARE ARROW-- AND HOPE THE LANTERN GETS THE MESSAGE!
IN THE LIGHT FROM THE FLARE, JOSHUA DISCERNS A DISTANT SILHOUETTE, AND CRIES--
AN INTRUDER--! OUR FIRST VICTIM! SHOOT!
BEEOW
UNNGH
VIIP
RELENTLESSLY, REMORSBLESSLY, THE MOB FOLLOWS ITS WILD-EYED LEADER, TREADING HEEDLESSLY UPON THE STILL FORM OF GREEN ARROW...
18

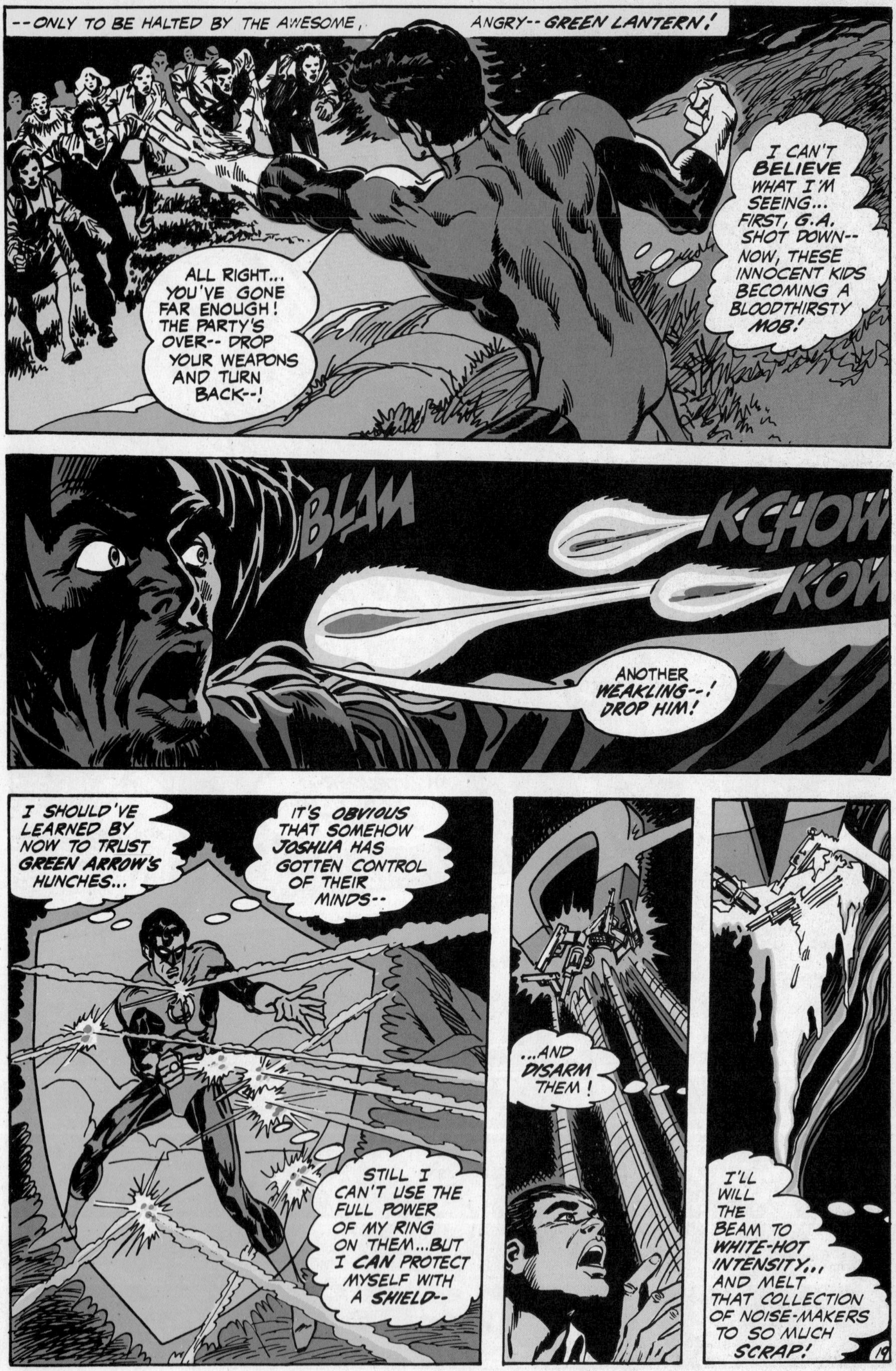
--ONLY TO BE HALTED BY THE AWESOME, ANGRY--GREEN LANTERN!
I CAN'T BELIEVE WHAT I'M SEEING... FIRST, G.A. SHOT DOWN-- NOW, THESE INNOCENT KIDS BECOMING A BLOODTHIRSTY MOB!
ALL RIGHT... YOU'VE GONE FAR ENOUGH! THE PARTY'S OVER-- DROP YOUR WEAPONS AND TURN BACK--!
BLAM
K-CHOW
KOW
ANOTHER WEAKLING--! DROP HIM!
I SHOULD'VE LEARNED BY NOW TO TRUST GREEN ARROW'S HUNCHES...
IT'S OBVIOUS THAT SOMEHOW JOSHUA HAS GOTTEN CONTROL OF THEIR MINDS--
STILL I CAN'T USE THE FULL POWER OF MY RING ON THEM...BUT I CAN PROTECT MYSELF WITH A SHIELD--
...AND DISARM THEM!
I'LL WILL THE BEAM TO WHITE-HOT INTENSITY... AND MELT THAT COLLECTION OF NOISE-MAKERS TO SO MUCH SCRAP!
19

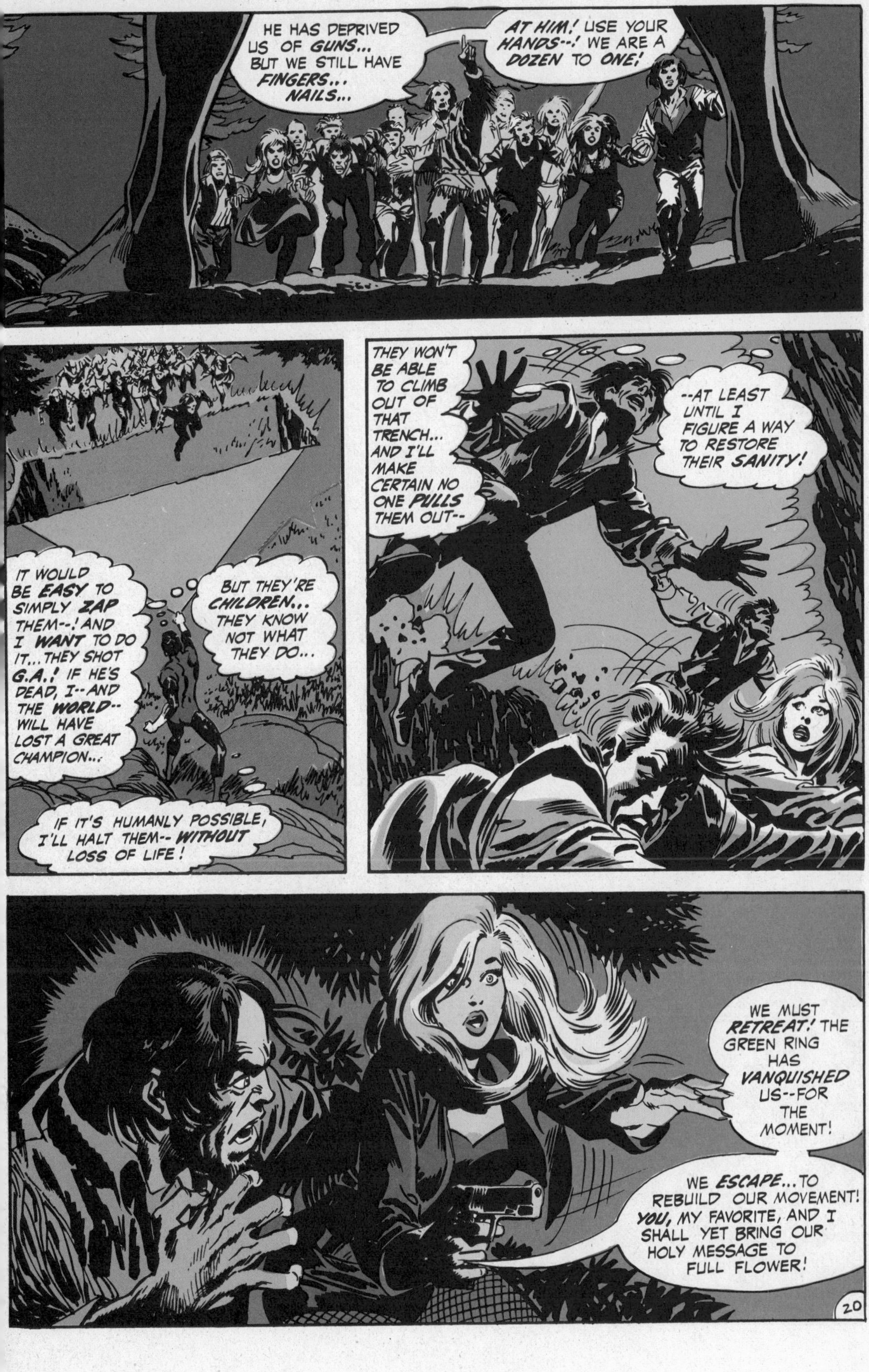
HE HAS DEPRIVED US OF GUNS... BUT WE STILL HAVE FINGERS... NAILS...
AT HIM! USE YOUR HANDS--! WE ARE A DOZEN TO ONE!
IT WOULD BE EASY TO SIMPLY ZAP THEM--! AND I WANT TO DO IT... THEY SHOT G.A.! IF HE'S DEAD, I--AND THE WORLD--WILL HAVE LOST A GREAT CHAMPION...
BUT THEY'RE CHILDREN... THEY KNOW NOT WHAT THEY DO...
IF IT'S HUMANLY POSSIBLE, I'LL HALT THEM--WITHOUT LOSS OF LIFE!
THEY WON'T BE ABLE TO CLIMB OUT OF THAT TRENCH... AND I'LL MAKE CERTAIN NO ONE PULLS THEM OUT--
--AT LEAST UNTIL I FIGURE A WAY TO RESTORE THEIR SANITY!
WE MUST RETREAT! THE GREEN RING HAS VANQUISHED US--FOR THE MOMENT!
WE ESCAPE... TO REBUILD OUR MOVEMENT! YOU, MY FAVORITE, AND I SHALL YET BRING OUR HOLY MESSAGE TO FULL FLOWER!
20

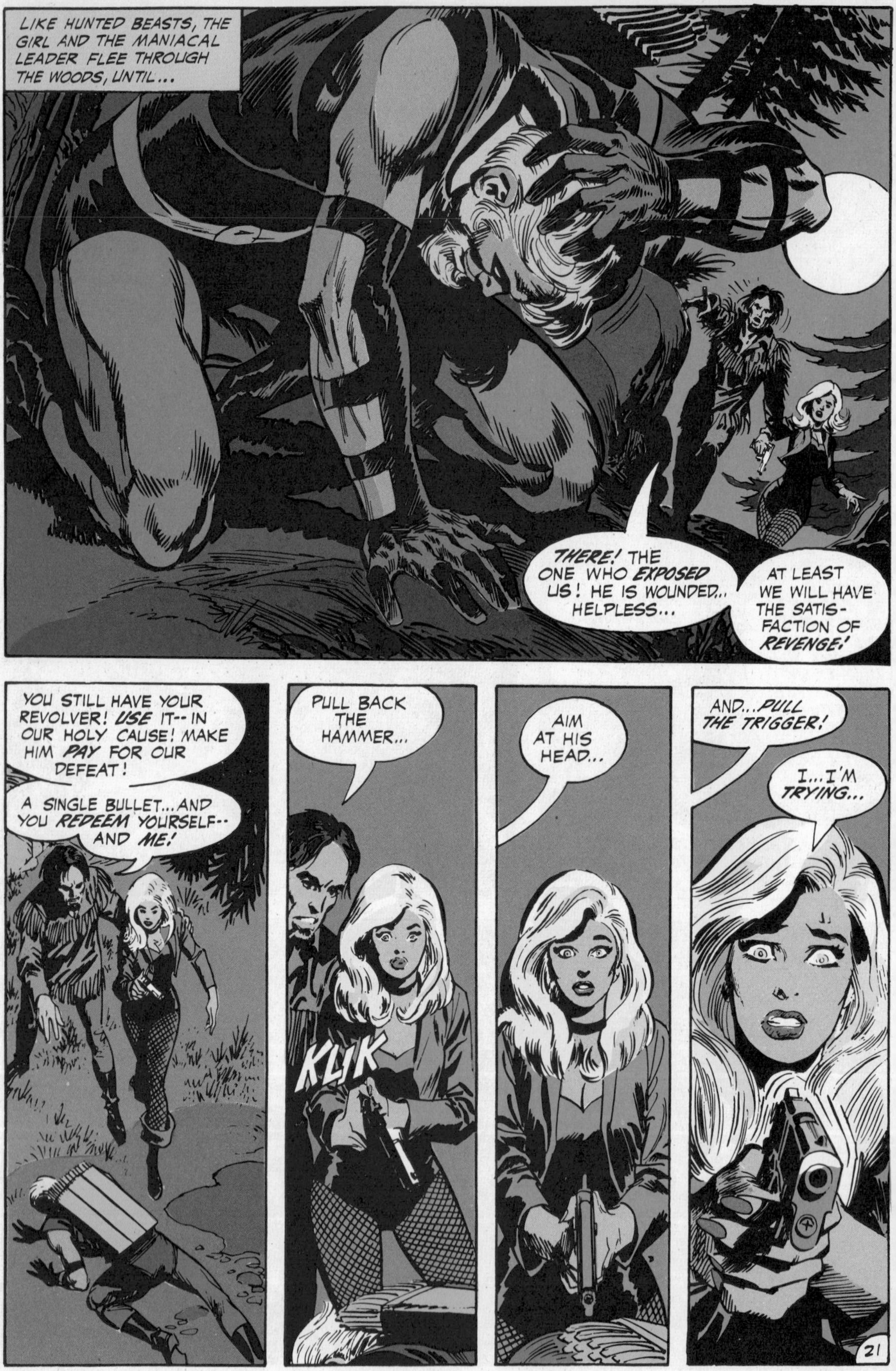
LIKE HUNTED BEASTS, THE GIRL AND THE MANIACAL LEADER FLEE THROUGH THE WOODS, UNTIL...
THERE! THE ONE WHO EXPOSED US! HE IS WOUNDED.. HELPLESS...
AT LEAST WE WILL HAVE THE SATIS-FACTION OF REVENGE!
YOU STILL HAVE YOUR REVOLVER! USE IT-- IN OUR HOLY CAUSE! MAKE HIM PAY FOR OUR DEFEAT!
A SINGLE BULLET...AND YOU REDEEM YOURSELF-- AND ME!
PULL BACK THE HAMMER...
KLIK
AIM AT HIS HEAD...
AND...PULL THE TRIGGER!
I...I'M TRYING...
21

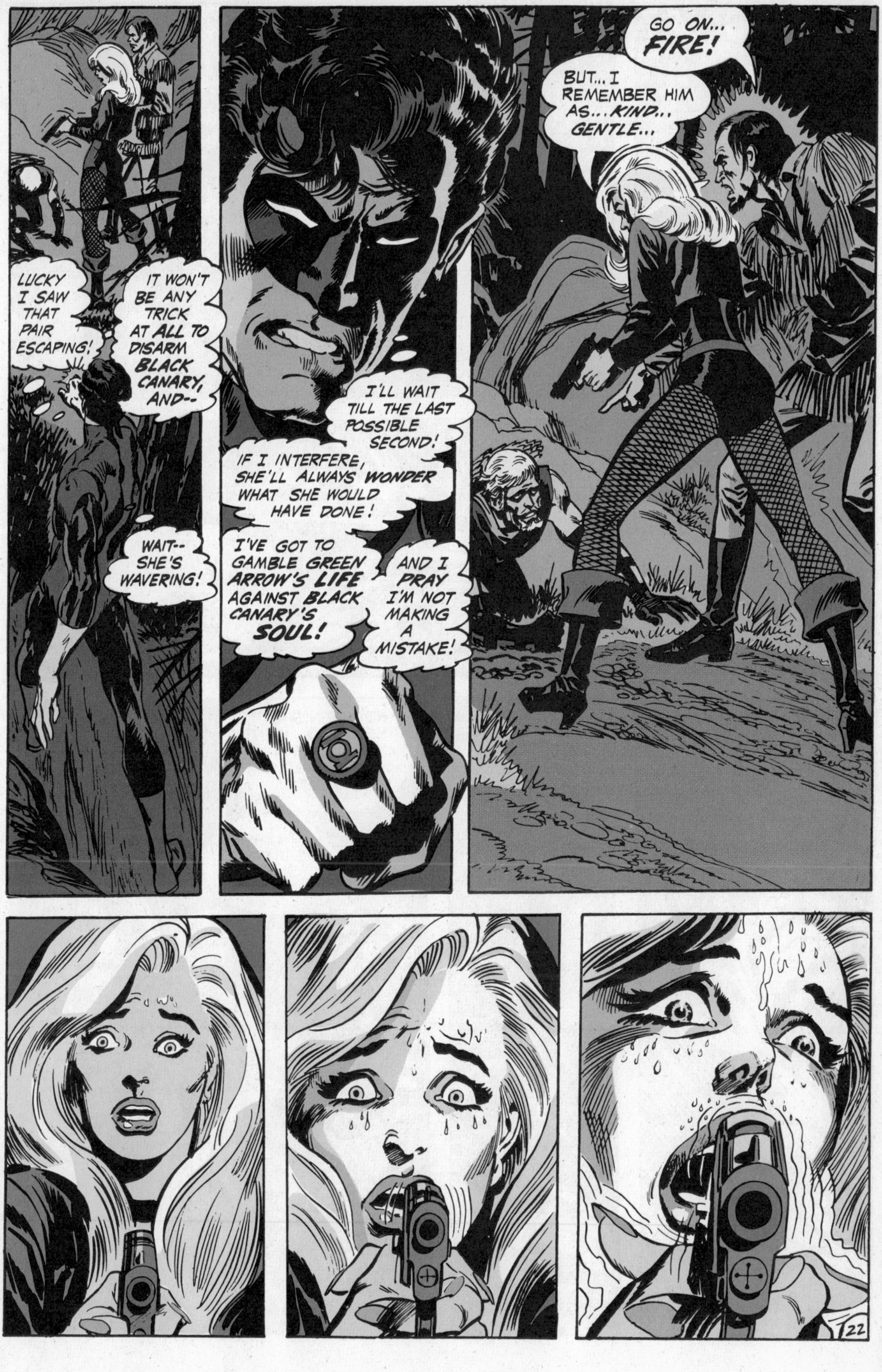
LUCKY I SAW THAT PAIR ESCAPING!
IT WON'T BE ANY TRICK AT ALL TO DISARM BLACK CANARY, AND--
WAIT-- SHE'S WAVERING!
I'LL WAIT TILL THE LAST POSSIBLE SECOND!
IF I INTERFERE, SHE'LL ALWAYS WONDER WHAT SHE WOULD HAVE DONE!
I'VE GOT TO GAMBLE GREEN ARROW'S LIFE AGAINST BLACK CANARY'S SOUL!
AND I PRAY I'M NOT MAKING A MISTAKE!
GO ON... FIRE!
BUT... I REMEMBER HIM AS... KIND... GENTLE...
22

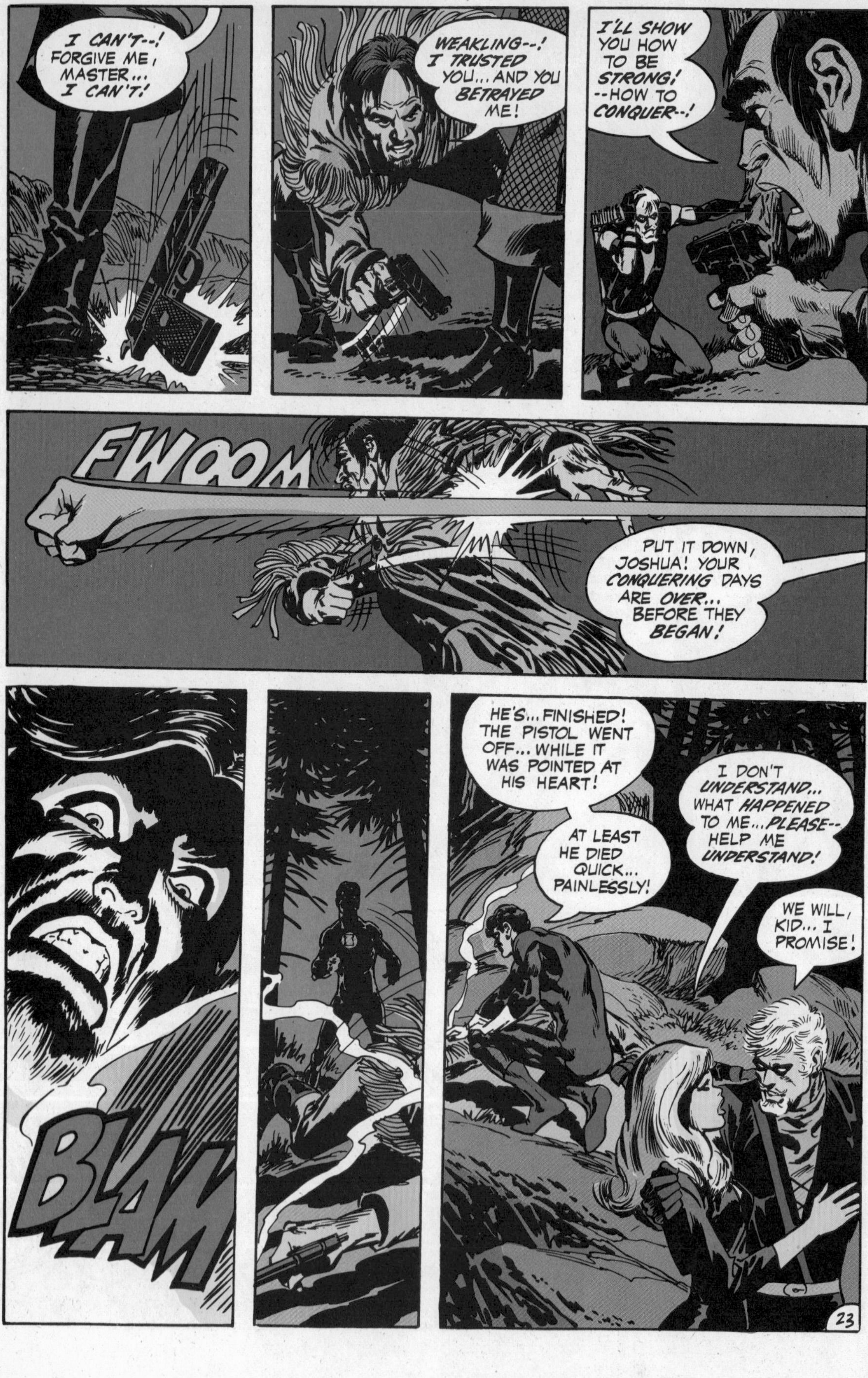
I CAN'T--! FORGIVE ME, MASTER... I CAN'T!
WEAKLING--! I TRUSTED YOU... AND YOU BETRAYED ME!
I'LL SHOW YOU HOW TO BE STRONG! --HOW TO CONQUER--!
FWOOM
PUT IT DOWN, JOSHUA! YOUR CONQUERING DAYS ARE OVER... BEFORE THEY BEGAN!
BLAM
HE'S... FINISHED! THE PISTOL WENT OFF... WHILE IT WAS POINTED AT HIS HEART!
AT LEAST HE DIED QUICK... PAINLESSLY!
I DON'T UNDERSTAND... WHAT HAPPENED TO ME... PLEASE-- HELP ME UNDERSTAND!
WE WILL, KID... I PROMISE!
23

AND MAYBE WHEN WE GET YOU STRAIGHTENED OUT, WE'LL LEARN SOMETHING... MAYBE WE'LL FINALLY KNOW HOW MANIACS LIKE JOSHUA CAN COME TO BE...
...HOW THEY CAN SEIZE THE HEARTS OF DECENT PEOPLE AND FILL THEM WITH THE POISON OF HATE... OF BIGOTRY!
HE... HYPNOTIZED US...
SURE, THAT'S PART OF IT... BUT THERE HAD TO BE A PART OF YOU THAT RESPONDED TO HIS INSANITY--
YOU...ME...ALL OF US! MAYBE NOW WE CAN GET RID OF THAT PART... FOREVER!
I HOPE SO, GREEN ARROW... BUT I CAN'T HELP DOUBTING IT! JOSHUA WASN'T THE FIRST OF HIS KIND...
...AND HE PROBABLY WON'T BE THE LAST!
END

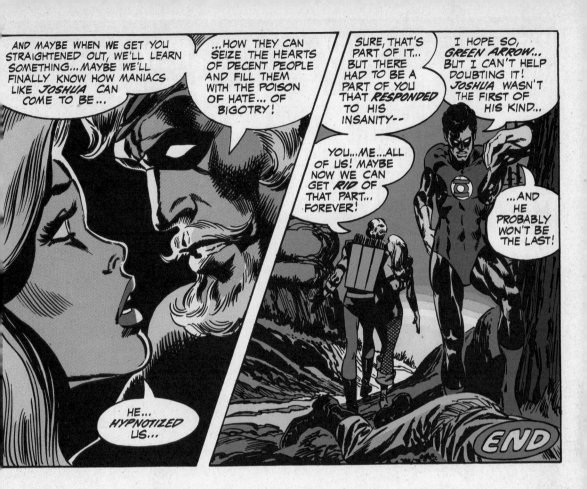

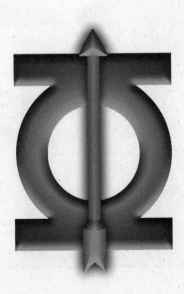

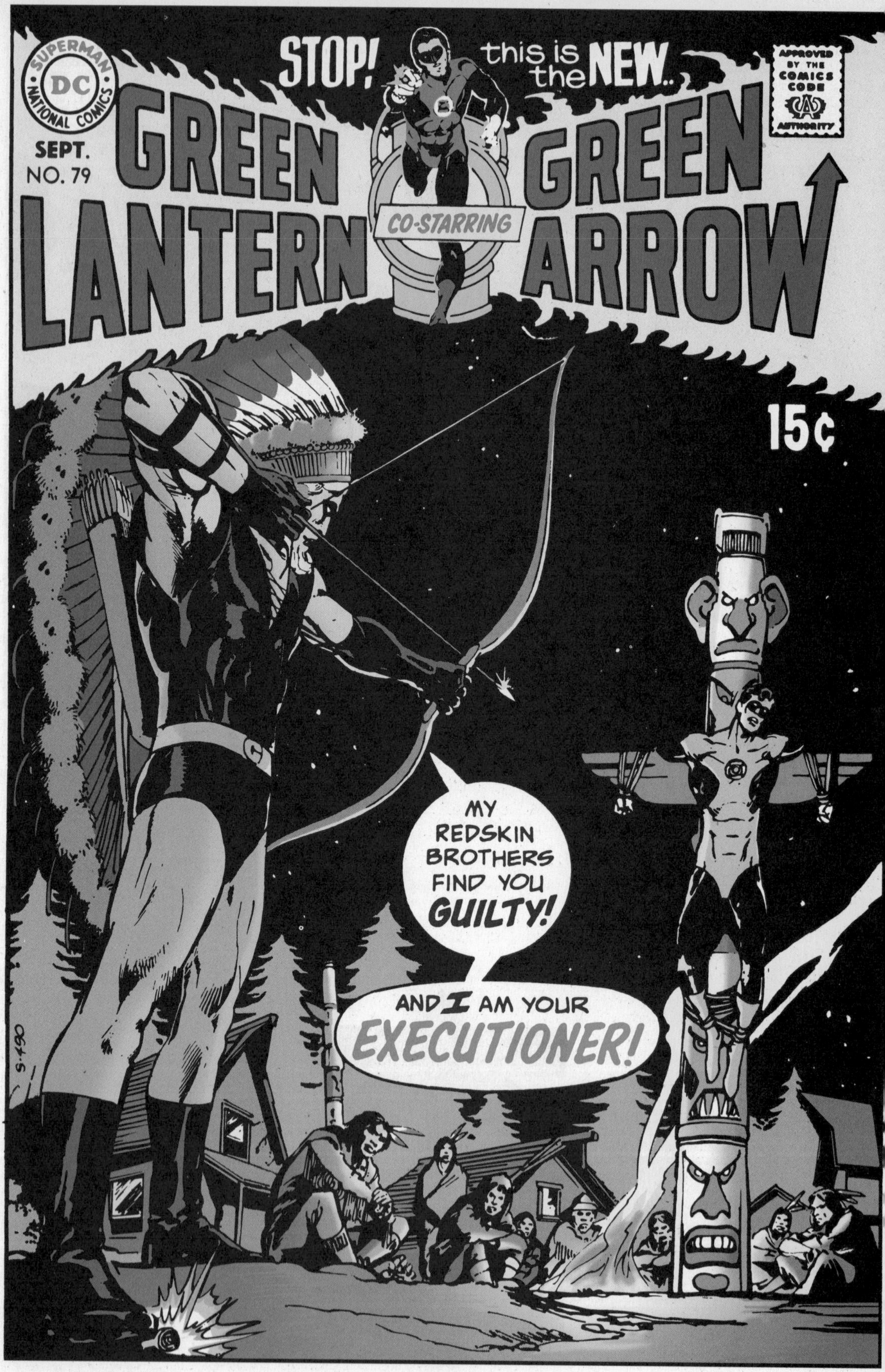
SUPERMAN DC NATIONAL COMICS
SEPT.
NO. 79
STOP! this is the NEW..
GREEN LANTERN
CO-STARRING
GREEN ARROW
APPROVED BY THE COMICS CODE AUTHORITY
15¢
MY REDSKIN BROTHERS FIND YOU GUILTY!
AND I AM YOUR EXECUTIONER!

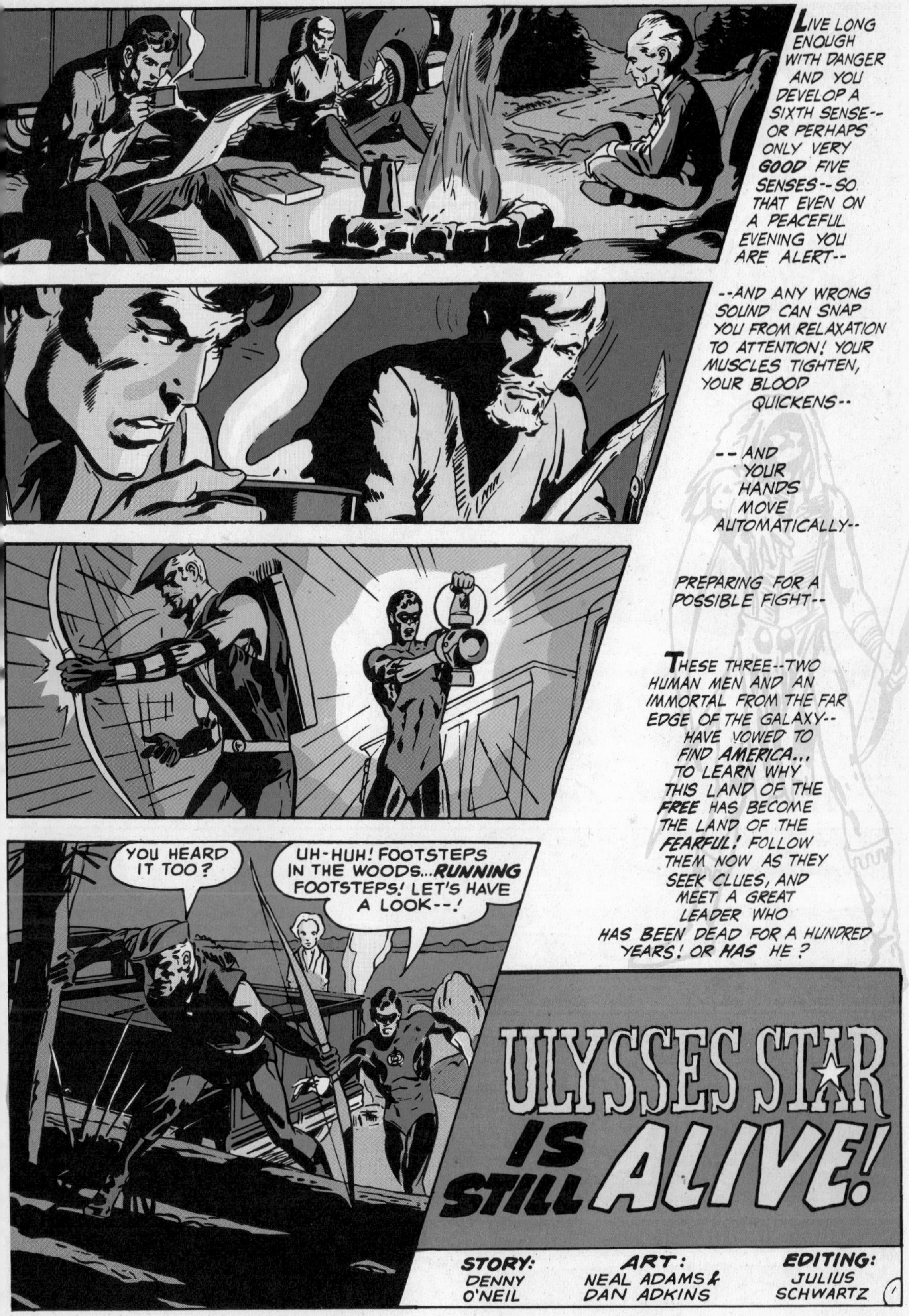
LIVE LONG ENOUGH WITH DANGER AND YOU DEVELOP A SIXTH SENSE--OR PERHAPS ONLY VERY GOOD FIVE SENSES--SO THAT EVEN ON A PEACEFUL EVENING YOU ARE ALERT--
--AND ANY WRONG SOUND CAN SNAP YOU FROM RELAXATION TO ATTENTION! YOUR MUSCLES TIGHTEN, YOUR BLOOD QUICKENS--
--AND YOUR HANDS MOVE AUTOMATICALLY--
PREPARING FOR A POSSIBLE FIGHT--
THESE THREE--TWO HUMAN MEN AND AN IMMORTAL FROM THE FAR EDGE OF THE GALAXY--HAVE VOWED TO FIND AMERICA... TO LEARN WHY THIS LAND OF THE FREE HAS BECOME THE LAND OF THE FEARFUL! FOLLOW THEM NOW AS THEY SEEK CLUES, AND MEET A GREAT LEADER WHO HAS BEEN DEAD FOR A HUNDRED YEARS! OR HAS HE?
YOU HEARD IT TOO?
UH-HUH! FOOTSTEPS IN THE WOODS...RUNNING FOOTSTEPS! LET'S HAVE A LOOK--!
ULYSSES STAR IS STILL ALIVE!
STORY: DENNY O'NEIL
ART: NEAL ADAMS & DAN ADKINS
EDITING: JULIUS SCHWARTZ
1

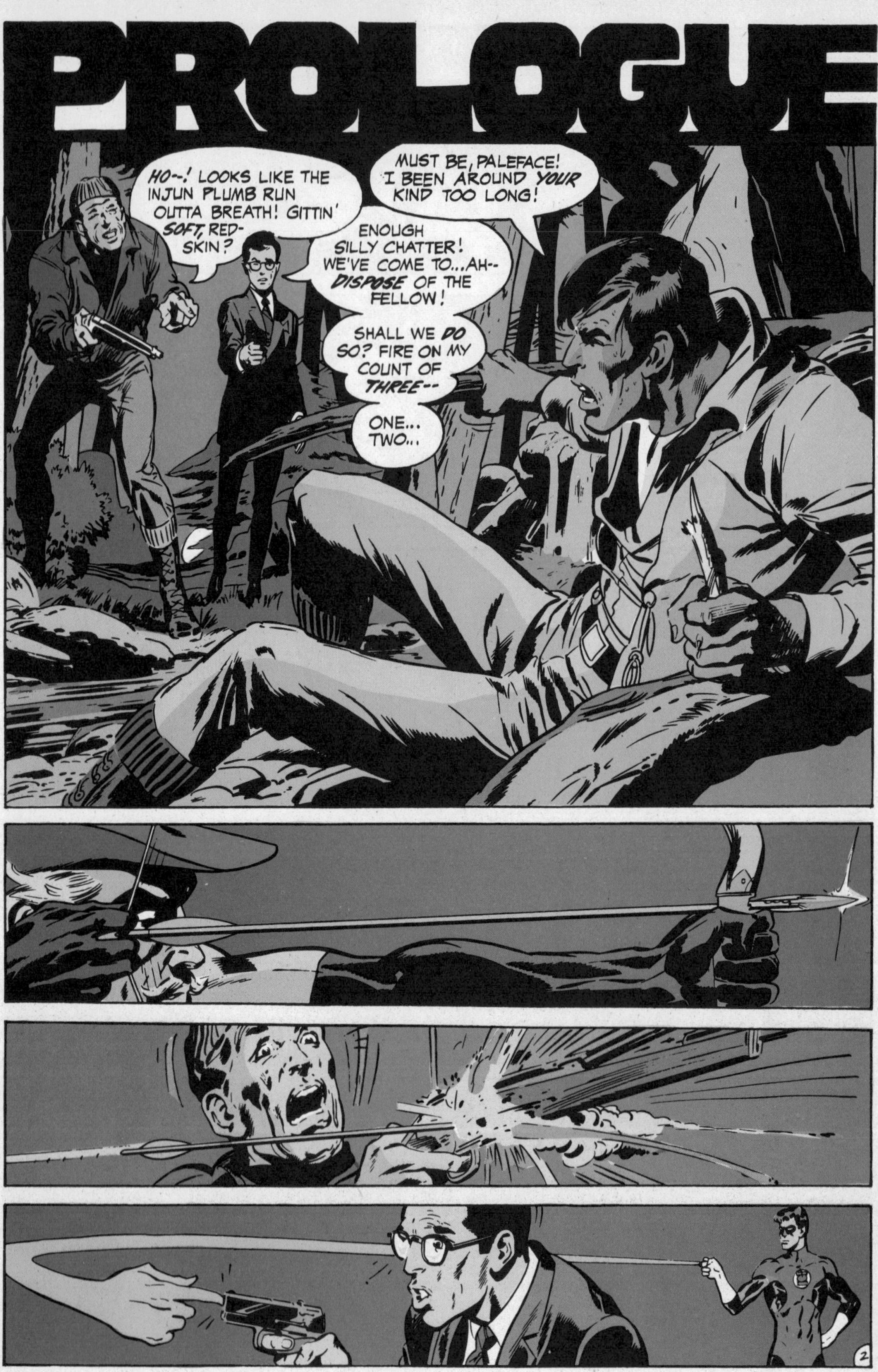
PROLOGUE
HO--! LOOKS LIKE THE INJUN PLUMB RUN OUTTA BREATH! GITTIN' SOFT, RED-SKIN?
MUST BE, PALEFACE! I BEEN AROUND YOUR KIND TOO LONG!
ENOUGH SILLY CHATTER! WE'VE COME TO...AH-- DISPOSE OF THE FELLOW!
SHALL WE DO SO? FIRE ON MY COUNT OF THREE--
ONE... TWO...
2

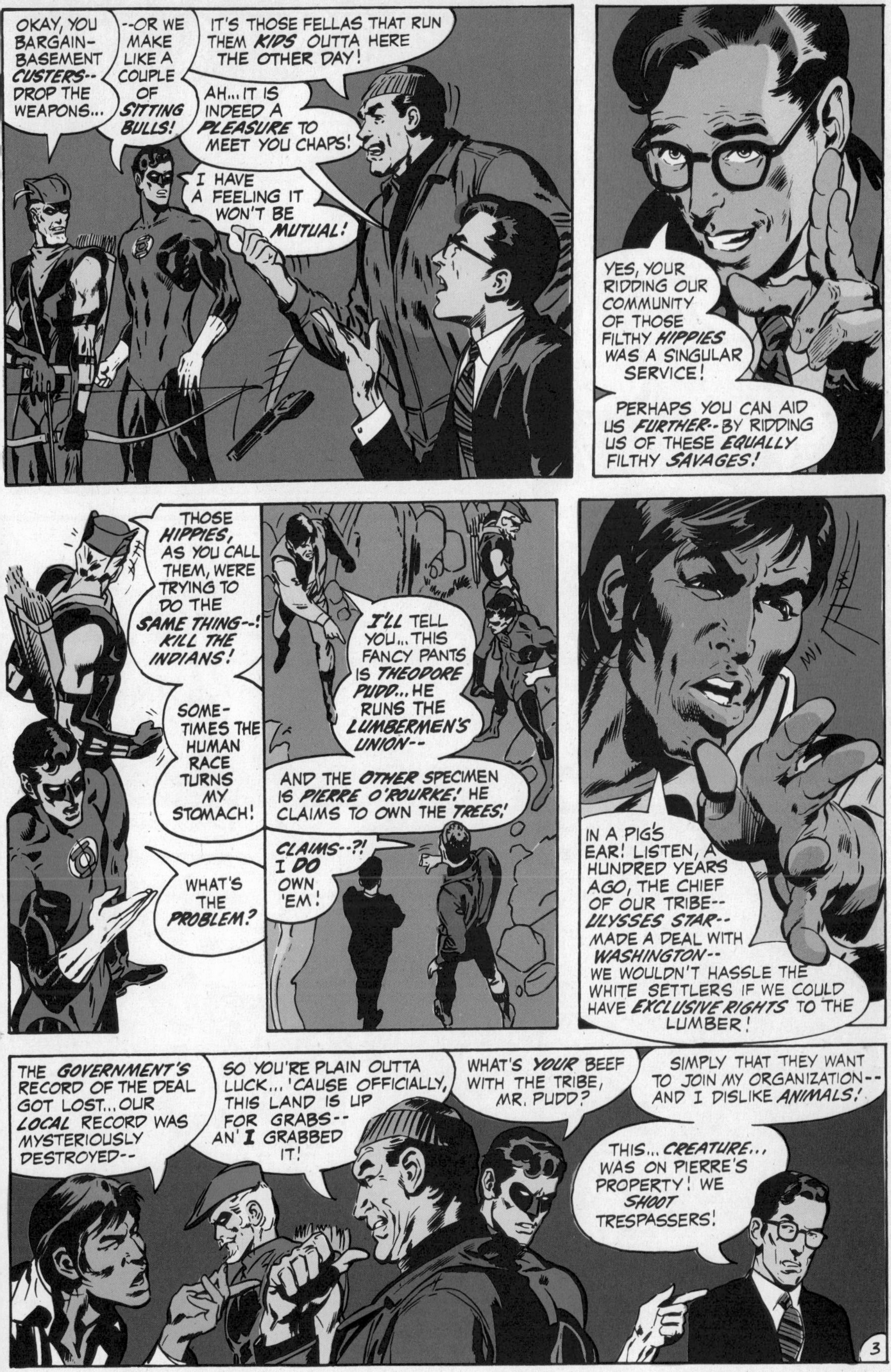
OKAY, YOU BARGAIN-BASEMENT CUSTERS-- DROP THE WEAPONS...
--OR WE MAKE LIKE A COUPLE OF SITTING BULLS!
IT'S THOSE FELLAS THAT RUN THEM KIDS OUTTA HERE THE OTHER DAY!
AH... IT IS INDEED A PLEASURE TO MEET YOU CHAPS!
I HAVE A FEELING IT WON'T BE MUTUAL!
YES, YOUR RIDDING OUR COMMUNITY OF THOSE FILTHY HIPPIES WAS A SINGULAR SERVICE!
PERHAPS YOU CAN AID US FURTHER-- BY RIDDING US OF THESE EQUALLY FILTHY SAVAGES!
THOSE HIPPIES, AS YOU CALL THEM, WERE TRYING TO DO THE SAME THING--! KILL THE INDIANS!
SOME-TIMES THE HUMAN RACE TURNS MY STOMACH!
WHAT'S THE PROBLEM?
I'LL TELL YOU... THIS FANCY PANTS IS THEODORE PUDD... HE RUNS THE LUMBERMEN'S UNION--
AND THE OTHER SPECIMEN IS PIERRE O'ROURKE! HE CLAIMS TO OWN THE TREES!
CLAIMS--?! I DO OWN 'EM!
IN A PIG'S EAR! LISTEN, A HUNDRED YEARS AGO, THE CHIEF OF OUR TRIBE-- ULYSSES STAR-- MADE A DEAL WITH WASHINGTON-- WE WOULDN'T HASSLE THE WHITE SETTLERS IF WE COULD HAVE EXCLUSIVE RIGHTS TO THE LUMBER!
THE GOVERNMENT'S RECORD OF THE DEAL GOT LOST... OUR LOCAL RECORD WAS MYSTERIOUSLY DESTROYED--
SO YOU'RE PLAIN OUTTA LUCK... 'CAUSE OFFICIALLY, THIS LAND IS UP FOR GRABS-- AN' I GRABBED IT!
WHAT'S YOUR BEEF WITH THE TRIBE, MR. PUDD?
SIMPLY THAT THEY WANT TO JOIN MY ORGANIZATION-- AND I DISLIKE ANIMALS!
THIS... CREATURE... WAS ON PIERRE'S PROPERTY! WE SHOOT TRESPASSERS!
3

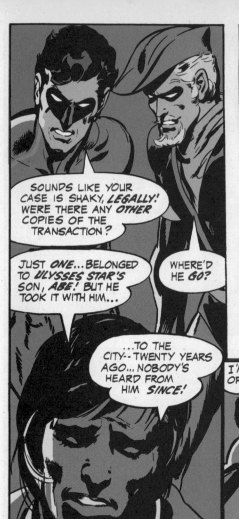

SOUNDS LIKE YOUR *CASE* IS SHAKY, *LEGALLY!* WERE THERE ANY *OTHER* COPIES OF THE TRANSACTION?

JUST *ONE*...BELONGED TO *ULYSSES STAR'S* SON, *ABE!* BUT HE TOOK IT WITH HIM...

WHERE'D HE *GO*?

...TO THE CITY--TWENTY YEARS AGO...NOBODY'S HEARD FROM HIM *SINCE!*

THEN THERE'S NOTHING WE CAN *DO* TO HELP!

THE *HECK* THERE ISN'T! WE CAN *STAY*... AND *FIGHT!* WE'RE SUPPOSED TO BE *GOOD* AT FIGHTING-- *REMEMBER*?!

I'M GETTING A BIT *TIRED* OF YOUR *LORDING* IT OVER ME...WITH YOUR *MORAL SUPERIORITY* ROUTINE...

IF YOU WANT TO BREAK THE *LAW--GO AHEAD!* BUT COUNT ME *OUT!*

THAT I WILL DO *GLADLY!*

THAT BLASTED *HOTHEAD!* HE STARTS *SWINGING* BEFORE HE BOTHERS TO *THINK!*

MAYBE I WAS WRONG, THOUGH...MAYBE I *CAN* HELP--!

I'LL BEGIN WITH A TRIP TO THE *RESERVATION*... THEN, I'LL HEAD FOR THE CITY...

4

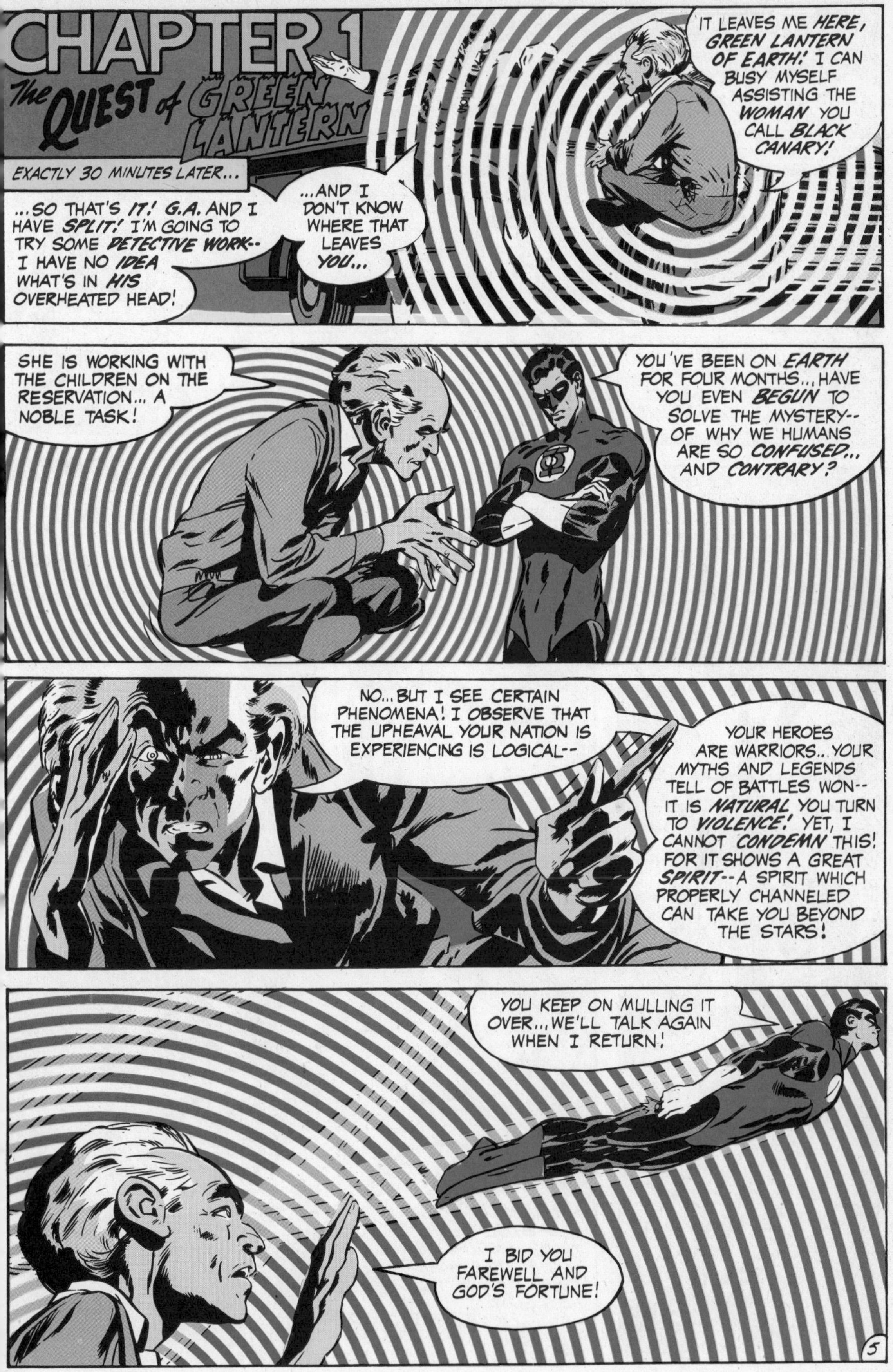
CHAPTER 1
The QUEST of GREEN LANTERN
EXACTLY 30 MINUTES LATER...
...SO THAT'S IT! G.A. AND I HAVE SPLIT! I'M GOING TO TRY SOME DETECTIVE WORK-- I HAVE NO IDEA WHAT'S IN HIS OVERHEATED HEAD!
...AND I DON'T KNOW WHERE THAT LEAVES YOU...
IT LEAVES ME HERE, GREEN LANTERN OF EARTH! I CAN BUSY MYSELF ASSISTING THE WOMAN YOU CALL BLACK CANARY!
SHE IS WORKING WITH THE CHILDREN ON THE RESERVATION... A NOBLE TASK!
YOU'VE BEEN ON EARTH FOR FOUR MONTHS... HAVE YOU EVEN BEGUN TO SOLVE THE MYSTERY-- OF WHY WE HUMANS ARE SO CONFUSED... AND CONTRARY?
NO... BUT I SEE CERTAIN PHENOMENA! I OBSERVE THAT THE UPHEAVAL YOUR NATION IS EXPERIENCING IS LOGICAL--
YOUR HEROES ARE WARRIORS... YOUR MYTHS AND LEGENDS TELL OF BATTLES WON-- IT IS NATURAL YOU TURN TO VIOLENCE! YET, I CANNOT CONDEMN THIS! FOR IT SHOWS A GREAT SPIRIT--A SPIRIT WHICH PROPERLY CHANNELED CAN TAKE YOU BEYOND THE STARS!
YOU KEEP ON MULLING IT OVER... WE'LL TALK AGAIN WHEN I RETURN!
I BID YOU FAREWELL AND GOD'S FORTUNE!
5

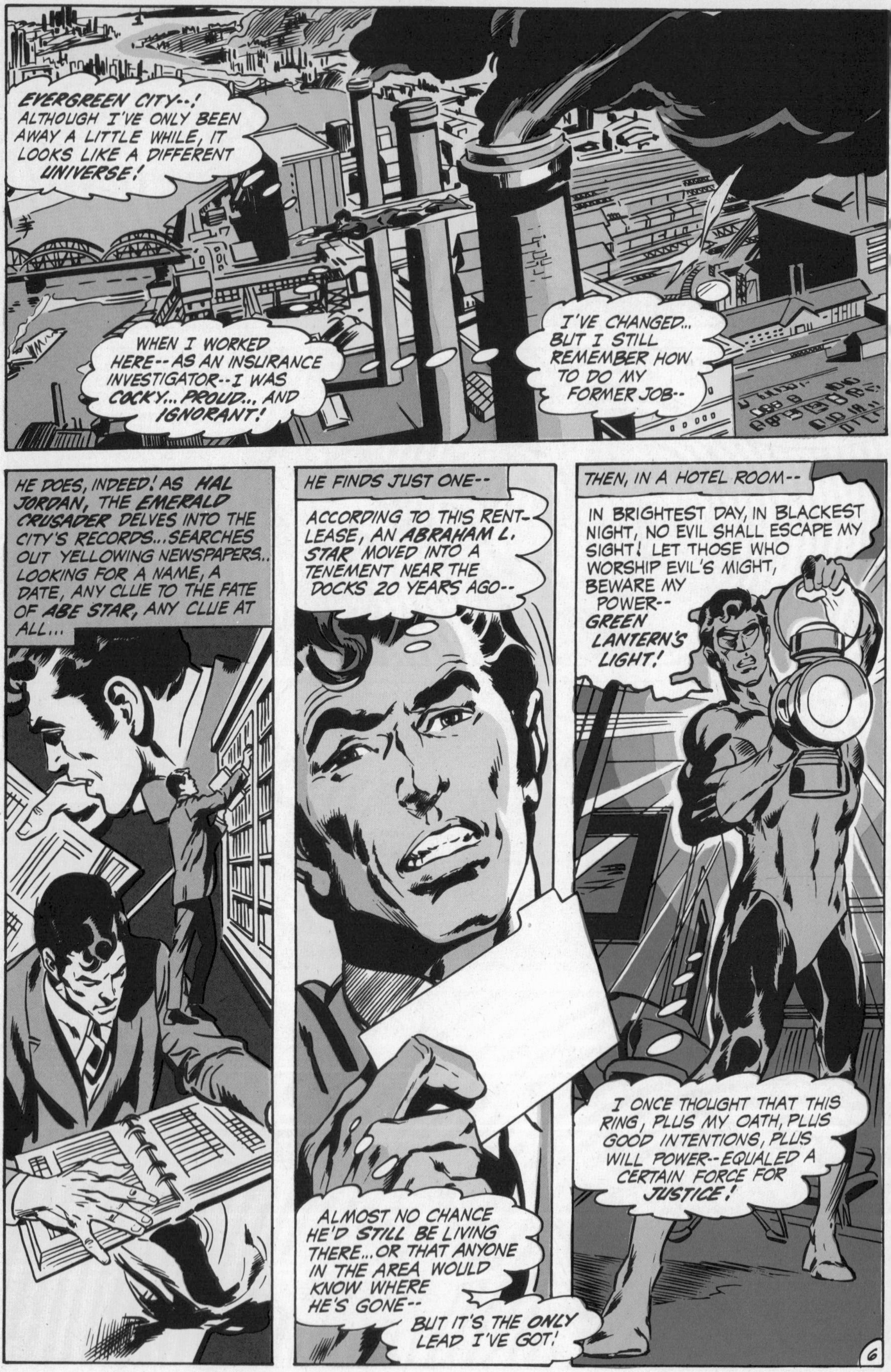
EVERGREEN CITY--! ALTHOUGH I'VE ONLY BEEN AWAY A LITTLE WHILE, IT LOOKS LIKE A DIFFERENT UNIVERSE!
WHEN I WORKED HERE--AS AN INSURANCE INVESTIGATOR--I WAS COCKY... PROUD... AND IGNORANT!
I'VE CHANGED... BUT I STILL REMEMBER HOW TO DO MY FORMER JOB--
HE DOES, INDEED! AS HAL JORDAN, THE EMERALD CRUSADER DELVES INTO THE CITY'S RECORDS...SEARCHES OUT YELLOWING NEWSPAPERS... LOOKING FOR A NAME, A DATE, ANY CLUE TO THE FATE OF ABE STAR, ANY CLUE AT ALL...
HE FINDS JUST ONE--
ACCORDING TO THIS RENT-LEASE, AN ABRAHAM L. STAR MOVED INTO A TENEMENT NEAR THE DOCKS 20 YEARS AGO--
ALMOST NO CHANCE HE'D STILL BE LIVING THERE...OR THAT ANYONE IN THE AREA WOULD KNOW WHERE HE'S GONE--
BUT IT'S THE ONLY LEAD I'VE GOT!
THEN, IN A HOTEL ROOM--
IN BRIGHTEST DAY, IN BLACKEST NIGHT, NO EVIL SHALL ESCAPE MY SIGHT! LET THOSE WHO WORSHIP EVIL'S MIGHT, BEWARE MY POWER-- GREEN LANTERN'S LIGHT!
I ONCE THOUGHT THAT THIS RING, PLUS MY OATH, PLUS GOOD INTENTIONS, PLUS WILL POWER--EQUALED A CERTAIN FORCE FOR JUSTICE!
6

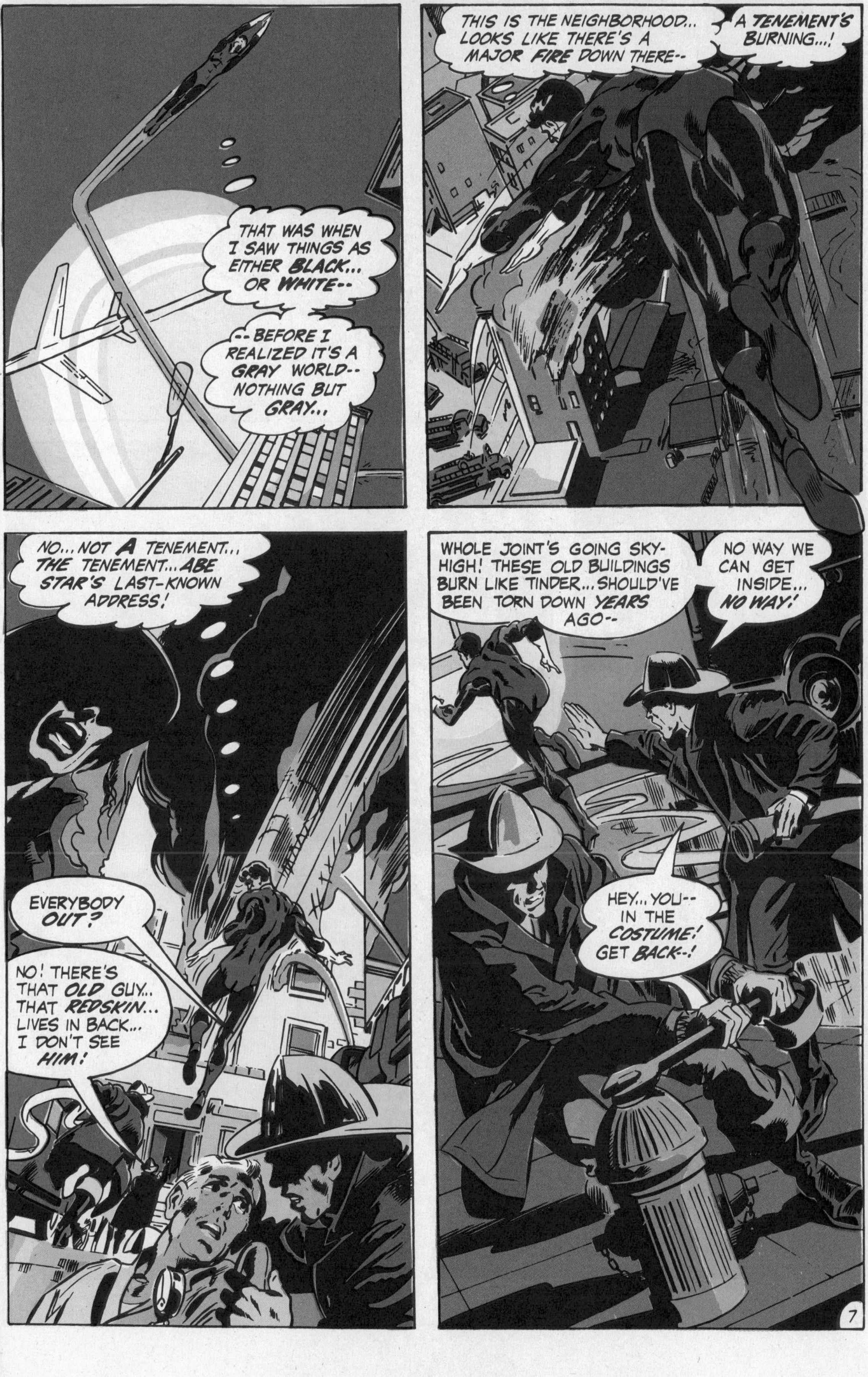
THAT WAS WHEN I SAW THINGS AS EITHER BLACK... OR WHITE--
--BEFORE I REALIZED IT'S A GRAY WORLD-- NOTHING BUT GRAY...
THIS IS THE NEIGHBORHOOD... LOOKS LIKE THERE'S A MAJOR FIRE DOWN THERE--
A TENEMENT'S BURNING...!
NO... NOT A TENEMENT... THE TENEMENT... ABE STAR'S LAST-KNOWN ADDRESS!
EVERYBODY OUT?
NO! THERE'S THAT OLD GUY.. THAT REDSKIN... LIVES IN BACK... I DON'T SEE HIM!
WHOLE JOINT'S GOING SKY-HIGH! THESE OLD BUILDINGS BURN LIKE TINDER... SHOULD'VE BEEN TORN DOWN YEARS AGO--
NO WAY WE CAN GET INSIDE... NO WAY!
HEY... YOU-- IN THE COSTUME! GET BACK-!
7

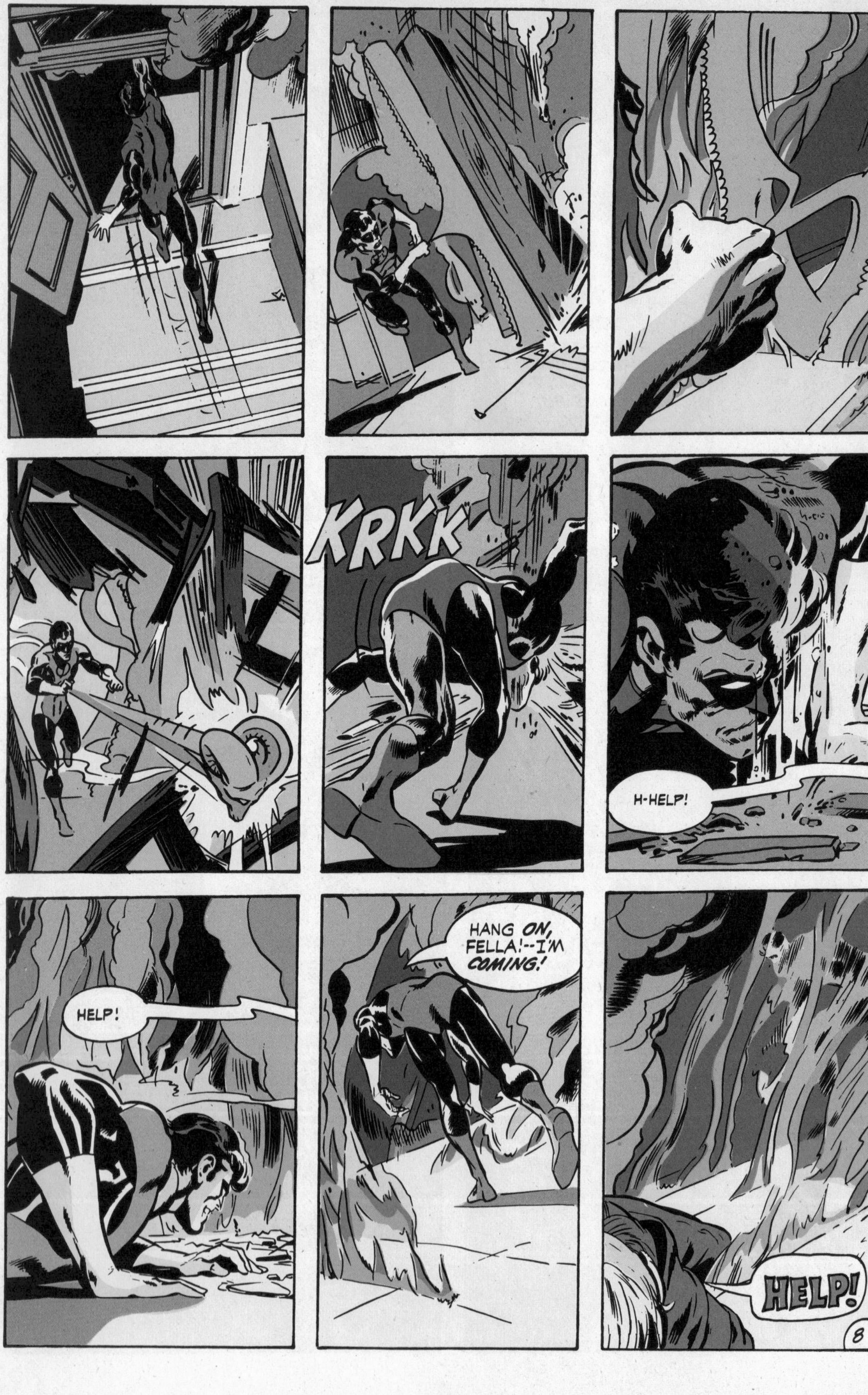
KRKK
H-HELP!
HELP!
HANG ON, FELLA!--I'M COMING!
HELP!
8

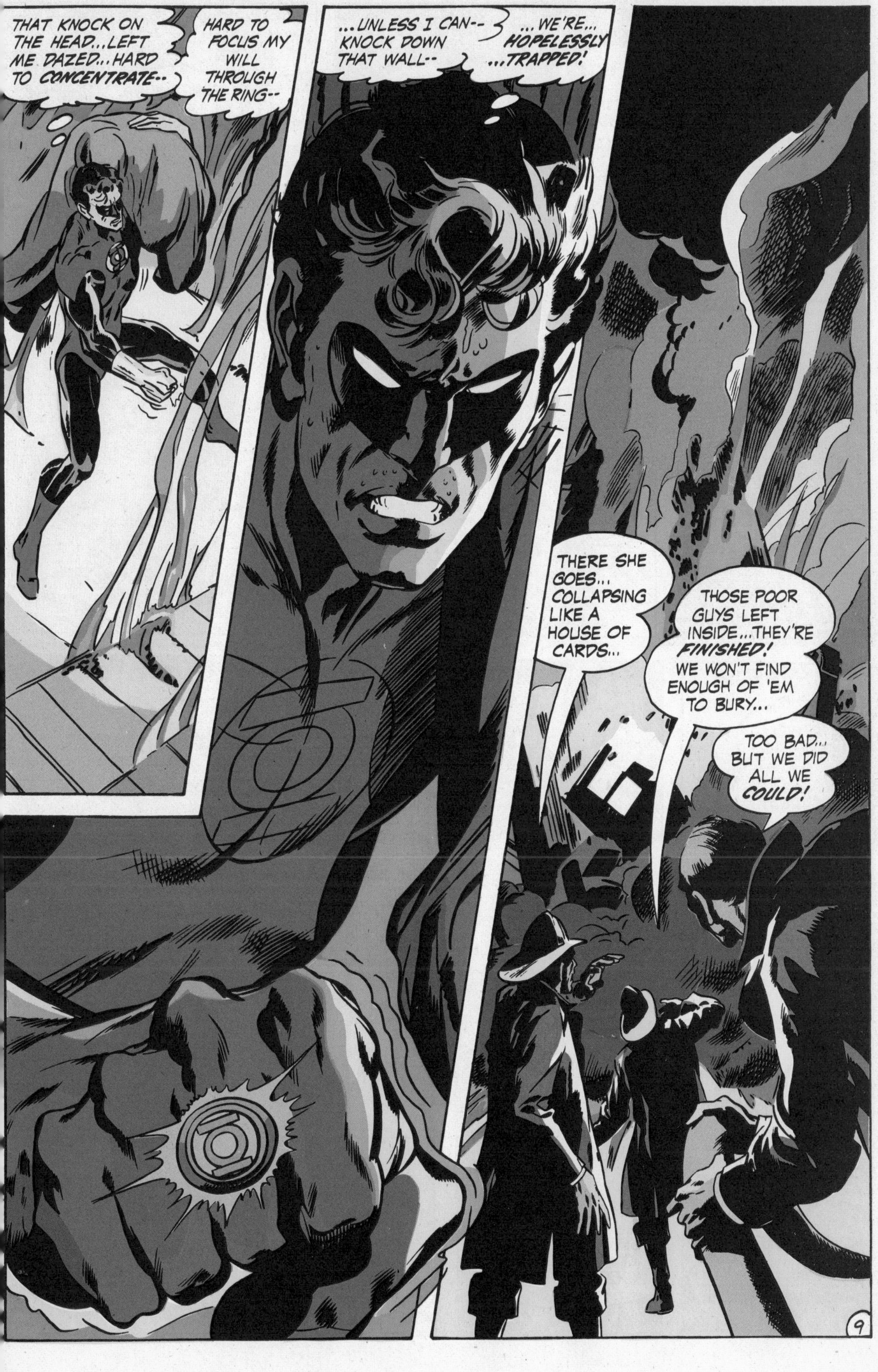
THAT KNOCK ON THE HEAD...LEFT ME DAZED...HARD TO CONCENTRATE--
HARD TO FOCUS MY WILL THROUGH THE RING--
...UNLESS I CAN--KNOCK DOWN THAT WALL--
...WE'RE... HOPELESSLY ...TRAPPED!
THERE SHE GOES... COLLAPSING LIKE A HOUSE OF CARDS...
THOSE POOR GUYS LEFT INSIDE...THEY'RE FINISHED! WE WON'T FIND ENOUGH OF 'EM TO BURY...
TOO BAD... BUT WE DID ALL WE COULD!
9

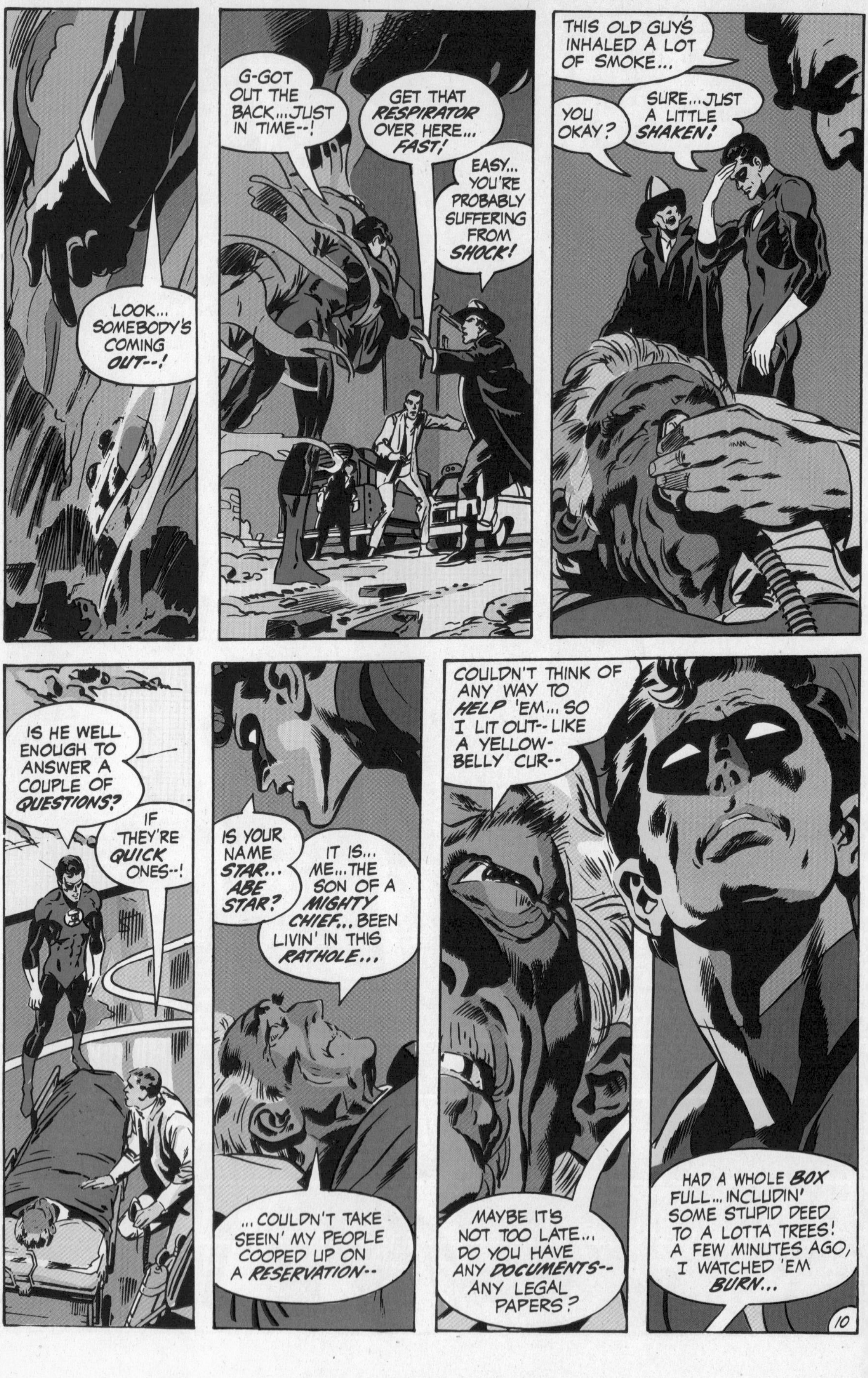
LOOK... SOMEBODY'S COMING OUT--!
G-GOT OUT THE BACK...JUST IN TIME--!
GET THAT RESPIRATOR OVER HERE... FAST!
EASY... YOU'RE PROBABLY SUFFERING FROM SHOCK!
THIS OLD GUY'S INHALED A LOT OF SMOKE...
YOU OKAY?
SURE...JUST A LITTLE SHAKEN!
IS HE WELL ENOUGH TO ANSWER A COUPLE OF QUESTIONS?
IF THEY'RE QUICK ONES--!
IS YOUR NAME STAR... ABE STAR?
IT IS... ME...THE SON OF A MIGHTY CHIEF... BEEN LIVIN' IN THIS RATHOLE...
...COULDN'T TAKE SEEIN' MY PEOPLE COOPED UP ON A RESERVATION--
COULDN'T THINK OF ANY WAY TO HELP 'EM... SO I LIT OUT-- LIKE A YELLOW-BELLY CUR--
MAYBE IT'S NOT TOO LATE... DO YOU HAVE ANY DOCUMENTS-- ANY LEGAL PAPERS?
HAD A WHOLE BOX FULL... INCLUDIN' SOME STUPID DEED TO A LOTTA TREES! A FEW MINUTES AGO, I WATCHED 'EM BURN...
10

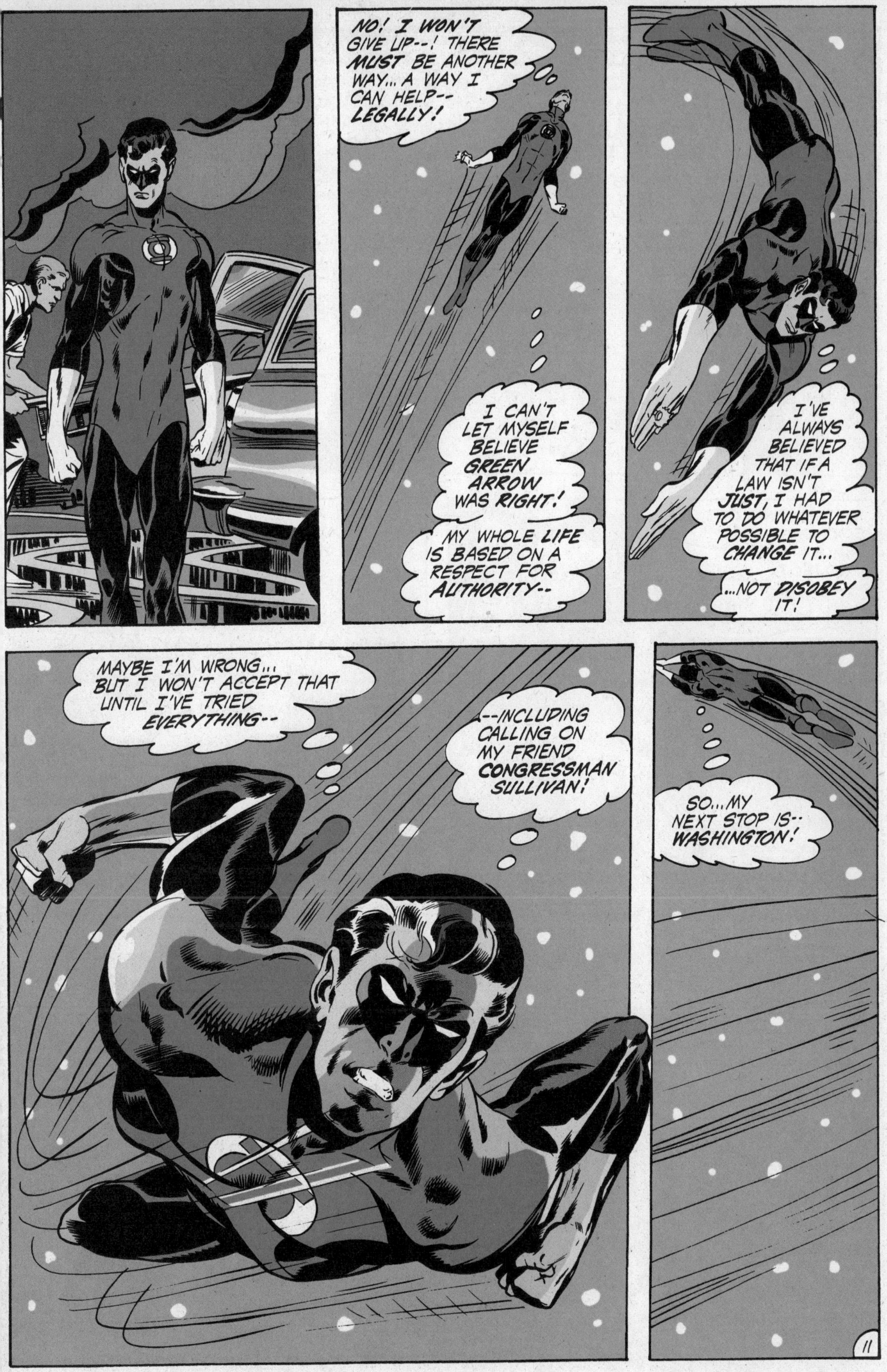
NO! I WON'T GIVE UP--! THERE MUST BE ANOTHER WAY... A WAY I CAN HELP-- LEGALLY!
I CAN'T LET MYSELF BELIEVE GREEN ARROW WAS RIGHT!
MY WHOLE LIFE IS BASED ON A RESPECT FOR AUTHORITY--
I'VE ALWAYS BELIEVED THAT IF A LAW ISN'T JUST, I HAD TO DO WHATEVER POSSIBLE TO CHANGE IT...
...NOT DISOBEY IT!
MAYBE I'M WRONG... BUT I WON'T ACCEPT THAT UNTIL I'VE TRIED EVERYTHING--
--INCLUDING CALLING ON MY FRIEND CONGRESSMAN SULLIVAN!
SO...MY NEXT STOP IS-- WASHINGTON!
11

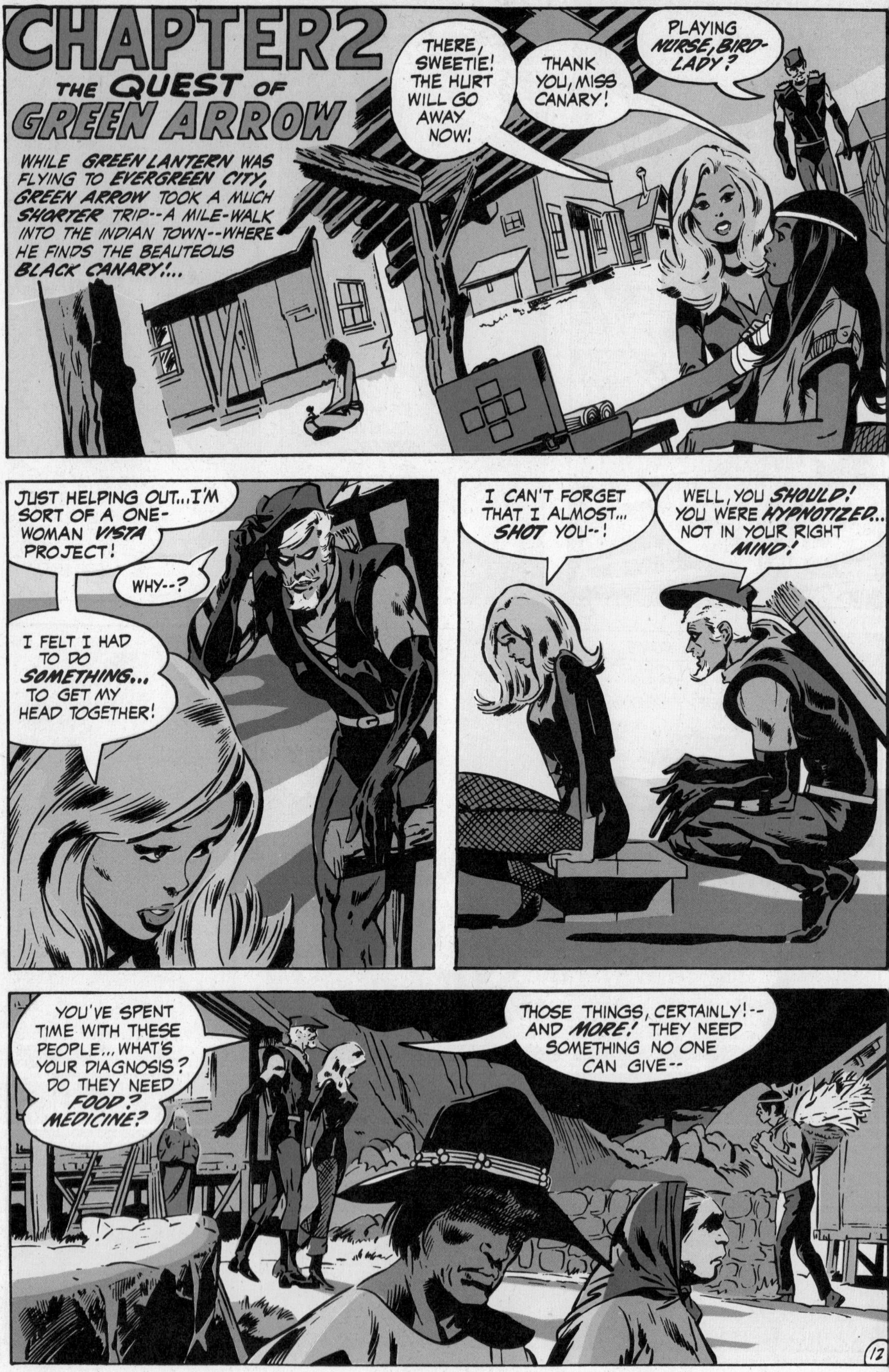
CHAPTER 2
THE QUEST OF GREEN ARROW
WHILE GREEN LANTERN WAS FLYING TO EVERGREEN CITY, GREEN ARROW TOOK A MUCH SHORTER TRIP--A MILE-WALK INTO THE INDIAN TOWN--WHERE HE FINDS THE BEAUTEOUS BLACK CANARY!...
THERE, SWEETIE! THE HURT WILL GO AWAY NOW!
THANK YOU, MISS CANARY!
PLAYING NURSE, BIRD-LADY?
JUST HELPING OUT...I'M SORT OF A ONE-WOMAN VISTA PROJECT!
WHY--?
I FELT I HAD TO DO SOMETHING... TO GET MY HEAD TOGETHER!
I CAN'T FORGET THAT I ALMOST... SHOT YOU--!
WELL, YOU SHOULD! YOU WERE HYPNOTIZED... NOT IN YOUR RIGHT MIND!
YOU'VE SPENT TIME WITH THESE PEOPLE... WHAT'S YOUR DIAGNOSIS? DO THEY NEED FOOD? MEDICINE?
THOSE THINGS, CERTAINLY!--AND MORE! THEY NEED SOMETHING NO ONE CAN GIVE--
12

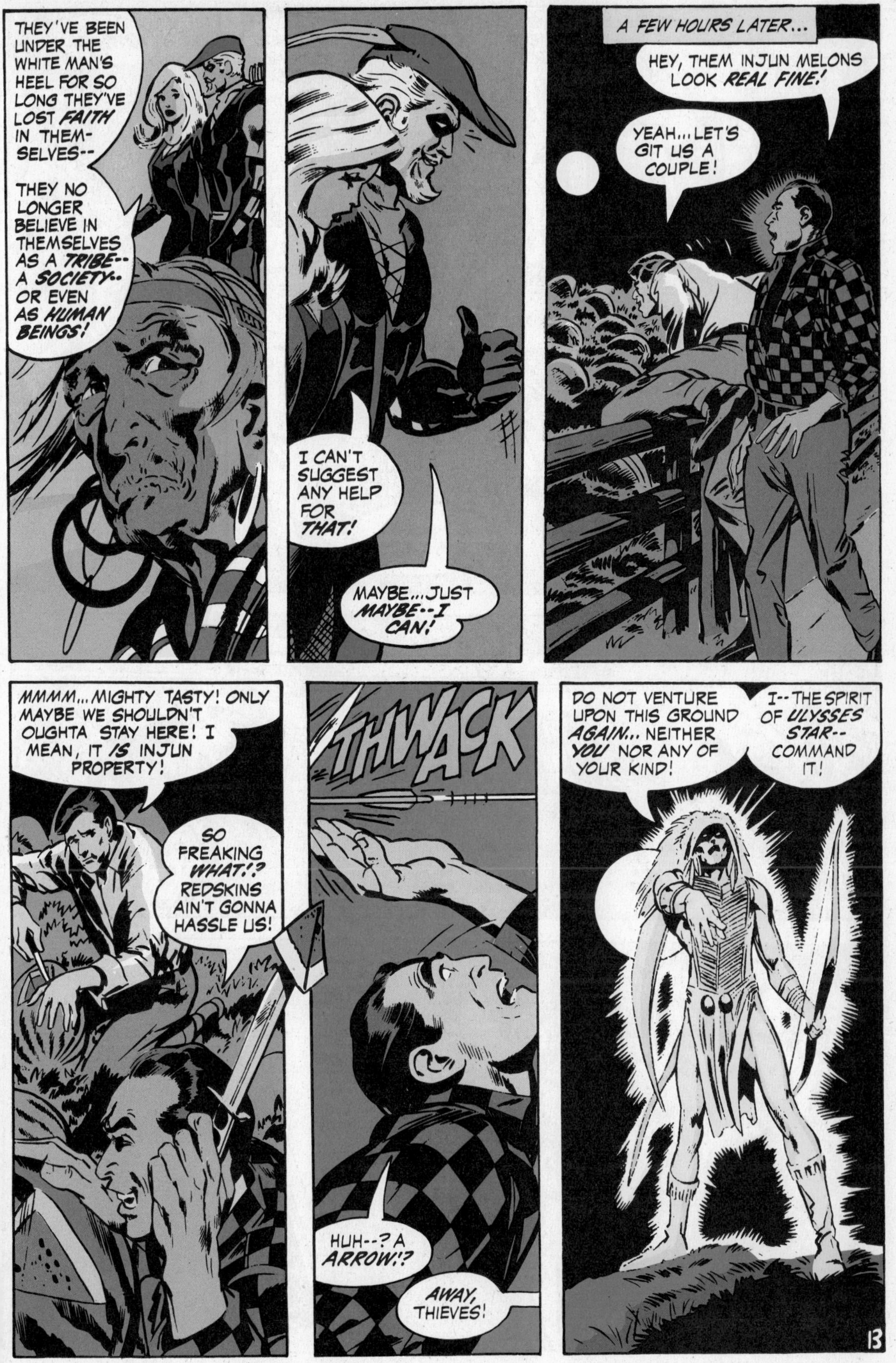
THEY'VE BEEN UNDER THE WHITE MAN'S HEEL FOR SO LONG THEY'VE LOST FAITH IN THEM-SELVES--
THEY NO LONGER BELIEVE IN THEMSELVES AS A TRIBE-- A SOCIETY-- OR EVEN AS HUMAN BEINGS!
I CAN'T SUGGEST ANY HELP FOR THAT!
MAYBE...JUST MAYBE--I CAN!
A FEW HOURS LATER...
HEY, THEM INJUN MELONS LOOK REAL FINE!
YEAH...LET'S GIT US A COUPLE!
MMMM...MIGHTY TASTY! ONLY MAYBE WE SHOULDN'T OUGHTA STAY HERE! I MEAN, IT IS INJUN PROPERTY!
SO FREAKING WHAT!? REDSKINS AIN'T GONNA HASSLE US!
THWACK
HUH--? A ARROW!?
AWAY, THIEVES!
DO NOT VENTURE UPON THIS GROUND AGAIN... NEITHER YOU NOR ANY OF YOUR KIND!
I--THE SPIRIT OF ULYSSES STAR-- COMMAND IT!
13

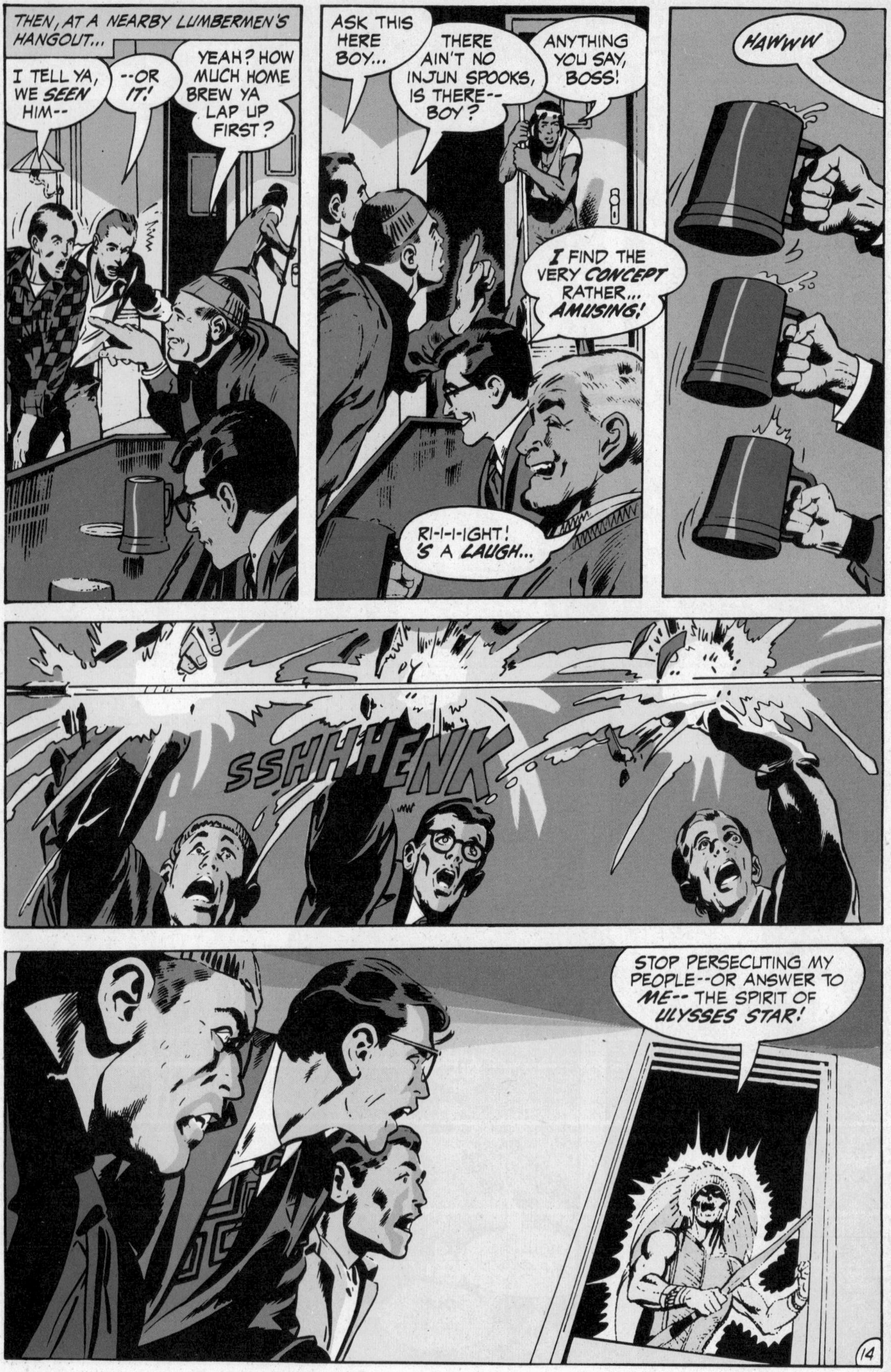
THEN, AT A NEARBY LUMBERMEN'S HANGOUT...
I TELL YA, WE SEEN HIM--
--OR IT!
YEAH? HOW MUCH HOME BREW YA LAP UP FIRST?
ASK THIS HERE BOY...
THERE AIN'T NO INJUN SPOOKS, IS THERE-- BOY?
ANYTHING YOU SAY, BOSS!
I FIND THE VERY CONCEPT RATHER... AMUSING!
RI-I-I-IGHT! 'S A LAUGH...
HAWWW
SSHHHENK
STOP PERSECUTING MY PEOPLE--OR ANSWER TO ME-- THE SPIRIT OF ULYSSES STAR!
14

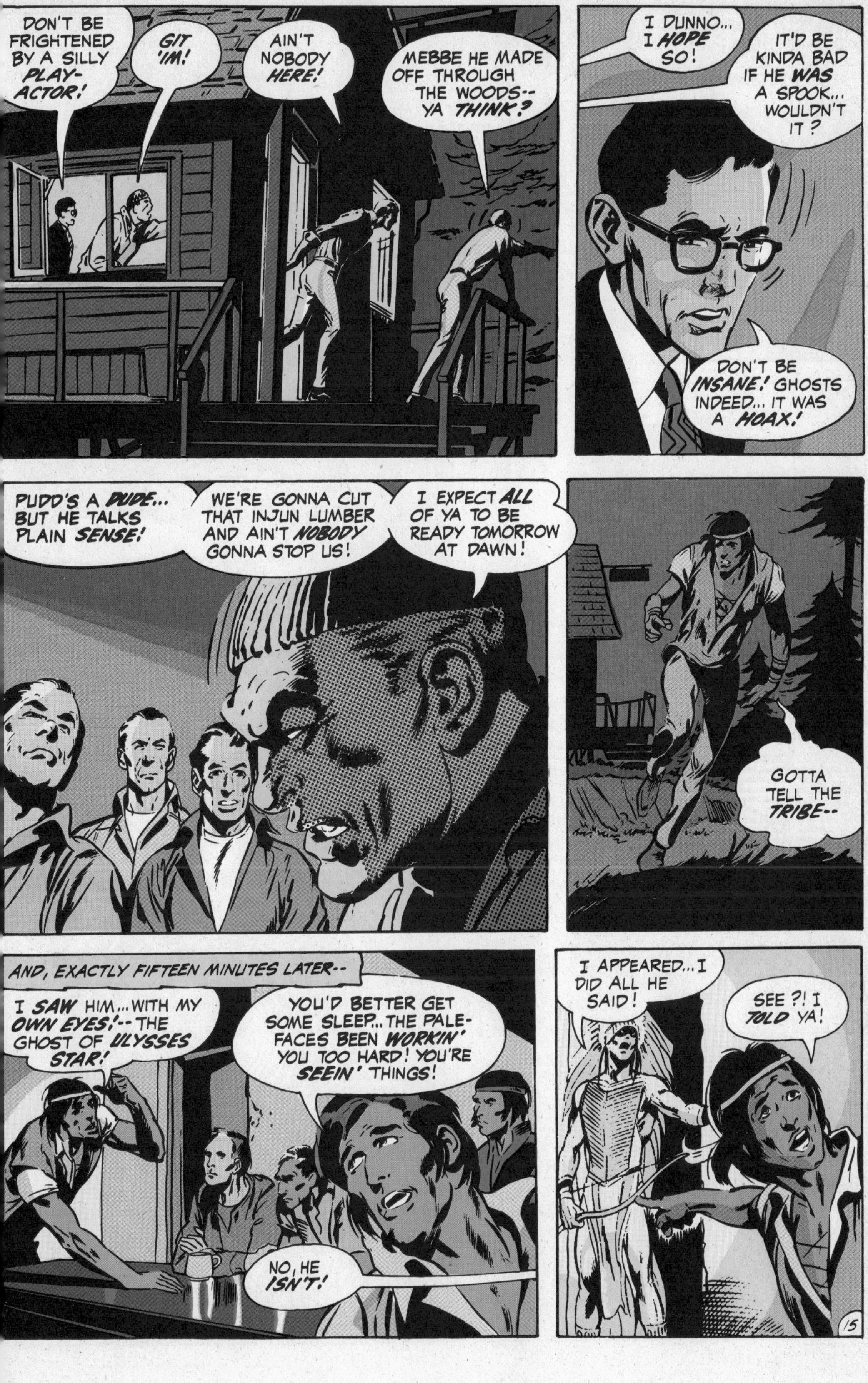

DON'T BE FRIGHTENED BY A SILLY PLAY-ACTOR!
GIT 'IM!
AIN'T NOBODY HERE!
MEBBE HE MADE OFF THROUGH THE WOODS-- YA THINK?
I DUNNO... I HOPE SO!
IT'D BE KINDA BAD IF HE WAS A SPOOK... WOULDN'T IT?
DON'T BE INSANE! GHOSTS INDEED... IT WAS A HOAX!
PUDD'S A DUDE... BUT HE TALKS PLAIN SENSE!
WE'RE GONNA CUT THAT INJUN LUMBER AND AIN'T NOBODY GONNA STOP US!
I EXPECT ALL OF YA TO BE READY TOMORROW AT DAWN!
GOTTA TELL THE TRIBE--
AND, EXACTLY FIFTEEN MINUTES LATER--
I SAW HIM... WITH MY OWN EYES!-- THE GHOST OF ULYSSES STAR!
YOU'D BETTER GET SOME SLEEP... THE PALE-FACES BEEN WORKIN' YOU TOO HARD! YOU'RE SEEIN' THINGS!
NO, HE ISN'T!
I APPEARED... I DID ALL HE SAID!
SEE?! I TOLD YA!
15

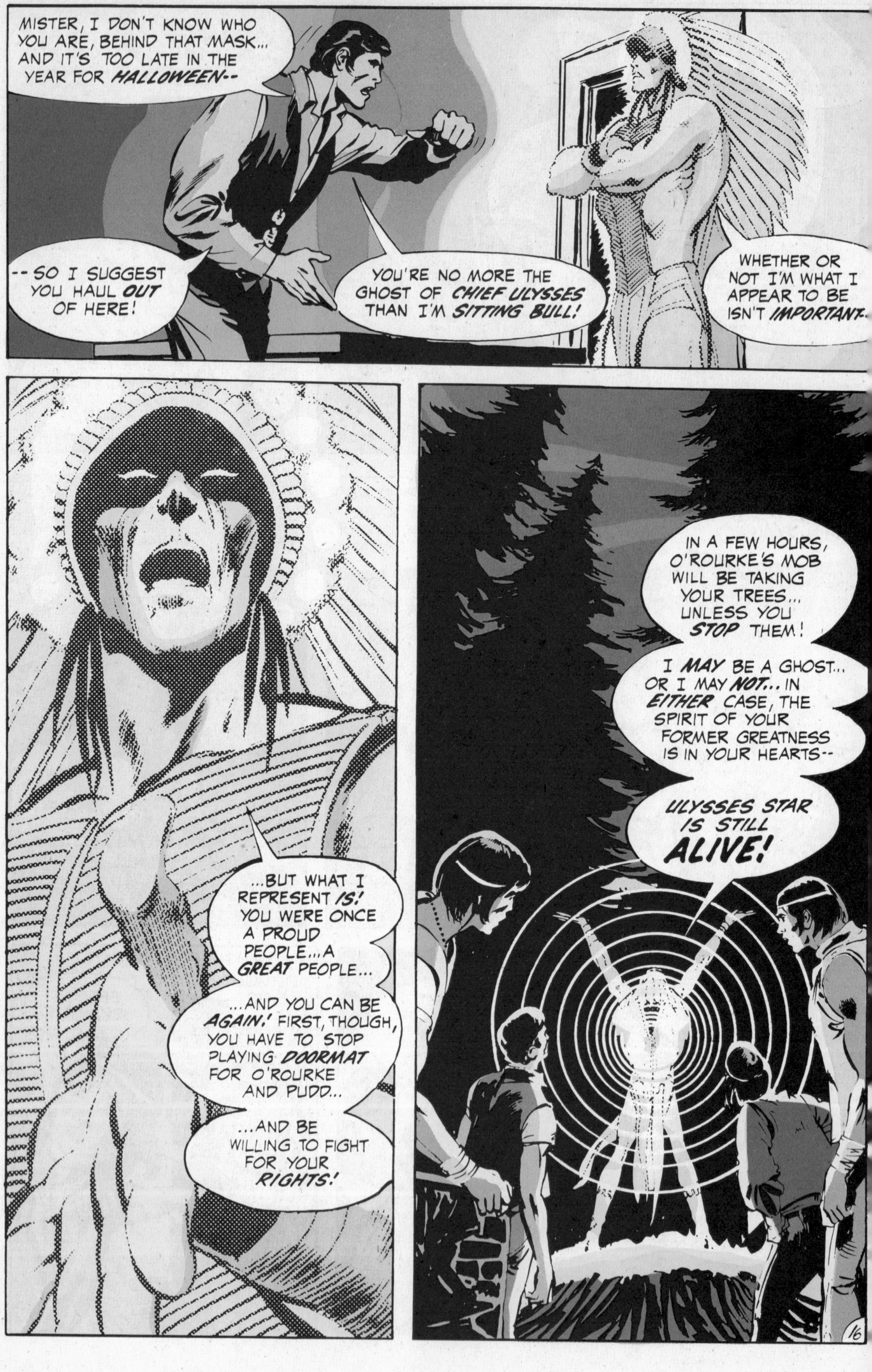

MISTER, I DON'T KNOW WHO YOU ARE, BEHIND THAT MASK... AND IT'S TOO LATE IN THE YEAR FOR HALLOWEEN--
-- SO I SUGGEST YOU HAUL OUT OF HERE!
YOU'RE NO MORE THE GHOST OF CHIEF ULYSSES THAN I'M SITTING BULL!
WHETHER OR NOT I'M WHAT I APPEAR TO BE ISN'T IMPORTANT--
...BUT WHAT I REPRESENT IS! YOU WERE ONCE A PROUD PEOPLE...A GREAT PEOPLE...
...AND YOU CAN BE AGAIN! FIRST, THOUGH, YOU HAVE TO STOP PLAYING DOORMAT FOR O'ROURKE AND PUDD...
...AND BE WILLING TO FIGHT FOR YOUR RIGHTS!
IN A FEW HOURS, O'ROURKE'S MOB WILL BE TAKING YOUR TREES... UNLESS YOU STOP THEM!
I MAY BE A GHOST... OR I MAY NOT... IN EITHER CASE, THE SPIRIT OF YOUR FORMER GREATNESS IS IN YOUR HEARTS--
ULYSSES STAR IS STILL ALIVE!
16

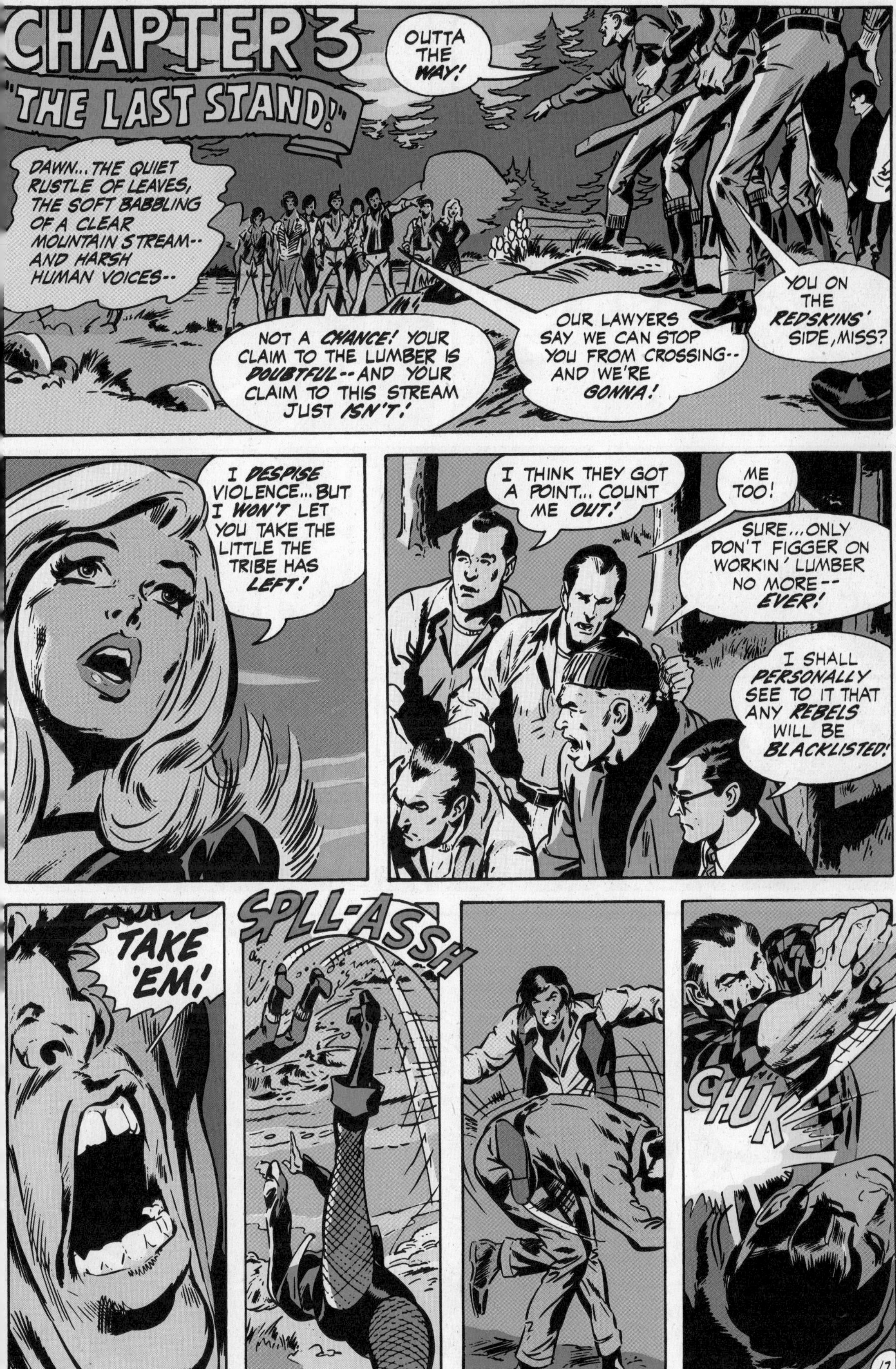
CHAPTER 3
"THE LAST STAND!"
OUTTA THE WAY!
DAWN... THE QUIET RUSTLE OF LEAVES, THE SOFT BABBLING OF A CLEAR MOUNTAIN STREAM-- AND HARSH HUMAN VOICES--
NOT A CHANCE! YOUR CLAIM TO THE LUMBER IS DOUBTFUL--AND YOUR CLAIM TO THIS STREAM JUST ISN'T!
OUR LAWYERS SAY WE CAN STOP YOU FROM CROSSING-- AND WE'RE GONNA!
YOU ON THE REDSKINS' SIDE, MISS?
I DESPISE VIOLENCE... BUT I WON'T LET YOU TAKE THE LITTLE THE TRIBE HAS LEFT!
I THINK THEY GOT A POINT... COUNT ME OUT!
ME TOO!
SURE... ONLY DON'T FIGGER ON WORKIN' LUMBER NO MORE-- EVER!
I SHALL PERSONALLY SEE TO IT THAT ANY REBELS WILL BE BLACKLISTED!
TAKE 'EM!
SPLL-ASSH
CHUK
17

I GOTTA *HAND* IT TO THE *REDSKINS...* THEY'RE MAKIN' A GOOD *FRACAS!*

TRUE! I TRUST, HOWEVER, THAT YOUR *STALWARTS* WILL *VANQUISH* THEM!

WHERE'S YER *GOL-DANG* SPOOK NOW THAT YA *NEED* HIM, HUH?

HERE!

STOP IT!

NOTHING WILL BE SETTLED LIKE... *THIS!* I'VE BROUGHT *U.S. REPRESENTATIVE* SULLIVAN! HE'S PROMISED TO LOOK INTO THE TRIBE'S CLAIMS!

UNTIL HE *DOES, GO HOME--* ALL OF YOU!

SURE...GO HOME-- SIT ON YOUR *HANDS!* --LIKE *ALWAYS!* BE *NICE* WHILE YOU'RE BEING ROBBED *BLIND!* CAN IT, *LANTERN!* GO, CRAWL BACK TO YOUR PALS, THE *GUARDIANS!*

THAT SOUNDS LIKE A *CHALLENGE!*

DARN *RIGHT* IT IS!

18

I *FIGURED* YOU MIGHT SHOW...AND START SLINGING THAT *POWER BEAM!* SO I PREPARED--

--MY COSTUME IS *YELLOW!* YOUR RING IS *USELESS* AGAINST ME!

YOU WANT TO MIX IT *WITHOUT* YOUR RING?

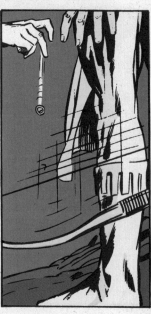

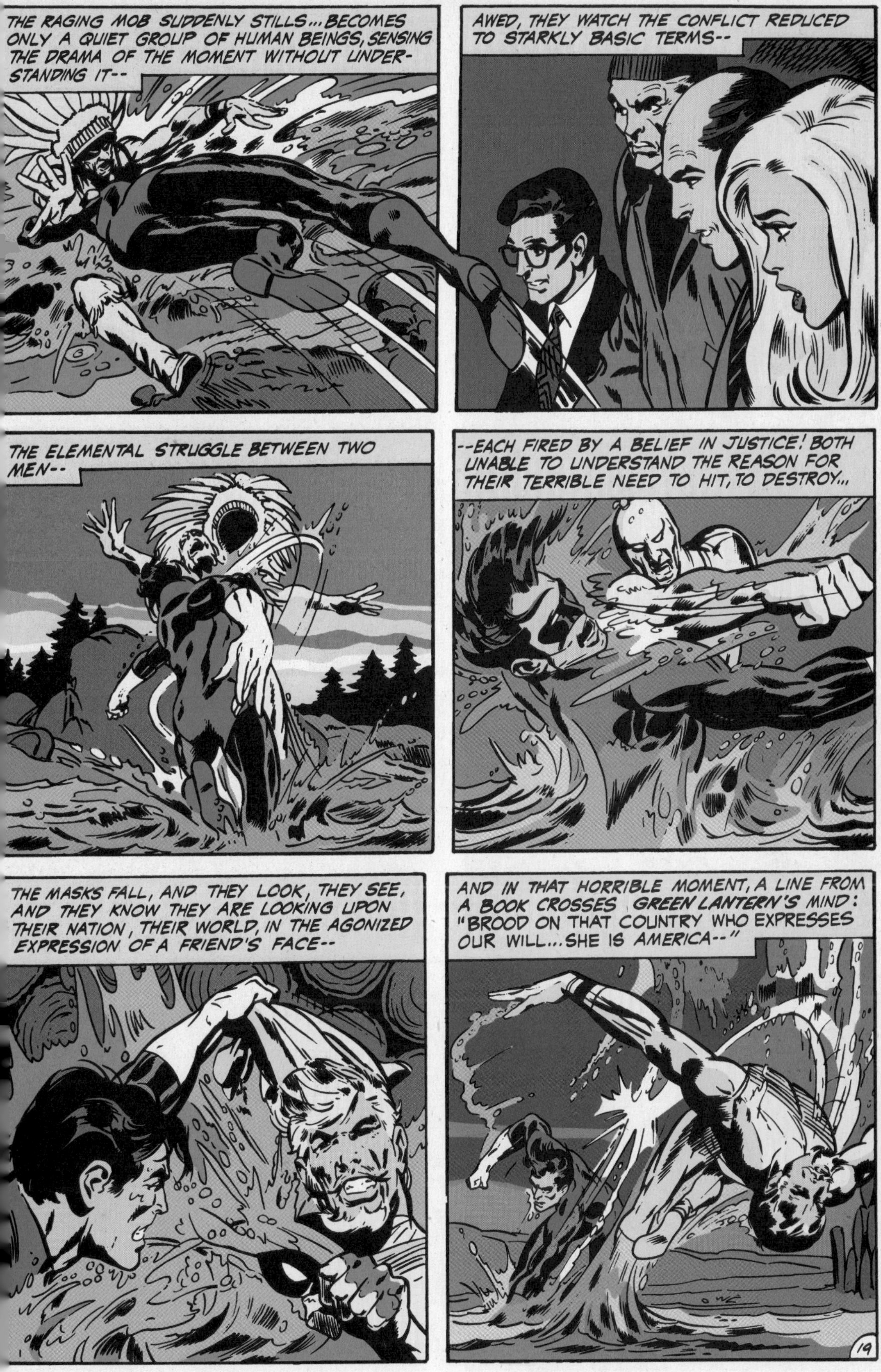
THE RAGING MOB SUDDENLY STILLS... BECOMES ONLY A QUIET GROUP OF HUMAN BEINGS, SENSING THE DRAMA OF THE MOMENT WITHOUT UNDER-STANDING IT--
AWED, THEY WATCH THE CONFLICT REDUCED TO STARKLY BASIC TERMS--
THE ELEMENTAL STRUGGLE BETWEEN TWO MEN--
--EACH FIRED BY A BELIEF IN JUSTICE! BOTH UNABLE TO UNDERSTAND THE REASON FOR THEIR TERRIBLE NEED TO HIT, TO DESTROY...
THE MASKS FALL, AND THEY LOOK, THEY SEE, AND THEY KNOW THEY ARE LOOKING UPON THEIR NATION, THEIR WORLD, IN THE AGONIZED EXPRESSION OF A FRIEND'S FACE--
AND IN THAT HORRIBLE MOMENT, A LINE FROM A BOOK CROSSES GREEN LANTERN'S MIND: "BROOD ON THAT COUNTRY WHO EXPRESSES OUR WILL... SHE IS AMERICA--"
19

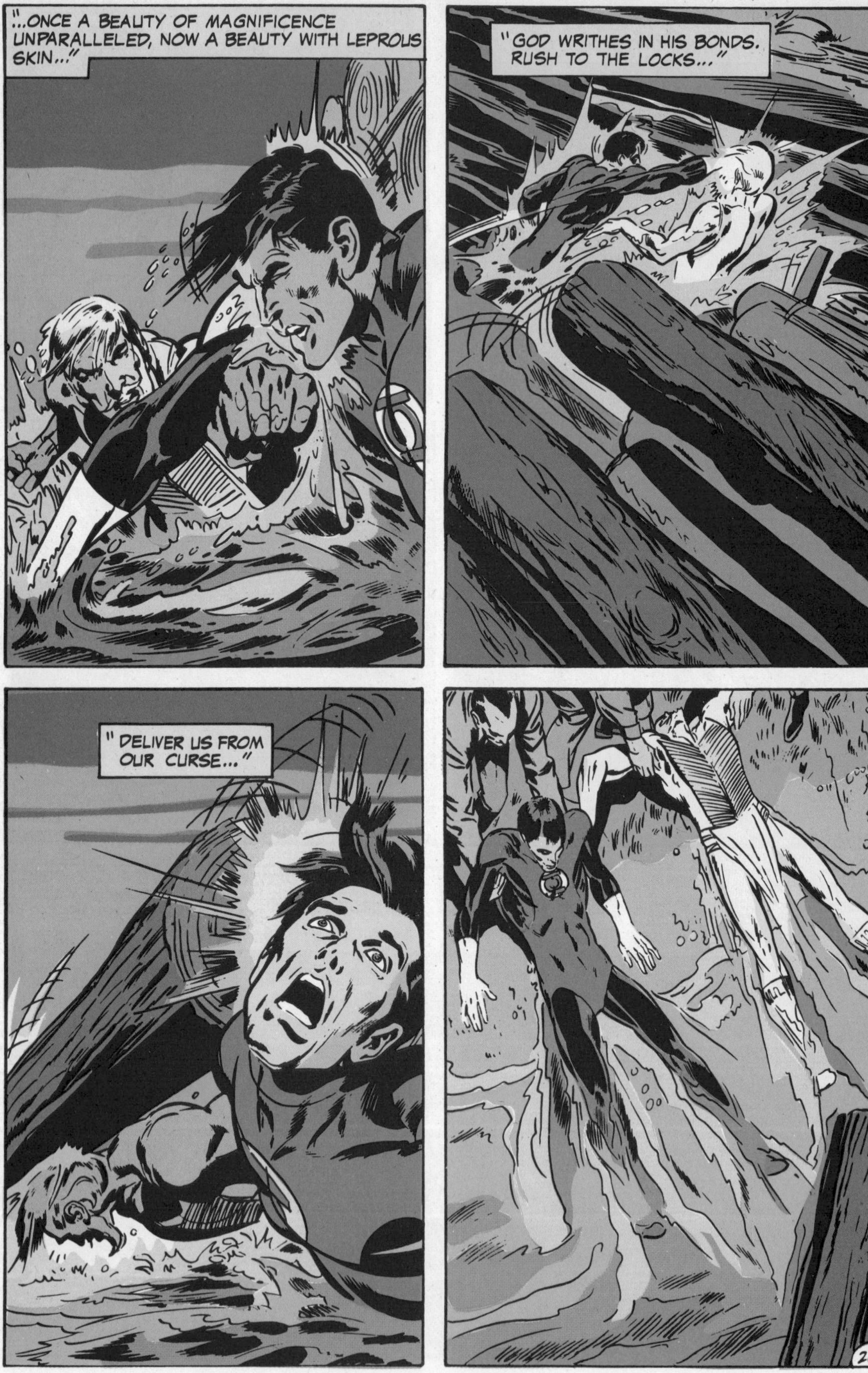
"...ONCE A BEAUTY OF MAGNIFICENCE UNPARALLELED, NOW A BEAUTY WITH LEPROUS SKIN..."
"GOD WRITHES IN HIS BONDS. RUSH TO THE LOCKS..."
"DELIVER US FROM OUR CURSE..."
20

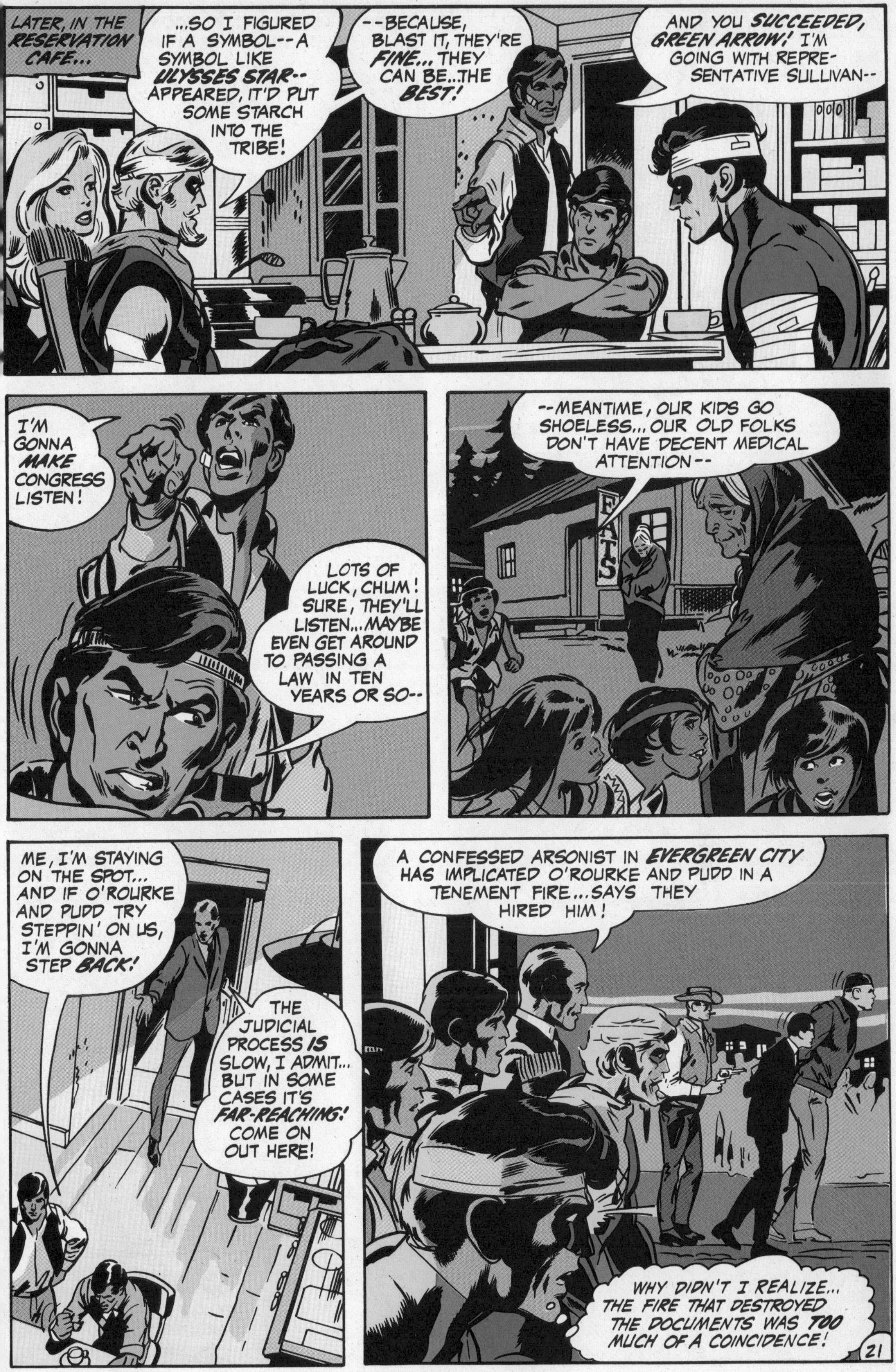
LATER, IN THE RESERVATION CAFE...
...SO I FIGURED IF A SYMBOL--A SYMBOL LIKE ULYSSES STAR--APPEARED, IT'D PUT SOME STARCH INTO THE TRIBE!
--BECAUSE, BLAST IT, THEY'RE FINE... THEY CAN BE...THE BEST!
AND YOU SUCCEEDED, GREEN ARROW! I'M GOING WITH REPRESENTATIVE SULLIVAN--
I'M GONNA MAKE CONGRESS LISTEN!
LOTS OF LUCK, CHUM! SURE, THEY'LL LISTEN... MAYBE EVEN GET AROUND TO PASSING A LAW IN TEN YEARS OR SO--
--MEANTIME, OUR KIDS GO SHOELESS... OUR OLD FOLKS DON'T HAVE DECENT MEDICAL ATTENTION--
EATS
ME, I'M STAYING ON THE SPOT... AND IF O'ROURKE AND PUDD TRY STEPPIN' ON US, I'M GONNA STEP BACK!
THE JUDICIAL PROCESS IS SLOW, I ADMIT... BUT IN SOME CASES IT'S FAR-REACHING! COME ON OUT HERE!
A CONFESSED ARSONIST IN EVERGREEN CITY HAS IMPLICATED O'ROURKE AND PUDD IN A TENEMENT FIRE...SAYS THEY HIRED HIM!
WHY DIDN'T I REALIZE... THE FIRE THAT DESTROYED THE DOCUMENTS WAS TOO MUCH OF A COINCIDENCE!
21

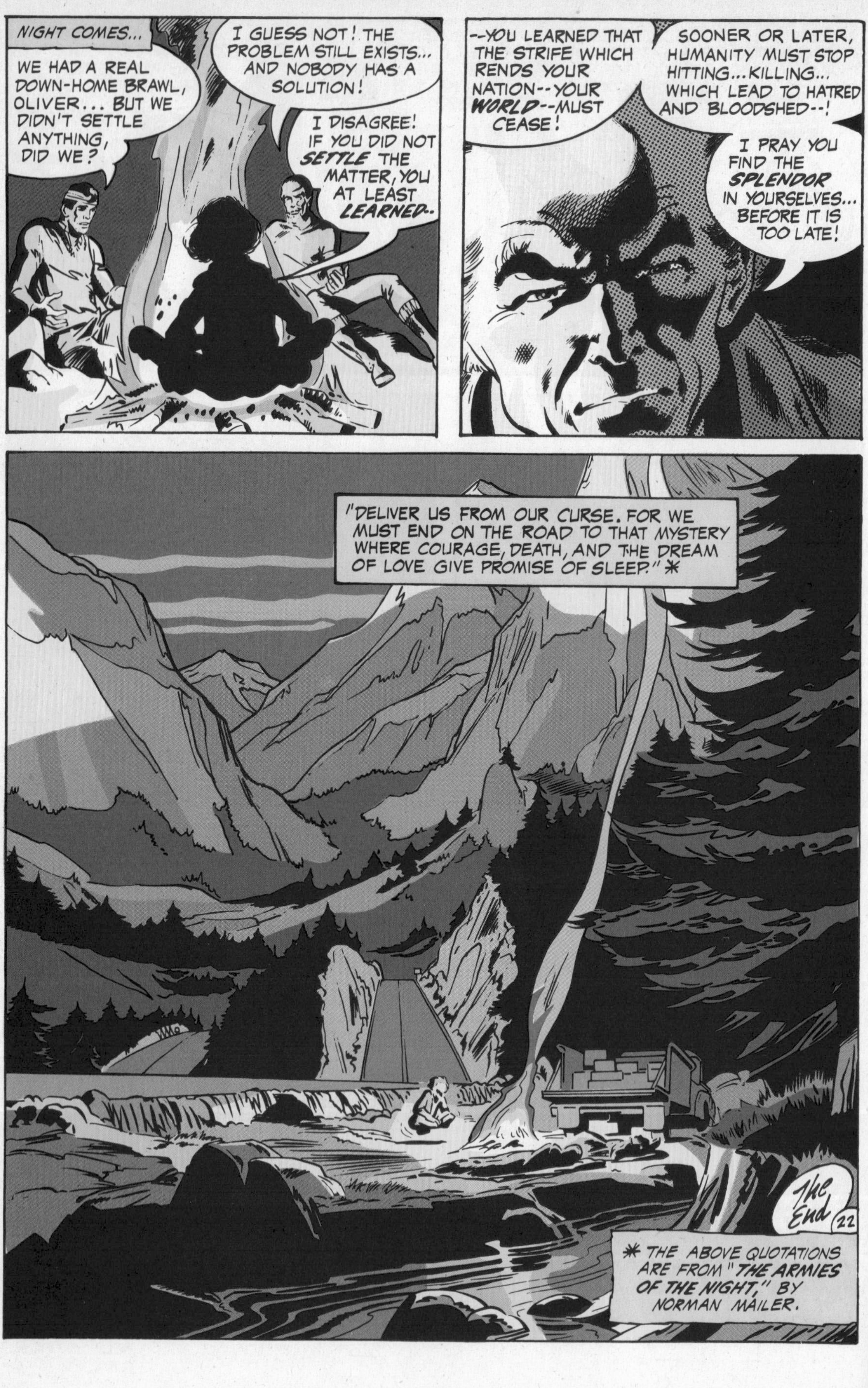

NIGHT COMES...
WE HAD A REAL DOWN-HOME BRAWL, OLIVER... BUT WE DIDN'T SETTLE ANYTHING, DID WE?
I GUESS NOT! THE PROBLEM STILL EXISTS... AND NOBODY HAS A SOLUTION!
I DISAGREE! IF YOU DID NOT SETTLE THE MATTER, YOU AT LEAST LEARNED..
--YOU LEARNED THAT THE STRIFE WHICH RENDS YOUR NATION--YOUR WORLD--MUST CEASE!
SOONER OR LATER, HUMANITY MUST STOP HITTING...KILLING... WHICH LEAD TO HATRED AND BLOODSHED--!
I PRAY YOU FIND THE SPLENDOR IN YOURSELVES... BEFORE IT IS TOO LATE!
"DELIVER US FROM OUR CURSE. FOR WE MUST END ON THE ROAD TO THAT MYSTERY WHERE COURAGE, DEATH, AND THE DREAM OF LOVE GIVE PROMISE OF SLEEP." *
The End
22
* THE ABOVE QUOTATIONS ARE FROM "THE ARMIES OF THE NIGHT," BY NORMAN MAILER.

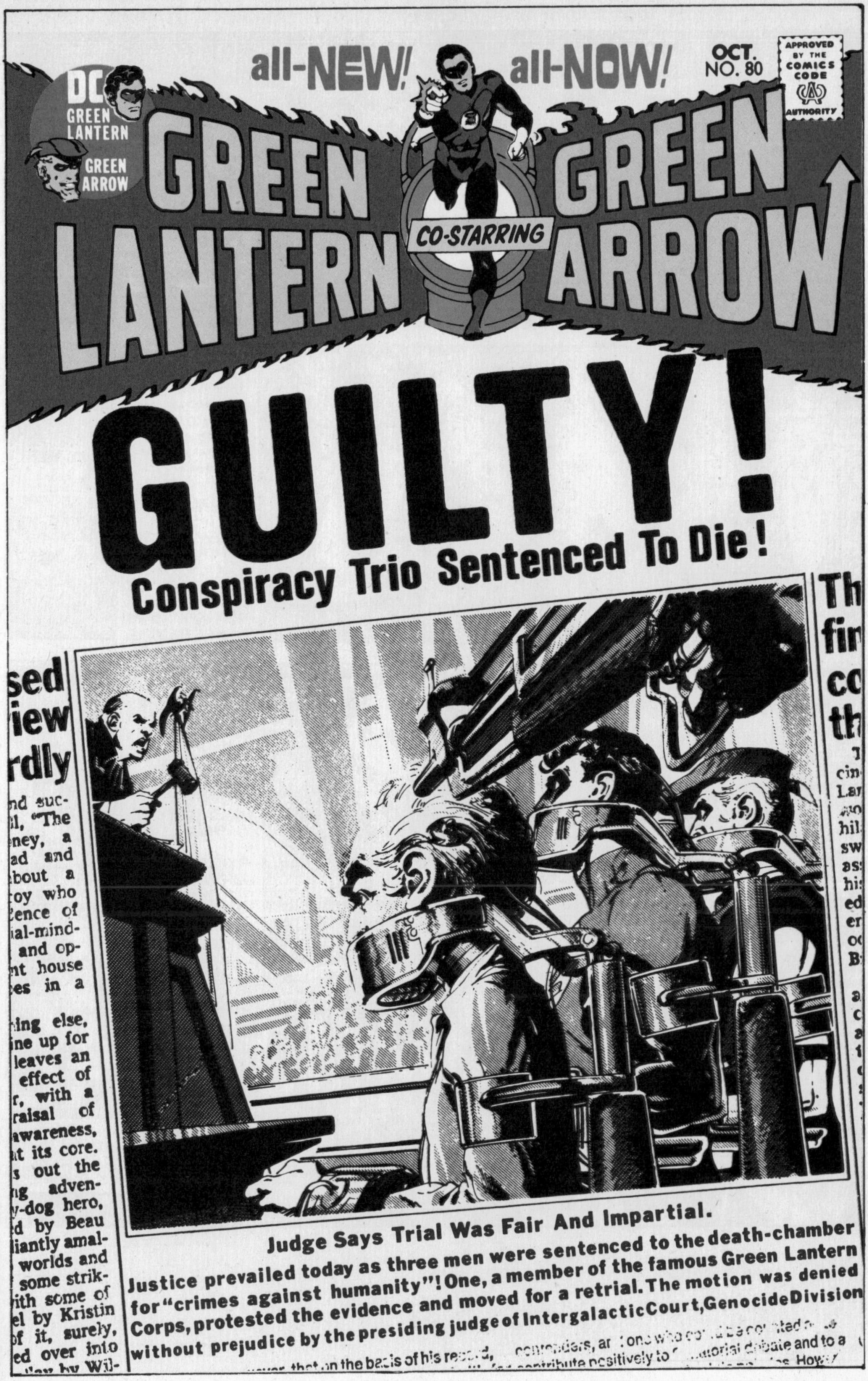

all-NEW! all-NOW!
OCT. NO. 80
APPROVED BY THE COMICS CODE AUTHORITY
DC GREEN LANTERN GREEN ARROW
GREEN LANTERN
CO-STARRING
GREEN ARROW
GUILTY!
Conspiracy Trio Sentenced To Die!
Judge Says Trial Was Fair And Impartial.
Justice prevailed today as three men were sentenced to the death-chamber for "crimes against humanity"! One, a member of the famous Green Lantern Corps, protested the evidence and moved for a retrial. The motion was denied without prejudice by the presiding judge of Intergalactic Court, Genocide Division

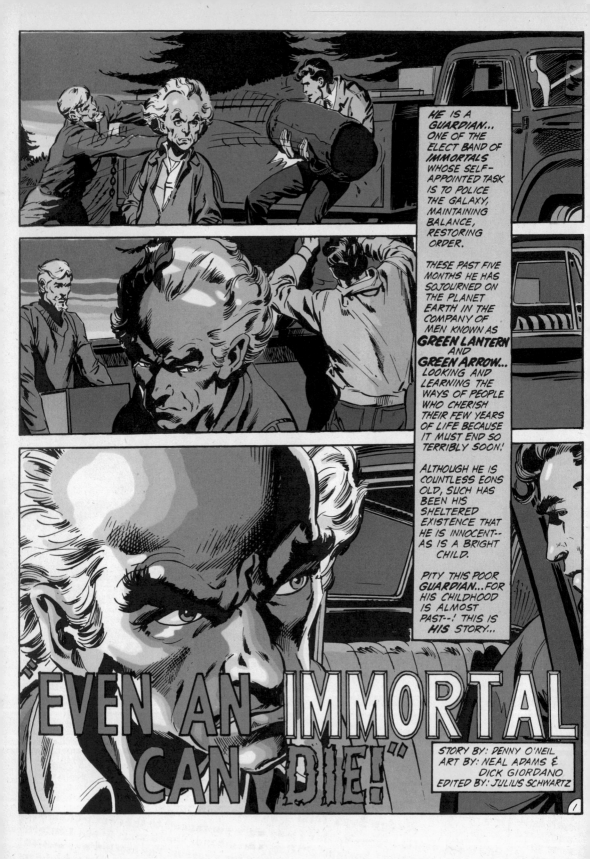

HE IS A GUARDIAN... ONE OF THE ELECT BAND OF **IMMORTALS** WHOSE SELF-APPOINTED TASK IS TO POLICE THE GALAXY, MAINTAINING BALANCE, RESTORING ORDER.

THESE PAST FIVE MONTHS HE HAS SOJOURNED ON THE PLANET EARTH IN THE COMPANY OF MEN KNOWN AS **GREEN LANTERN** AND **GREEN ARROW**... LOOKING AND LEARNING THE WAYS OF PEOPLE WHO CHERISH THEIR FEW YEARS OF LIFE BECAUSE IT MUST END SO TERRIBLY SOON!

ALTHOUGH HE IS COUNTLESS EONS OLD, SUCH HAS BEEN HIS SHELTERED EXISTENCE THAT HE IS INNOCENT-- AS IS A BRIGHT CHILD.

PITY THIS POOR GUARDIAN...FOR HIS CHILDHOOD IS ALMOST PAST--! THIS IS **HIS** STORY...

"EVEN AN IMMORTAL CAN DIE!"

STORY BY: DENNY O'NEIL
ART BY: NEAL ADAMS & DICK GIORDANO
EDITED BY: JULIUS SCHWARTZ

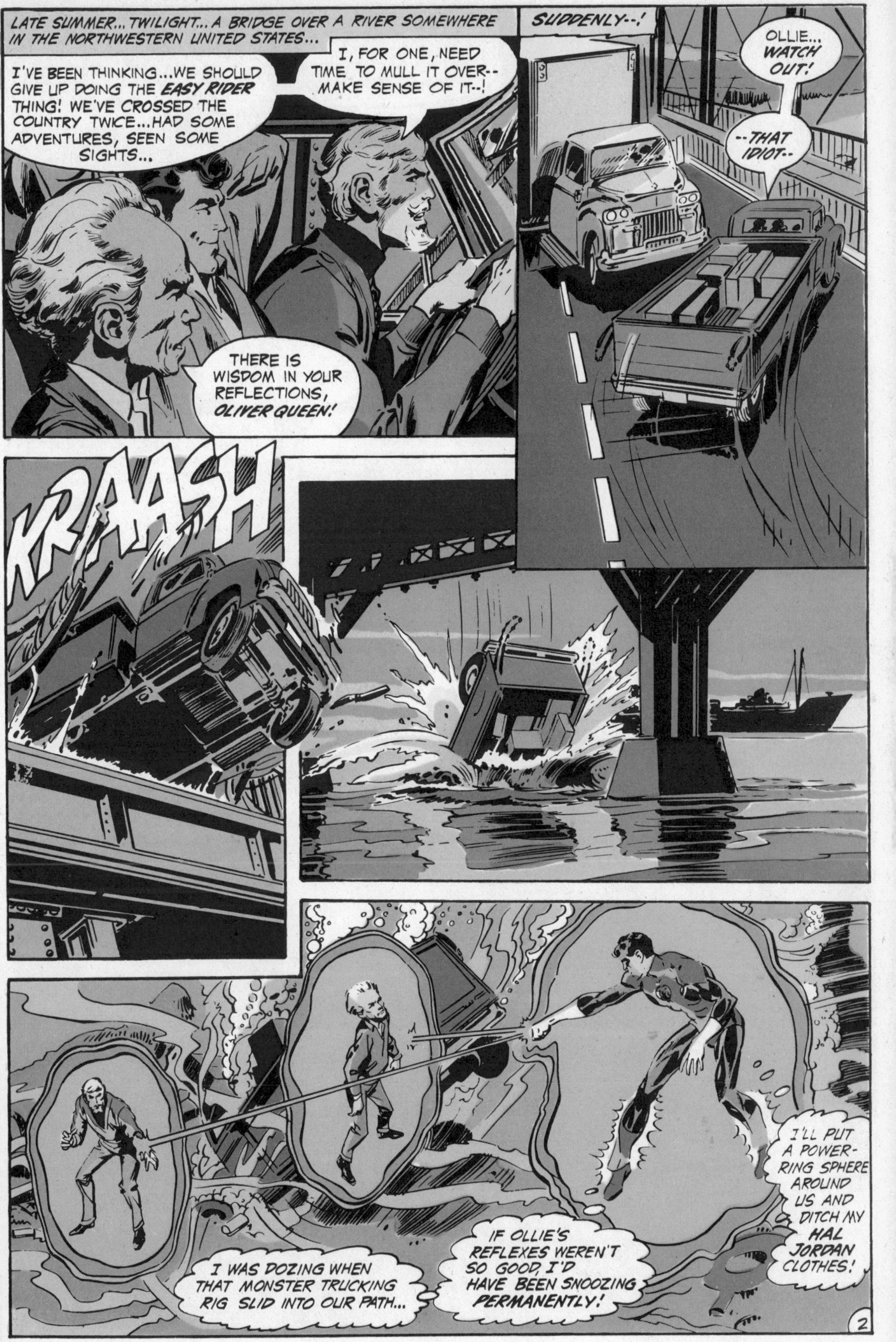

LATE SUMMER... TWILIGHT... A BRIDGE OVER A RIVER SOMEWHERE IN THE NORTHWESTERN UNITED STATES...
I'VE BEEN THINKING...WE SHOULD GIVE UP DOING THE EASY RIDER THING! WE'VE CROSSED THE COUNTRY TWICE...HAD SOME ADVENTURES, SEEN SOME SIGHTS...
I, FOR ONE, NEED TIME TO MULL IT OVER-- MAKE SENSE OF IT--!
THERE IS WISDOM IN YOUR REFLECTIONS, OLIVER QUEEN!
SUDDENLY--!
OLLIE... WATCH OUT!
--THAT IDIOT--
KRAASH
I WAS DOZING WHEN THAT MONSTER TRUCKING RIG SLID INTO OUR PATH...
IF OLLIE'S REFLEXES WEREN'T SO GOOD, I'D HAVE BEEN SNOOZING PERMANENTLY!
I'LL PUT A POWER-RING SPHERE AROUND US AND DITCH MY HAL JORDAN CLOTHES!
2

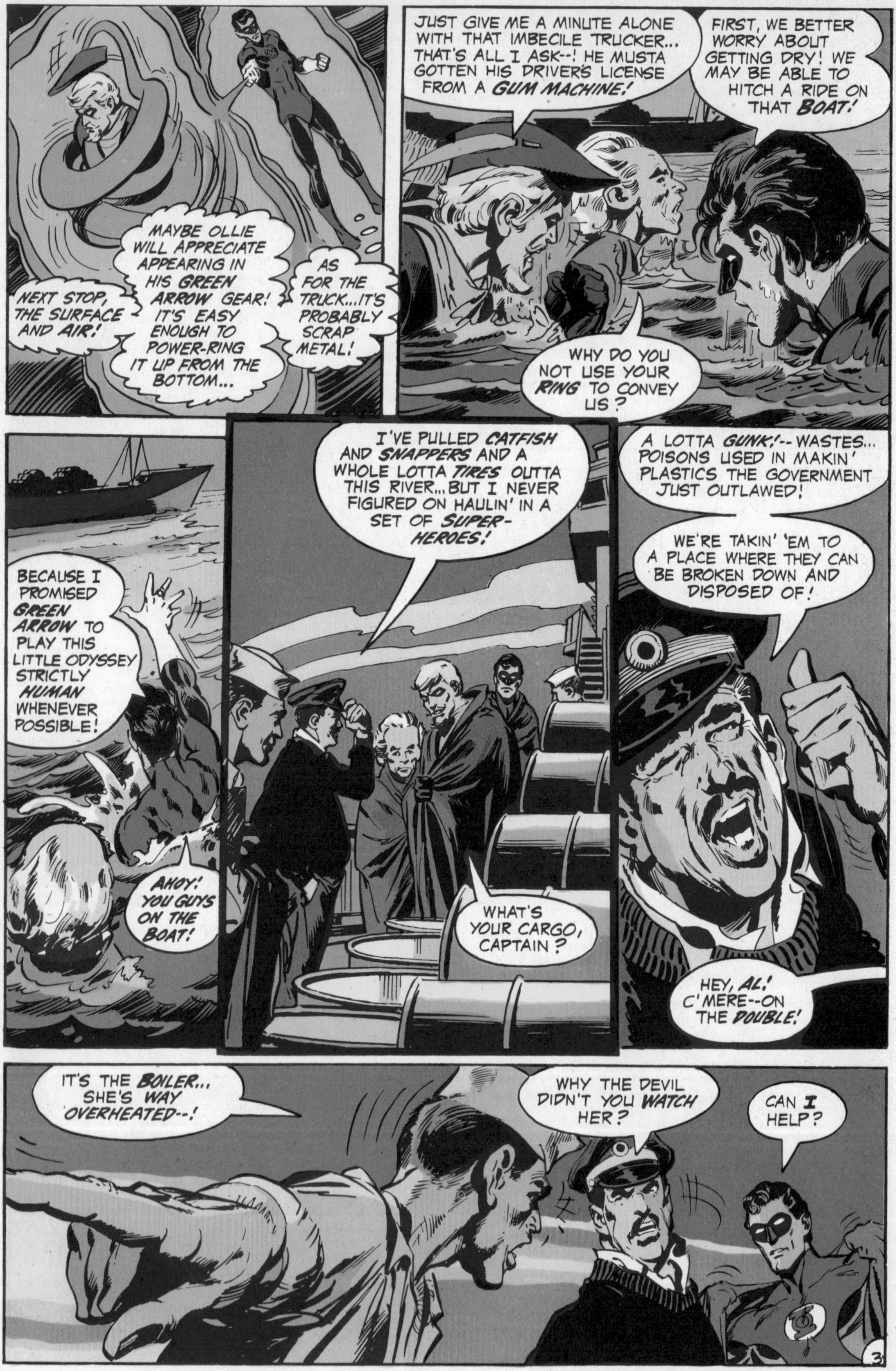
MAYBE OLLIE WILL APPRECIATE APPEARING IN HIS GREEN ARROW GEAR! IT'S EASY ENOUGH TO POWER-RING IT UP FROM THE BOTTOM...
NEXT STOP, THE SURFACE AND AIR!
AS FOR THE TRUCK...IT'S PROBABLY SCRAP METAL!
JUST GIVE ME A MINUTE ALONE WITH THAT IMBECILE TRUCKER... THAT'S ALL I ASK--! HE MUSTA GOTTEN HIS DRIVER'S LICENSE FROM A GUM MACHINE!
FIRST, WE BETTER WORRY ABOUT GETTING DRY! WE MAY BE ABLE TO HITCH A RIDE ON THAT BOAT!
WHY DO YOU NOT USE YOUR RING TO CONVEY US?
BECAUSE I PROMISED GREEN ARROW TO PLAY THIS LITTLE ODYSSEY STRICTLY HUMAN WHENEVER POSSIBLE!
AHOY! YOU GUYS ON THE BOAT!
I'VE PULLED CATFISH AND SNAPPERS AND A WHOLE LOTTA TIRES OUTTA THIS RIVER...BUT I NEVER FIGURED ON HAULIN' IN A SET OF SUPER-HEROES!
WHAT'S YOUR CARGO, CAPTAIN?
A LOTTA GUNK!--WASTES... POISONS USED IN MAKIN' PLASTICS THE GOVERNMENT JUST OUTLAWED!
WE'RE TAKIN' 'EM TO A PLACE WHERE THEY CAN BE BROKEN DOWN AND DISPOSED OF!
HEY, AL! C'MERE--ON THE DOUBLE!
IT'S THE BOILER... SHE'S WAY OVERHEATED--!
WHY THE DEVIL DIDN'T YOU WATCH HER?
CAN I HELP?
3

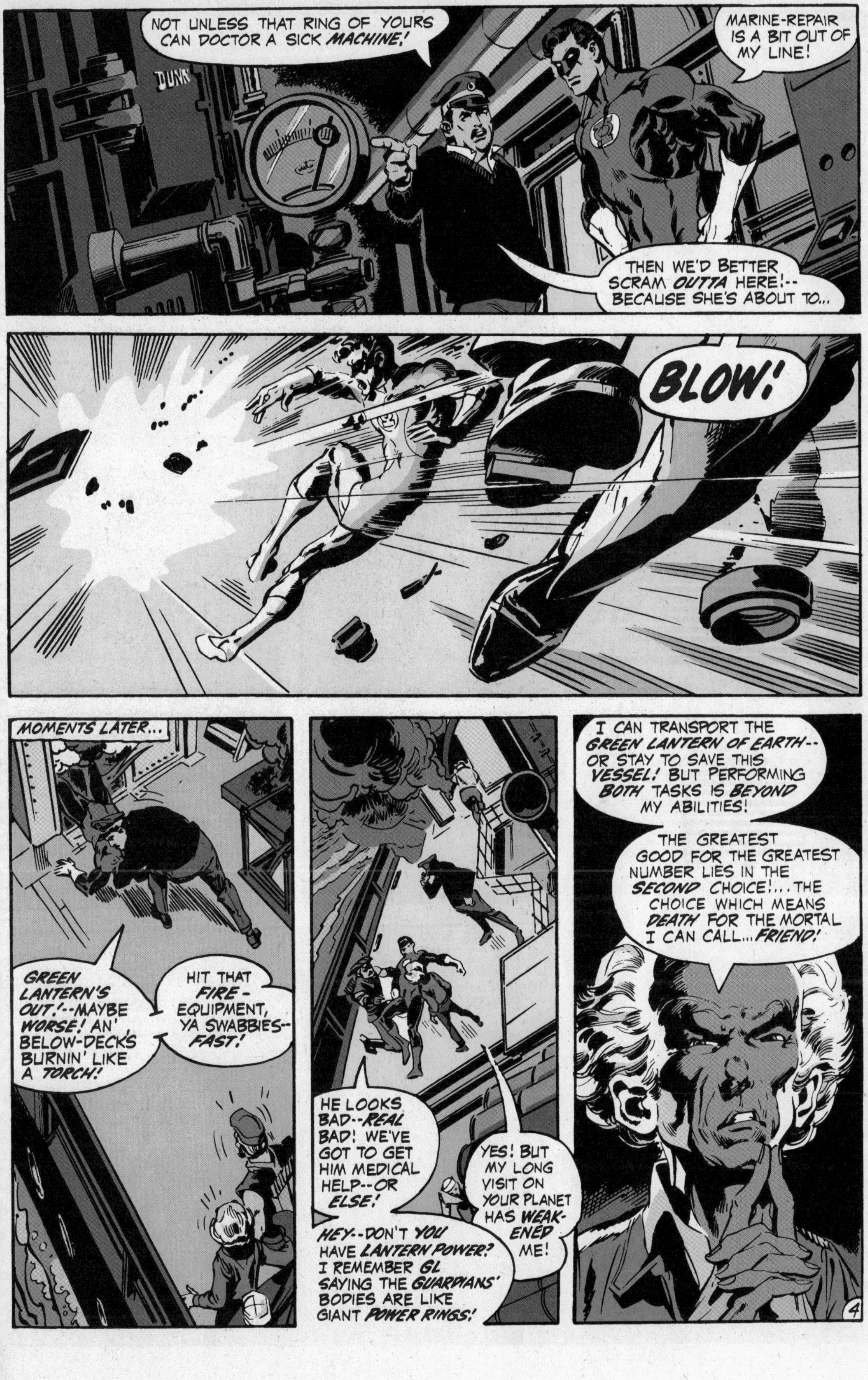
NOT UNLESS THAT RING OF YOURS CAN DOCTOR A SICK MACHINE!
MARINE-REPAIR IS A BIT OUT OF MY LINE!
DUNK
THEN WE'D BETTER SCRAM OUTTA HERE!--BECAUSE SHE'S ABOUT TO...
BLOW!
MOMENTS LATER...
GREEN LANTERN'S OUT!--MAYBE WORSE! AN' BELOW-DECKS BURNIN' LIKE A TORCH!
HIT THAT FIRE-EQUIPMENT, YA SWABBIES--FAST!
HE LOOKS BAD--REAL BAD! WE'VE GOT TO GET HIM MEDICAL HELP--OR ELSE!
HEY--DON'T YOU HAVE LANTERN POWER? I REMEMBER GL SAYING THE GUARDIANS' BODIES ARE LIKE GIANT POWER RINGS!
YES! BUT MY LONG VISIT ON YOUR PLANET HAS WEAKENED ME!
I CAN TRANSPORT THE GREEN LANTERN OF EARTH--OR STAY TO SAVE THIS VESSEL! BUT PERFORMING BOTH TASKS IS BEYOND MY ABILITIES!
THE GREATEST GOOD FOR THE GREATEST NUMBER LIES IN THE SECOND CHOICE!... THE CHOICE WHICH MEANS DEATH FOR THE MORTAL I CAN CALL...FRIEND!
4

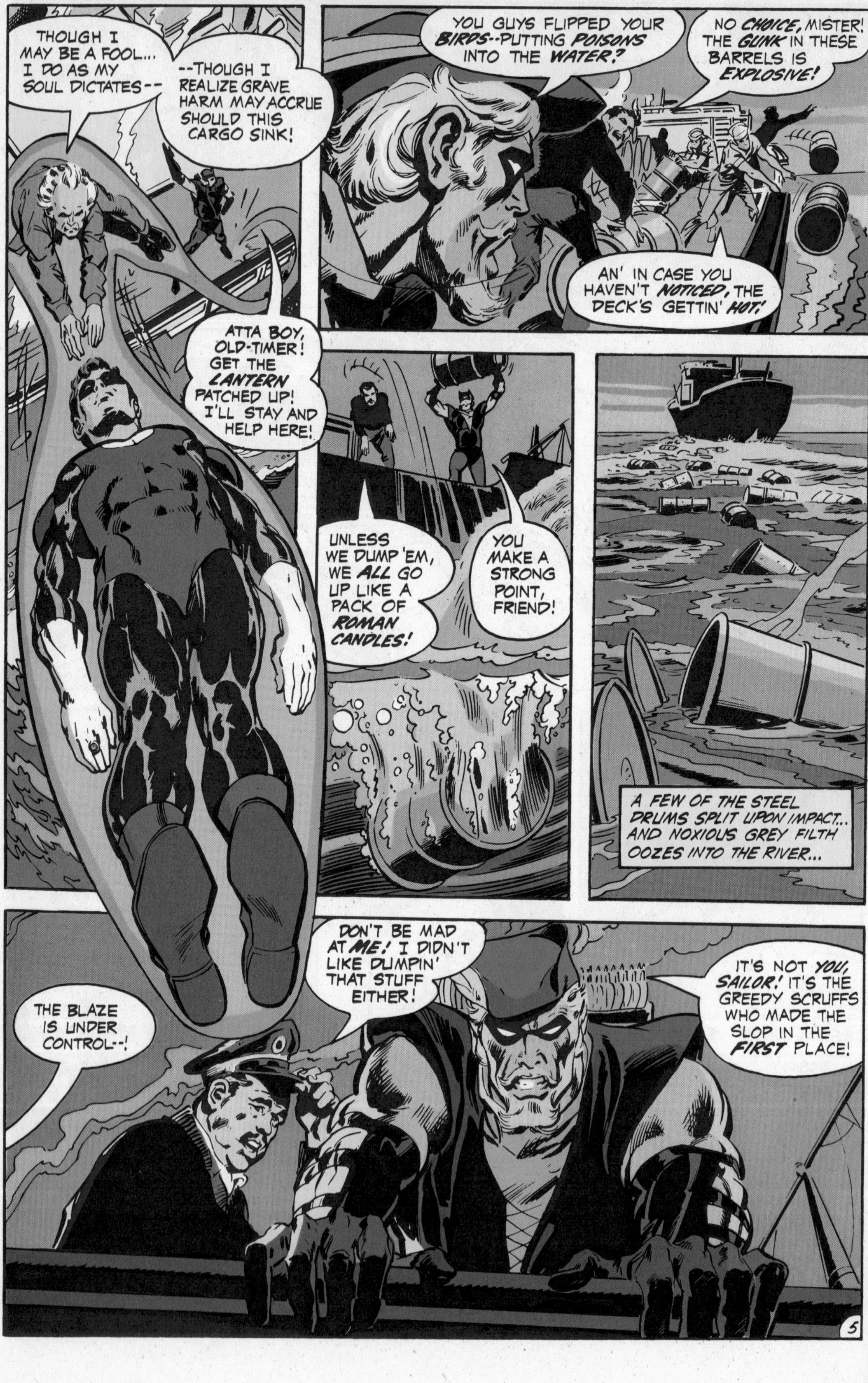
THOUGH I MAY BE A FOOL... I DO AS MY SOUL DICTATES--
--THOUGH I REALIZE GRAVE HARM MAY ACCRUE SHOULD THIS CARGO SINK!
ATTA BOY, OLD-TIMER! GET THE LANTERN PATCHED UP! I'LL STAY AND HELP HERE!
YOU GUYS FLIPPED YOUR BIRDS--PUTTING POISONS INTO THE WATER?
NO CHOICE, MISTER! THE GUNK IN THESE BARRELS IS EXPLOSIVE!
AN' IN CASE YOU HAVEN'T NOTICED, THE DECK'S GETTIN' HOT!
UNLESS WE DUMP 'EM, WE ALL GO UP LIKE A PACK OF ROMAN CANDLES!
YOU MAKE A STRONG POINT, FRIEND!
A FEW OF THE STEEL DRUMS SPLIT UPON IMPACT... AND NOXIOUS GREY FILTH OOZES INTO THE RIVER...
THE BLAZE IS UNDER CONTROL--!
DON'T BE MAD AT ME! I DIDN'T LIKE DUMPIN' THAT STUFF EITHER!
IT'S NOT YOU, SAILOR! IT'S THE GREEDY SCRUFFS WHO MADE THE SLOP IN THE FIRST PLACE!
5

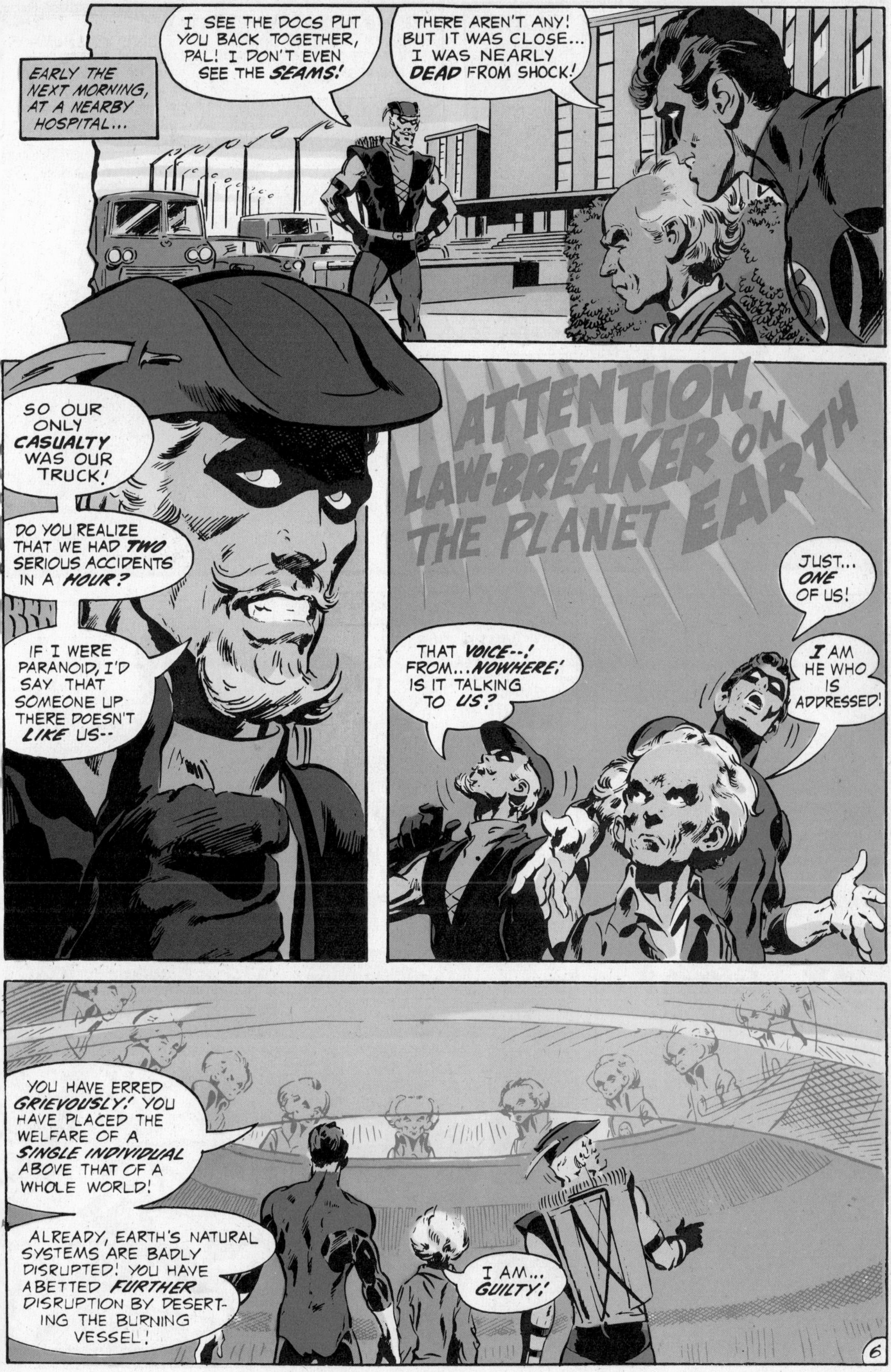

EARLY THE NEXT MORNING, AT A NEARBY HOSPITAL...
I SEE THE DOCS PUT YOU BACK TOGETHER, PAL! I DON'T EVEN SEE THE SEAMS!
THERE AREN'T ANY! BUT IT WAS CLOSE... I WAS NEARLY DEAD FROM SHOCK!
SO OUR ONLY CASUALTY WAS OUR TRUCK!
DO YOU REALIZE THAT WE HAD TWO SERIOUS ACCIDENTS IN A HOUR?
IF I WERE PARANOID, I'D SAY THAT SOMEONE UP THERE DOESN'T LIKE US--
ATTENTION, LAW-BREAKER ON THE PLANET EARTH
JUST... ONE OF US!
THAT VOICE--! FROM... NOWHERE! IS IT TALKING TO US?
I AM HE WHO IS ADDRESSED!
YOU HAVE ERRED GRIEVOUSLY! YOU HAVE PLACED THE WELFARE OF A SINGLE INDIVIDUAL ABOVE THAT OF A WHOLE WORLD!
ALREADY, EARTH'S NATURAL SYSTEMS ARE BADLY DISRUPTED! YOU HAVE ABETTED FURTHER DISRUPTION BY DESERTING THE BURNING VESSEL!
I AM... GUILTY!
6

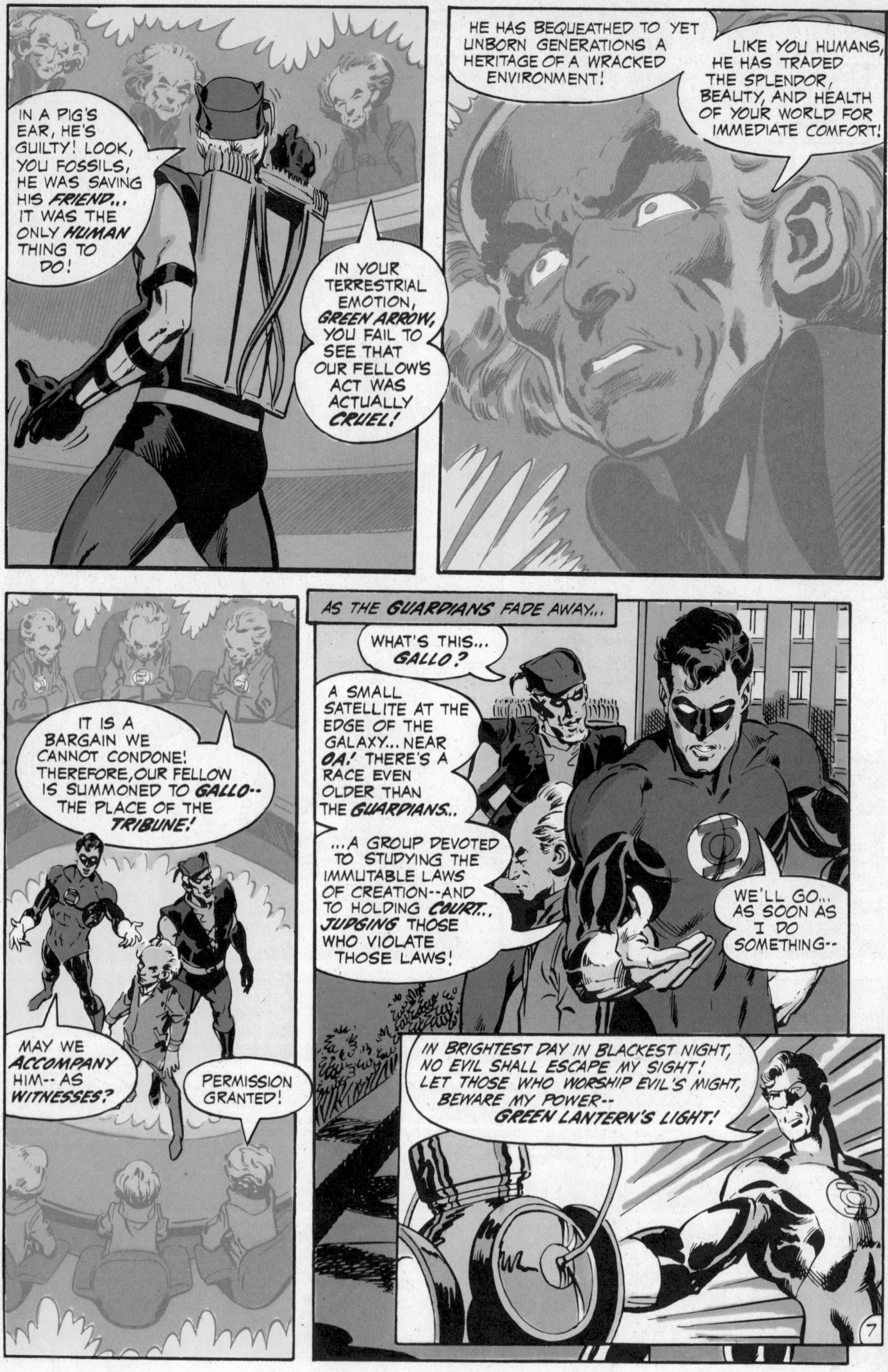
IN A PIG'S EAR, HE'S GUILTY! LOOK, YOU FOSSILS, HE WAS SAVING HIS FRIEND... IT WAS THE ONLY HUMAN THING TO DO!
IN YOUR TERRESTRIAL EMOTION, GREEN ARROW, YOU FAIL TO SEE THAT OUR FELLOW'S ACT WAS ACTUALLY CRUEL!
HE HAS BEQUEATHED TO YET UNBORN GENERATIONS A HERITAGE OF A WRACKED ENVIRONMENT!
LIKE YOU HUMANS, HE HAS TRADED THE SPLENDOR, BEAUTY, AND HEALTH OF YOUR WORLD FOR IMMEDIATE COMFORT!
IT IS A BARGAIN WE CANNOT CONDONE! THEREFORE, OUR FELLOW IS SUMMONED TO GALLO-- THE PLACE OF THE TRIBUNE!
MAY WE ACCOMPANY HIM-- AS WITNESSES?
PERMISSION GRANTED!
AS THE GUARDIANS FADE AWAY...
WHAT'S THIS... GALLO?
A SMALL SATELLITE AT THE EDGE OF THE GALAXY... NEAR OA! THERE'S A RACE EVEN OLDER THAN THE GUARDIANS..
...A GROUP DEVOTED TO STUDYING THE IMMUTABLE LAWS OF CREATION--AND TO HOLDING COURT... JUDGING THOSE WHO VIOLATE THOSE LAWS!
WE'LL GO... AS SOON AS I DO SOMETHING--
IN BRIGHTEST DAY IN BLACKEST NIGHT, NO EVIL SHALL ESCAPE MY SIGHT! LET THOSE WHO WORSHIP EVIL'S MIGHT, BEWARE MY POWER-- GREEN LANTERN'S LIGHT!
7

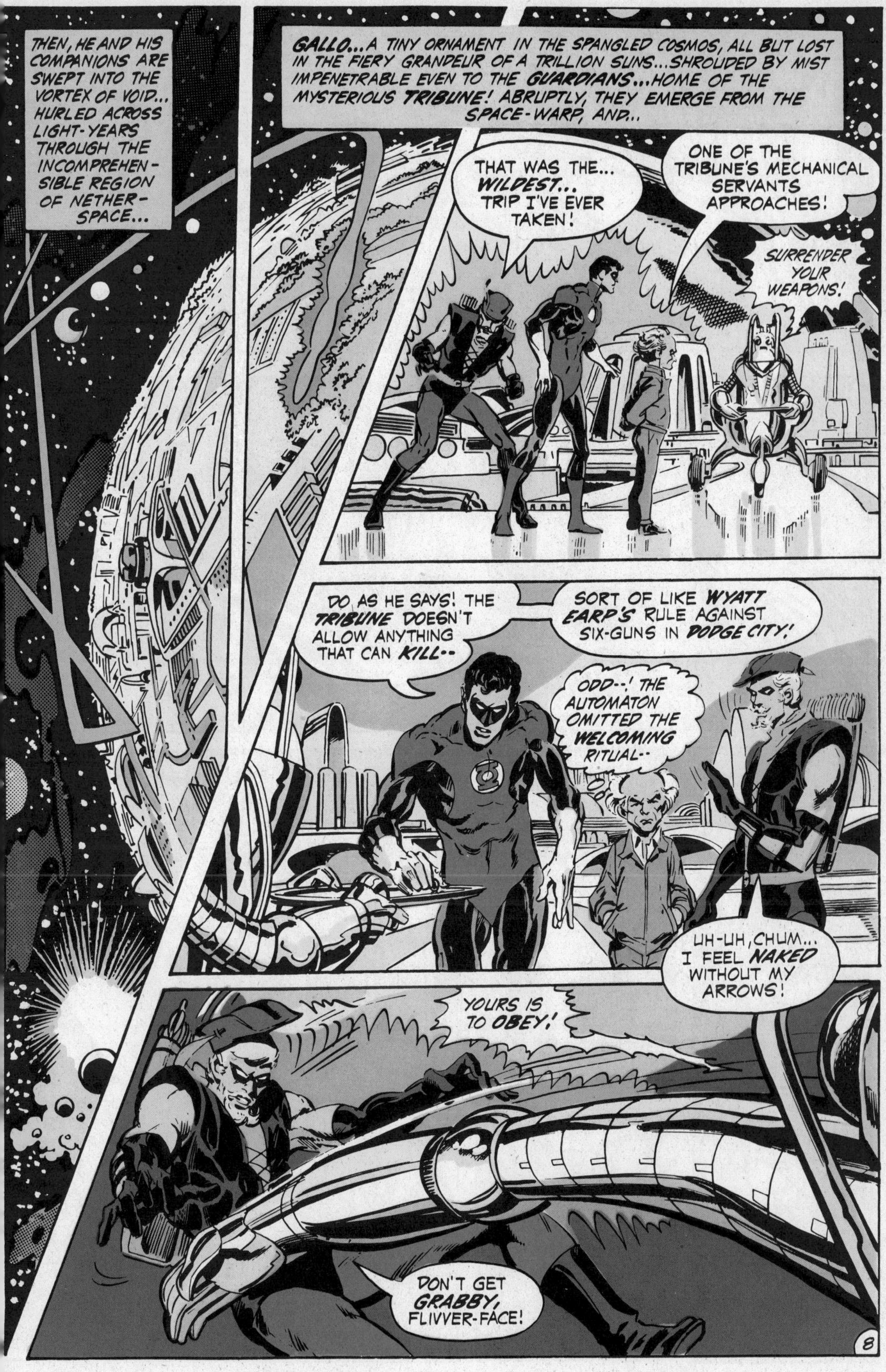
THEN, HE AND HIS COMPANIONS ARE SWEPT INTO THE VORTEX OF VOID... HURLED ACROSS LIGHT-YEARS THROUGH THE INCOMPREHENSIBLE REGION OF NETHER-SPACE...
GALLO... A TINY ORNAMENT IN THE SPANGLED COSMOS, ALL BUT LOST IN THE FIERY GRANDEUR OF A TRILLION SUNS... SHROUDED BY MIST IMPENETRABLE EVEN TO THE GUARDIANS... HOME OF THE MYSTERIOUS TRIBUNE! ABRUPTLY, THEY EMERGE FROM THE SPACE-WARP, AND...
THAT WAS THE... WILDEST... TRIP I'VE EVER TAKEN!
ONE OF THE TRIBUNE'S MECHANICAL SERVANTS APPROACHES!
SURRENDER YOUR WEAPONS!
DO AS HE SAYS! THE TRIBUNE DOESN'T ALLOW ANYTHING THAT CAN KILL--
SORT OF LIKE WYATT EARP'S RULE AGAINST SIX-GUNS IN DODGE CITY!
ODD--! THE AUTOMATON OMITTED THE WELCOMING RITUAL--
UH-UH, CHUM... I FEEL NAKED WITHOUT MY ARROWS!
YOURS IS TO OBEY!
DON'T GET GRABBY, FLIVVER-FACE!
8

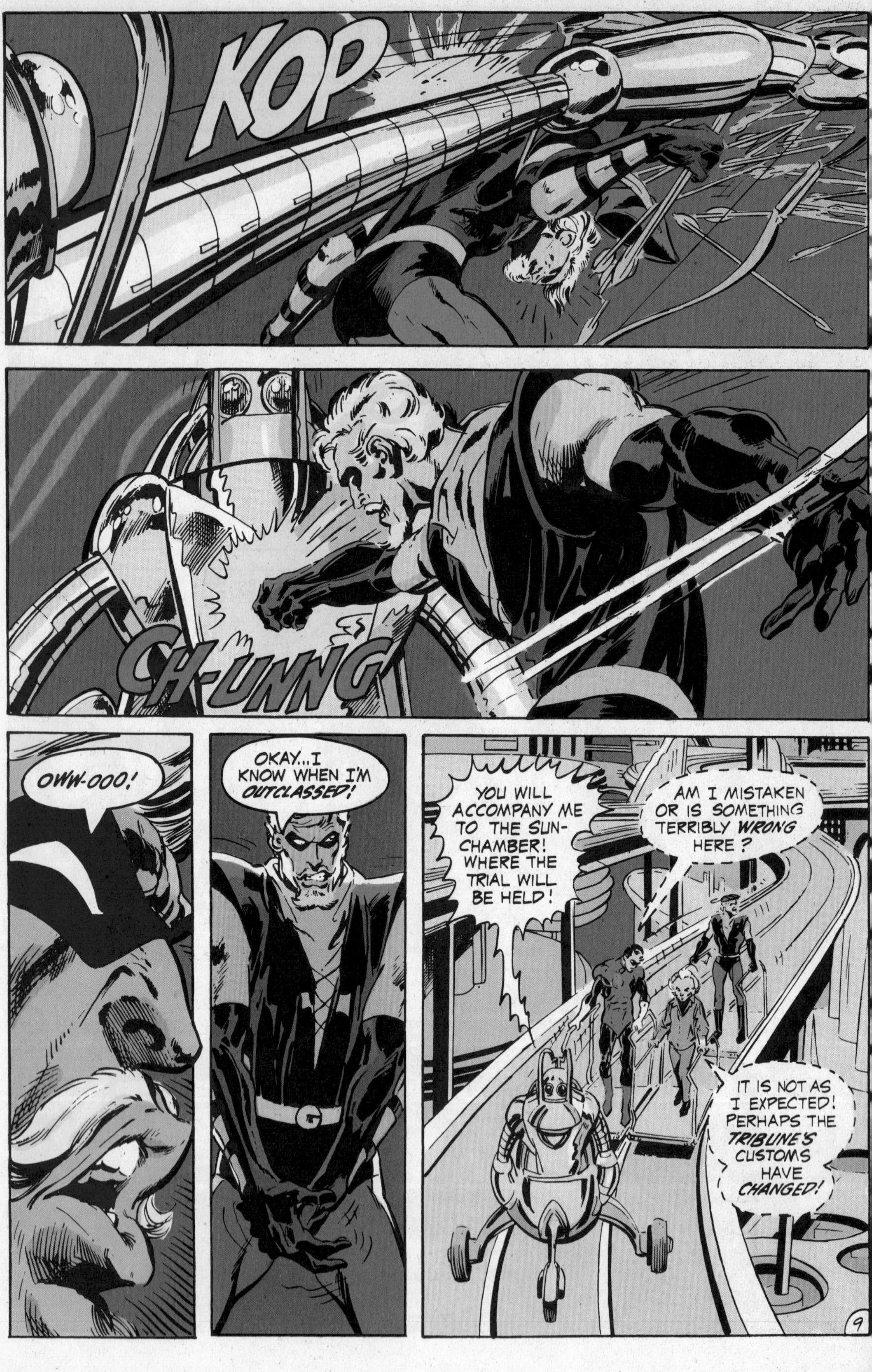
KOP
CH-UNNG
OWW-OOO!
OKAY...I KNOW WHEN I'M OUTCLASSED!
YOU WILL ACCOMPANY ME TO THE SUN-CHAMBER! WHERE THE TRIAL WILL BE HELD!
AM I MISTAKEN OR IS SOMETHING TERRIBLY WRONG HERE ?
IT IS NOT AS I EXPECTED! PERHAPS THE TRIBUNE'S CUSTOMS HAVE CHANGED!
9

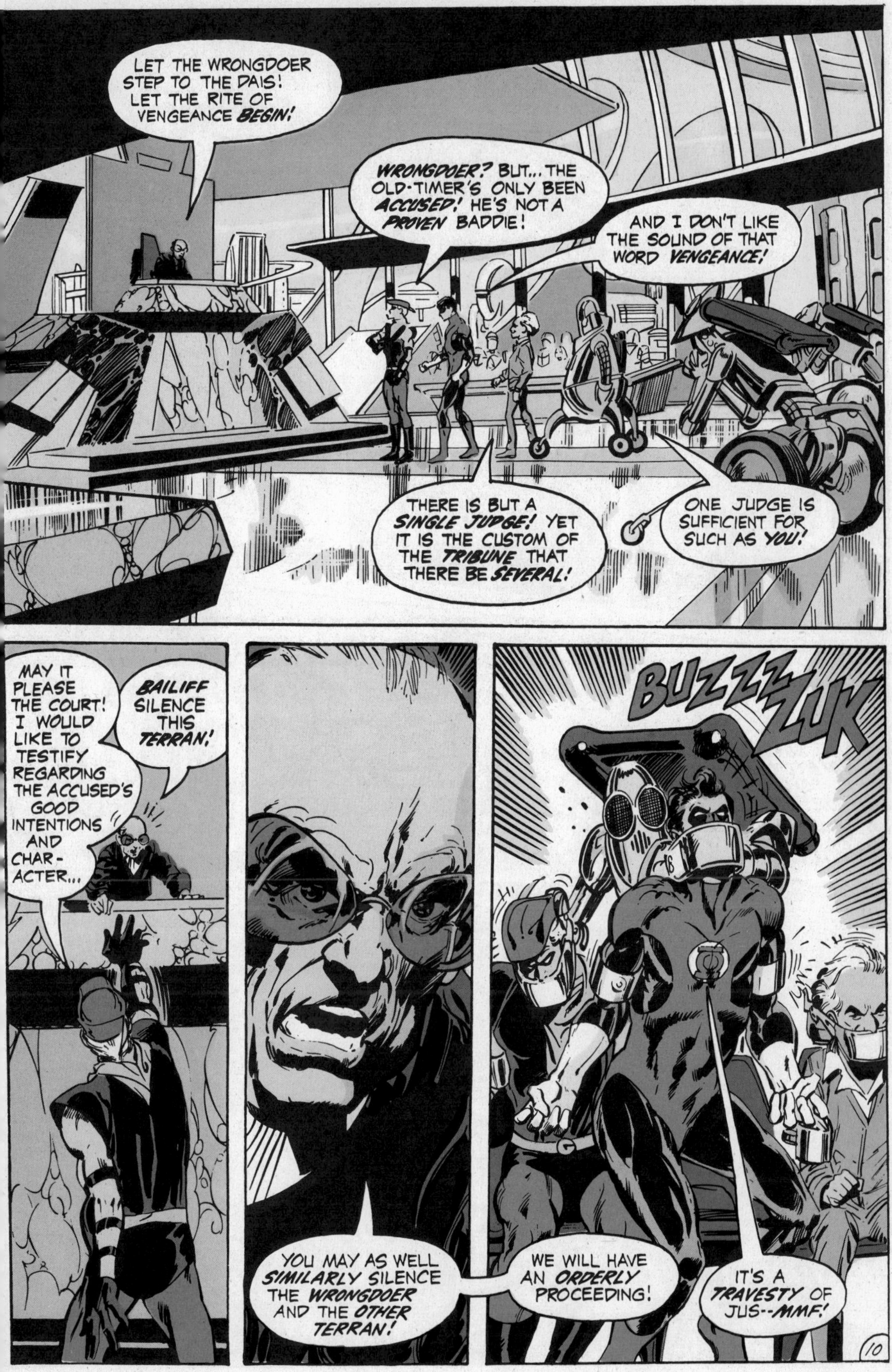
LET THE WRONGDOER STEP TO THE DAIS! LET THE RITE OF VENGEANCE BEGIN!
WRONGDOER? BUT... THE OLD-TIMER'S ONLY BEEN ACCUSED! HE'S NOT A PROVEN BADDIE!
AND I DON'T LIKE THE SOUND OF THAT WORD VENGEANCE!
THERE IS BUT A SINGLE JUDGE! YET IT IS THE CUSTOM OF THE TRIBUNE THAT THERE BE SEVERAL!
ONE JUDGE IS SUFFICIENT FOR SUCH AS YOU!
MAY IT PLEASE THE COURT! I WOULD LIKE TO TESTIFY REGARDING THE ACCUSED'S GOOD INTENTIONS AND CHAR-ACTER...
BAILIFF SILENCE THIS TERRAN!
YOU MAY AS WELL SIMILARLY SILENCE THE WRONGDOER AND THE OTHER TERRAN!
WE WILL HAVE AN ORDERLY PROCEEDING!
BUZZZ ZUK
IT'S A TRAVESTY OF JUS--MMF!
10

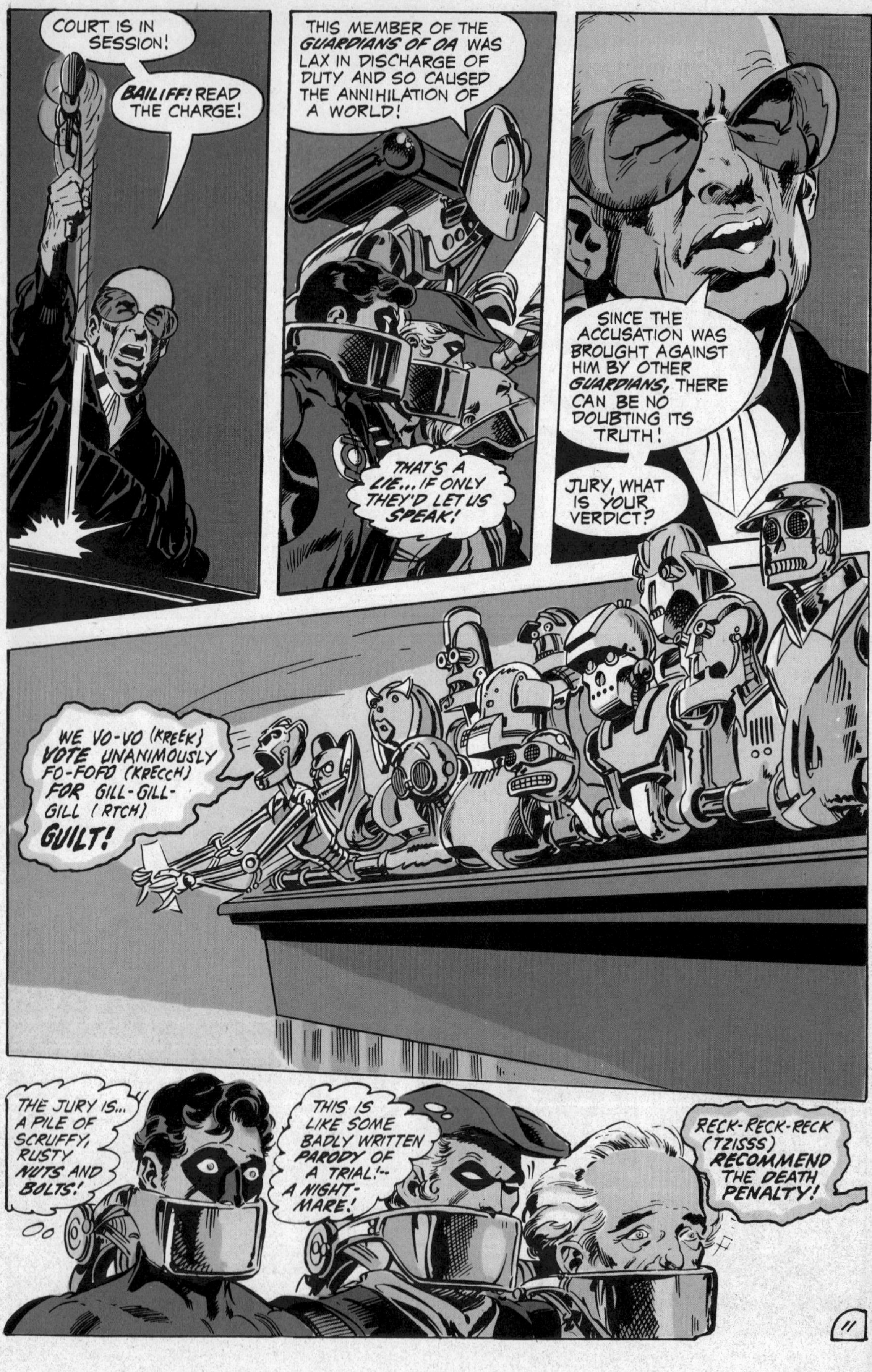
COURT IS IN SESSION!
BAILIFF! READ THE CHARGE!
THIS MEMBER OF THE GUARDIANS OF OA WAS LAX IN DISCHARGE OF DUTY AND SO CAUSED THE ANNIHILATION OF A WORLD!
THAT'S A LIE... IF ONLY THEY'D LET US SPEAK!
SINCE THE ACCUSATION WAS BROUGHT AGAINST HIM BY OTHER GUARDIANS, THERE CAN BE NO DOUBTING ITS TRUTH!
JURY, WHAT IS YOUR VERDICT?
WE VO-VO (KREEK) VOTE UNANIMOUSLY FO-FOFO (KRECCH) FOR GILL-GILL-GILL (RTCH) GUILT!
THE JURY IS... A PILE OF SCRUFFY, RUSTY NUTS AND BOLTS!
THIS IS LIKE SOME BADLY WRITTEN PARODY OF A TRIAL!-- A NIGHTMARE!
RECK-RECK-RECK (TZISSS) RECOMMEND THE DEATH PENALTY!
11

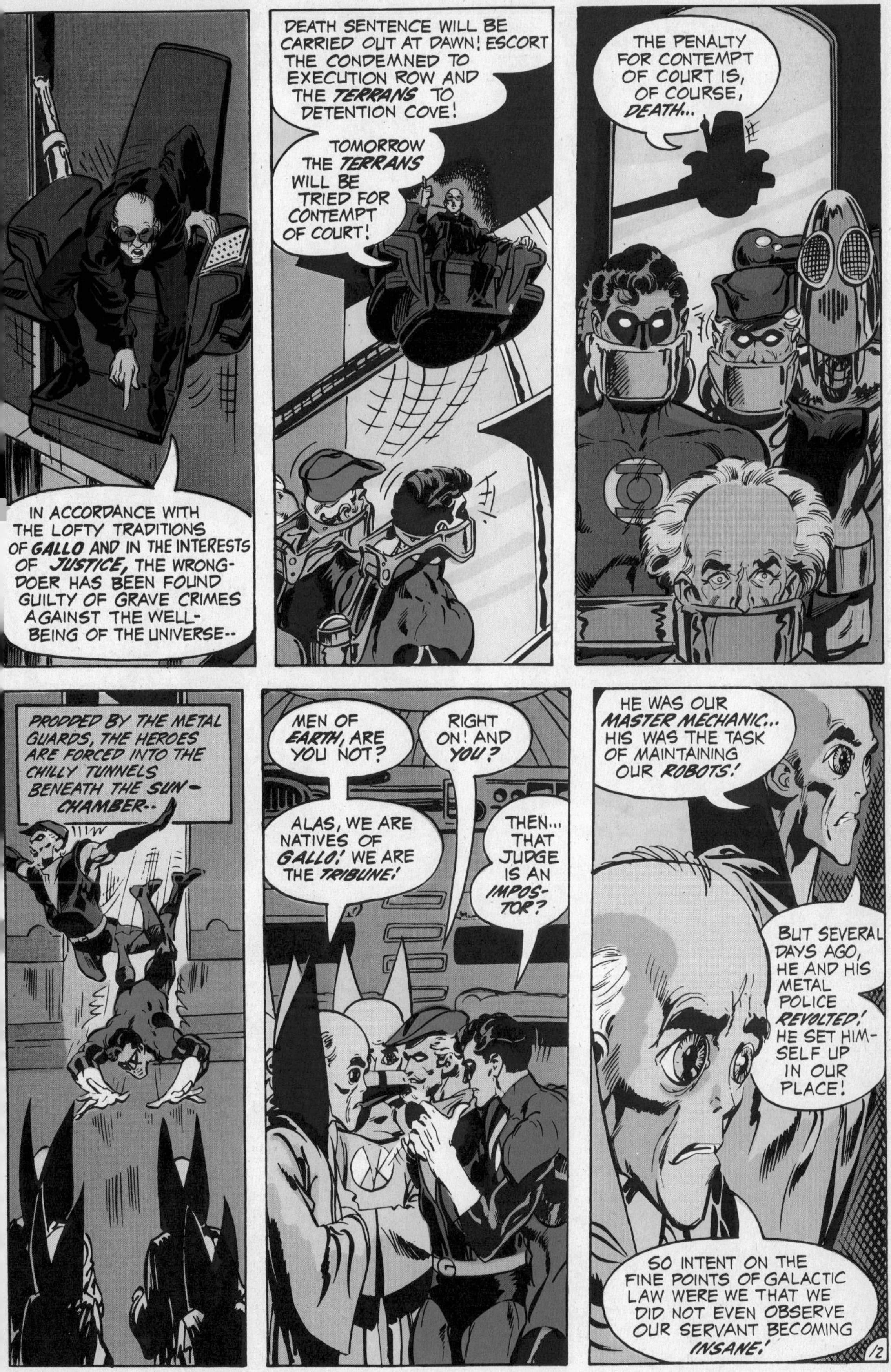
IN ACCORDANCE WITH THE LOFTY TRADITIONS OF GALLO AND IN THE INTERESTS OF JUSTICE, THE WRONG-DOER HAS BEEN FOUND GUILTY OF GRAVE CRIMES AGAINST THE WELL-BEING OF THE UNIVERSE--
DEATH SENTENCE WILL BE CARRIED OUT AT DAWN! ESCORT THE CONDEMNED TO EXECUTION ROW AND THE TERRANS TO DETENTION COVE!
TOMORROW THE TERRANS WILL BE TRIED FOR CONTEMPT OF COURT!
THE PENALTY FOR CONTEMPT OF COURT IS, OF COURSE, DEATH...
PRODDED BY THE METAL GUARDS, THE HEROES ARE FORCED INTO THE CHILLY TUNNELS BENEATH THE SUN-CHAMBER--
MEN OF EARTH, ARE YOU NOT?
RIGHT ON! AND YOU?
ALAS, WE ARE NATIVES OF GALLO! WE ARE THE TRIBUNE!
THEN... THAT JUDGE IS AN IMPOSTOR?
HE WAS OUR MASTER MECHANIC... HIS WAS THE TASK OF MAINTAINING OUR ROBOTS!
BUT SEVERAL DAYS AGO, HE AND HIS METAL POLICE REVOLTED! HE SET HIMSELF UP IN OUR PLACE!
SO INTENT ON THE FINE POINTS OF GALACTIC LAW WERE WE THAT WE DID NOT EVEN OBSERVE OUR SERVANT BECOMING INSANE!
12

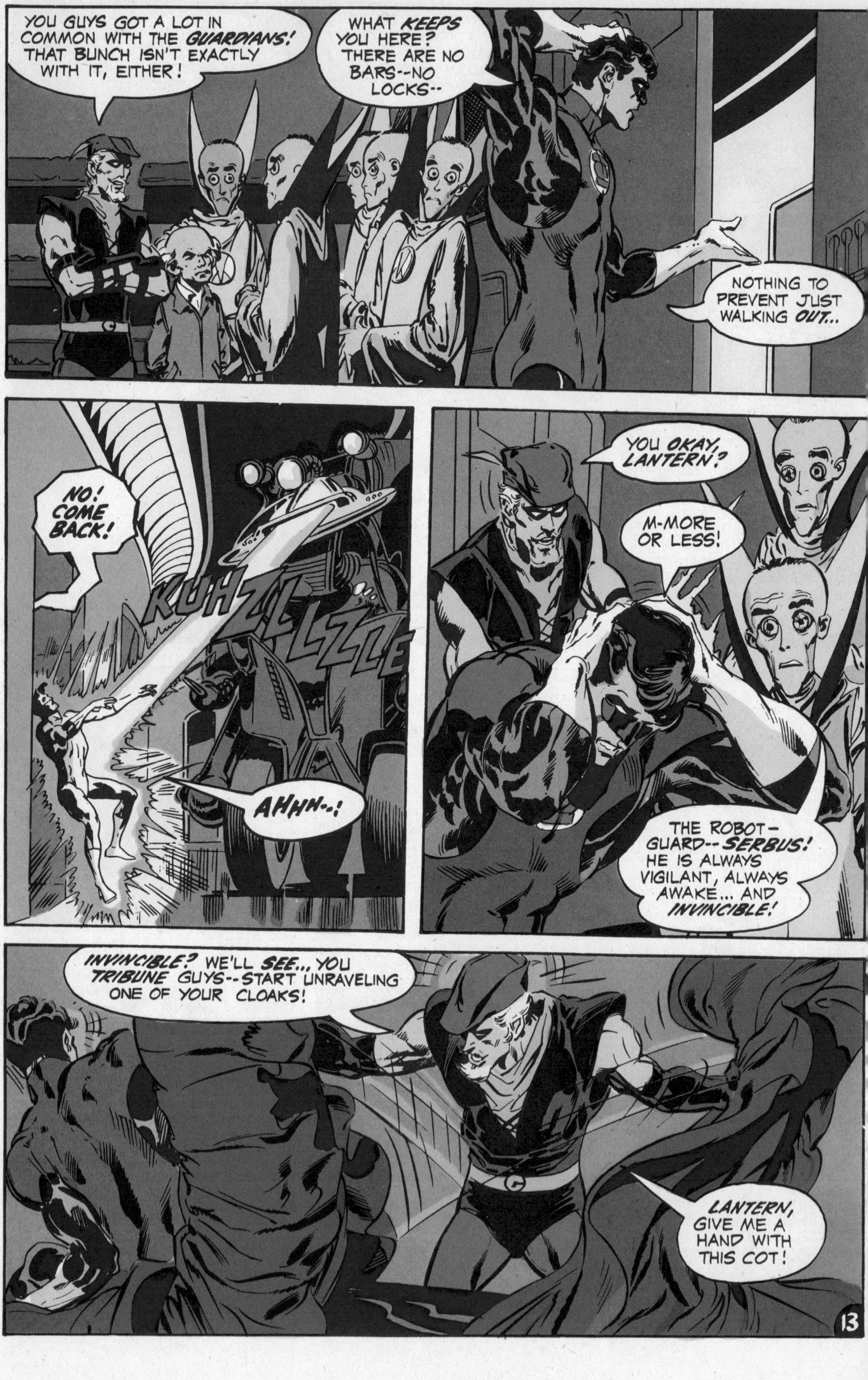
YOU GUYS GOT A LOT IN COMMON WITH THE GUARDIANS! THAT BUNCH ISN'T EXACTLY WITH IT, EITHER!
WHAT KEEPS YOU HERE? THERE ARE NO BARS--NO LOCKS--
NOTHING TO PREVENT JUST WALKING OUT...
NO! COME BACK!
KUHZZZLLZZLE
AHHH--!
YOU OKAY, LANTERN?
M-MORE OR LESS!
THE ROBOT-GUARD--SERBUS! HE IS ALWAYS VIGILANT, ALWAYS AWAKE... AND INVINCIBLE!
INVINCIBLE? WE'LL SEE..., YOU TRIBUNE GUYS--START UNRAVELING ONE OF YOUR CLOAKS!
LANTERN, GIVE ME A HAND WITH THIS COT!
13

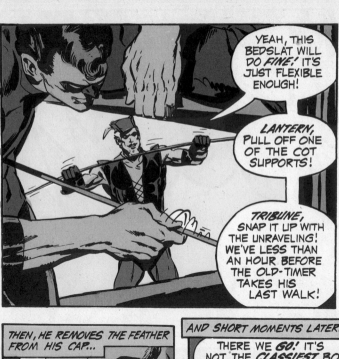

YEAH, THIS BEDSLAT WILL DO *FINE!* IT'S JUST FLEXIBLE ENOUGH!

LANTERN, PULL OFF ONE OF THE COT SUPPORTS!

TRIBUNE, SNAP IT UP WITH THE UNRAVELING! WE'VE LESS THAN AN HOUR BEFORE THE OLD-TIMER TAKES HIS LAST WALK!

HIS DEFT, PRACTICED FINGERS FLASHING, THE ARCHER TIES THE THREAD FROM THE CLOAK TO THE PLASTIC SLAT!

THEN, HE REMOVES THE FEATHER FROM HIS CAP...

AND SHORT MOMENTS LATER...

THERE WE *GO!* IT'S NOT THE *CLASSIEST* BOW I'VE EVER MADE, BUT IT'LL DO!

SERBUS IS ABOUT TO HAVE HIS GEARS SCRAMBLED!

SURELY YOU DON'T THINK A SINGLE *SHAFT*--WITHOUT AN *ARROWHEAD*--WILL STOP THAT *MONSTER!*

I HAVE A LITTLE *SURPRISE!* I SMELLED A RAT THE MOMENT WE LANDED ON THIS FORSAKEN MUD-BALL--

--SO WHILE I WAS SCRAPPING WITH THE *FIRST* GUARD WE MET, I MANAGED TO BREAK OFF THE HEAD OF ONE OF MY REGULAR ARROWS!

DIG IT! A GIMMICK CONTAINING ENOUGH *EXPLOSIVE* TO FIX *TEN* SERBUSES!

14

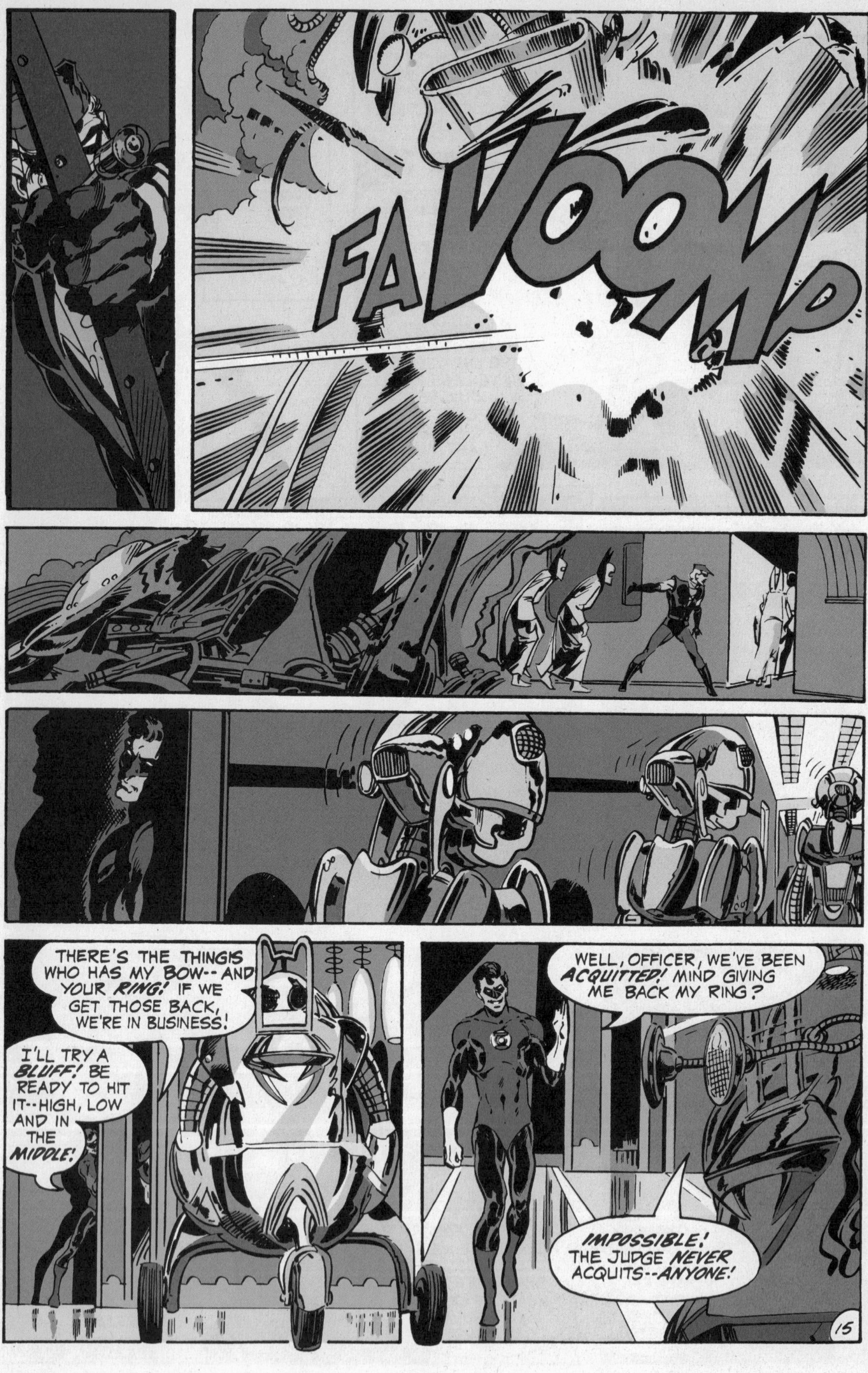
FAVOOMP
THERE'S THE THINGIS WHO HAS MY BOW-- AND YOUR RING! IF WE GET THOSE BACK, WE'RE IN BUSINESS!
I'LL TRY A BLUFF! BE READY TO HIT IT--HIGH, LOW AND IN THE MIDDLE!
WELL, OFFICER, WE'VE BEEN ACQUITTED! MIND GIVING ME BACK MY RING?
IMPOSSIBLE! THE JUDGE NEVER ACQUITS--ANYONE!
15

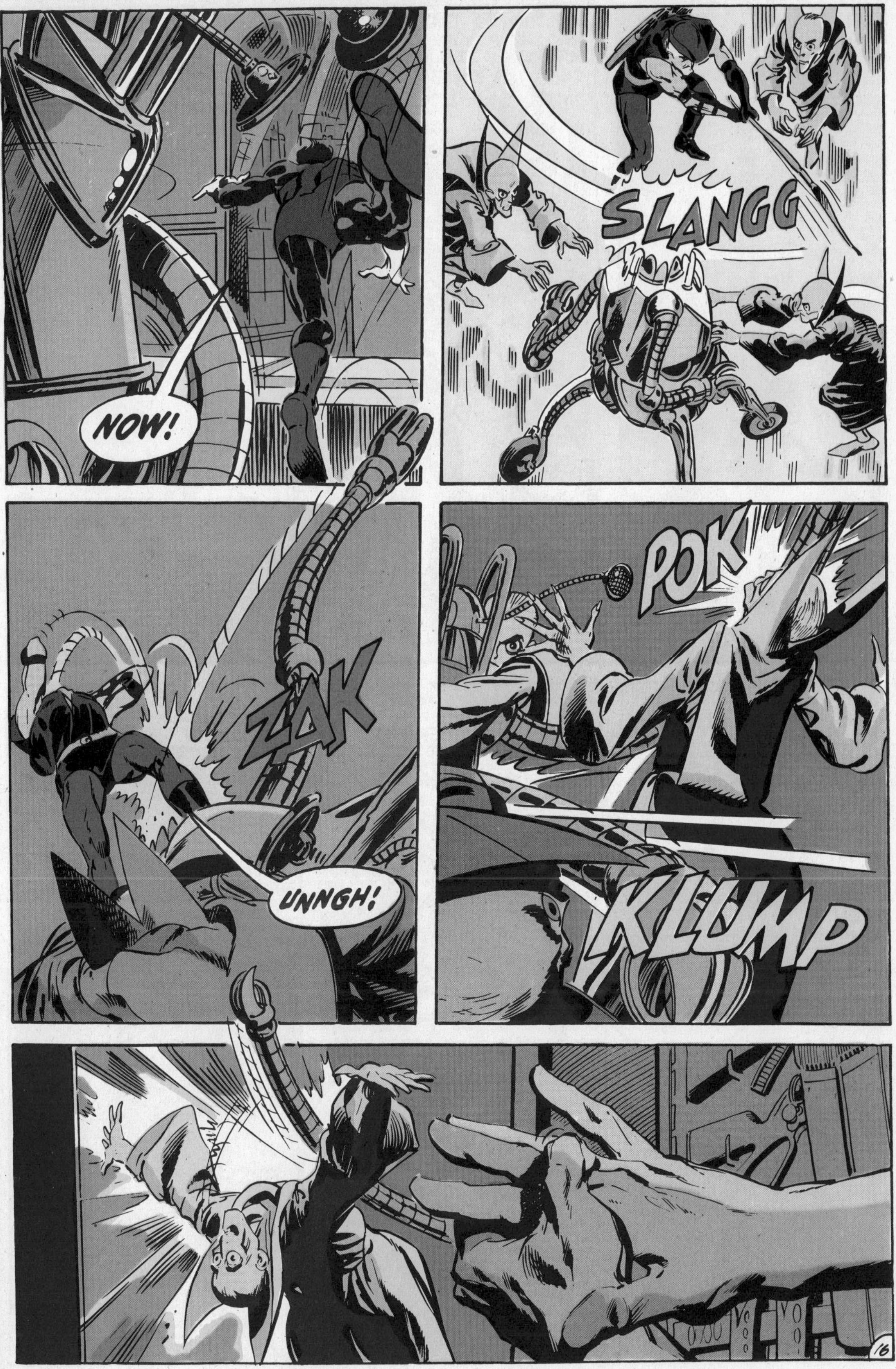
NOW!
SLANGG
ZAK
UNNGH!
POK
KLUMP
16

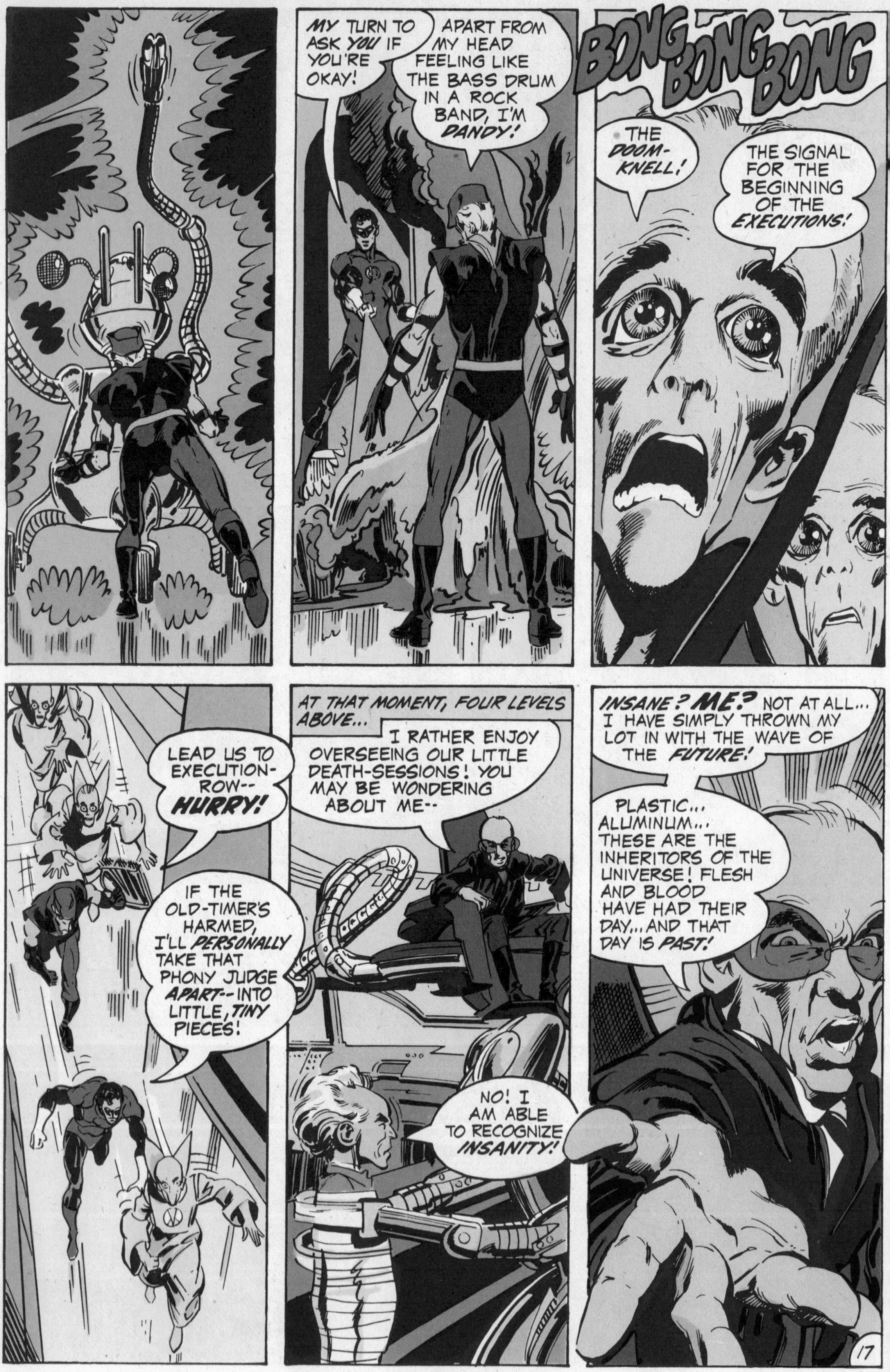
MY TURN TO ASK YOU IF YOU'RE OKAY!
APART FROM MY HEAD FEELING LIKE THE BASS DRUM IN A ROCK BAND, I'M DANDY!
BONG BONG BONG
THE DOOM-KNELL!
THE SIGNAL FOR THE BEGINNING OF THE EXECUTIONS!
LEAD US TO EXECUTION-ROW-- HURRY!
IF THE OLD-TIMER'S HARMED, I'LL PERSONALLY TAKE THAT PHONY JUDGE APART--INTO LITTLE, TINY PIECES!
AT THAT MOMENT, FOUR LEVELS ABOVE...
I RATHER ENJOY OVERSEEING OUR LITTLE DEATH-SESSIONS! YOU MAY BE WONDERING ABOUT ME--
NO! I AM ABLE TO RECOGNIZE INSANITY!
INSANE? ME? NOT AT ALL... I HAVE SIMPLY THROWN MY LOT IN WITH THE WAVE OF THE FUTURE!
PLASTIC... ALUMINUM... THESE ARE THE INHERITORS OF THE UNIVERSE! FLESH AND BLOOD HAVE HAD THEIR DAY... AND THAT DAY IS PAST!
17

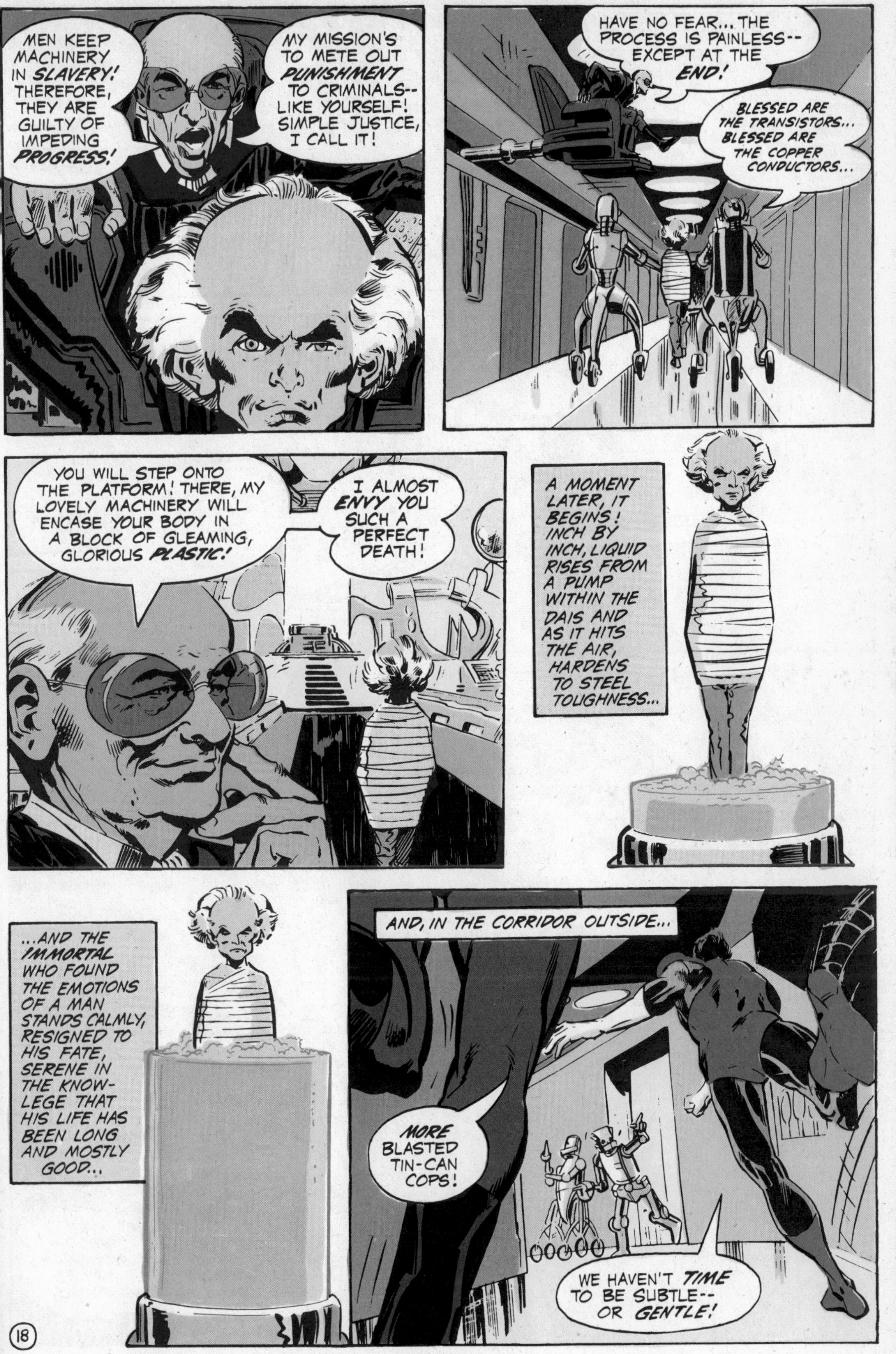
MEN KEEP MACHINERY IN SLAVERY! THEREFORE, THEY ARE GUILTY OF IMPEDING PROGRESS!
MY MISSION'S TO METE OUT PUNISHMENT TO CRIMINALS-- LIKE YOURSELF! SIMPLE JUSTICE, I CALL IT!
HAVE NO FEAR... THE PROCESS IS PAINLESS-- EXCEPT AT THE END!
BLESSED ARE THE TRANSISTORS... BLESSED ARE THE COPPER CONDUCTORS...
YOU WILL STEP ONTO THE PLATFORM! THERE, MY LOVELY MACHINERY WILL ENCASE YOUR BODY IN A BLOCK OF GLEAMING, GLORIOUS PLASTIC!
I ALMOST ENVY YOU SUCH A PERFECT DEATH!
A MOMENT LATER, IT BEGINS! INCH BY INCH, LIQUID RISES FROM A PUMP WITHIN THE DAIS AND AS IT HITS THE AIR, HARDENS TO STEEL TOUGHNESS...
...AND THE IMMORTAL WHO FOUND THE EMOTIONS OF A MAN STANDS CALMLY, RESIGNED TO HIS FATE, SERENE IN THE KNOW-LEGE THAT HIS LIFE HAS BEEN LONG AND MOSTLY GOOD...
18
AND, IN THE CORRIDOR OUTSIDE...
MORE BLASTED TIN-CAN COPS!
WE HAVEN'T TIME TO BE SUBTLE-- OR GENTLE!

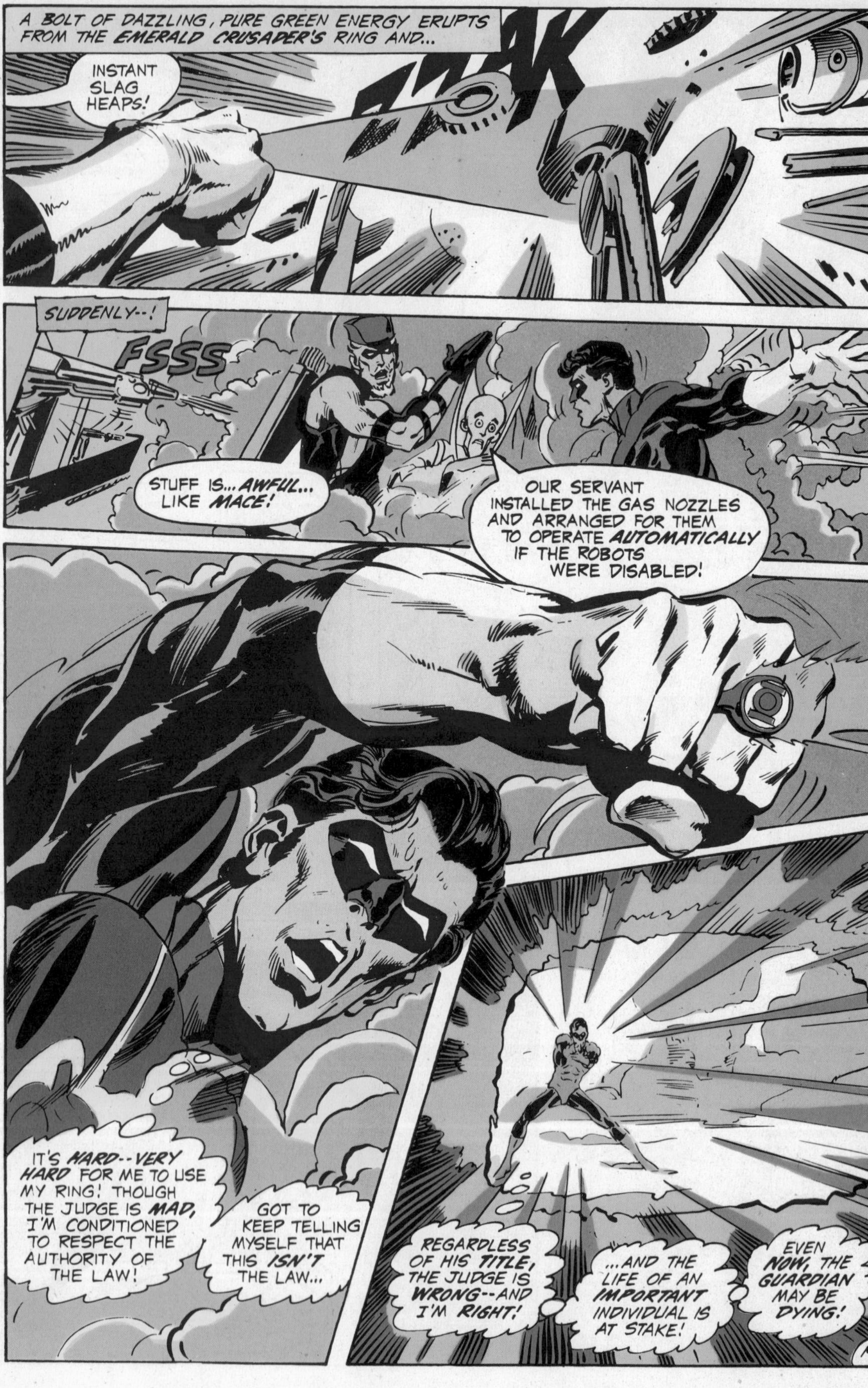
A BOLT OF DAZZLING, PURE GREEN ENERGY ERUPTS FROM THE EMERALD CRUSADER'S RING AND...
INSTANT SLAG HEAPS!
ZHAK
SUDDENLY--!
FSSS
STUFF IS... AWFUL... LIKE MACE!
OUR SERVANT INSTALLED THE GAS NOZZLES AND ARRANGED FOR THEM TO OPERATE AUTOMATICALLY IF THE ROBOTS WERE DISABLED!
IT'S HARD--VERY HARD FOR ME TO USE MY RING! THOUGH THE JUDGE IS MAD, I'M CONDITIONED TO RESPECT THE AUTHORITY OF THE LAW!
GOT TO KEEP TELLING MYSELF THAT THIS ISN'T THE LAW...
REGARDLESS OF HIS TITLE, THE JUDGE IS WRONG--AND I'M RIGHT!
...AND THE LIFE OF AN IMPORTANT INDIVIDUAL IS AT STAKE!
EVEN NOW, THE GUARDIAN MAY BE DYING!
19

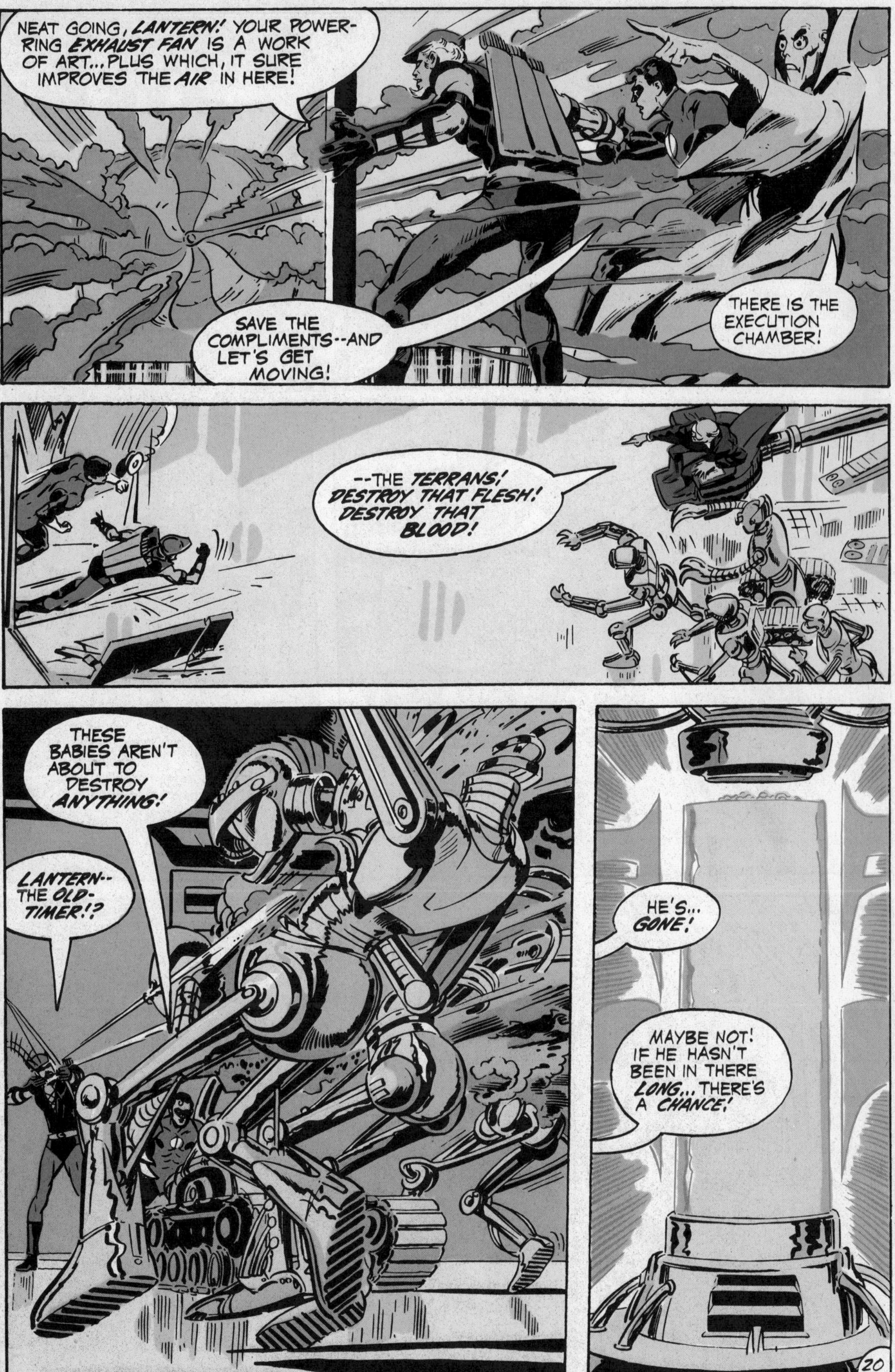

NEAT GOING, LANTERN! YOUR POWER-RING EXHAUST FAN IS A WORK OF ART...PLUS WHICH, IT SURE IMPROVES THE AIR IN HERE!
SAVE THE COMPLIMENTS--AND LET'S GET MOVING!
THERE IS THE EXECUTION CHAMBER!
--THE TERRANS! DESTROY THAT FLESH! DESTROY THAT BLOOD!
THESE BABIES AREN'T ABOUT TO DESTROY ANYTHING!
LANTERN-- THE OLD-TIMER!?
HE'S... GONE!
MAYBE NOT! IF HE HASN'T BEEN IN THERE LONG... THERE'S A CHANCE!
20

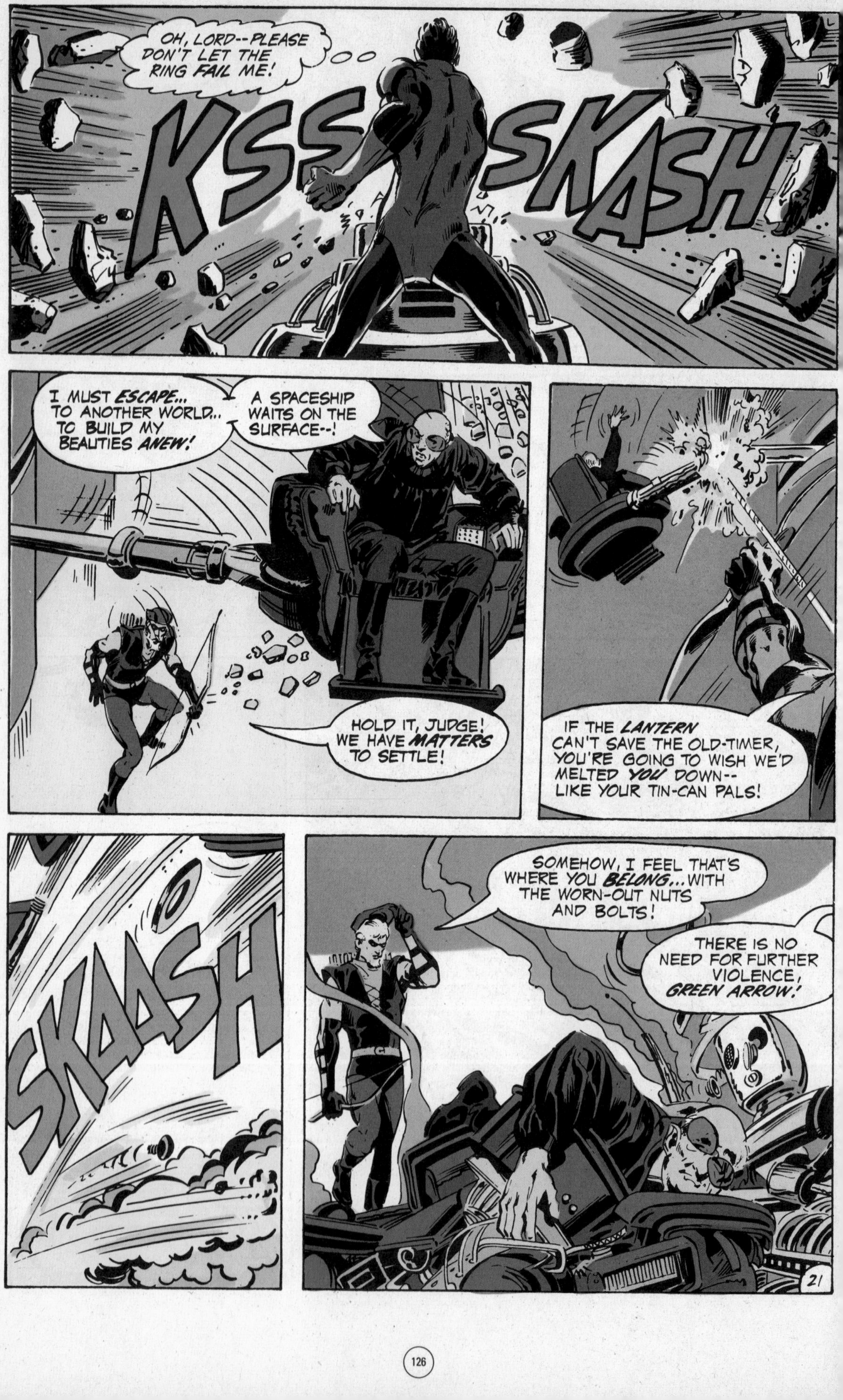
OH, LORD--PLEASE DON'T LET THE RING FAIL ME!
KSSSSKASH
I MUST ESCAPE... TO ANOTHER WORLD... TO BUILD MY BEAUTIES ANEW!
A SPACESHIP WAITS ON THE SURFACE--!
HOLD IT, JUDGE! WE HAVE MATTERS TO SETTLE!
IF THE LANTERN CAN'T SAVE THE OLD-TIMER, YOU'RE GOING TO WISH WE'D MELTED YOU DOWN-- LIKE YOUR TIN-CAN PALS!
SKAASH
SOMEHOW, I FEEL THAT'S WHERE YOU BELONG... WITH THE WORN-OUT NUTS AND BOLTS!
THERE IS NO NEED FOR FURTHER VIOLENCE, GREEN ARROW!
21

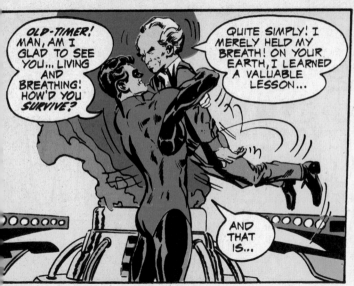

OLD-TIMER! MAN, AM I GLAD TO SEE YOU... LIVING AND BREATHING! HOW'D YOU *SURVIVE?*

QUITE SIMPLY! I MERELY HELD MY BREATH! ON YOUR EARTH, I LEARNED A VALUABLE LESSON...

AND THAT IS...

WHERE THERE IS LIFE, THERE IS HOPE!

WE CANNOT EXPRESS OUR GRATITUDE! WE SHALL REINSTATE OURSELVES ON THE BENCH OF JUSTICE!

YOU CERTAIN YOU *WANT* TO..? I MEAN, YOU BLEW IT *ONCE,* RIGHT? CAN YOU GUARANTEE YOU WON'T *AGAIN?*

THE OBJECTION OF THE *TERRAN* BEARS MUCH CONSIDERATION...

COME ON! WE'LL RETURN TO EARTH AND...

YOU MUST GO WITHOUT ME! I STAND ACCUSED OF A CRIME! I SHALL ASK JUDGMENT OF MY FELLOW GUARDIANS!

IF THAT'S THE WAY YOU WANT IT, OLD-TIMER... SO LONG... AND GOD BLESS!

I HOPE THEY WON'T BE HARSH ON HIM! HE'S GOOD PEOPLE!

YEAH...LET'S LEAVE THIS MUD-BALL...

22

THE END

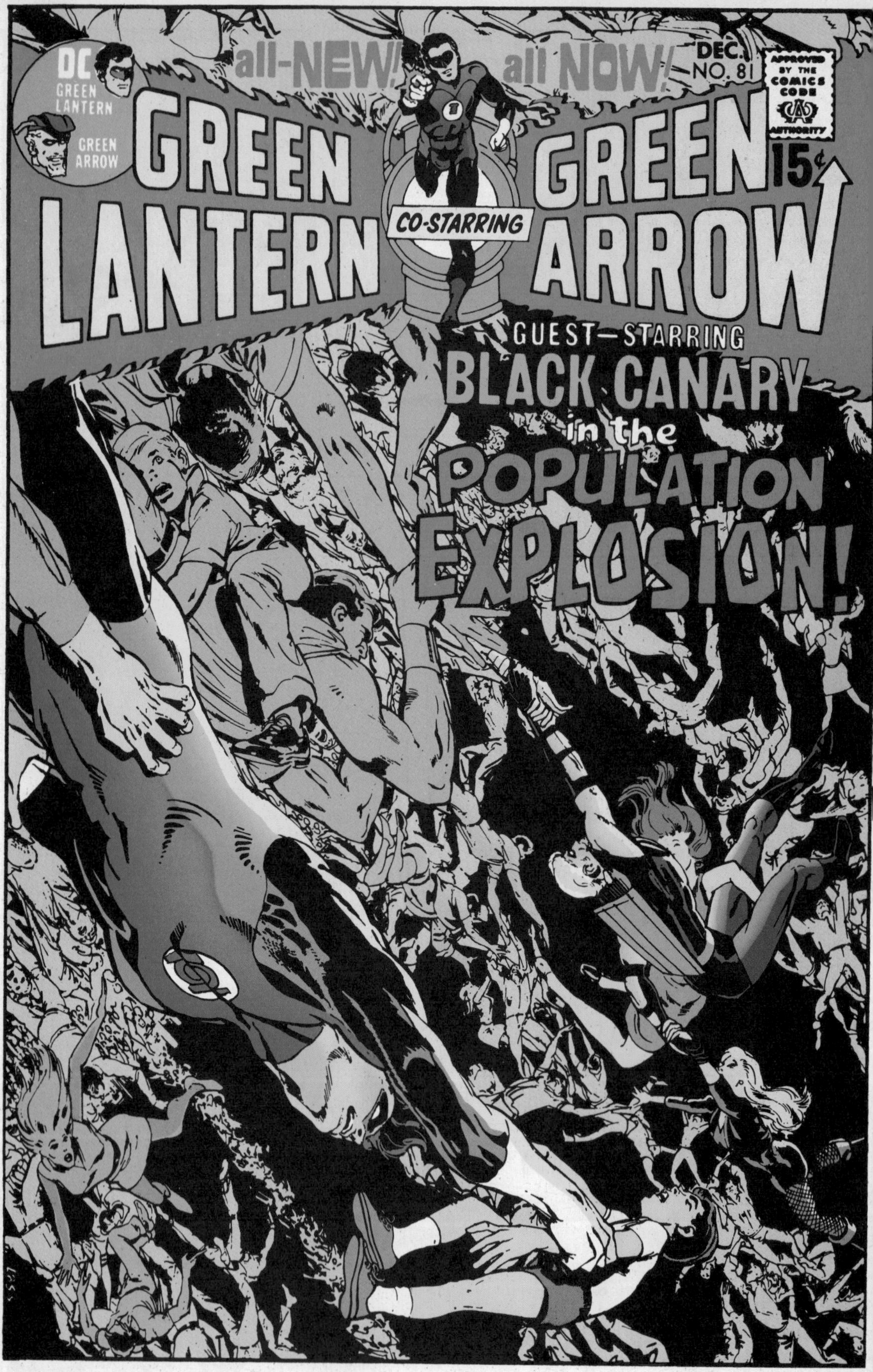
DC
GREEN LANTERN
GREEN ARROW
all-NEW! all NOW!
DEC. NO. 81
APPROVED BY THE COMICS CODE AUTHORITY
GREEN LANTERN
CO-STARRING
GREEN ARROW
15¢
GUEST-STARRING
BLACK CANARY
in the
POPULATION
EXPLOSION!

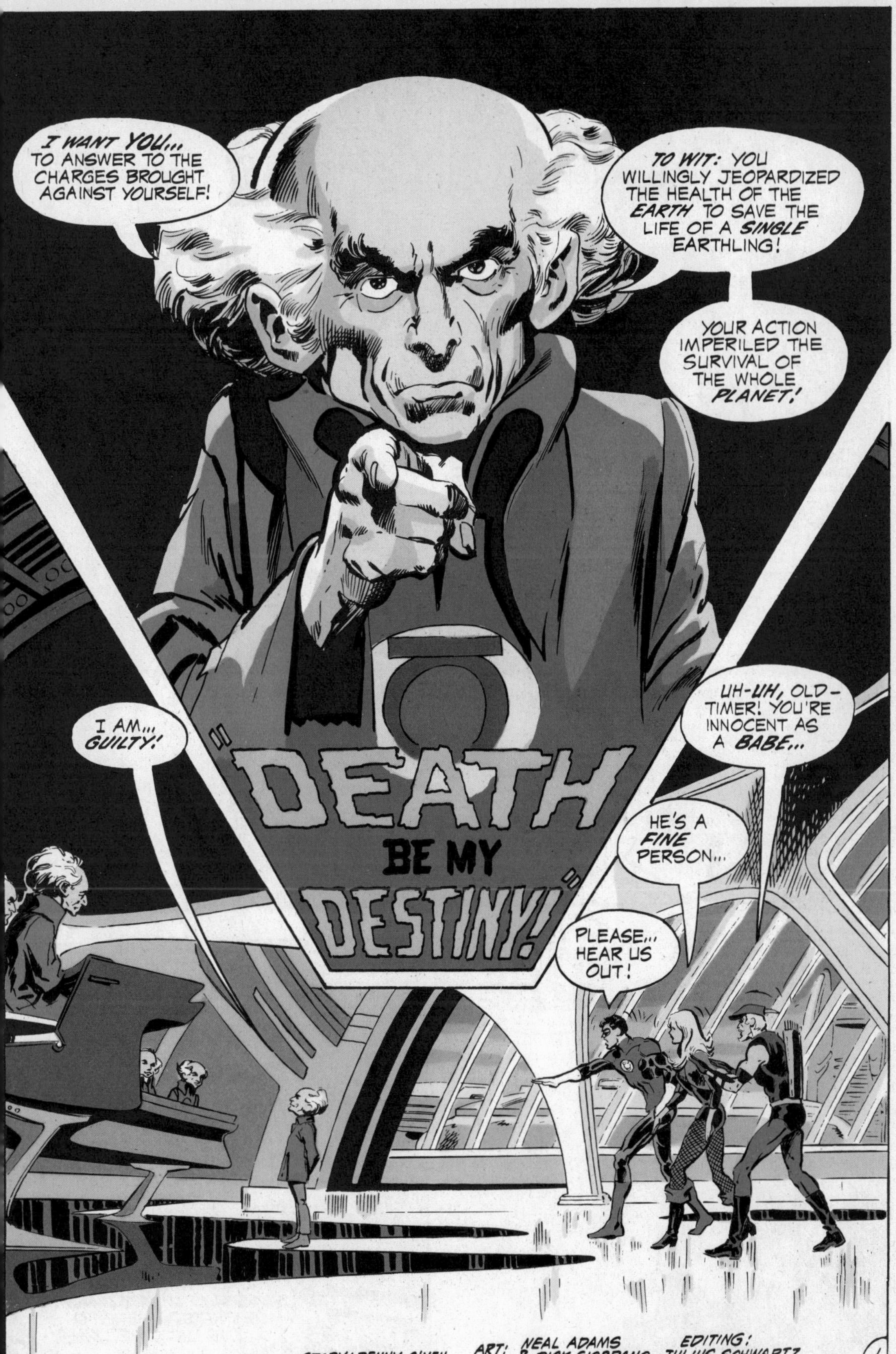
I WANT YOU... TO ANSWER TO THE CHARGES BROUGHT AGAINST YOURSELF!
TO WIT: YOU WILLINGLY JEOPARDIZED THE HEALTH OF THE EARTH TO SAVE THE LIFE OF A SINGLE EARTHLING!
YOUR ACTION IMPERILED THE SURVIVAL OF THE WHOLE PLANET!
"DEATH BE MY DESTINY!"
I AM... GUILTY!
UH-UH, OLD-TIMER! YOU'RE INNOCENT AS A BABE...
HE'S A FINE PERSON...
PLEASE... HEAR US OUT!
STORY: DENNY O'NEIL ART: NEAL ADAMS & DICK GIORDANO EDITING: JULIUS SCHWARTZ
1

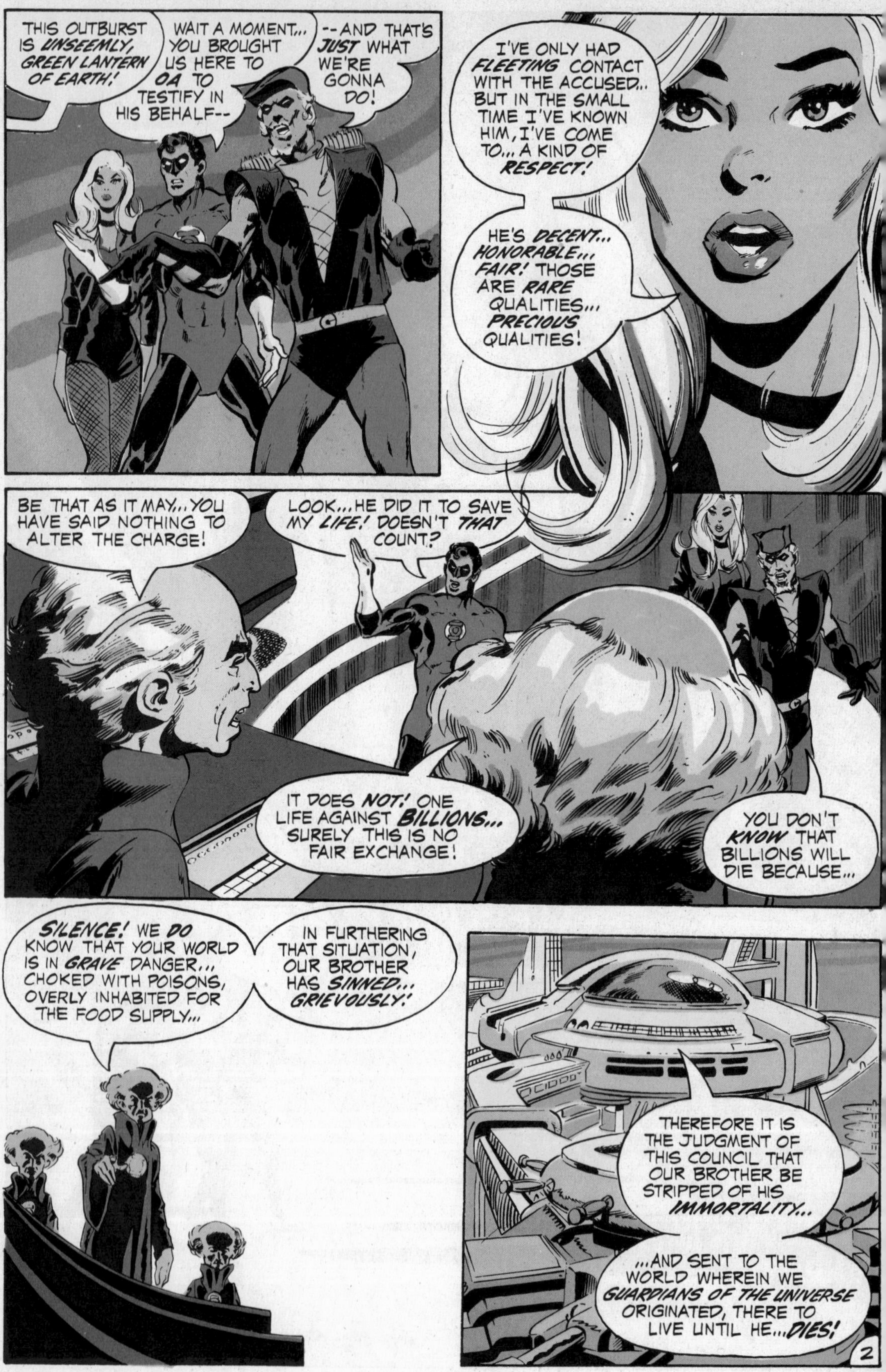
THIS OUTBURST IS UNSEEMLY, GREEN LANTERN OF EARTH!
WAIT A MOMENT... YOU BROUGHT US HERE TO OA TO TESTIFY IN HIS BEHALF--
--AND THAT'S JUST WHAT WE'RE GONNA DO!
I'VE ONLY HAD FLEETING CONTACT WITH THE ACCUSED.. BUT IN THE SMALL TIME I'VE KNOWN HIM, I'VE COME TO... A KIND OF RESPECT!
HE'S DECENT... HONORABLE... FAIR! THOSE ARE RARE QUALITIES... PRECIOUS QUALITIES!
BE THAT AS IT MAY... YOU HAVE SAID NOTHING TO ALTER THE CHARGE!
LOOK... HE DID IT TO SAVE MY LIFE! DOESN'T THAT COUNT?
IT DOES NOT! ONE LIFE AGAINST BILLIONS... SURELY THIS IS NO FAIR EXCHANGE!
YOU DON'T KNOW THAT BILLIONS WILL DIE BECAUSE...
SILENCE! WE DO KNOW THAT YOUR WORLD IS IN GRAVE DANGER... CHOKED WITH POISONS, OVERLY INHABITED FOR THE FOOD SUPPLY...
IN FURTHERING THAT SITUATION, OUR BROTHER HAS SINNED... GRIEVOUSLY!
THEREFORE IT IS THE JUDGMENT OF THIS COUNCIL THAT OUR BROTHER BE STRIPPED OF HIS IMMORTALITY...
...AND SENT TO THE WORLD WHEREIN WE GUARDIANS OF THE UNIVERSE ORIGINATED, THERE TO LIVE UNTIL HE...DIES!
2

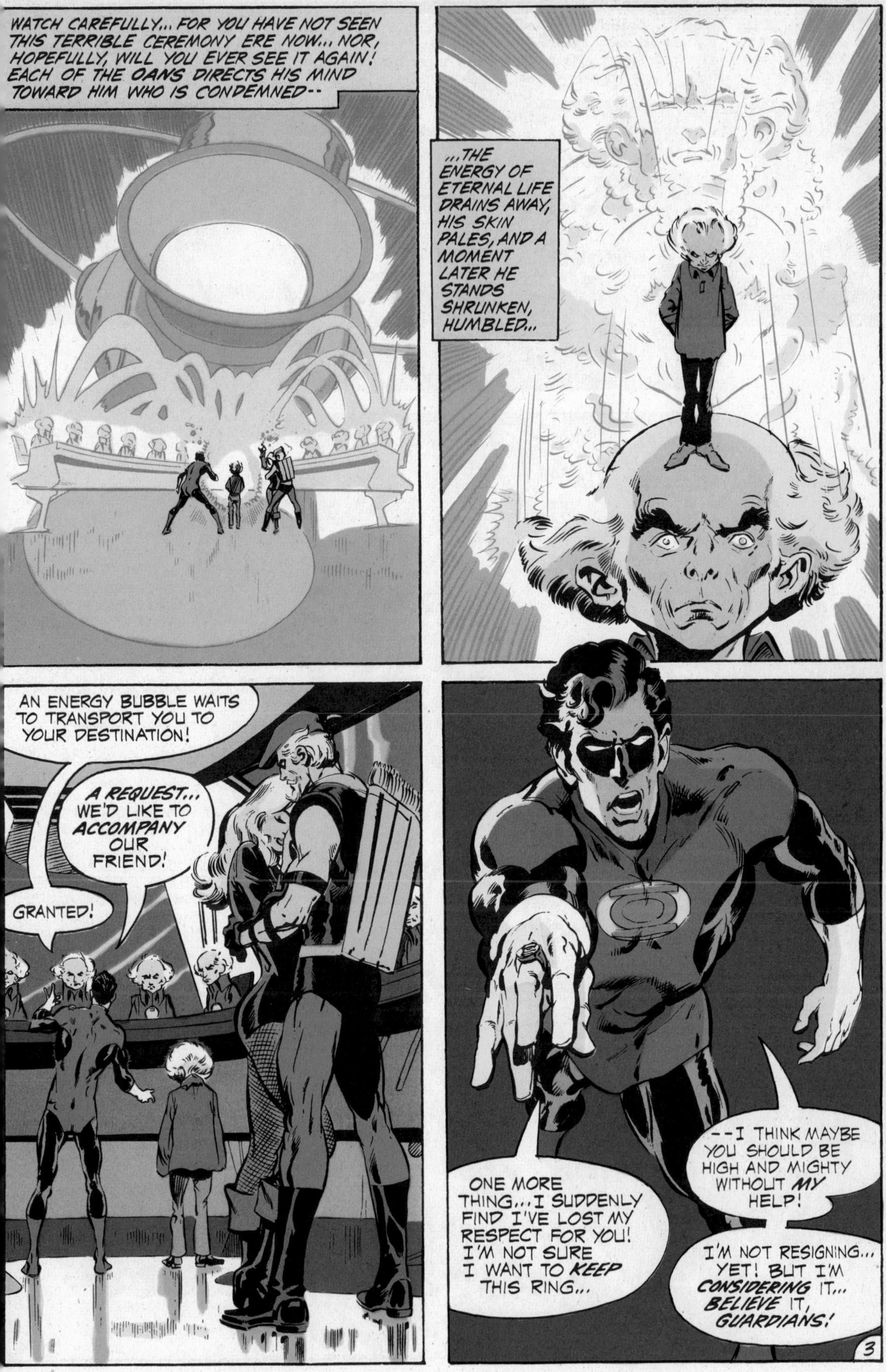
WATCH CAREFULLY... FOR YOU HAVE NOT SEEN THIS TERRIBLE CEREMONY ERE NOW... NOR, HOPEFULLY, WILL YOU EVER SEE IT AGAIN! EACH OF THE OANS DIRECTS HIS MIND TOWARD HIM WHO IS CONDEMNED--
...THE ENERGY OF ETERNAL LIFE DRAINS AWAY, HIS SKIN PALES, AND A MOMENT LATER HE STANDS SHRUNKEN, HUMBLED...
AN ENERGY BUBBLE WAITS TO TRANSPORT YOU TO YOUR DESTINATION!
A REQUEST... WE'D LIKE TO ACCOMPANY OUR FRIEND!
GRANTED!
ONE MORE THING... I SUDDENLY FIND I'VE LOST MY RESPECT FOR YOU! I'M NOT SURE I WANT TO KEEP THIS RING...
--I THINK MAYBE YOU SHOULD BE HIGH AND MIGHTY WITHOUT MY HELP!
I'M NOT RESIGNING... YET! BUT I'M CONSIDERING IT... BELIEVE IT, GUARDIANS!
3

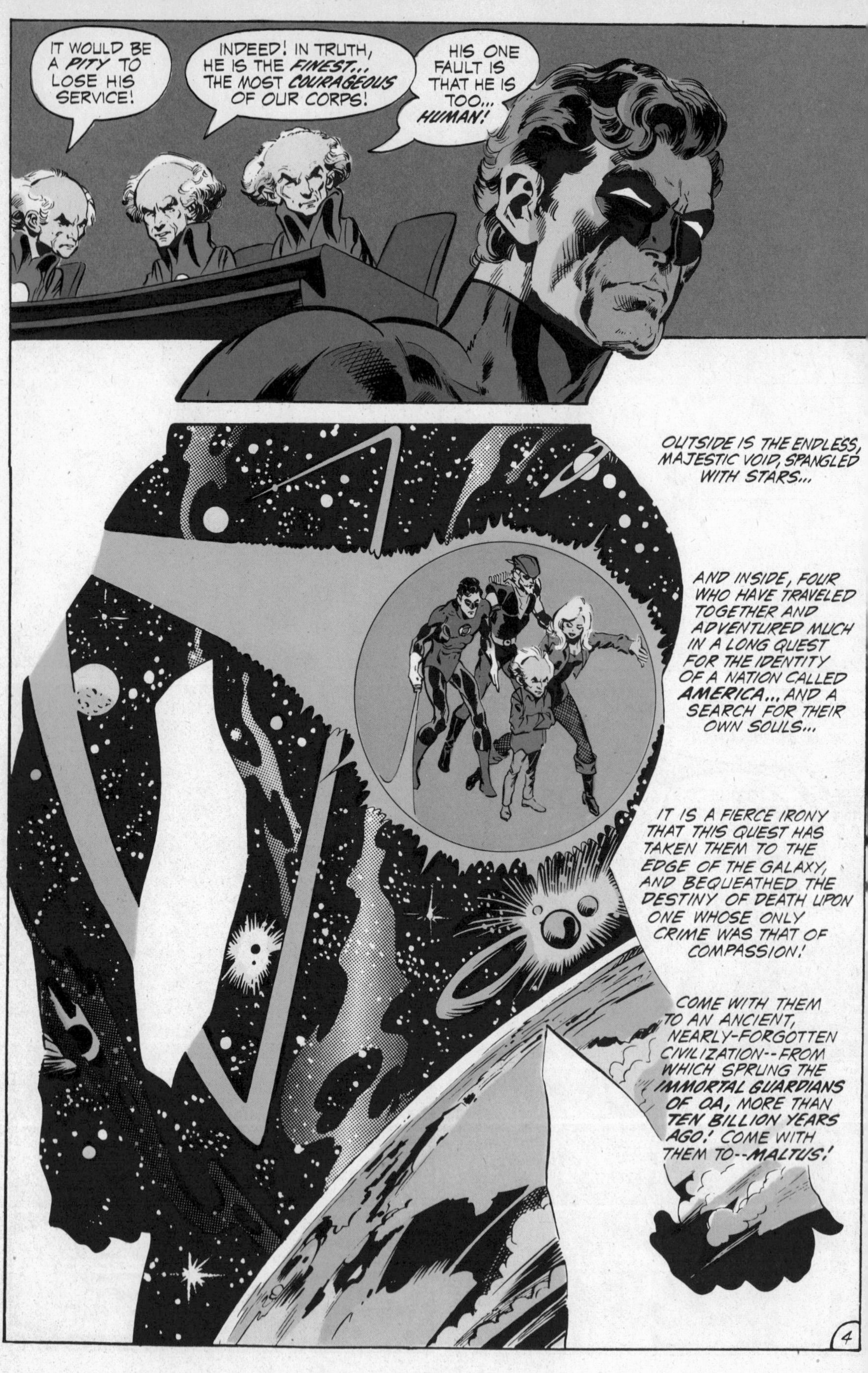
IT WOULD BE A PITY TO LOSE HIS SERVICE!
INDEED! IN TRUTH, HE IS THE FINEST... THE MOST COURAGEOUS OF OUR CORPS!
HIS ONE FAULT IS THAT HE IS TOO... HUMAN!
OUTSIDE IS THE ENDLESS, MAJESTIC VOID, SPANGLED WITH STARS...
AND INSIDE, FOUR WHO HAVE TRAVELED TOGETHER AND ADVENTURED MUCH IN A LONG QUEST FOR THE IDENTITY OF A NATION CALLED AMERICA... AND A SEARCH FOR THEIR OWN SOULS...
IT IS A FIERCE IRONY THAT THIS QUEST HAS TAKEN THEM TO THE EDGE OF THE GALAXY, AND BEQUEATHED THE DESTINY OF DEATH UPON ONE WHOSE ONLY CRIME WAS THAT OF COMPASSION!
COME WITH THEM TO AN ANCIENT, NEARLY-FORGOTTEN CIVILIZATION--FROM WHICH SPRUNG THE IMMORTAL GUARDIANS OF OA, MORE THAN TEN BILLION YEARS AGO! COME WITH THEM TO--MALTUS!
4

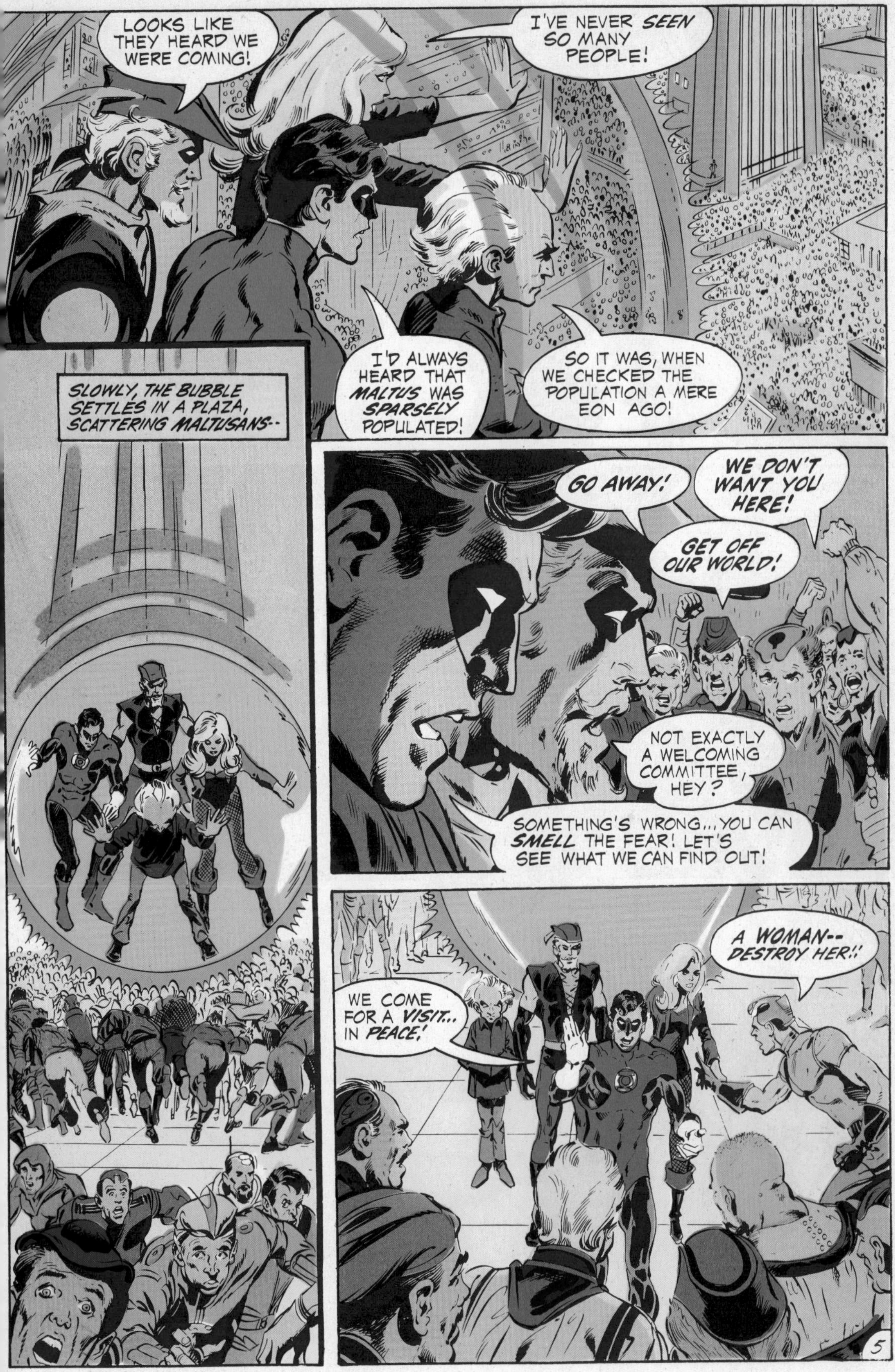

LOOKS LIKE THEY HEARD WE WERE COMING!
I'VE NEVER SEEN SO MANY PEOPLE!
I'D ALWAYS HEARD THAT MALTUS WAS SPARSELY POPULATED!
SO IT WAS, WHEN WE CHECKED THE POPULATION A MERE EON AGO!
SLOWLY, THE BUBBLE SETTLES IN A PLAZA, SCATTERING MALTUSANS--
GO AWAY!
WE DON'T WANT YOU HERE!
GET OFF OUR WORLD!
NOT EXACTLY A WELCOMING COMMITTEE, HEY?
SOMETHING'S WRONG... YOU CAN SMELL THE FEAR! LET'S SEE WHAT WE CAN FIND OUT!
WE COME FOR A VISIT... IN PEACE!
A WOMAN-- DESTROY HER!!
5

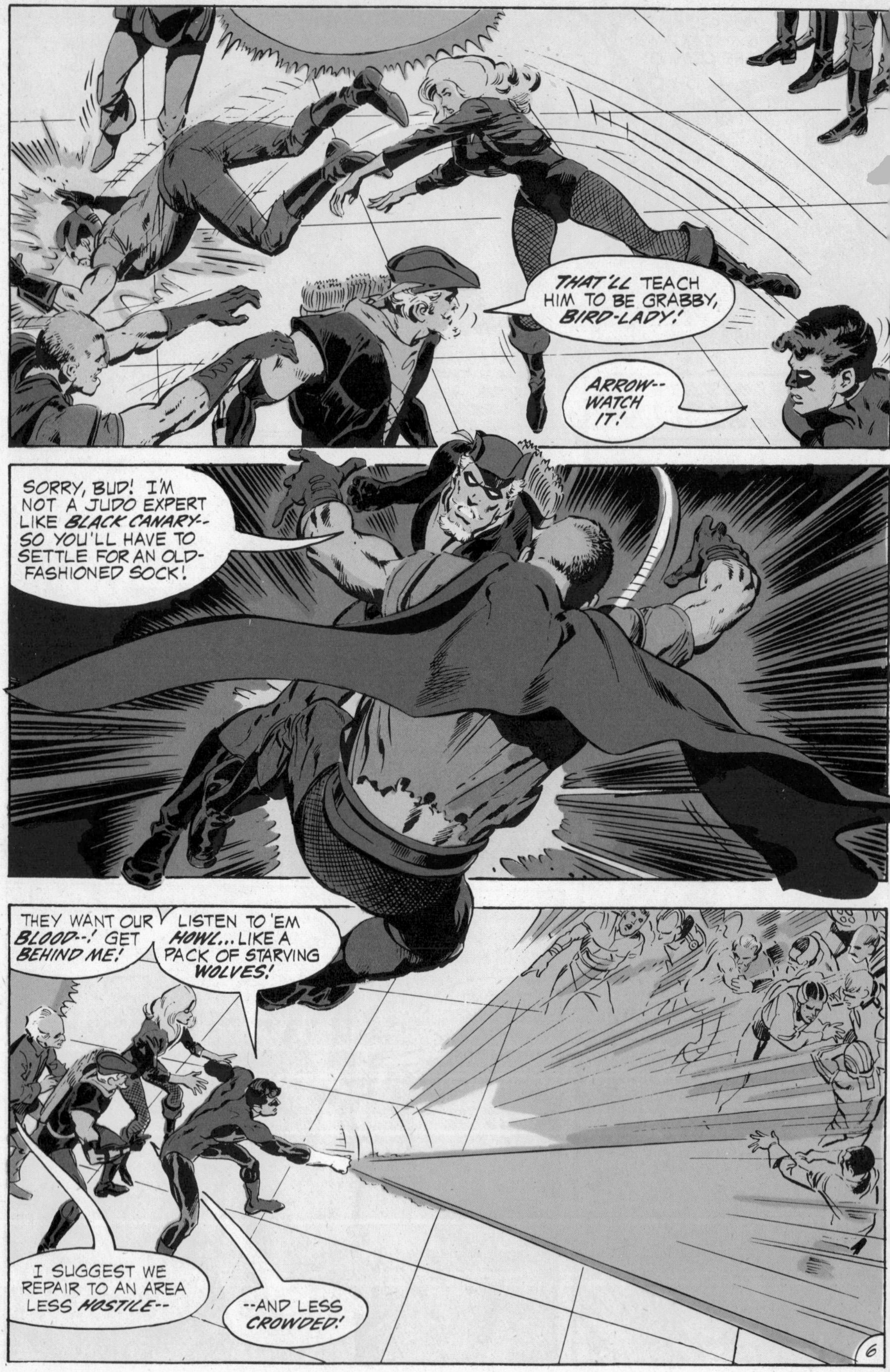
THAT'LL TEACH HIM TO BE GRABBY, BIRD-LADY!
ARROW-- WATCH IT!
SORRY, BUD! I'M NOT A JUDO EXPERT LIKE BLACK CANARY-- SO YOU'LL HAVE TO SETTLE FOR AN OLD-FASHIONED SOCK!
THEY WANT OUR BLOOD--! GET BEHIND ME!
LISTEN TO 'EM HOWL... LIKE A PACK OF STARVING WOLVES!
I SUGGEST WE REPAIR TO AN AREA LESS HOSTILE--
--AND LESS CROWDED!
6

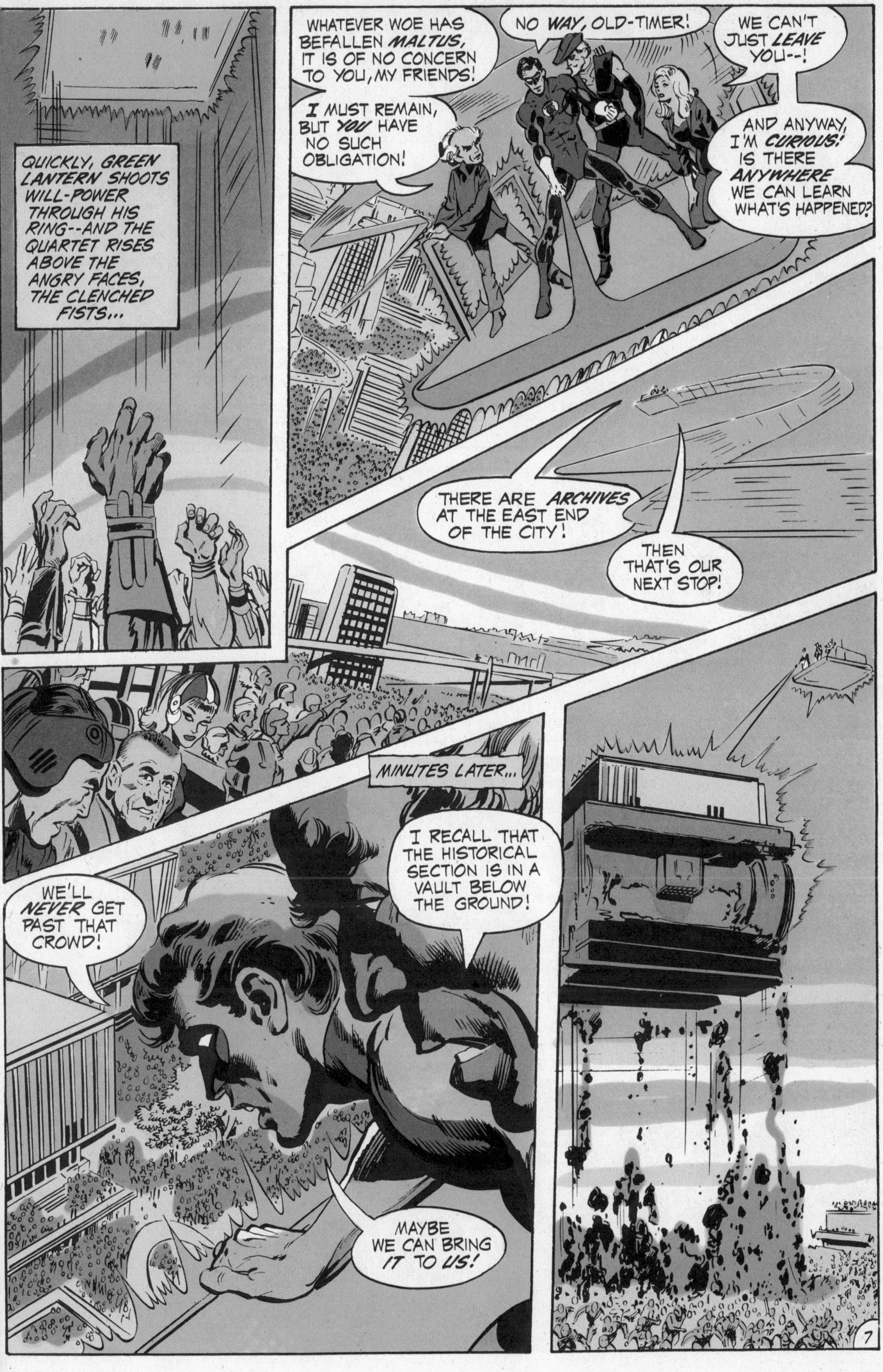
QUICKLY, GREEN LANTERN SHOOTS WILL-POWER THROUGH HIS RING--AND THE QUARTET RISES ABOVE THE ANGRY FACES, THE CLENCHED FISTS...
WHATEVER WOE HAS BEFALLEN MALTUS, IT IS OF NO CONCERN TO YOU, MY FRIENDS!
I MUST REMAIN, BUT YOU HAVE NO SUCH OBLIGATION!
NO WAY, OLD-TIMER!
WE CAN'T JUST LEAVE YOU--!
AND ANYWAY, I'M CURIOUS! IS THERE ANYWHERE WE CAN LEARN WHAT'S HAPPENED?
THERE ARE ARCHIVES AT THE EAST END OF THE CITY!
THEN THAT'S OUR NEXT STOP!
MINUTES LATER...
WE'LL NEVER GET PAST THAT CROWD!
I RECALL THAT THE HISTORICAL SECTION IS IN A VAULT BELOW THE GROUND!
MAYBE WE CAN BRING IT TO US!
7

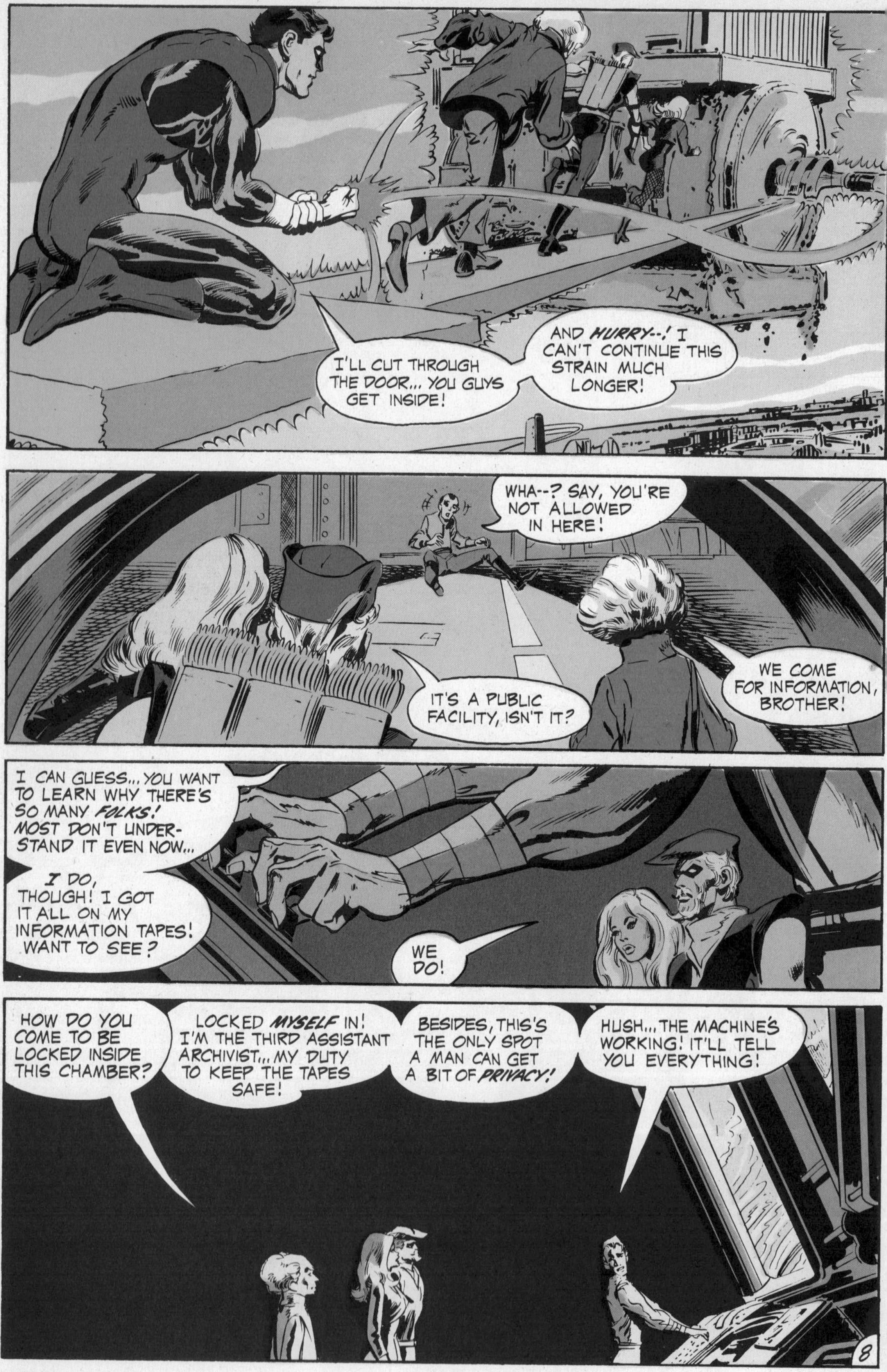
I'LL CUT THROUGH THE DOOR... YOU GUYS GET INSIDE!
AND HURRY--! I CAN'T CONTINUE THIS STRAIN MUCH LONGER!
WHA--? SAY, YOU'RE NOT ALLOWED IN HERE!
IT'S A PUBLIC FACILITY, ISN'T IT?
WE COME FOR INFORMATION, BROTHER!
I CAN GUESS... YOU WANT TO LEARN WHY THERE'S SO MANY FOLKS! MOST DON'T UNDERSTAND IT EVEN NOW...
I DO, THOUGH! I GOT IT ALL ON MY INFORMATION TAPES! WANT TO SEE?
WE DO!
HOW DO YOU COME TO BE LOCKED INSIDE THIS CHAMBER?
LOCKED MYSELF IN! I'M THE THIRD ASSISTANT ARCHIVIST... MY DUTY TO KEEP THE TAPES SAFE!
BESIDES, THIS'S THE ONLY SPOT A MAN CAN GET A BIT OF PRIVACY!
HUSH... THE MACHINE'S WORKING! IT'LL TELL YOU EVERYTHING!
8

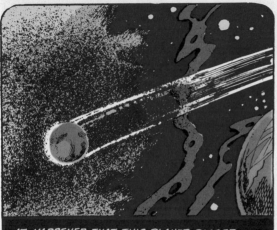

IT HAPPENED THAT THIS PLANET PASSED THROUGH A CLOUD OF COSMIC DUST.

THE PEOPLE REJOICED WHEN THEY SAW THAT THE DUST HAD NO APPARENT EFFECT ON THEIR HEALTH OR WELFARE.

YET, WHEN SEVENTY SOLAR CYCLES PASSED, A DELAYED EFFECT BECAME MANIFEST. FOR THERE WERE NO CHILDREN BORN, AND THE PEOPLE WERE ALL AGED. A GREAT FEAR SWEPT THE MOUNTAINS AND VALLEYS ALIKE.

IN THE MOMENT OF DARKEST DESPAIR THERE CAME A SAVIOR, WHO CALLED HERSELF MOTHER JUNA. FROM THE CITIZENS SHE COLLECTED SPECIMENS OF FLESH AND DROPS OF BLOOD.

THESE DID MOTHER JUNA TAKE INTO HER LABORATORY. WITH GREAT SCIENTIFIC SKILL, SHE CULTURED THEM.

AND FROM EACH SHE CREATED A BABY MALTUSAN, AND THESE GREW TO A FULL ADULTHOOD IN MERE DAYS!

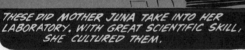

9

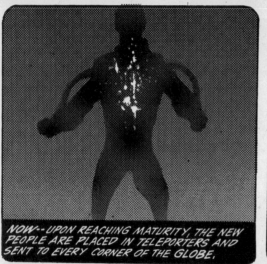

NOW--UPON REACHING MATURITY, THE NEW PEOPLE ARE PLACED IN TELEPORTERS AND SENT TO EVERY CORNER OF THE GLOBE.

EACH ARRIVES WITH A FULL SET OF PSEUDO-MEMORIES AND A PRE-DESIGNED IDENTITY. IT'S IMPOSSIBLE TO DISTINGUISH JUNA'S SYNTHETIC CHILDREN FROM THE NATURAL-BORN.

MOTHER JUNA SAYSSS

SO *THAT'S* IT! MALTUS IS SUFFERING FROM *OVER-POPULATION!*

WORST PART IS, FOLKS *RECOVERED* FROM THE COSMIC DUST! HAVING *REAL* CHILDREN NOW!

WE'VE GOT TO *FIND* THAT WOMAN-- AND *STOP* HER MADNESS!

AND WHEN THE MONOLITH IS REPLACED...

BIRD-LADY IS *RIGHT!* MOTHER JUNA'S OVERDUE FOR A *ZAPPING...*

WE GOT THE WHOLE UGLY STORY, *LANTERN!* IT SEEMS...

I *KNOW!* I MONITORED THE TAPE WITH MY *RING!*

WE'LL DISCUSS IT *AFTER* I GET RID OF THAT VAULT! EITHER *IT* GOES DOWN-- OR *I* DO!

HOLD ON, *ARROW!* MAYBE THE SITUATION ISN'T AS BAD AS WE *THINK!*

I'M NEARLY EXHAUSTED... SO WE'LL HAVE TO USE THE *OAN* BUBBLE TO TAKE A TOUR OF THIS WORLD AND SEE THE EFFECTS OF *POPULATION EXPLOSION* FIRST-HAND!

10

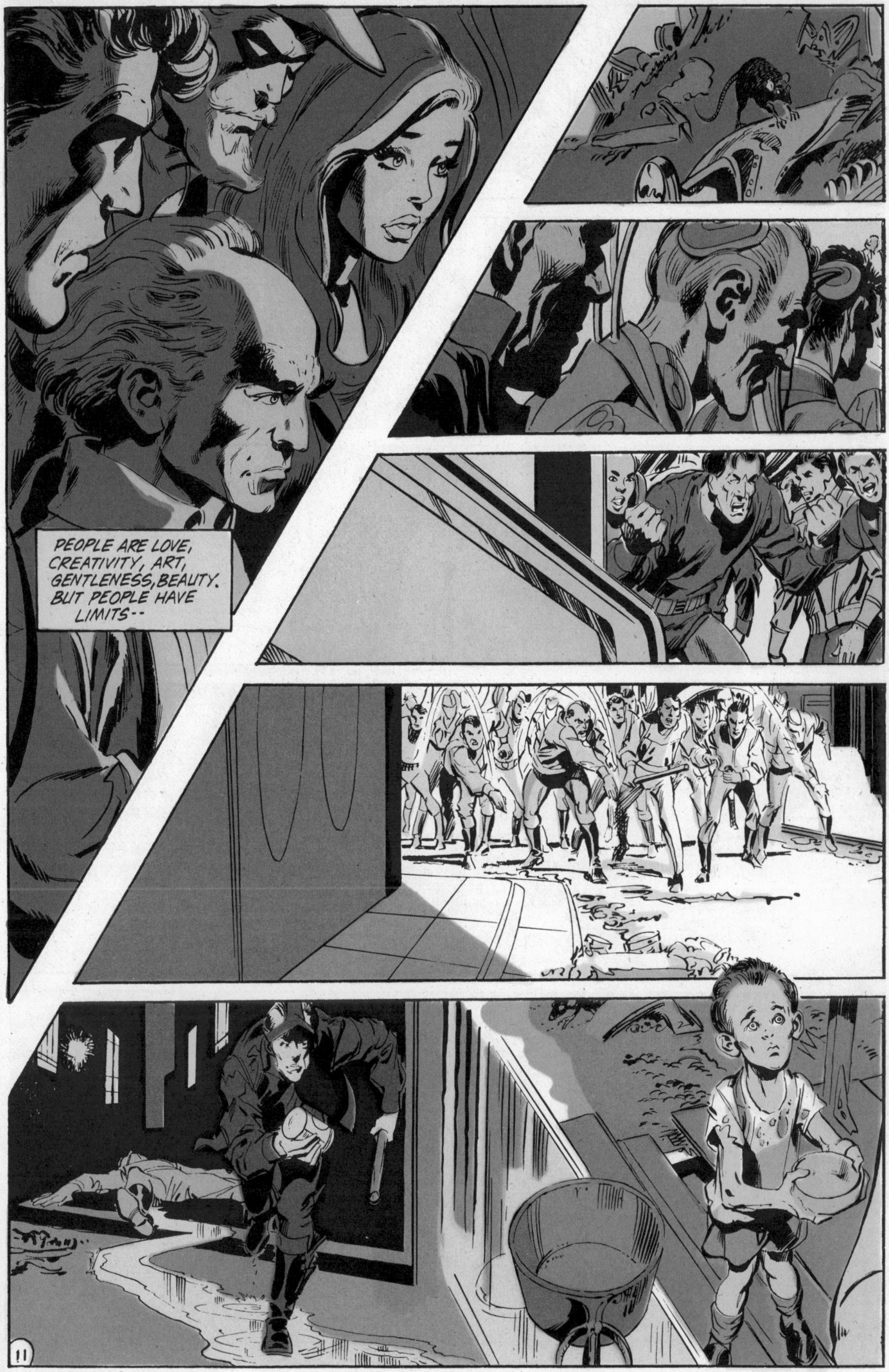
PEOPLE ARE LOVE, CREATIVITY, ART, GENTLENESS, BEAUTY. BUT PEOPLE HAVE LIMITS--
11

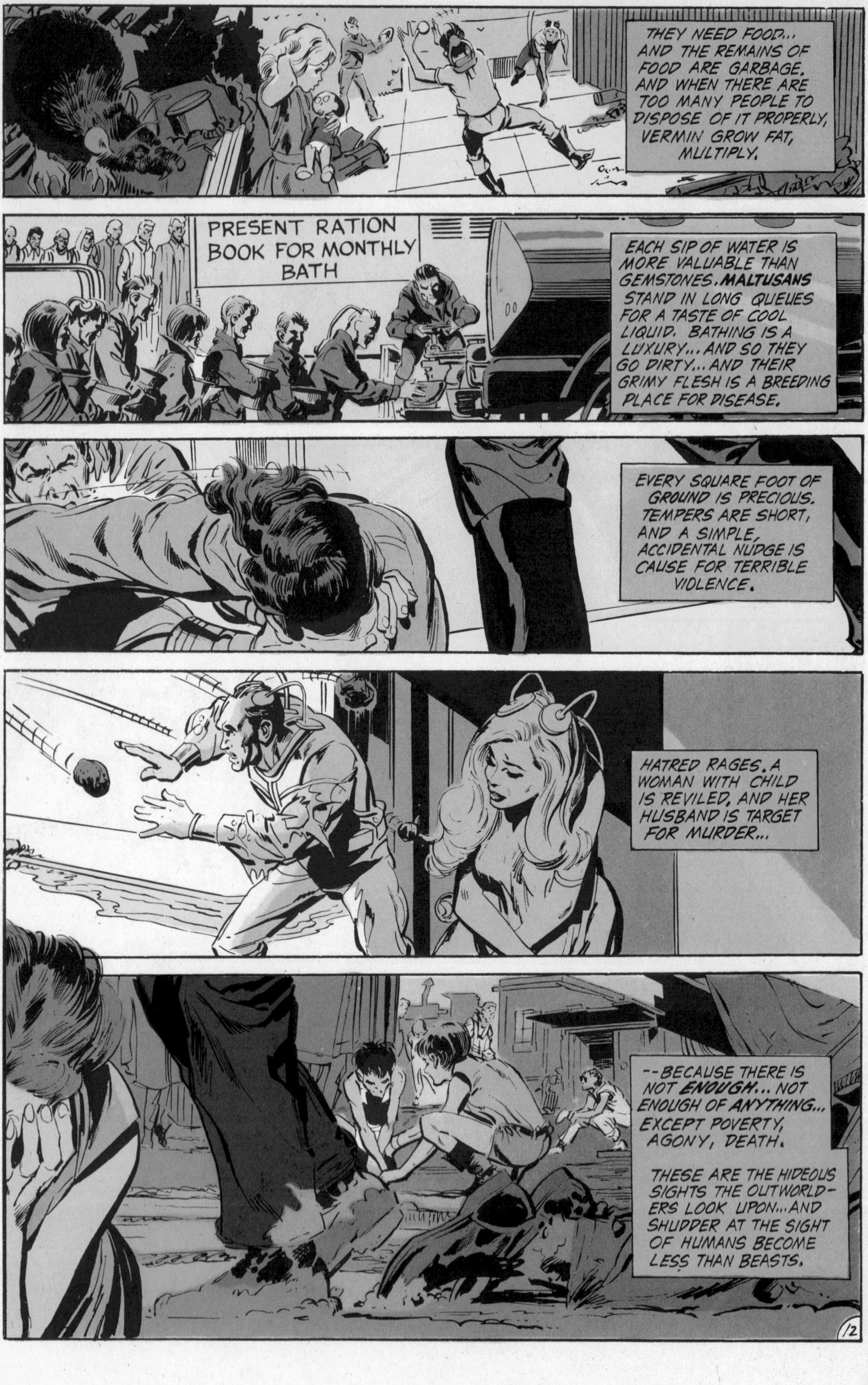
THEY NEED FOOD... AND THE REMAINS OF FOOD ARE GARBAGE. AND WHEN THERE ARE TOO MANY PEOPLE TO DISPOSE OF IT PROPERLY, VERMIN GROW FAT, MULTIPLY.
PRESENT RATION BOOK FOR MONTHLY BATH
EACH SIP OF WATER IS MORE VALUABLE THAN GEMSTONES. MALTUSANS STAND IN LONG QUEUES FOR A TASTE OF COOL LIQUID. BATHING IS A LUXURY... AND SO THEY GO DIRTY... AND THEIR GRIMY FLESH IS A BREEDING PLACE FOR DISEASE.
EVERY SQUARE FOOT OF GROUND IS PRECIOUS. TEMPERS ARE SHORT, AND A SIMPLE, ACCIDENTAL NUDGE IS CAUSE FOR TERRIBLE VIOLENCE.
HATRED RAGES. A WOMAN WITH CHILD IS REVILED, AND HER HUSBAND IS TARGET FOR MURDER...
--BECAUSE THERE IS NOT ENOUGH... NOT ENOUGH OF ANYTHING... EXCEPT POVERTY, AGONY, DEATH.
THESE ARE THE HIDEOUS SIGHTS THE OUTWORLDERS LOOK UPON... AND SHUDDER AT THE SIGHT OF HUMANS BECOME LESS THAN BEASTS.
12

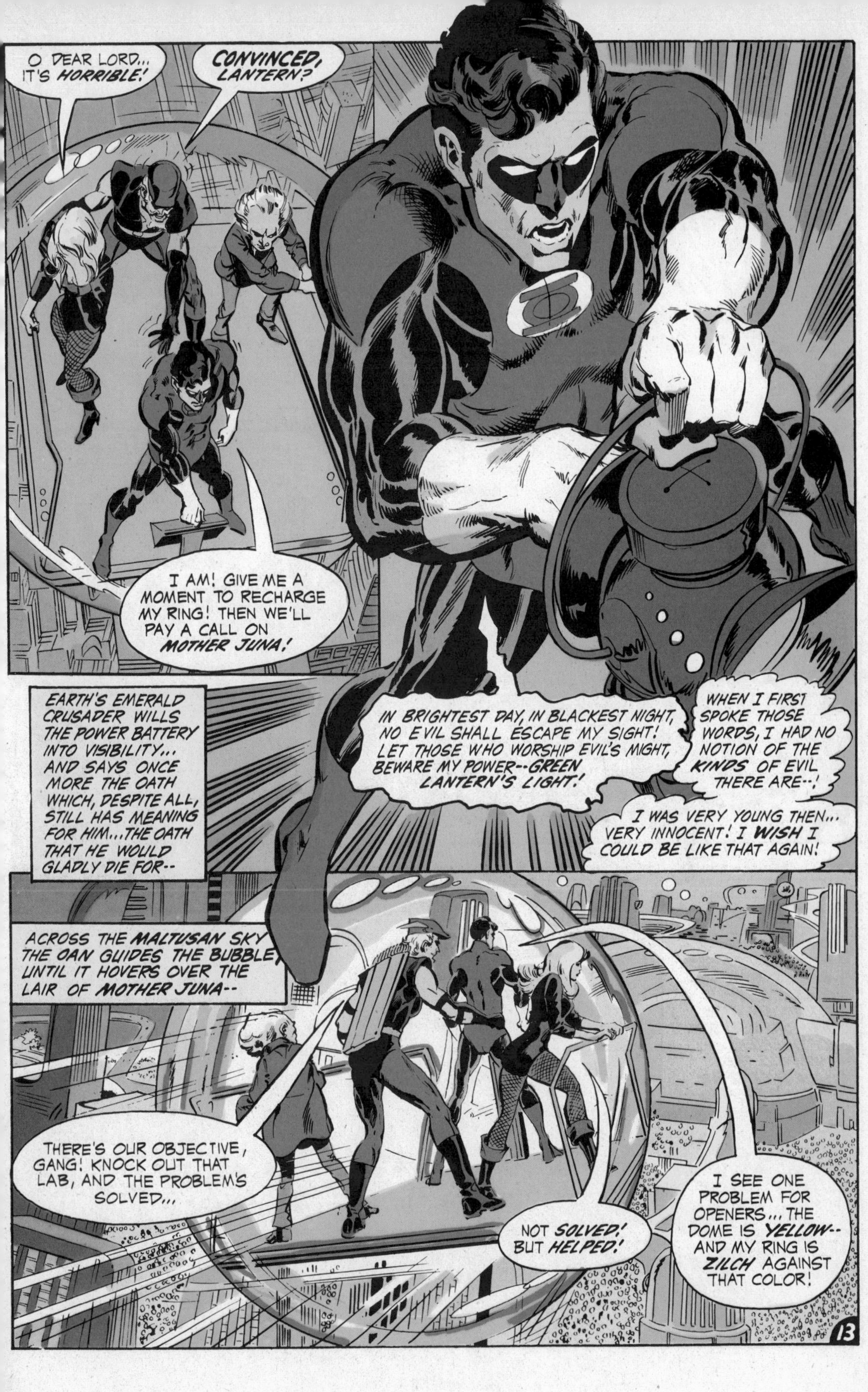

O DEAR LORD... IT'S HORRIBLE!
CONVINCED, LANTERN?
I AM! GIVE ME A MOMENT TO RECHARGE MY RING! THEN WE'LL PAY A CALL ON MOTHER JUNA!
EARTH'S EMERALD CRUSADER WILLS THE POWER BATTERY INTO VISIBILITY... AND SAYS ONCE MORE THE OATH WHICH, DESPITE ALL, STILL HAS MEANING FOR HIM... THE OATH THAT HE WOULD GLADLY DIE FOR--
IN BRIGHTEST DAY, IN BLACKEST NIGHT, NO EVIL SHALL ESCAPE MY SIGHT! LET THOSE WHO WORSHIP EVIL'S MIGHT, BEWARE MY POWER--GREEN LANTERN'S LIGHT!
WHEN I FIRST SPOKE THOSE WORDS, I HAD NO NOTION OF THE KINDS OF EVIL THERE ARE--!
I WAS VERY YOUNG THEN... VERY INNOCENT! I WISH I COULD BE LIKE THAT AGAIN!
ACROSS THE MALTUSAN SKY THE OAN GUIDES THE BUBBLE, UNTIL IT HOVERS OVER THE LAIR OF MOTHER JUNA--
THERE'S OUR OBJECTIVE, GANG! KNOCK OUT THAT LAB, AND THE PROBLEM'S SOLVED...
NOT SOLVED! BUT HELPED!
I SEE ONE PROBLEM FOR OPENERS... THE DOME IS YELLOW-- AND MY RING IS ZILCH AGAINST THAT COLOR!
13

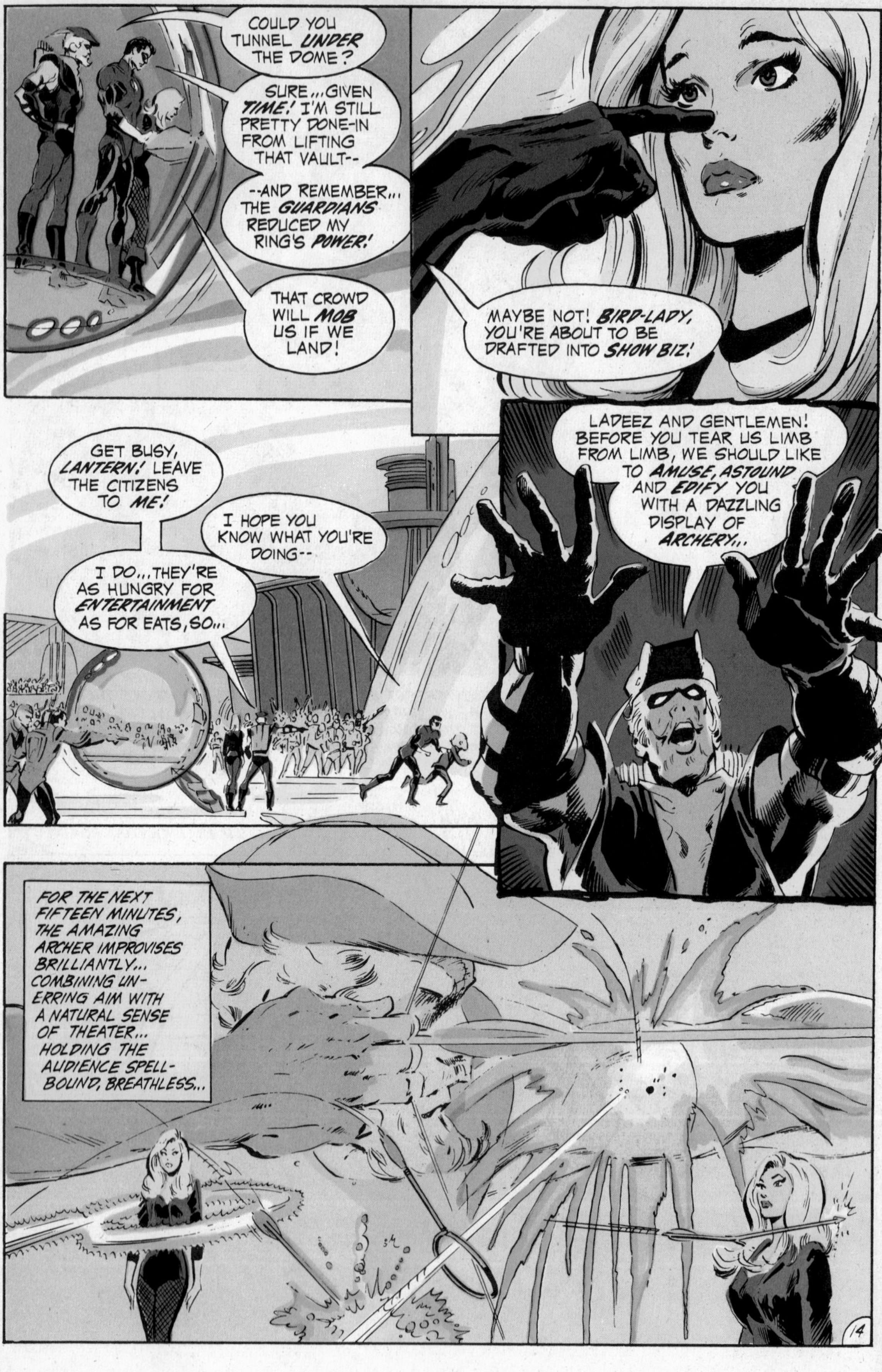
COULD YOU TUNNEL UNDER THE DOME?
SURE... GIVEN TIME! I'M STILL PRETTY DONE-IN FROM LIFTING THAT VAULT--
--AND REMEMBER... THE GUARDIANS REDUCED MY RING'S POWER!
THAT CROWD WILL MOB US IF WE LAND!
MAYBE NOT! BIRD-LADY, YOU'RE ABOUT TO BE DRAFTED INTO SHOW BIZ!
GET BUSY, LANTERN! LEAVE THE CITIZENS TO ME!
I HOPE YOU KNOW WHAT YOU'RE DOING--
I DO... THEY'RE AS HUNGRY FOR ENTERTAINMENT AS FOR EATS, SO...
LADEEZ AND GENTLEMEN! BEFORE YOU TEAR US LIMB FROM LIMB, WE SHOULD LIKE TO AMUSE, ASTOUND AND EDIFY YOU WITH A DAZZLING DISPLAY OF ARCHERY...
FOR THE NEXT FIFTEEN MINUTES, THE AMAZING ARCHER IMPROVISES BRILLIANTLY... COMBINING UNERRING AIM WITH A NATURAL SENSE OF THEATER... HOLDING THE AUDIENCE SPELLBOUND, BREATHLESS...
14

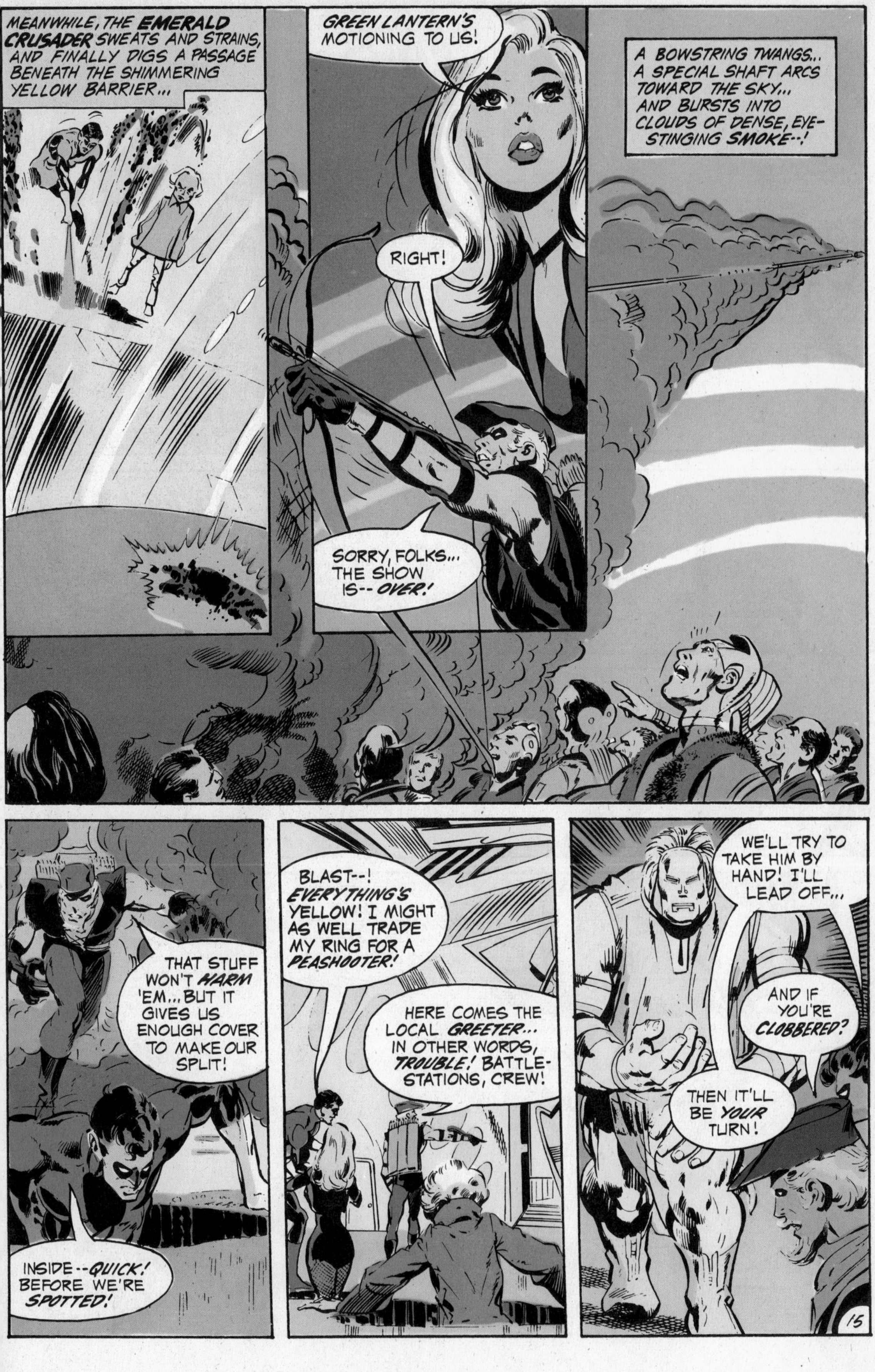
MEANWHILE, THE EMERALD CRUSADER SWEATS AND STRAINS, AND FINALLY DIGS A PASSAGE BENEATH THE SHIMMERING YELLOW BARRIER...
GREEN LANTERN'S MOTIONING TO US!
RIGHT!
SORRY, FOLKS... THE SHOW IS--OVER!
A BOWSTRING TWANGS... A SPECIAL SHAFT ARCS TOWARD THE SKY... AND BURSTS INTO CLOUDS OF DENSE, EYE-STINGING SMOKE--!
THAT STUFF WON'T HARM 'EM... BUT IT GIVES US ENOUGH COVER TO MAKE OUR SPLIT!
INSIDE--QUICK! BEFORE WE'RE SPOTTED!
BLAST--! EVERYTHING'S YELLOW! I MIGHT AS WELL TRADE MY RING FOR A PEASHOOTER!
HERE COMES THE LOCAL GREETER... IN OTHER WORDS, TROUBLE! BATTLE-STATIONS, CREW!
WE'LL TRY TO TAKE HIM BY HAND! I'LL LEAD OFF...
AND IF YOU'RE CLOBBERED?
THEN IT'LL BE YOUR TURN!
15

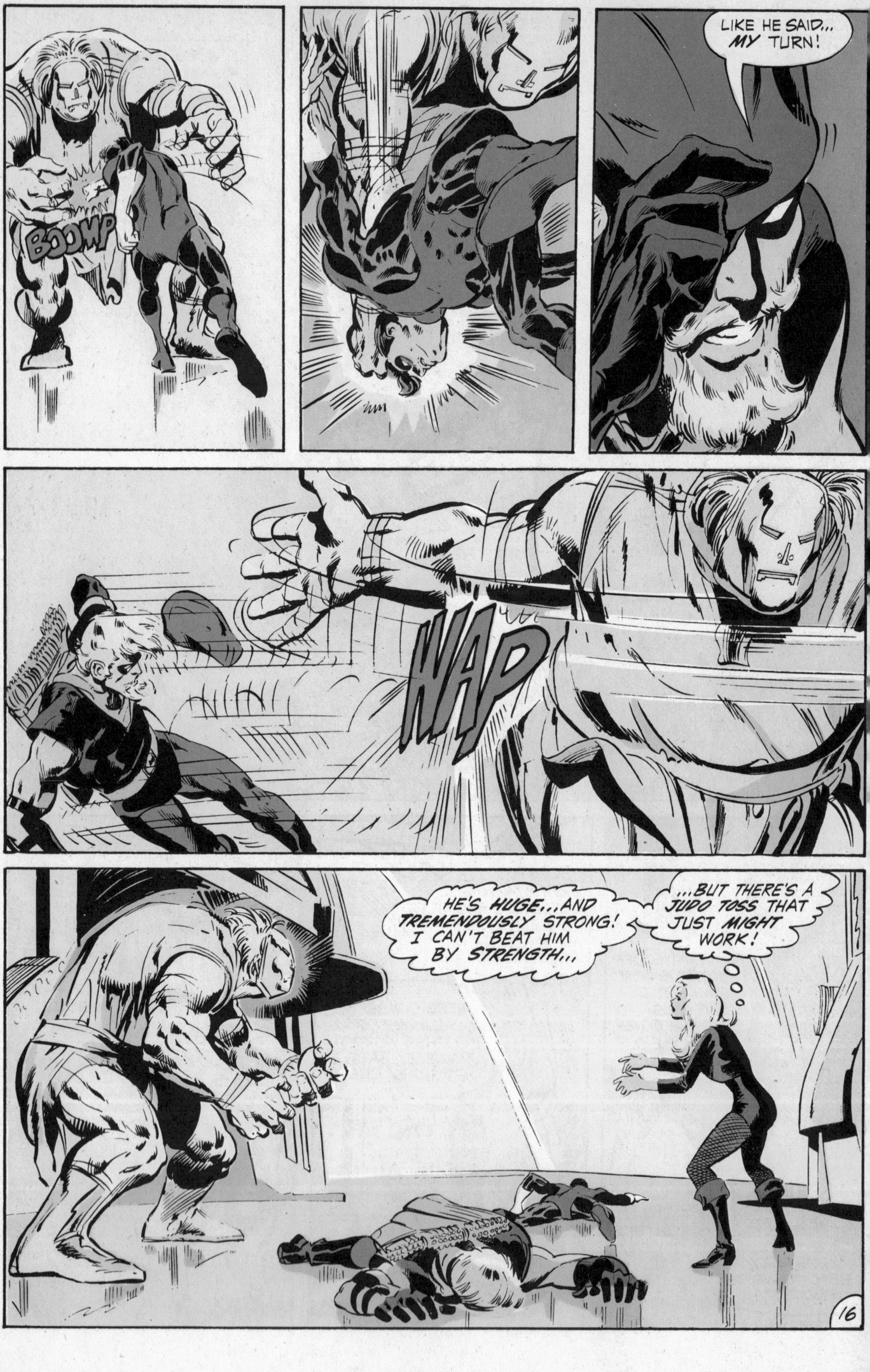
BOOMP
LIKE HE SAID... MY TURN!
WAP
HE'S HUGE...AND TREMENDOUSLY STRONG! I CAN'T BEAT HIM BY STRENGTH...
...BUT THERE'S A JUDO TOSS THAT JUST MIGHT WORK!
16

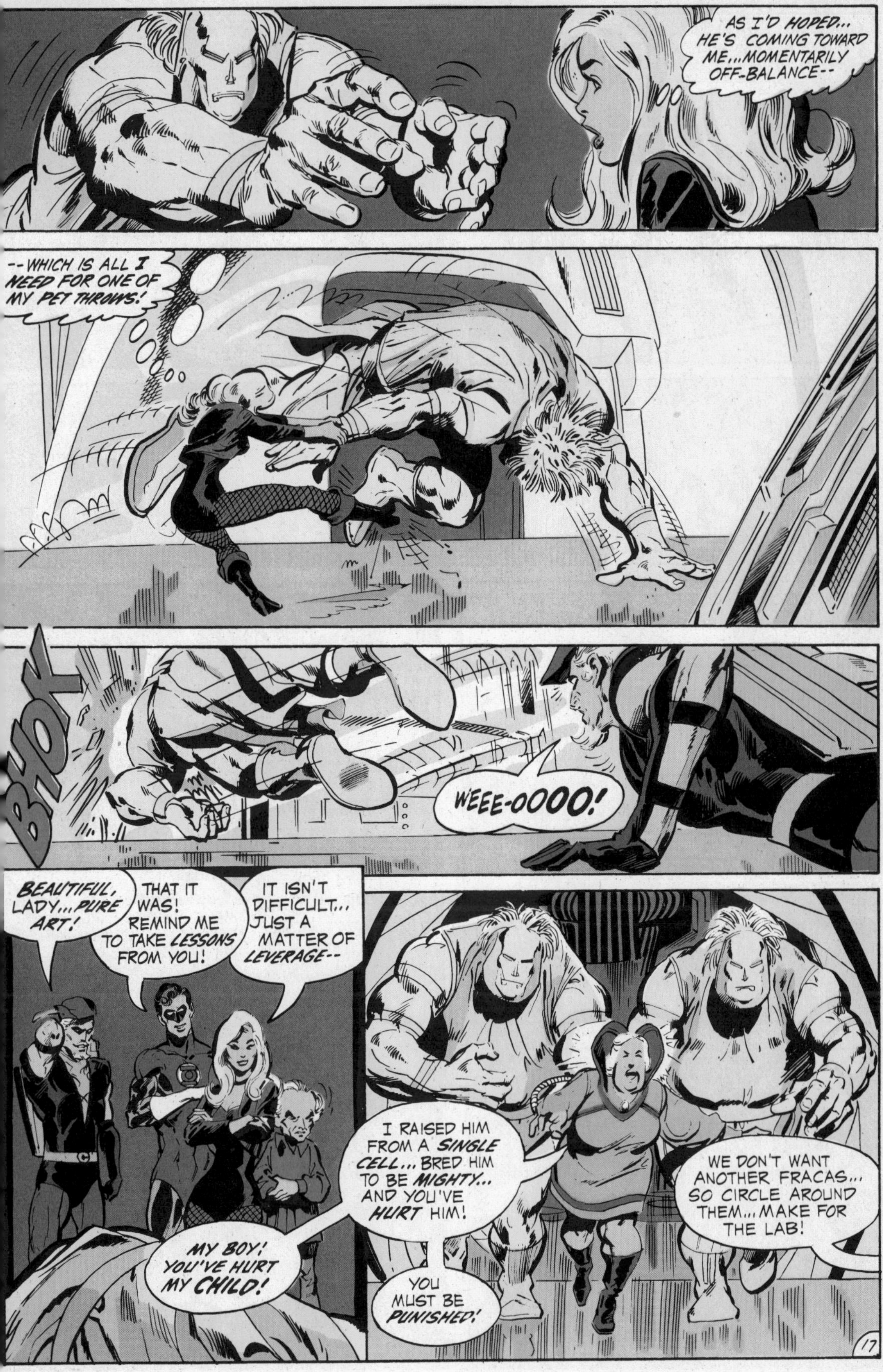
AS I'D HOPED... HE'S COMING TOWARD ME...MOMENTARILY OFF-BALANCE--
--WHICH IS ALL I NEED FOR ONE OF MY PET THROWS!
BHOK
WEEE-OOOO!
BEAUTIFUL, LADY...PURE ART!
THAT IT WAS! REMIND ME TO TAKE LESSONS FROM YOU!
IT ISN'T DIFFICULT... JUST A MATTER OF LEVERAGE--
MY BOY! YOU'VE HURT MY CHILD!
I RAISED HIM FROM A SINGLE CELL... BRED HIM TO BE MIGHTY... AND YOU'VE HURT HIM!
YOU MUST BE PUNISHED!
WE DON'T WANT ANOTHER FRACAS... SO CIRCLE AROUND THEM... MAKE FOR THE LAB!
17

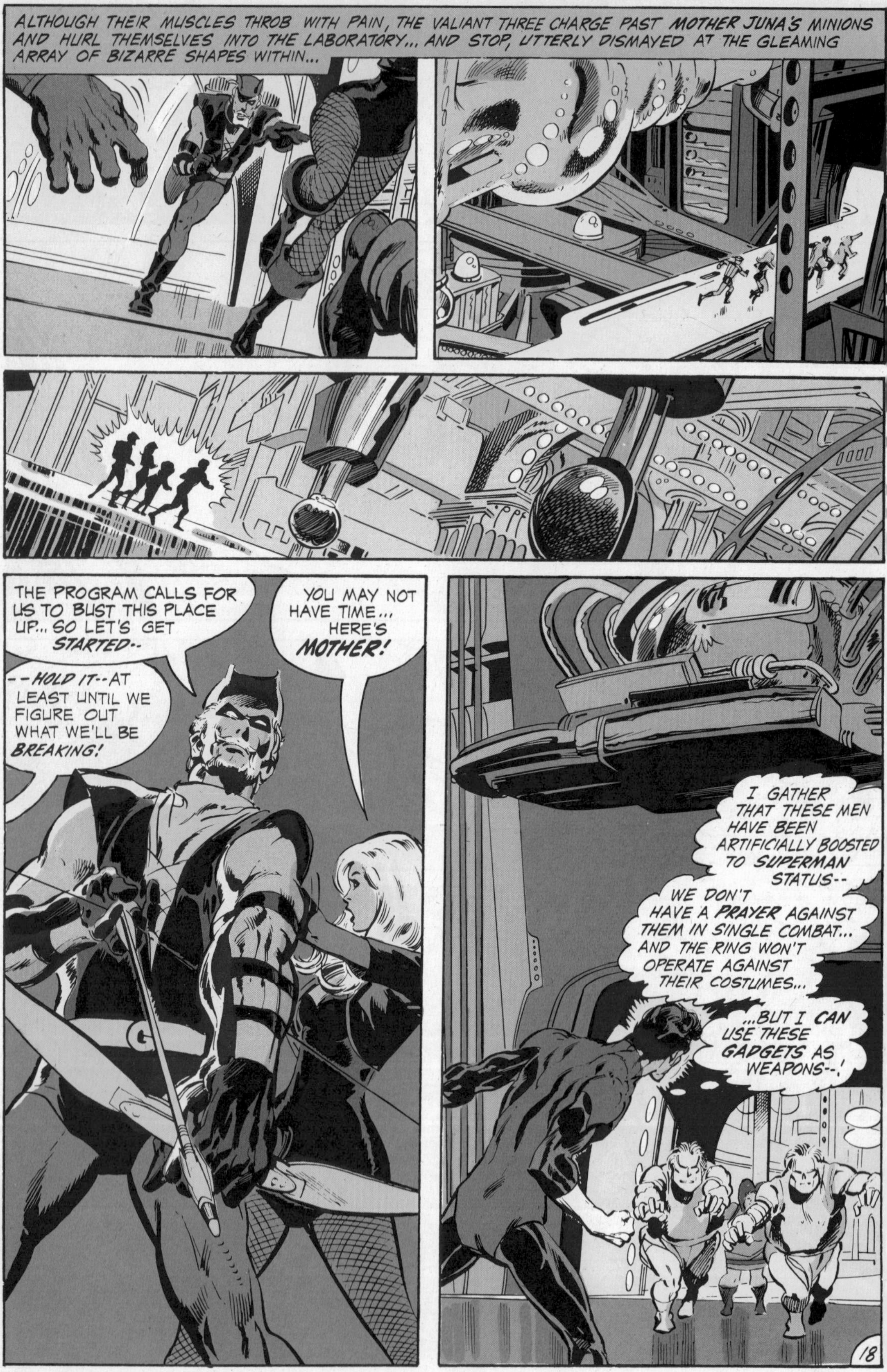
ALTHOUGH THEIR MUSCLES THROB WITH PAIN, THE VALIANT THREE CHARGE PAST MOTHER JUNA'S MINIONS AND HURL THEMSELVES INTO THE LABORATORY... AND STOP, UTTERLY DISMAYED AT THE GLEAMING ARRAY OF BIZARRE SHAPES WITHIN...
THE PROGRAM CALLS FOR US TO BUST THIS PLACE UP... SO LET'S GET STARTED--
--HOLD IT--AT LEAST UNTIL WE FIGURE OUT WHAT WE'LL BE BREAKING!
YOU MAY NOT HAVE TIME... HERE'S MOTHER!
I GATHER THAT THESE MEN HAVE BEEN ARTIFICIALLY BOOSTED TO SUPERMAN STATUS--
WE DON'T HAVE A PRAYER AGAINST THEM IN SINGLE COMBAT... AND THE RING WON'T OPERATE AGAINST THEIR COSTUMES...
...BUT I CAN USE THESE GADGETS AS WEAPONS--!
18

UNLESS HE HAS A SKULL LIKE *GRANITE,* A CLUNK ON THE HEAD WITH *THAT* THING SHOULD PUT HIM OUT!

NOPE...NO *GRANITE!*

MY MISTAKE WAS TRYING TO PLAY REASONABLY *FAIR* WITH THESE GOONS... NOT USING *ARROWS* AGAINST THEM!

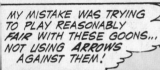

WELL, I LEARN... I *LEARN!*

YOU...*HUSSY!* YOU AND YOUR BULLY BOYFRIENDS ATTACKING MY *DARLINGS*--!

SHE'S INSANE--! I HOPE I CAN SUBDUE HER... GENTLY!

19

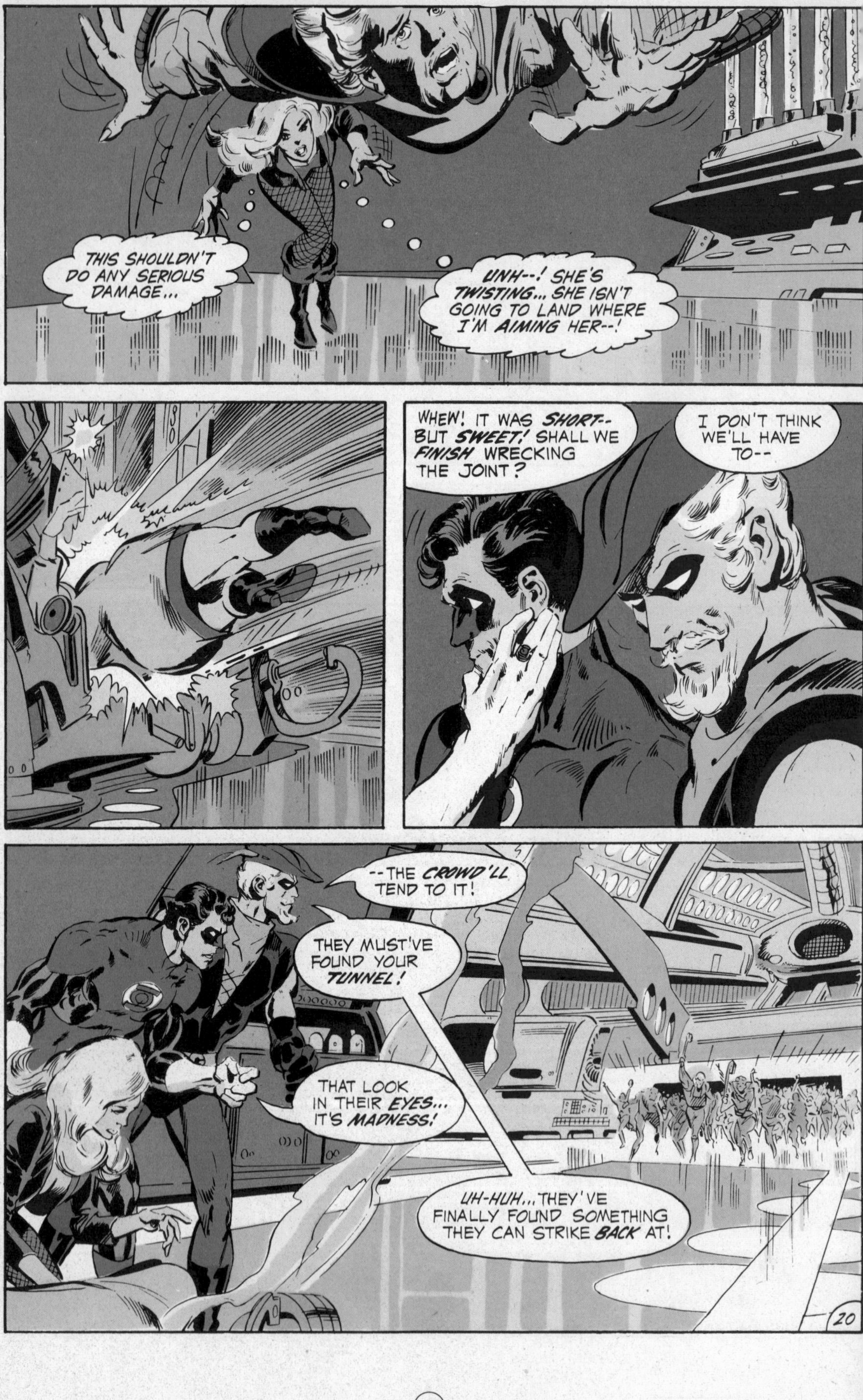
THIS SHOULDN'T DO ANY SERIOUS DAMAGE...
UNH--! SHE'S TWISTING... SHE ISN'T GOING TO LAND WHERE I'M AIMING HER--!
WHEW! IT WAS SHORT--BUT SWEET! SHALL WE FINISH WRECKING THE JOINT?
I DON'T THINK WE'LL HAVE TO--
--THE CROWD'LL TEND TO IT!
THEY MUST'VE FOUND YOUR TUNNEL!
THAT LOOK IN THEIR EYES... IT'S MADNESS!
UH-HUH... THEY'VE FINALLY FOUND SOMETHING THEY CAN STRIKE BACK AT!
20

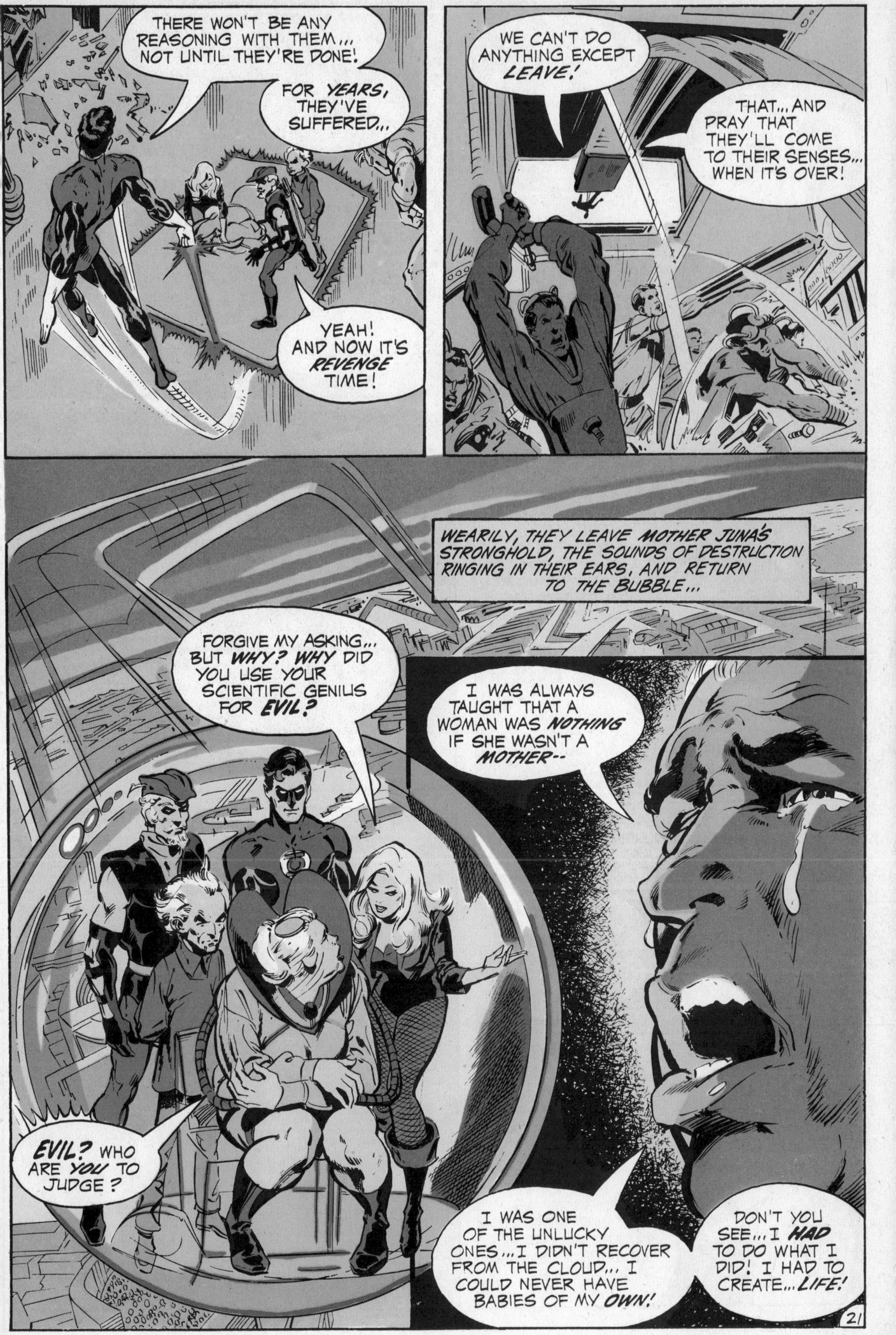
THERE WON'T BE ANY REASONING WITH THEM... NOT UNTIL THEY'RE DONE!
FOR YEARS, THEY'VE SUFFERED...
YEAH! AND NOW IT'S REVENGE TIME!
WE CAN'T DO ANYTHING EXCEPT LEAVE!
THAT... AND PRAY THAT THEY'LL COME TO THEIR SENSES... WHEN IT'S OVER!
WEARILY, THEY LEAVE MOTHER JUNA'S STRONGHOLD, THE SOUNDS OF DESTRUCTION RINGING IN THEIR EARS, AND RETURN TO THE BUBBLE...
FORGIVE MY ASKING... BUT WHY? WHY DID YOU USE YOUR SCIENTIFIC GENIUS FOR EVIL?
EVIL? WHO ARE YOU TO JUDGE?
I WAS ALWAYS TAUGHT THAT A WOMAN WAS NOTHING IF SHE WASN'T A MOTHER--
I WAS ONE OF THE UNLUCKY ONES... I DIDN'T RECOVER FROM THE CLOUD... I COULD NEVER HAVE BABIES OF MY OWN!
DON'T YOU SEE... I HAD TO DO WHAT I DID! I HAD TO CREATE... LIFE!
21

I'M SORRY... SO SORRY--

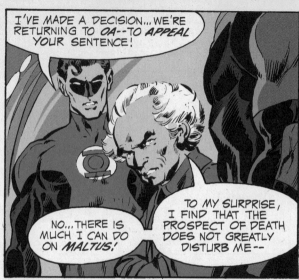

I'VE MADE A DECISION... WE'RE RETURNING TO OA--TO APPEAL YOUR SENTENCE!

NO... THERE IS MUCH I CAN DO ON MALTUS!

TO MY SURPRISE, I FIND THAT THE PROSPECT OF DEATH DOES NOT GREATLY DISTURB ME--

KNOWING IT WILL COME, I WILL WORK, I WILL FILL MY DAYS WITH DEEDS...

PERHAPS I CAN ACCOMPLISH MORE IN A DECADE THAN MY IMMORTAL BROTHERS DO IN CENTURIES!

I WILL GO IN PEACE, I AM SURE...

TAKE IT EASY, OLD-TIMER!

GOOD-BYE...

GOD BLESS...

SILENTLY, MOURNFULLY, THEY CROSS THE GALAXY AND THEIR SOULS ARE COLD, THEIR MEMORIES BLEAK...

...THE LONG TREK ENDS WHERE IT BEGAN, IN STAR CITY! GREEN LANTERN BIDS HIS COMPANIONS FAREWELL AND BLACK CANARY AND THE ARCHER ARE LEFT...

I WISH I COULD TELL YOU TO BE CHEERFUL... BUT IT'S NOT A CHEERFUL UNIVERSE, IS IT?

I DON'T KNOW... I'M SO CONFUSED! I THINK PERHAPS THERE'S NOTHING THAT MATTERS EXCEPT WHATEVER LOVE PEOPLE CAN FIND FOR ONE ANOTHER...

PLEASE... BE KIND... BE GENTLE!

22

THUS, THE JOURNEY IS DONE! PERHAPS THEY HAVE FOUND WHAT THEY SOUGHT... AND PERHAPS NOT... End

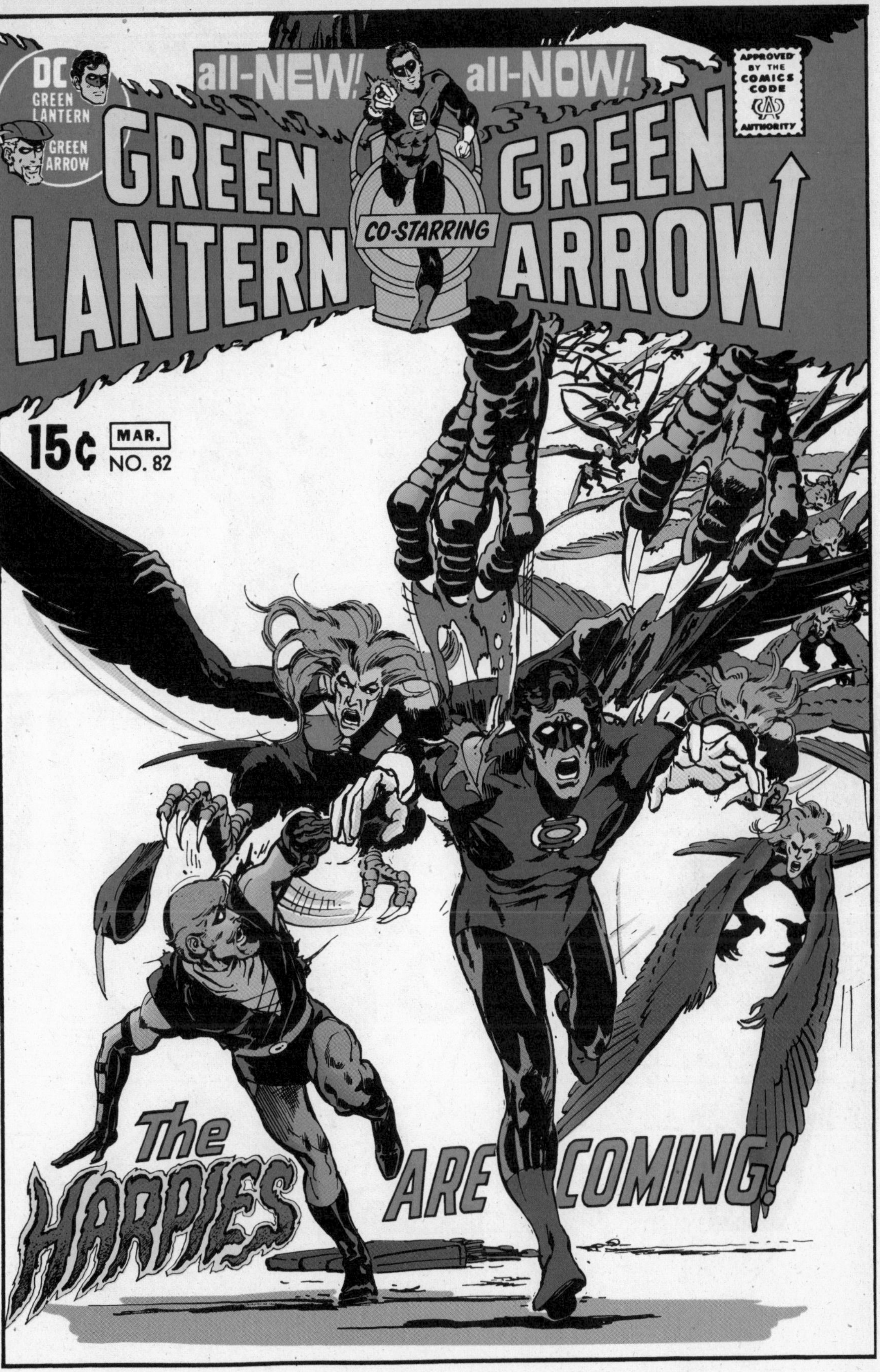
DC GREEN LANTERN GREEN ARROW
all-NEW! all-NOW!
APPROVED BY THE COMICS CODE AUTHORITY
GREEN LANTERN
CO-STARRING
GREEN ARROW
15¢
MAR.
NO. 82
The HARPIES ARE COMING!

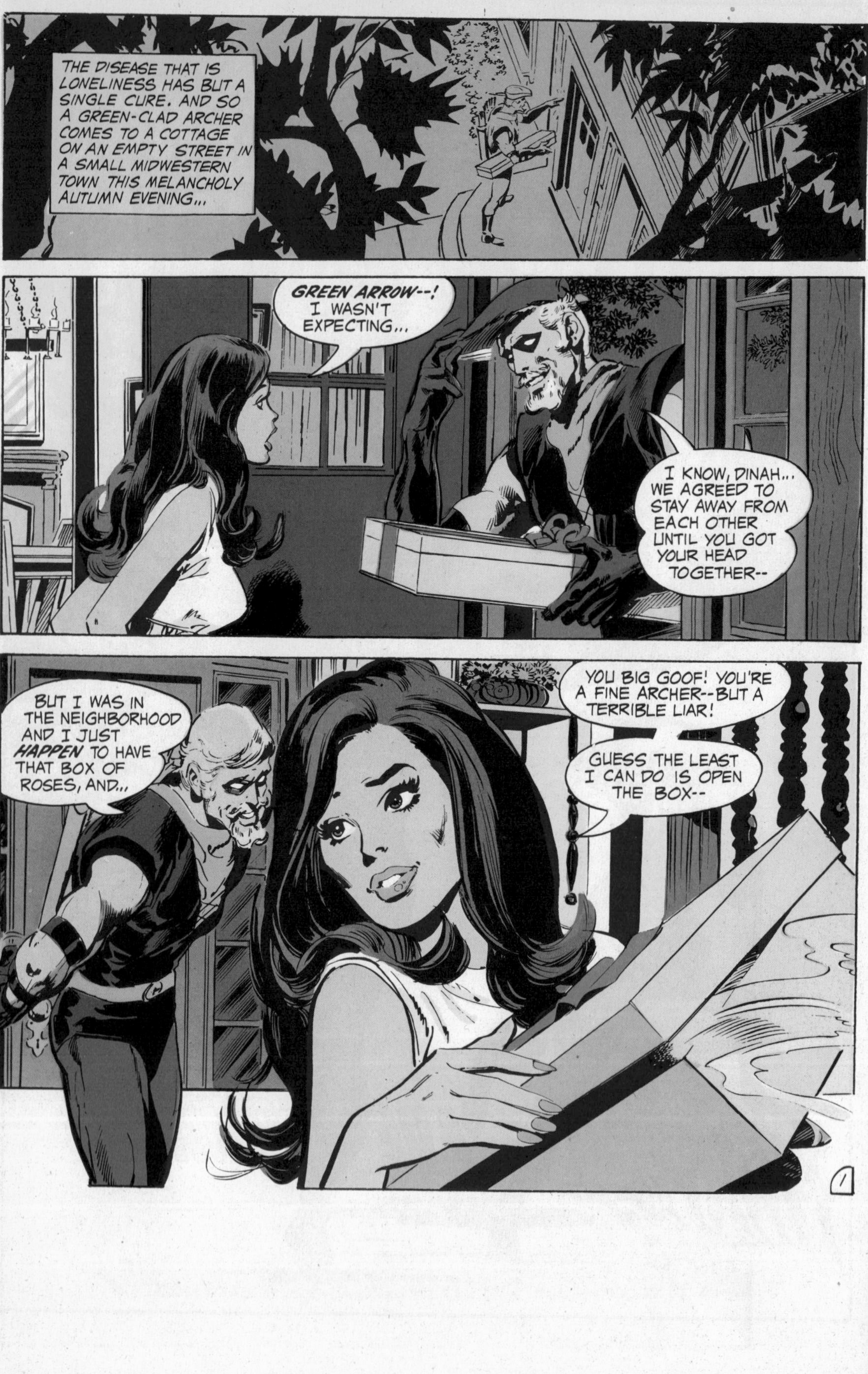
THE DISEASE THAT IS LONELINESS HAS BUT A SINGLE CURE. AND SO A GREEN-CLAD ARCHER COMES TO A COTTAGE ON AN EMPTY STREET IN A SMALL MIDWESTERN TOWN THIS MELANCHOLY AUTUMN EVENING...
GREEN ARROW--! I WASN'T EXPECTING...
I KNOW, DINAH... WE AGREED TO STAY AWAY FROM EACH OTHER UNTIL YOU GOT YOUR HEAD TOGETHER--
BUT I WAS IN THE NEIGHBORHOOD AND I JUST HAPPEN TO HAVE THAT BOX OF ROSES, AND...
YOU BIG GOOF! YOU'RE A FINE ARCHER--BUT A TERRIBLE LIAR!
GUESS THE LEAST I CAN DO IS OPEN THE BOX--
1

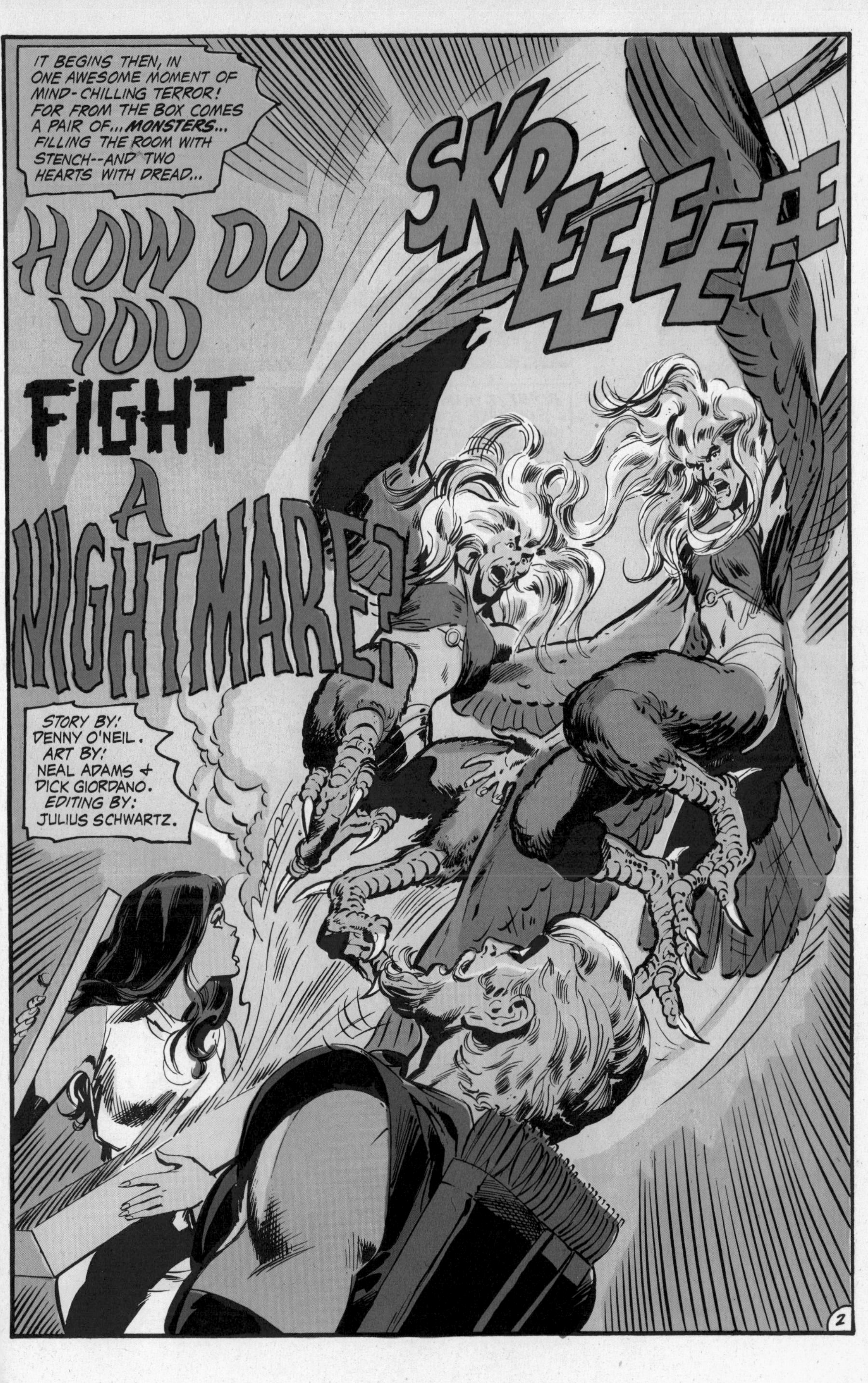

IT BEGINS THEN, IN ONE AWESOME MOMENT OF MIND-CHILLING TERROR! FOR FROM THE BOX COMES A PAIR OF... MONSTERS... FILLING THE ROOM WITH STENCH--AND TWO HEARTS WITH DREAD...
SKREEEEEE
HOW DO YOU FIGHT A NIGHTMARE?
STORY BY: DENNY O'NEIL. ART BY: NEAL ADAMS & DICK GIORDANO. EDITING BY: JULIUS SCHWARTZ.
2

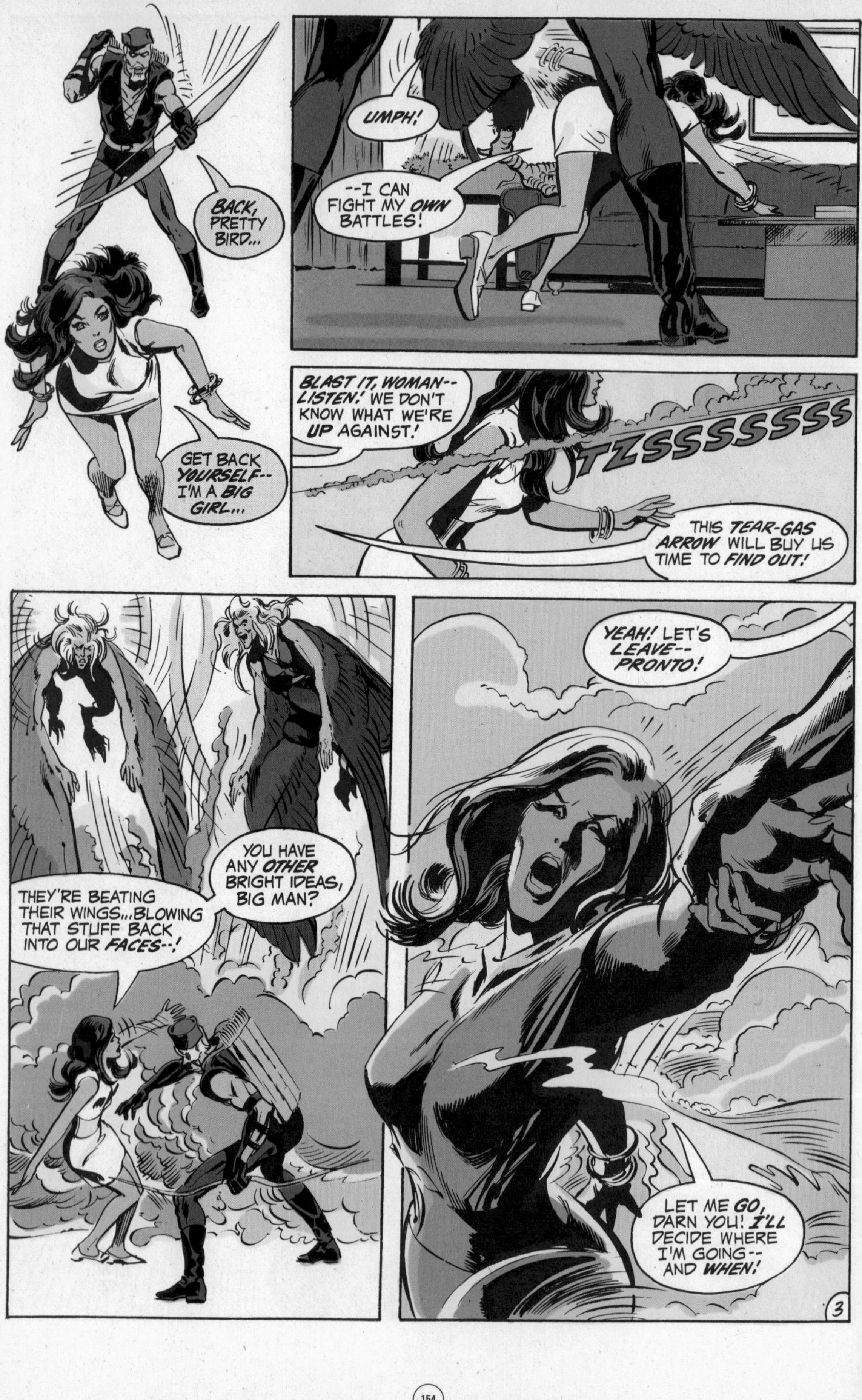
BACK, PRETTY BIRD...
GET BACK YOURSELF-- I'M A BIG GIRL...
UMPH!
--I CAN FIGHT MY OWN BATTLES!
BLAST IT, WOMAN-- LISTEN! WE DON'T KNOW WHAT WE'RE UP AGAINST!
TZSSSSSSSS
THIS TEAR-GAS ARROW WILL BUY US TIME TO FIND OUT!
THEY'RE BEATING THEIR WINGS...BLOWING THAT STUFF BACK INTO OUR FACES--!
YOU HAVE ANY OTHER BRIGHT IDEAS, BIG MAN?
YEAH! LET'S LEAVE-- PRONTO!
LET ME GO, DARN YOU! I'LL DECIDE WHERE I'M GOING-- AND WHEN!
3

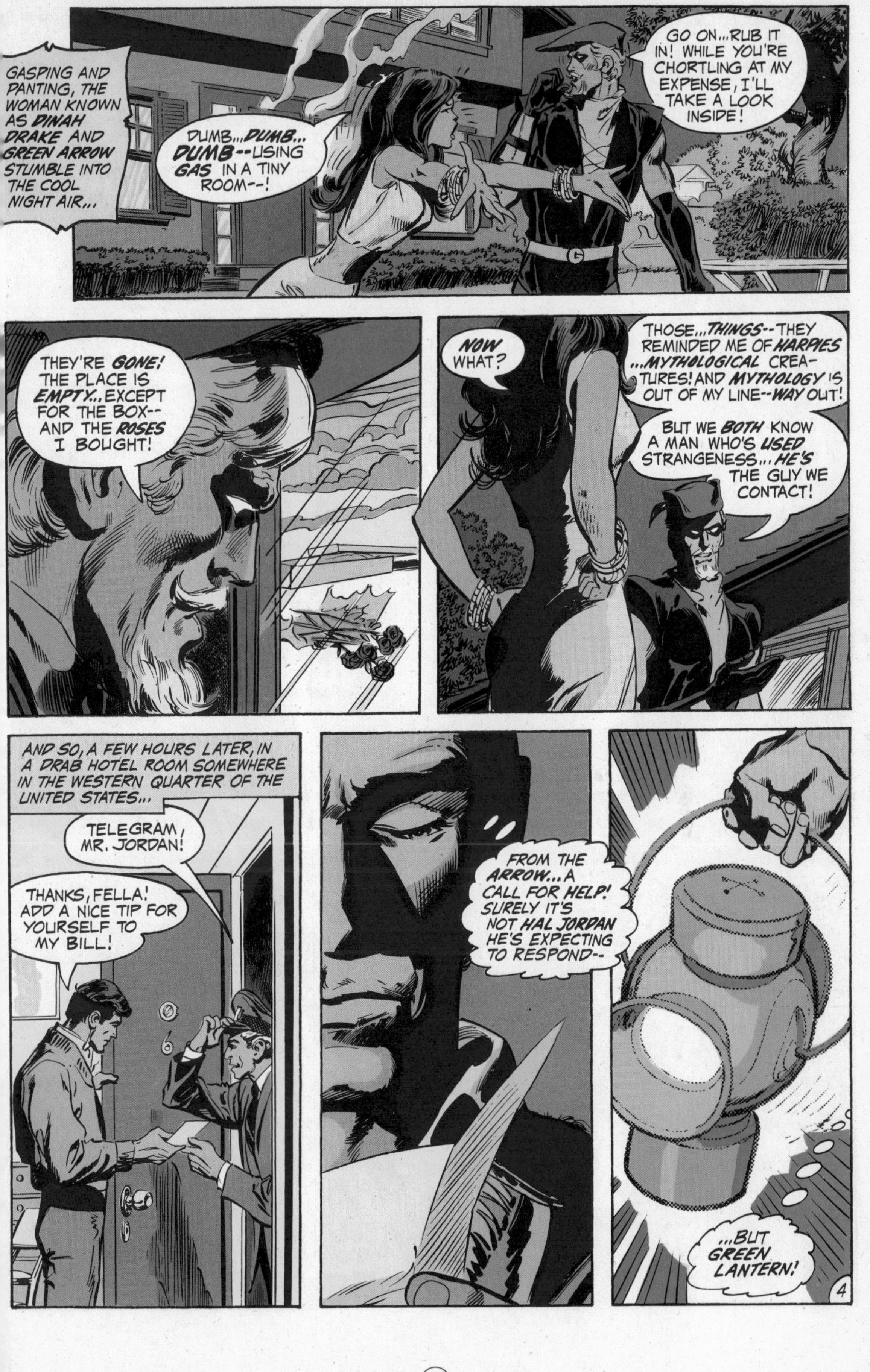
GASPING AND PANTING, THE WOMAN KNOWN AS DINAH DRAKE AND GREEN ARROW STUMBLE INTO THE COOL NIGHT AIR...
DUMB...DUMB... DUMB--USING GAS IN A TINY ROOM--!
GO ON...RUB IT IN! WHILE YOU'RE CHORTLING AT MY EXPENSE, I'LL TAKE A LOOK INSIDE!
THEY'RE GONE! THE PLACE IS EMPTY...EXCEPT FOR THE BOX-- AND THE ROSES I BOUGHT!
NOW WHAT?
THOSE...THINGS--THEY REMINDED ME OF HARPIES ...MYTHOLOGICAL CREATURES! AND MYTHOLOGY IS OUT OF MY LINE--WAY OUT!
BUT WE BOTH KNOW A MAN WHO'S USED STRANGENESS... HE'S THE GUY WE CONTACT!
AND SO, A FEW HOURS LATER, IN A DRAB HOTEL ROOM SOMEWHERE IN THE WESTERN QUARTER OF THE UNITED STATES...
TELEGRAM, MR. JORDAN!
THANKS, FELLA! ADD A NICE TIP FOR YOURSELF TO MY BILL!
FROM THE ARROW...A CALL FOR HELP! SURELY IT'S NOT HAL JORDAN HE'S EXPECTING TO RESPOND--
...BUT GREEN LANTERN!
4

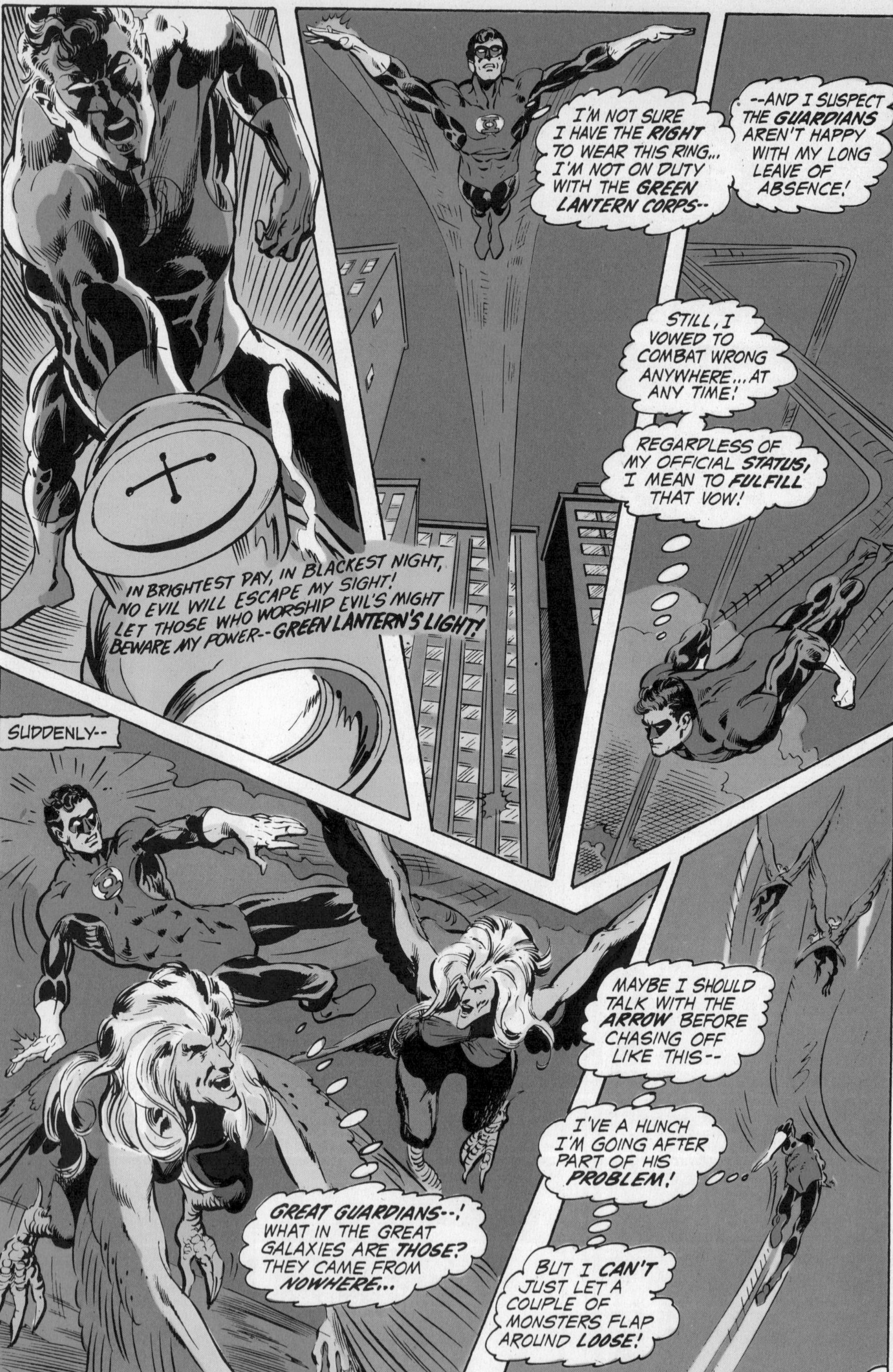
IN BRIGHTEST DAY, IN BLACKEST NIGHT,
NO EVIL WILL ESCAPE MY SIGHT!
LET THOSE WHO WORSHIP EVIL'S MIGHT
BEWARE MY POWER--GREEN LANTERN'S LIGHT!
I'M NOT SURE I HAVE THE RIGHT TO WEAR THIS RING... I'M NOT ON DUTY WITH THE GREEN LANTERN CORPS--
--AND I SUSPECT THE GUARDIANS AREN'T HAPPY WITH MY LONG LEAVE OF ABSENCE!
STILL, I VOWED TO COMBAT WRONG ANYWHERE... AT ANY TIME!
REGARDLESS OF MY OFFICIAL STATUS, I MEAN TO FULFILL THAT VOW!
SUDDENLY--
GREAT GUARDIANS--! WHAT IN THE GREAT GALAXIES ARE THOSE? THEY CAME FROM NOWHERE...
MAYBE I SHOULD TALK WITH THE ARROW BEFORE CHASING OFF LIKE THIS--
I'VE A HUNCH I'M GOING AFTER PART OF HIS PROBLEM!
BUT I CAN'T JUST LET A COUPLE OF MONSTERS FLAP AROUND LOOSE!
5

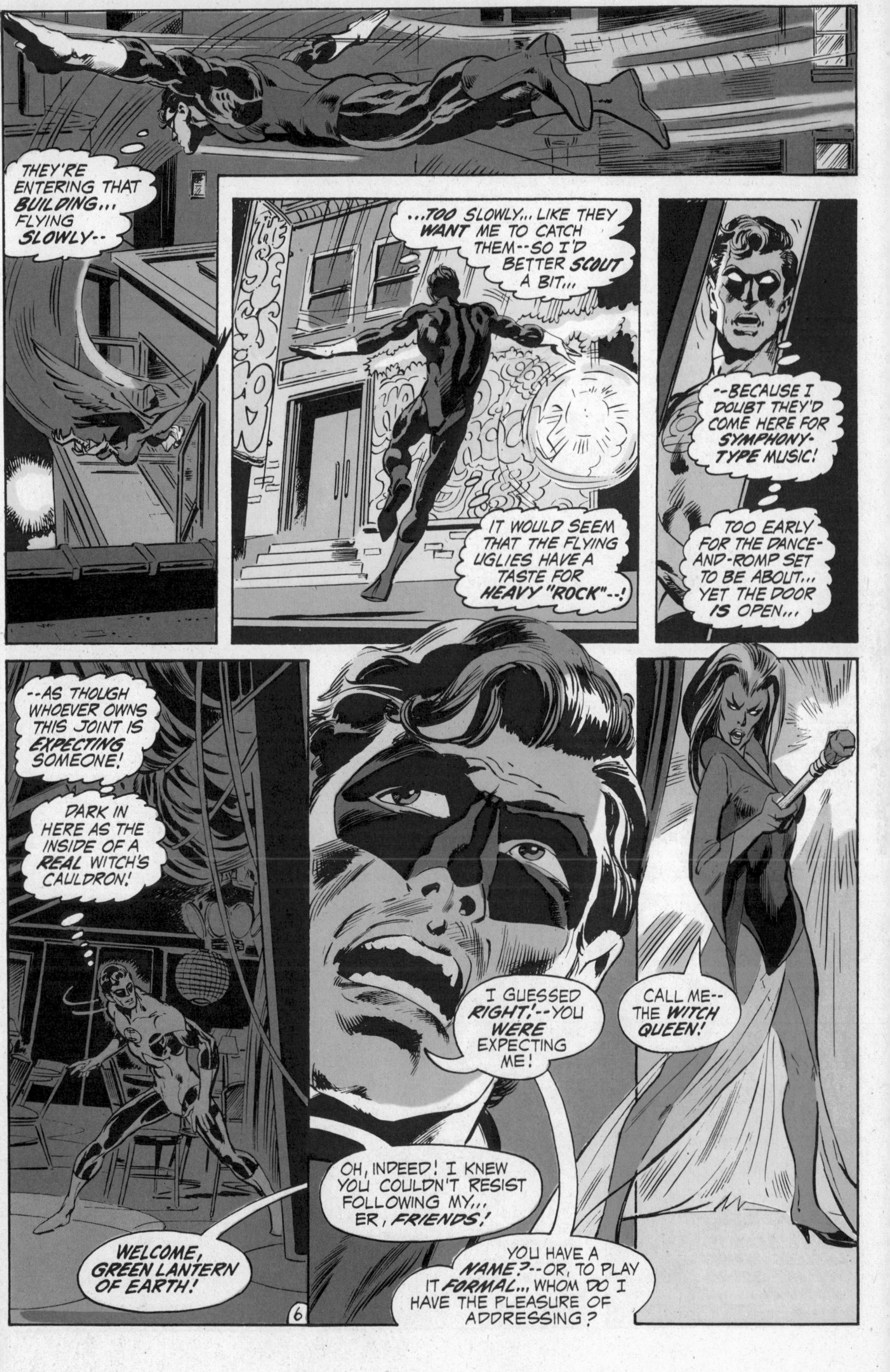

THEY'RE ENTERING THAT BUILDING... FLYING SLOWLY--
...TOO SLOWLY... LIKE THEY WANT ME TO CATCH THEM--SO I'D BETTER SCOUT A BIT...
IT WOULD SEEM THAT THE FLYING UGLIES HAVE A TASTE FOR HEAVY "ROCK"--!
--BECAUSE I DOUBT THEY'D COME HERE FOR SYMPHONY-TYPE MUSIC!
TOO EARLY FOR THE DANCE-AND-ROMP SET TO BE ABOUT... YET THE DOOR IS OPEN...
--AS THOUGH WHOEVER OWNS THIS JOINT IS EXPECTING SOMEONE!
DARK IN HERE AS THE INSIDE OF A REAL WITCH'S CAULDRON!
WELCOME, GREEN LANTERN OF EARTH!
6
I GUESSED RIGHT!--YOU WERE EXPECTING ME!
OH, INDEED! I KNEW YOU COULDN'T RESIST FOLLOWING MY... ER, FRIENDS!
YOU HAVE A NAME?--OR, TO PLAY IT FORMAL... WHOM DO I HAVE THE PLEASURE OF ADDRESSING?
CALL ME--THE WITCH QUEEN!

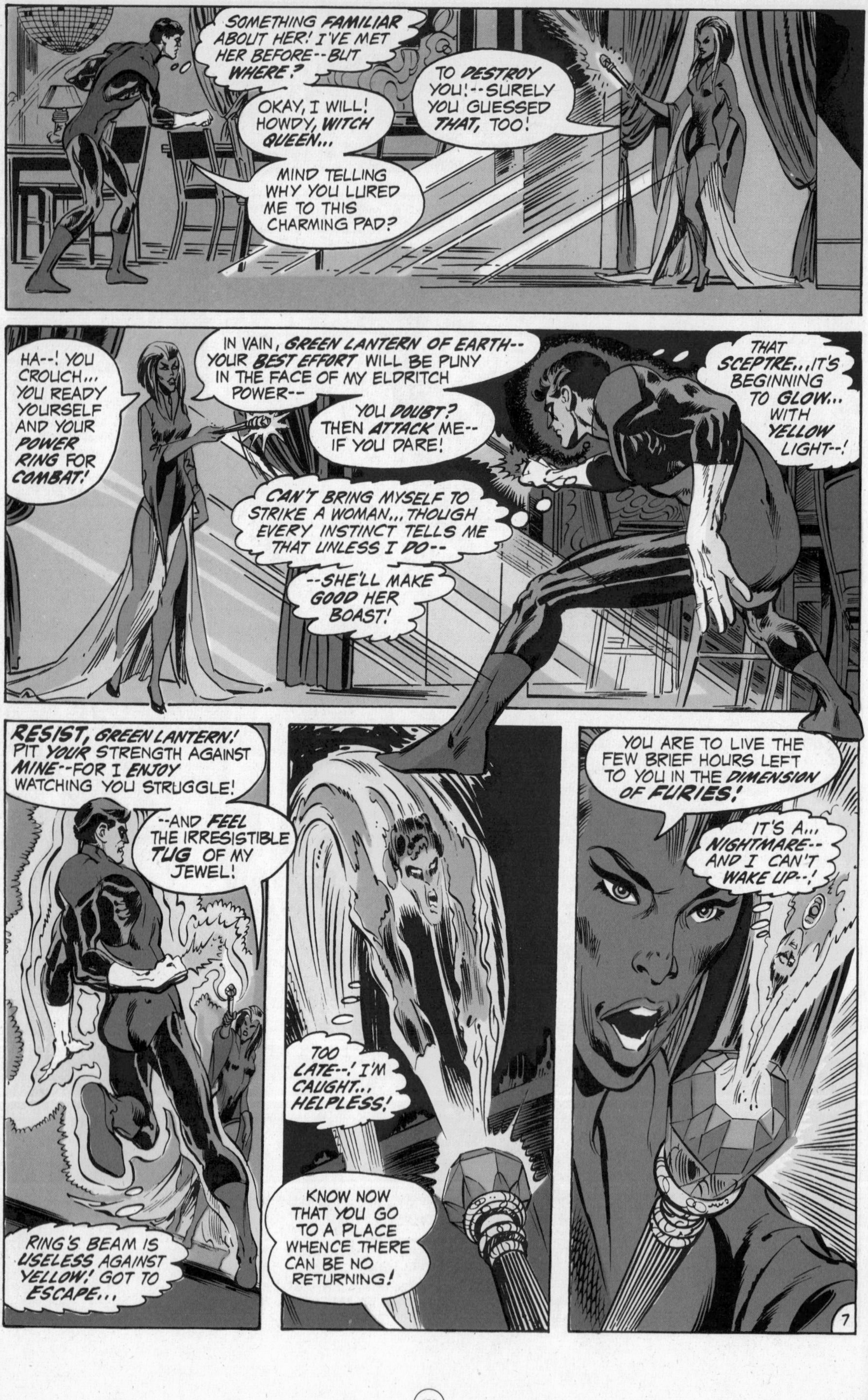
SOMETHING FAMILIAR ABOUT HER! I'VE MET HER BEFORE--BUT WHERE?
OKAY, I WILL! HOWDY, WITCH QUEEN...
MIND TELLING WHY YOU LURED ME TO THIS CHARMING PAD?
TO DESTROY YOU!--SURELY YOU GUESSED THAT, TOO!
HA--! YOU CROUCH... YOU READY YOURSELF AND YOUR POWER RING FOR COMBAT!
IN VAIN, GREEN LANTERN OF EARTH--YOUR BEST EFFORT WILL BE PUNY IN THE FACE OF MY ELDRITCH POWER--
YOU DOUBT? THEN ATTACK ME--IF YOU DARE!
THAT SCEPTRE...IT'S BEGINNING TO GLOW... WITH YELLOW LIGHT--!
CAN'T BRING MYSELF TO STRIKE A WOMAN...THOUGH EVERY INSTINCT TELLS ME THAT UNLESS I DO--
--SHE'LL MAKE GOOD HER BOAST!
RESIST, GREEN LANTERN! PIT YOUR STRENGTH AGAINST MINE--FOR I ENJOY WATCHING YOU STRUGGLE!
--AND FEEL THE IRRESISTIBLE TUG OF MY JEWEL!
RING'S BEAM IS USELESS AGAINST YELLOW! GOT TO ESCAPE...
TOO LATE--! I'M CAUGHT... HELPLESS!
KNOW NOW THAT YOU GO TO A PLACE WHENCE THERE CAN BE NO RETURNING!
YOU ARE TO LIVE THE FEW BRIEF HOURS LEFT TO YOU IN THE DIMENSION OF FURIES!
IT'S A... NIGHTMARE--AND I CAN'T WAKE UP--!
7

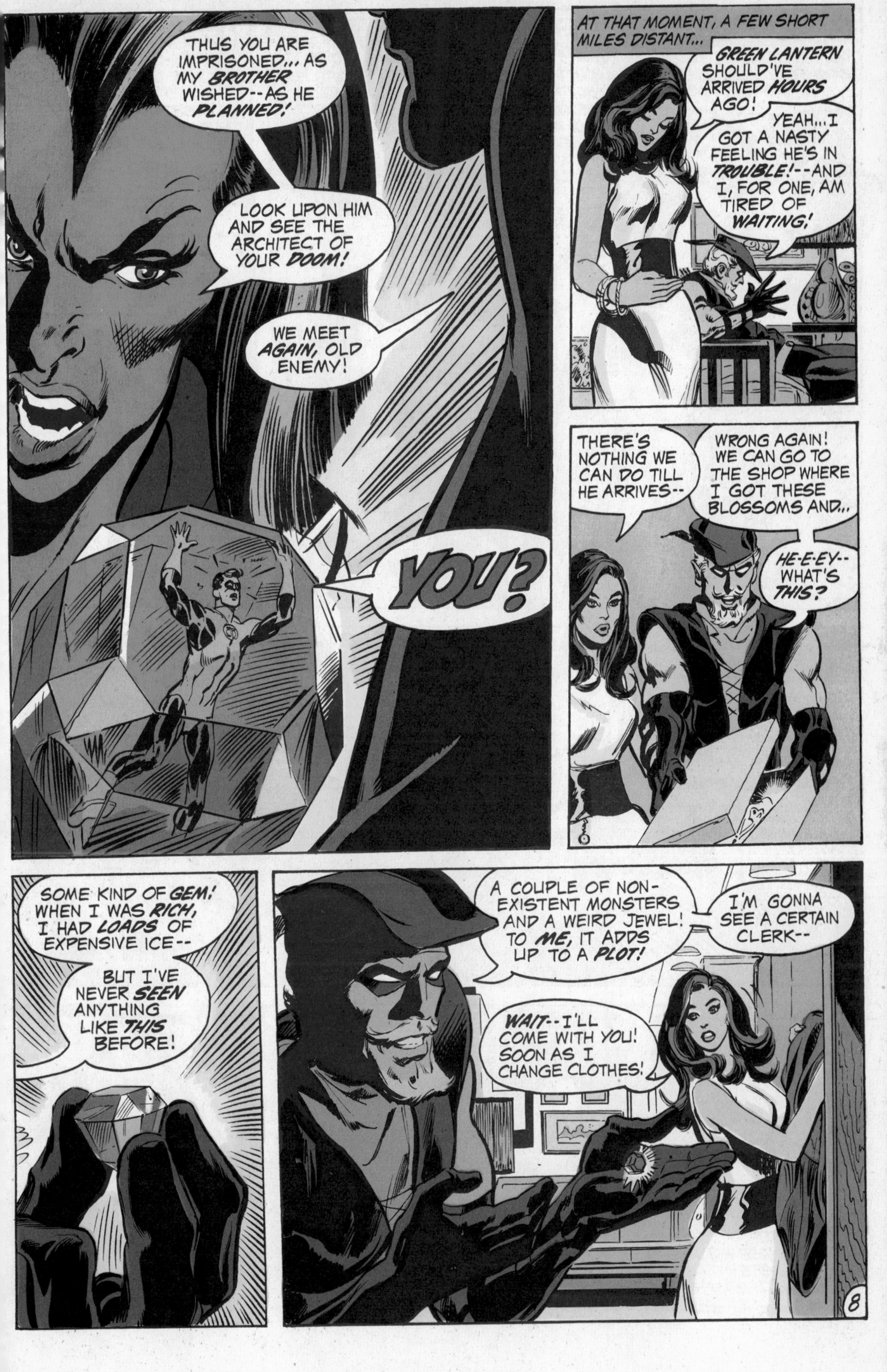
THUS YOU ARE IMPRISONED... AS MY BROTHER WISHED--AS HE PLANNED!
LOOK UPON HIM AND SEE THE ARCHITECT OF YOUR DOOM!
WE MEET AGAIN, OLD ENEMY!
YOU?
AT THAT MOMENT, A FEW SHORT MILES DISTANT...
GREEN LANTERN SHOULD'VE ARRIVED HOURS AGO!
YEAH...I GOT A NASTY FEELING HE'S IN TROUBLE!--AND I, FOR ONE, AM TIRED OF WAITING!
THERE'S NOTHING WE CAN DO TILL HE ARRIVES--
WRONG AGAIN! WE CAN GO TO THE SHOP WHERE I GOT THESE BLOSSOMS AND...
HE-E-EY--WHAT'S THIS?
SOME KIND OF GEM! WHEN I WAS RICH, I HAD LOADS OF EXPENSIVE ICE--
BUT I'VE NEVER SEEN ANYTHING LIKE THIS BEFORE!
A COUPLE OF NON-EXISTENT MONSTERS AND A WEIRD JEWEL! TO ME, IT ADDS UP TO A PLOT!
I'M GONNA SEE A CERTAIN CLERK--
WAIT--I'LL COME WITH YOU! SOON AS I CHANGE CLOTHES!
8

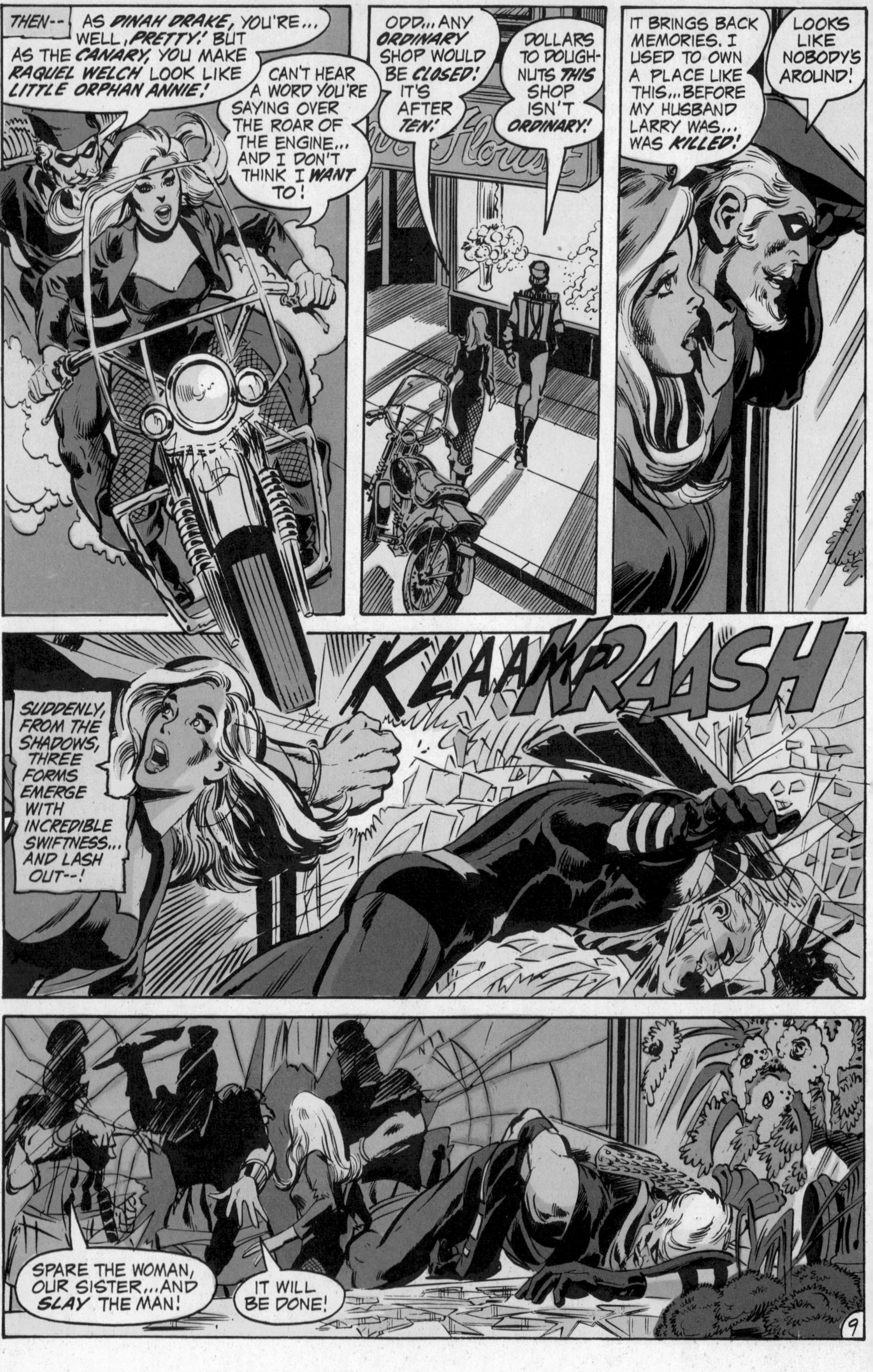
THEN--
AS DINAH DRAKE, YOU'RE... WELL, PRETTY! BUT AS THE CANARY, YOU MAKE RAQUEL WELCH LOOK LIKE LITTLE ORPHAN ANNIE!
CAN'T HEAR A WORD YOU'RE SAYING OVER THE ROAR OF THE ENGINE... AND I DON'T THINK I WANT TO!
ODD... ANY ORDINARY SHOP WOULD BE CLOSED! IT'S AFTER TEN!
DOLLARS TO DOUGH-NUTS THIS SHOP ISN'T ORDINARY!
IT BRINGS BACK MEMORIES. I USED TO OWN A PLACE LIKE THIS... BEFORE MY HUSBAND LARRY WAS... WAS KILLED!
LOOKS LIKE NOBODY'S AROUND!
KLAAKRAASH
SUDDENLY, FROM THE SHADOWS, THREE FORMS EMERGE WITH INCREDIBLE SWIFTNESS... AND LASH OUT--!
SPARE THE WOMAN, OUR SISTER... AND SLAY THE MAN!
IT WILL BE DONE!
9

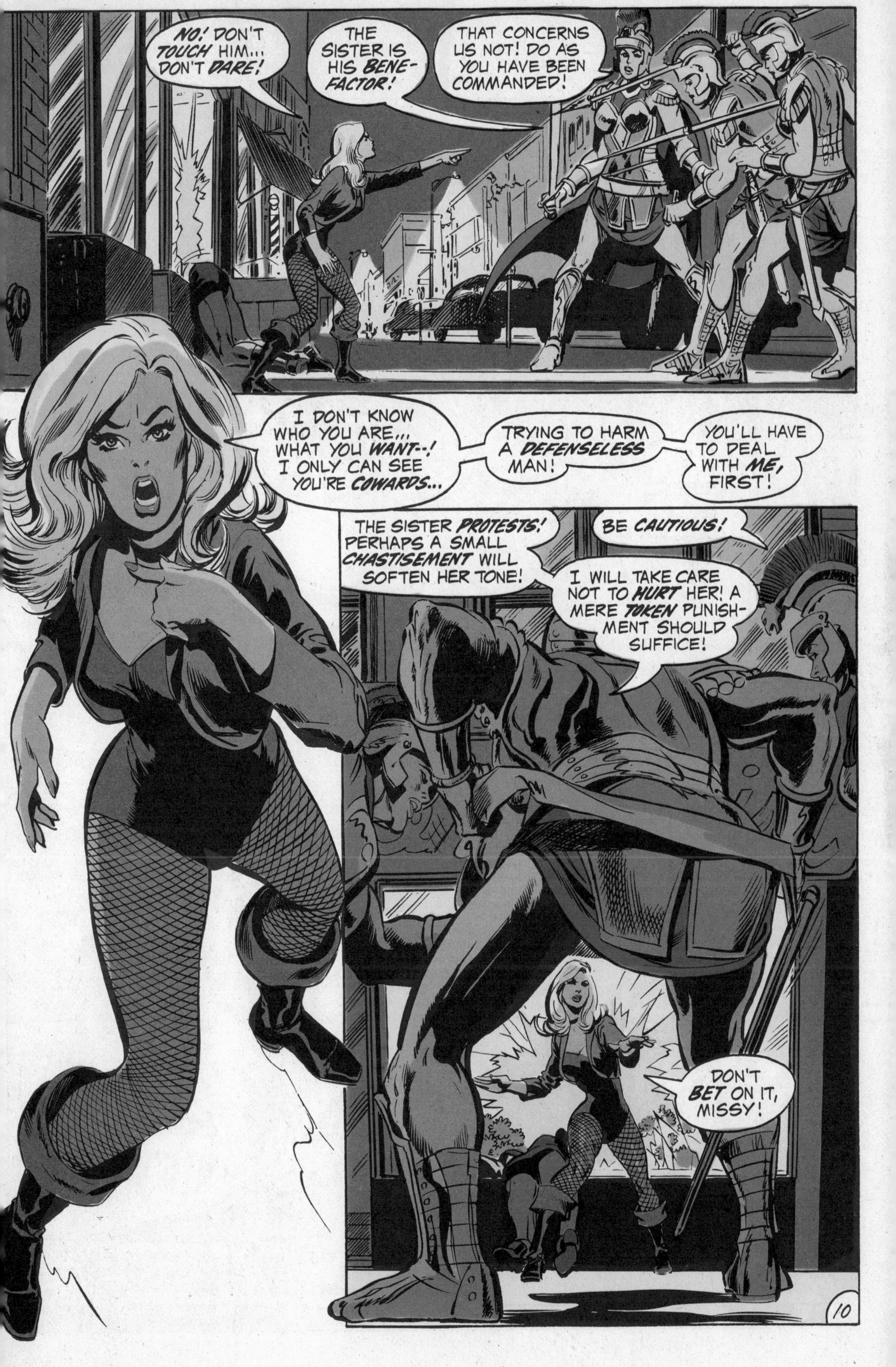

NO! DON'T TOUCH HIM... DON'T DARE!
THE SISTER IS HIS BENE-FACTOR!
THAT CONCERNS US NOT! DO AS YOU HAVE BEEN COMMANDED!
I DON'T KNOW WHO YOU ARE... WHAT YOU WANT--! I ONLY CAN SEE YOU'RE COWARDS...
TRYING TO HARM A DEFENSELESS MAN!
YOU'LL HAVE TO DEAL WITH ME, FIRST!
THE SISTER PROTESTS! PERHAPS A SMALL CHASTISEMENT WILL SOFTEN HER TONE!
BE CAUTIOUS!
I WILL TAKE CARE NOT TO HURT HER! A MERE TOKEN PUNISH-MENT SHOULD SUFFICE!
DON'T BET ON IT, MISSY!
10

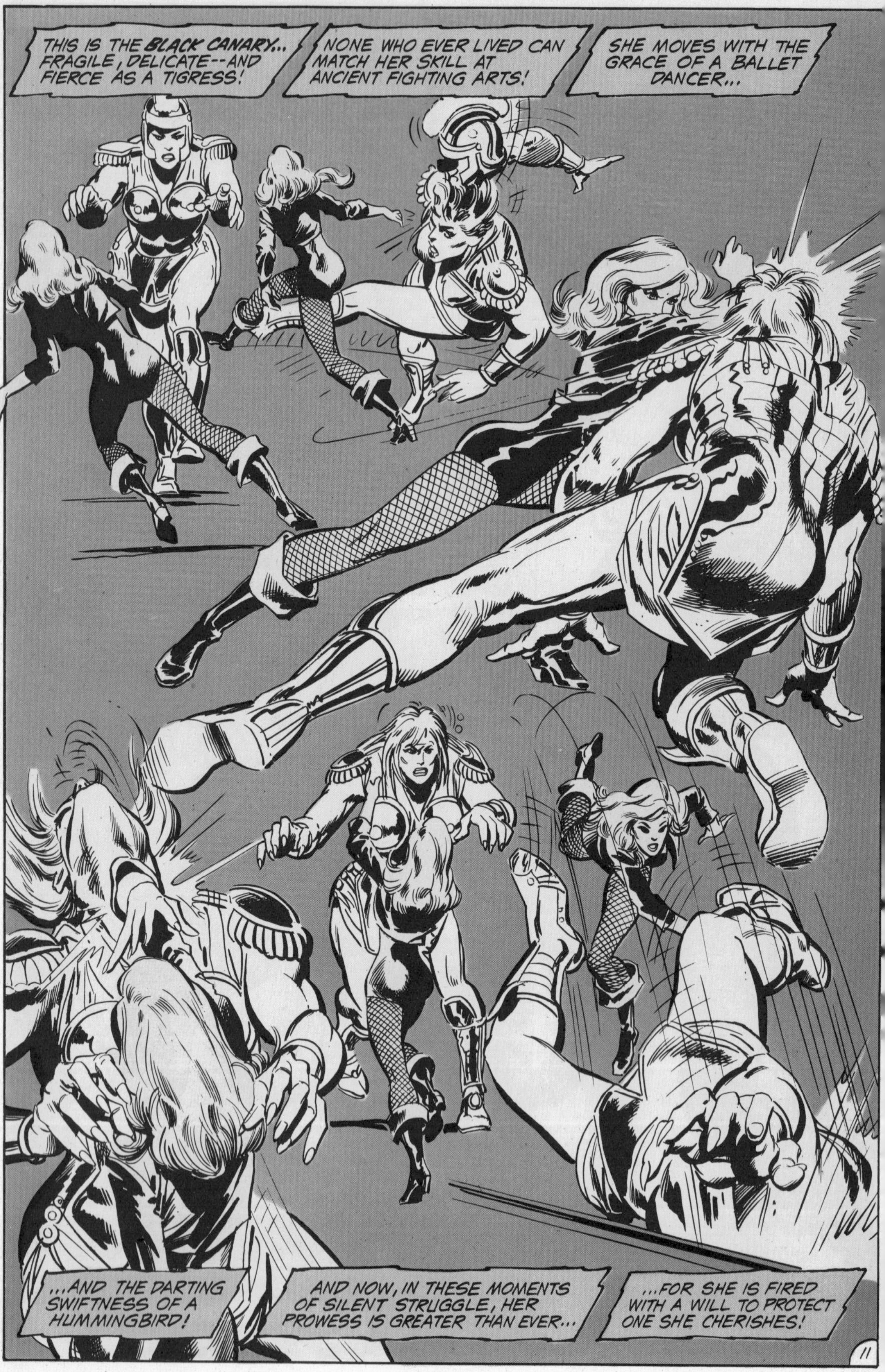
THIS IS THE BLACK CANARY... FRAGILE, DELICATE--AND FIERCE AS A TIGRESS!
NONE WHO EVER LIVED CAN MATCH HER SKILL AT ANCIENT FIGHTING ARTS!
SHE MOVES WITH THE GRACE OF A BALLET DANCER...
...AND THE DARTING SWIFTNESS OF A HUMMINGBIRD!
AND NOW, IN THESE MOMENTS OF SILENT STRUGGLE, HER PROWESS IS GREATER THAN EVER...
...FOR SHE IS FIRED WITH A WILL TO PROTECT ONE SHE CHERISHES!
11

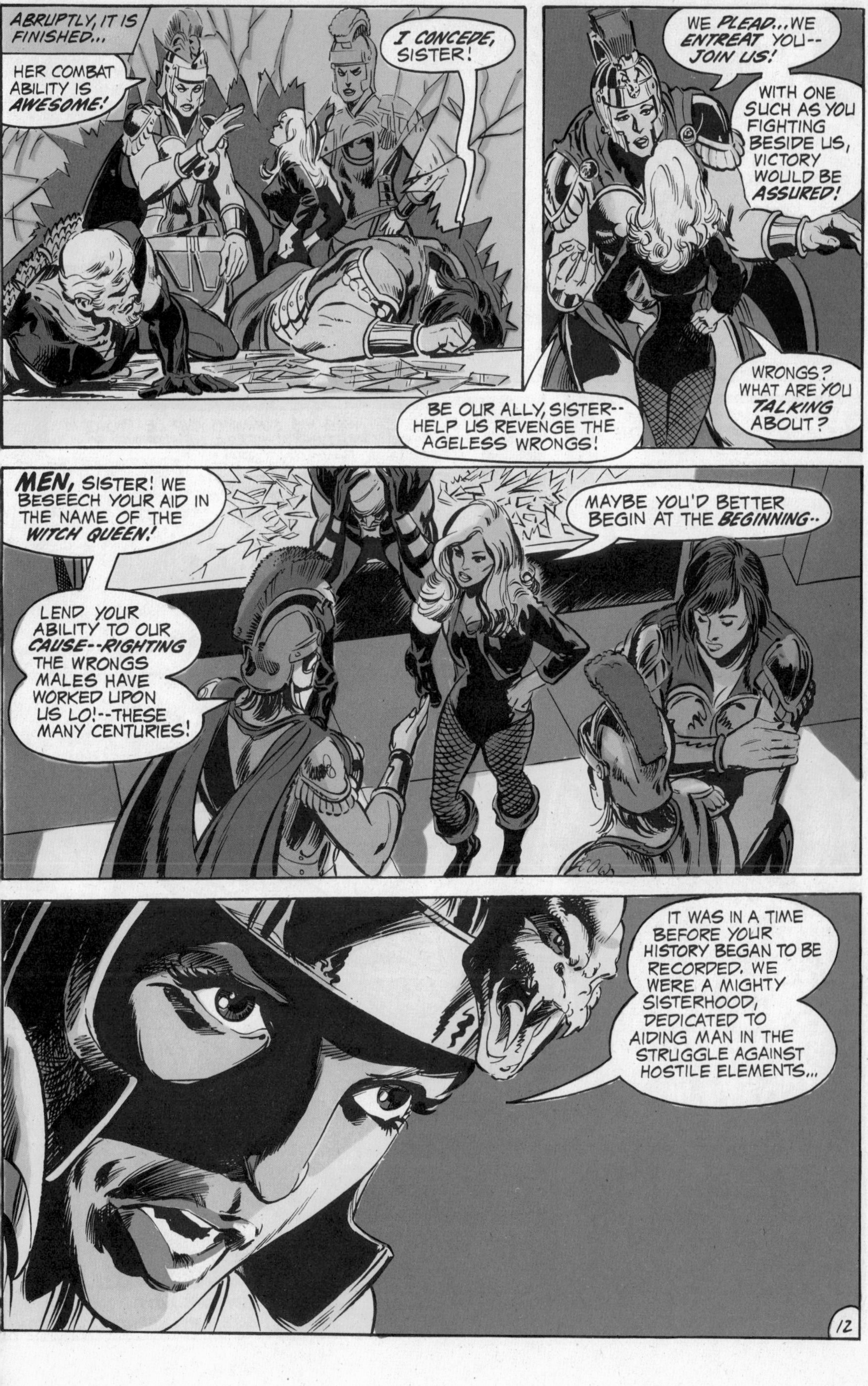
ABRUPTLY, IT IS FINISHED...
HER COMBAT ABILITY IS AWESOME!
I CONCEDE, SISTER!
WE PLEAD...WE ENTREAT YOU-- JOIN US!
WITH ONE SUCH AS YOU FIGHTING BESIDE US, VICTORY WOULD BE ASSURED!
BE OUR ALLY, SISTER-- HELP US REVENGE THE AGELESS WRONGS!
WRONGS? WHAT ARE YOU TALKING ABOUT?
MEN, SISTER! WE BESEECH YOUR AID IN THE NAME OF THE WITCH QUEEN!
LEND YOUR ABILITY TO OUR CAUSE--RIGHTING THE WRONGS MALES HAVE WORKED UPON US LO!--THESE MANY CENTURIES!
MAYBE YOU'D BETTER BEGIN AT THE BEGINNING..
IT WAS IN A TIME BEFORE YOUR HISTORY BEGAN TO BE RECORDED. WE WERE A MIGHTY SISTERHOOD, DEDICATED TO AIDING MAN IN THE STRUGGLE AGAINST HOSTILE ELEMENTS...
12

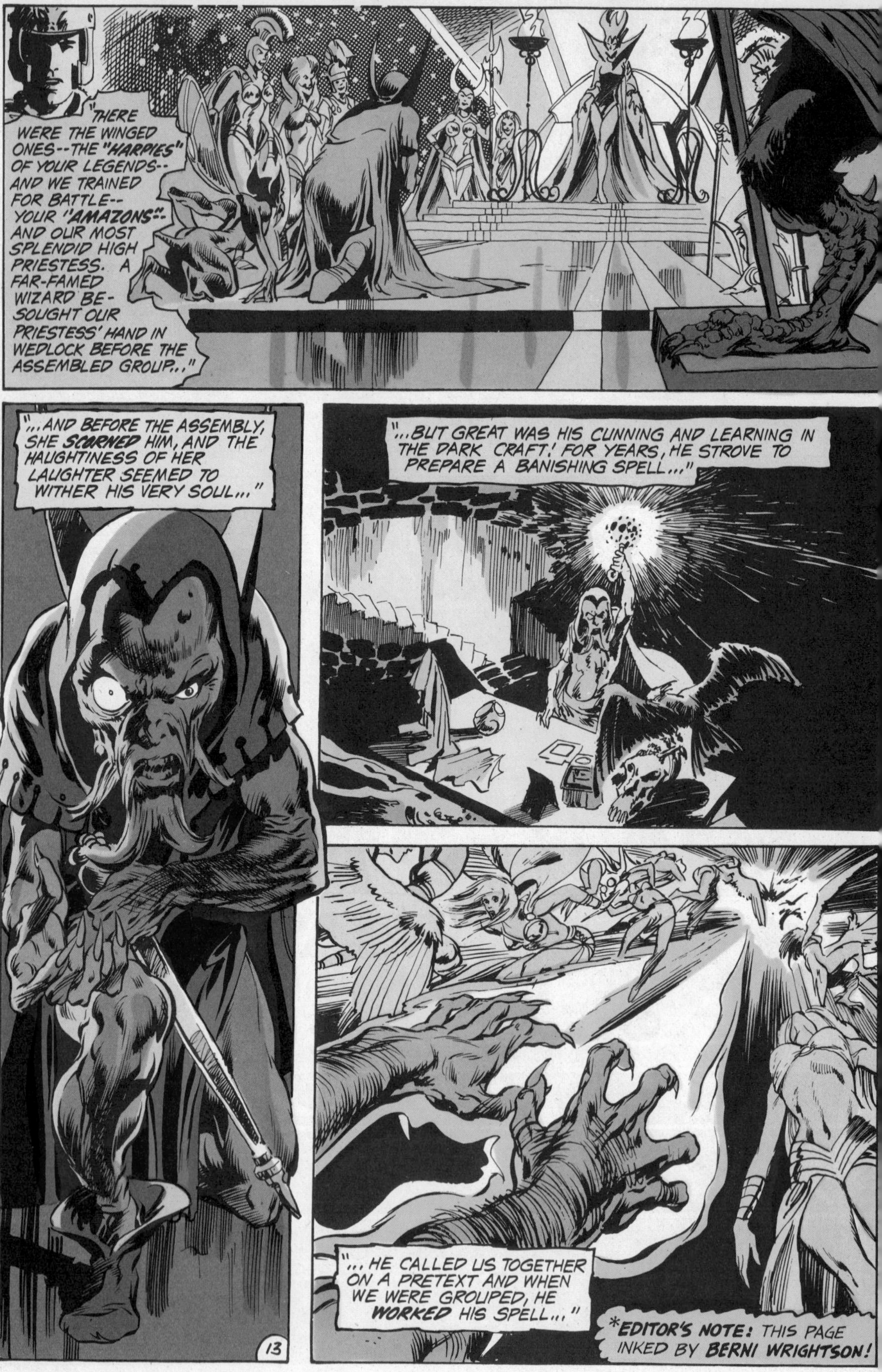
"THERE WERE THE WINGED ONES--THE "HARPIES" OF YOUR LEGENDS-- AND WE TRAINED FOR BATTLE-- YOUR "AMAZONS"*-- AND OUR MOST SPLENDID HIGH PRIESTESS. A FAR-FAMED WIZARD BE-SOUGHT OUR PRIESTESS' HAND IN WEDLOCK BEFORE THE ASSEMBLED GROUP..."
"...AND BEFORE THE ASSEMBLY, SHE SCORNED HIM, AND THE HAUGHTINESS OF HER LAUGHTER SEEMED TO WITHER HIS VERY SOUL..."
"...BUT GREAT WAS HIS CUNNING AND LEARNING IN THE DARK CRAFT! FOR YEARS, HE STROVE TO PREPARE A BANISHING SPELL..."
"...HE CALLED US TOGETHER ON A PRETEXT AND WHEN WE WERE GROUPED, HE WORKED HIS SPELL..."
*EDITOR'S NOTE: THIS PAGE INKED BY BERNI WRIGHTSON!
13

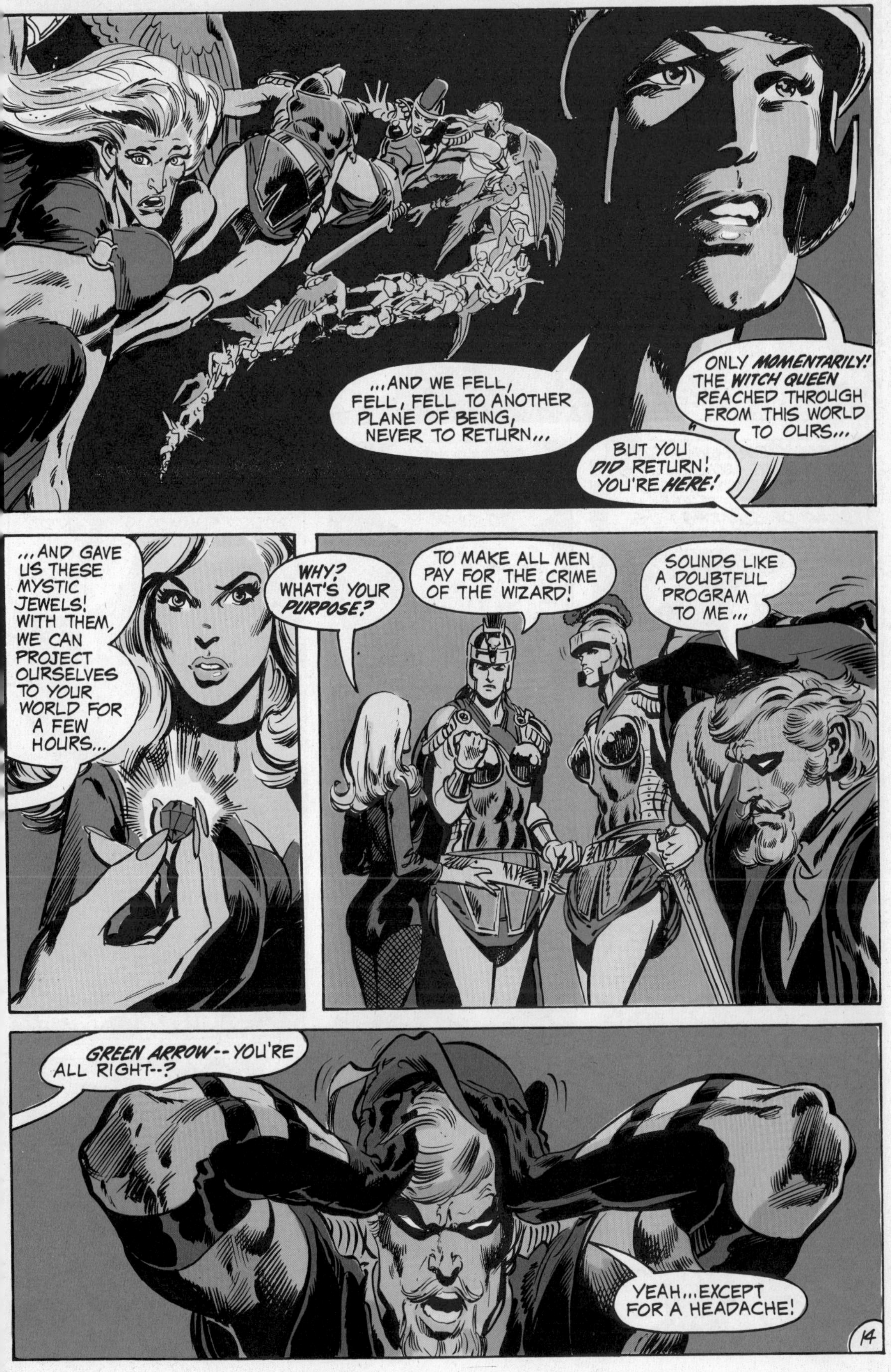
...AND WE FELL, FELL, FELL TO ANOTHER PLANE OF BEING, NEVER TO RETURN...
ONLY MOMENTARILY! THE WITCH QUEEN REACHED THROUGH FROM THIS WORLD TO OURS...
BUT YOU DID RETURN! YOU'RE HERE!
...AND GAVE US THESE MYSTIC JEWELS! WITH THEM, WE CAN PROJECT OURSELVES TO YOUR WORLD FOR A FEW HOURS...
WHY? WHAT'S YOUR PURPOSE?
TO MAKE ALL MEN PAY FOR THE CRIME OF THE WIZARD!
SOUNDS LIKE A DOUBTFUL PROGRAM TO ME...
GREEN ARROW--YOU'RE ALL RIGHT--?
YEAH...EXCEPT FOR A HEADACHE!
14

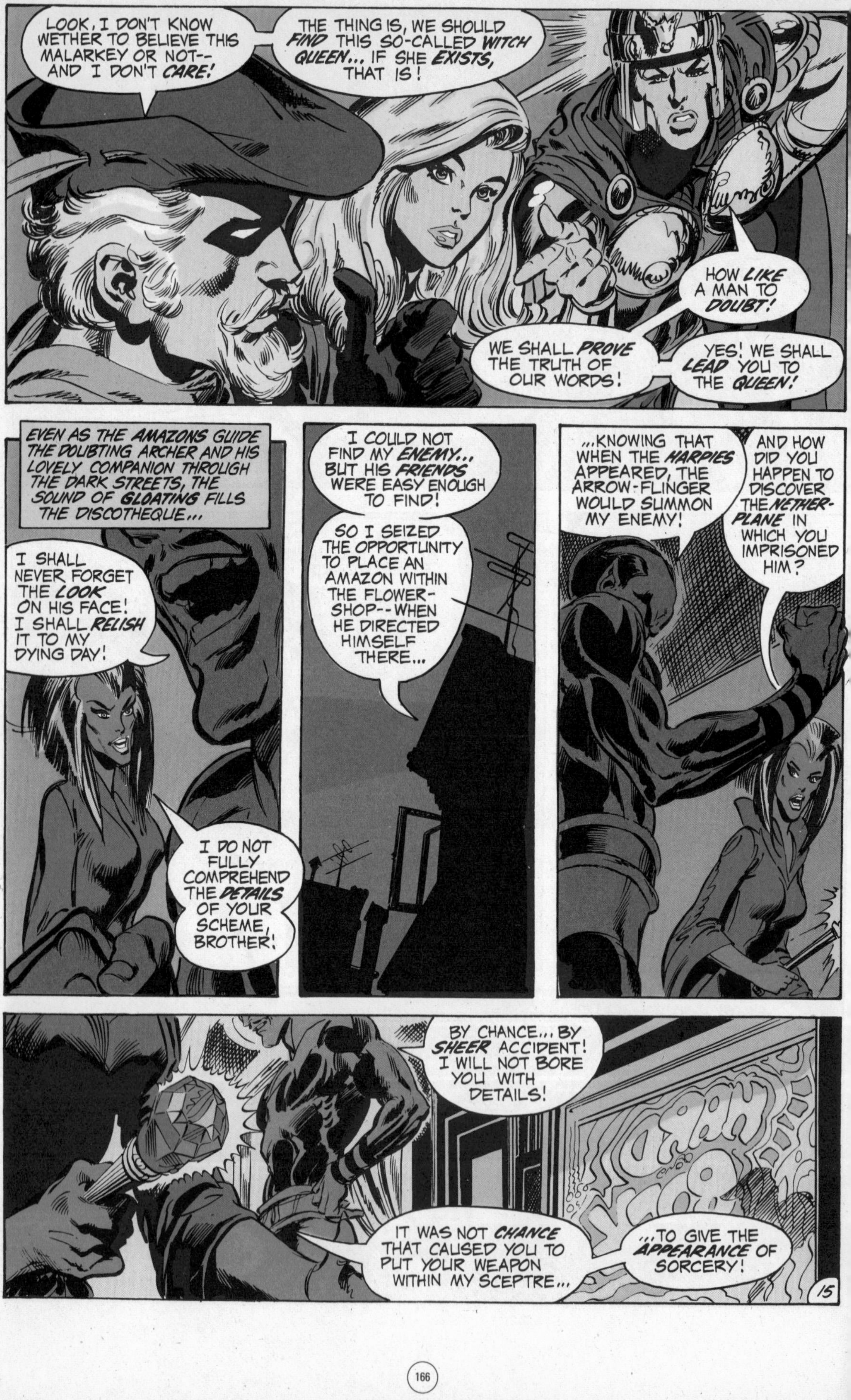
LOOK, I DON'T KNOW WETHER TO BELIEVE THIS MALARKEY OR NOT-- AND I DON'T CARE!
THE THING IS, WE SHOULD FIND THIS SO-CALLED WITCH QUEEN... IF SHE EXISTS, THAT IS!
HOW LIKE A MAN TO DOUBT!
WE SHALL PROVE THE TRUTH OF OUR WORDS!
YES! WE SHALL LEAD YOU TO THE QUEEN!
EVEN AS THE AMAZONS GUIDE THE DOUBTING ARCHER AND HIS LOVELY COMPANION THROUGH THE DARK STREETS, THE SOUND OF GLOATING FILLS THE DISCOTHEQUE...
I SHALL NEVER FORGET THE LOOK ON HIS FACE! I SHALL RELISH IT TO MY DYING DAY!
I DO NOT FULLY COMPREHEND THE DETAILS OF YOUR SCHEME, BROTHER!
I COULD NOT FIND MY ENEMY... BUT HIS FRIENDS WERE EASY ENOUGH TO FIND!
SO I SEIZED THE OPPORTUNITY TO PLACE AN AMAZON WITHIN THE FLOWER-SHOP--WHEN HE DIRECTED HIMSELF THERE...
...KNOWING THAT WHEN THE HARPIES APPEARED, THE ARROW-FLINGER WOULD SUMMON MY ENEMY!
AND HOW DID YOU HAPPEN TO DISCOVER THE NETHER-PLANE IN WHICH YOU IMPRISONED HIM?
BY CHANCE... BY SHEER ACCIDENT! I WILL NOT BORE YOU WITH DETAILS!
IT WAS NOT CHANCE THAT CAUSED YOU TO PUT YOUR WEAPON WITHIN MY SCEPTRE...
...TO GIVE THE APPEARANCE OF SORCERY!
15

NO... THAT WAS CLEVERNESS! I COUNTED ON MY FOE'S BEWILDERMENT...

PERHAPS YOU HAD BEST TAKE IT BACK!

UH-UH, LADY... IT LOOKS BETTER ON YOU!

--THE ARCHER! QUICKLY, MY BROTHER... USE YOUR WEAPON!

SKLAAASH

I HAVE IT... MY RING! HIS SHAFTS ARE NOTHING AGAINST IT!

THINK NOT? OKAY, WE'LL SEE!

NO EYE CAN FOLLOW GREEN ARROW'S HAND AS IT REACHES INTO HIS QUIVER, SELECTS AN ARROW BY TOUCH AND FITS IT TO BOWSTRING!

THERE IS THE TWANG OF THE STRING, BUT BEFORE ANY HEARS THAT SOUND, THE SHAFT IS ALREADY SPEEDING TOWARD THE TARGET--!

16

SINESTRO: YOU'RE CALLED *SINESTRO,* I BELIEVE... THE *RENEGADE* MEMBER OF THE *GREEN LANTERN CORPS!*

GREEN ARROW: FAIR'S FAIR... I WON'T USE MY *BOW* EITHER!

SINESTRO: I DO NOT *NEED* MY RING TO HUMBLE A PUNY *EARTHLING!*

WOMAN: YOU *STRUCK* HIM... WITH YOUR *FIST?* YOU HIT MY *BROTHER?!*

GREEN ARROW: IT WAS ONLY A *TAP,* DEARIE... MUSTN'T GET *EXCITED!*

GREEN ARROW: *BEE-YOU-TI-FUL,* PRETTY BIRD! THAT'S THE *SECOND* TIME TONIGHT YOU'VE SAVED MY HIDE!

BLACK CANARY: I'D DO IT FOR *ANYONE...* A STRAY CAT, A POLITICIAN-- JUST ANYONE AT ALL!

17

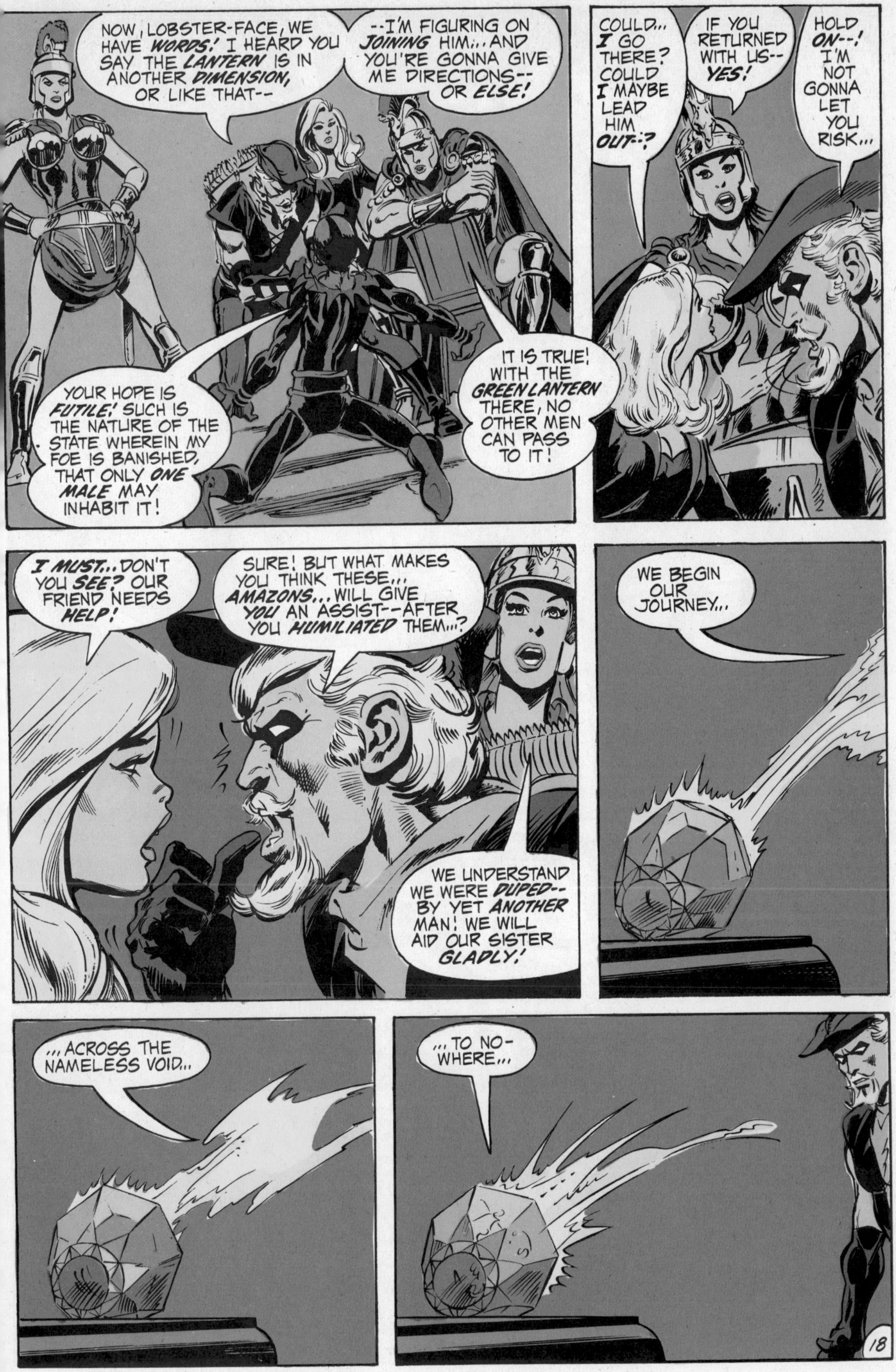

NOW, LOBSTER-FACE, WE HAVE WORDS! I HEARD YOU SAY THE LANTERN IS IN ANOTHER DIMENSION, OR LIKE THAT--
--I'M FIGURING ON JOINING HIM... AND YOU'RE GONNA GIVE ME DIRECTIONS-- OR ELSE!
YOUR HOPE IS FUTILE! SUCH IS THE NATURE OF THE STATE WHEREIN MY FOE IS BANISHED, THAT ONLY ONE MALE MAY INHABIT IT!
IT IS TRUE! WITH THE GREEN LANTERN THERE, NO OTHER MEN CAN PASS TO IT!
COULD... I GO THERE? COULD I MAYBE LEAD HIM OUT--?
IF YOU RETURNED WITH US-- YES!
HOLD ON--! I'M NOT GONNA LET YOU RISK...
I MUST... DON'T YOU SEE? OUR FRIEND NEEDS HELP!
SURE! BUT WHAT MAKES YOU THINK THESE... AMAZONS... WILL GIVE YOU AN ASSIST--AFTER YOU HUMILIATED THEM...?
WE UNDERSTAND WE WERE DUPED-- BY YET ANOTHER MAN! WE WILL AID OUR SISTER GLADLY!
WE BEGIN OUR JOURNEY...
...ACROSS THE NAMELESS VOID...
...TO NO-WHERE...
18

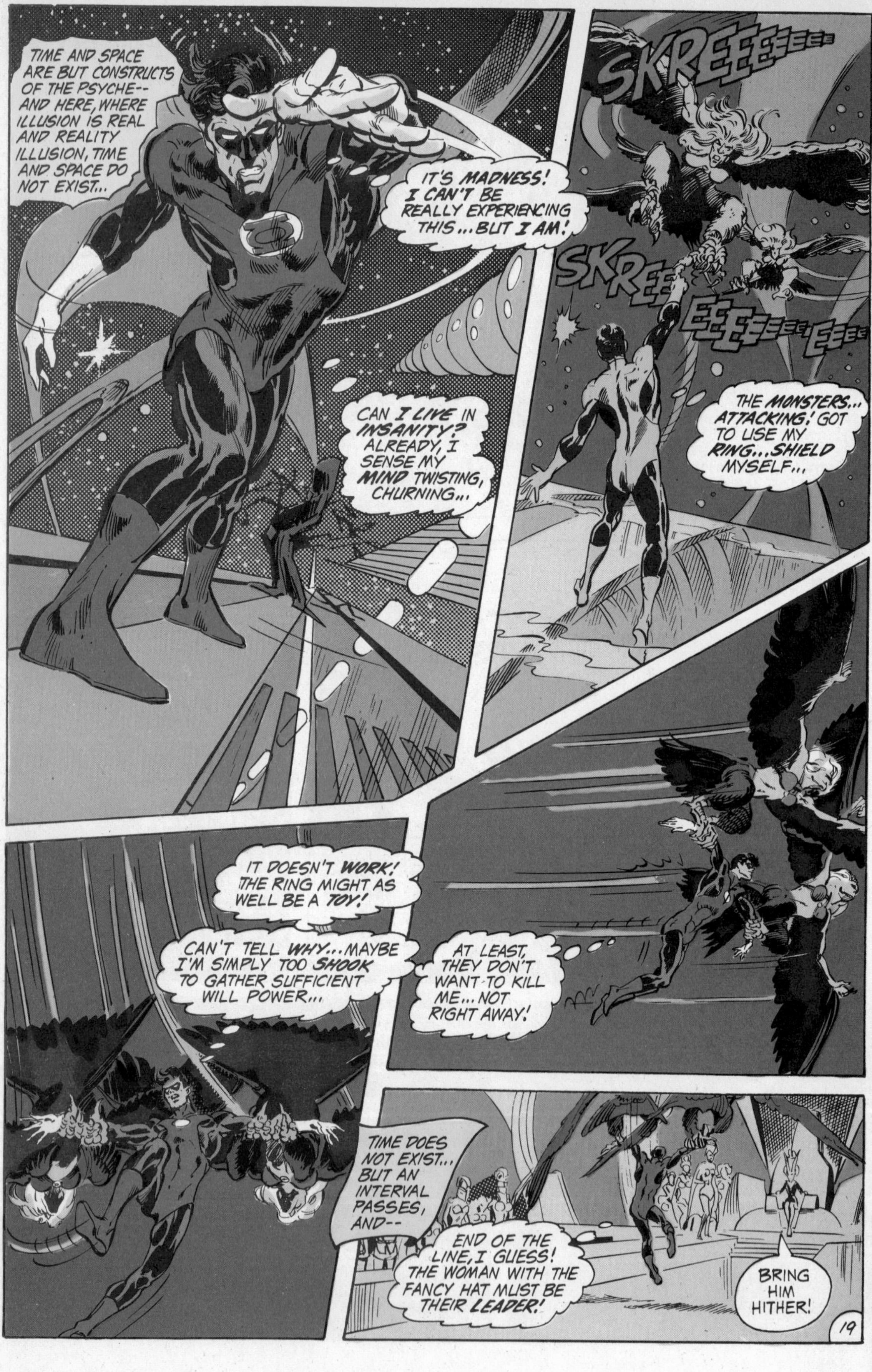
TIME AND SPACE ARE BUT CONSTRUCTS OF THE PSYCHE-- AND HERE, WHERE ILLUSION IS REAL AND REALITY ILLUSION, TIME AND SPACE DO NOT EXIST...
IT'S MADNESS! I CAN'T BE REALLY EXPERIENCING THIS... BUT I AM!
CAN I LIVE IN INSANITY? ALREADY, I SENSE MY MIND TWISTING, CHURNING...
SKREEEEEEE
SKREEEEEEEEEEEE
THE MONSTERS... ATTACKING! GOT TO USE MY RING... SHIELD MYSELF...
IT DOESN'T WORK! THE RING MIGHT AS WELL BE A TOY!
CAN'T TELL WHY... MAYBE I'M SIMPLY TOO SHOOK TO GATHER SUFFICIENT WILL POWER...
AT LEAST, THEY DON'T WANT TO KILL ME... NOT RIGHT AWAY!
TIME DOES NOT EXIST... BUT AN INTERVAL PASSES, AND--
END OF THE LINE, I GUESS! THE WOMAN WITH THE FANCY HAT MUST BE THEIR LEADER!
BRING HIM HITHER!
19

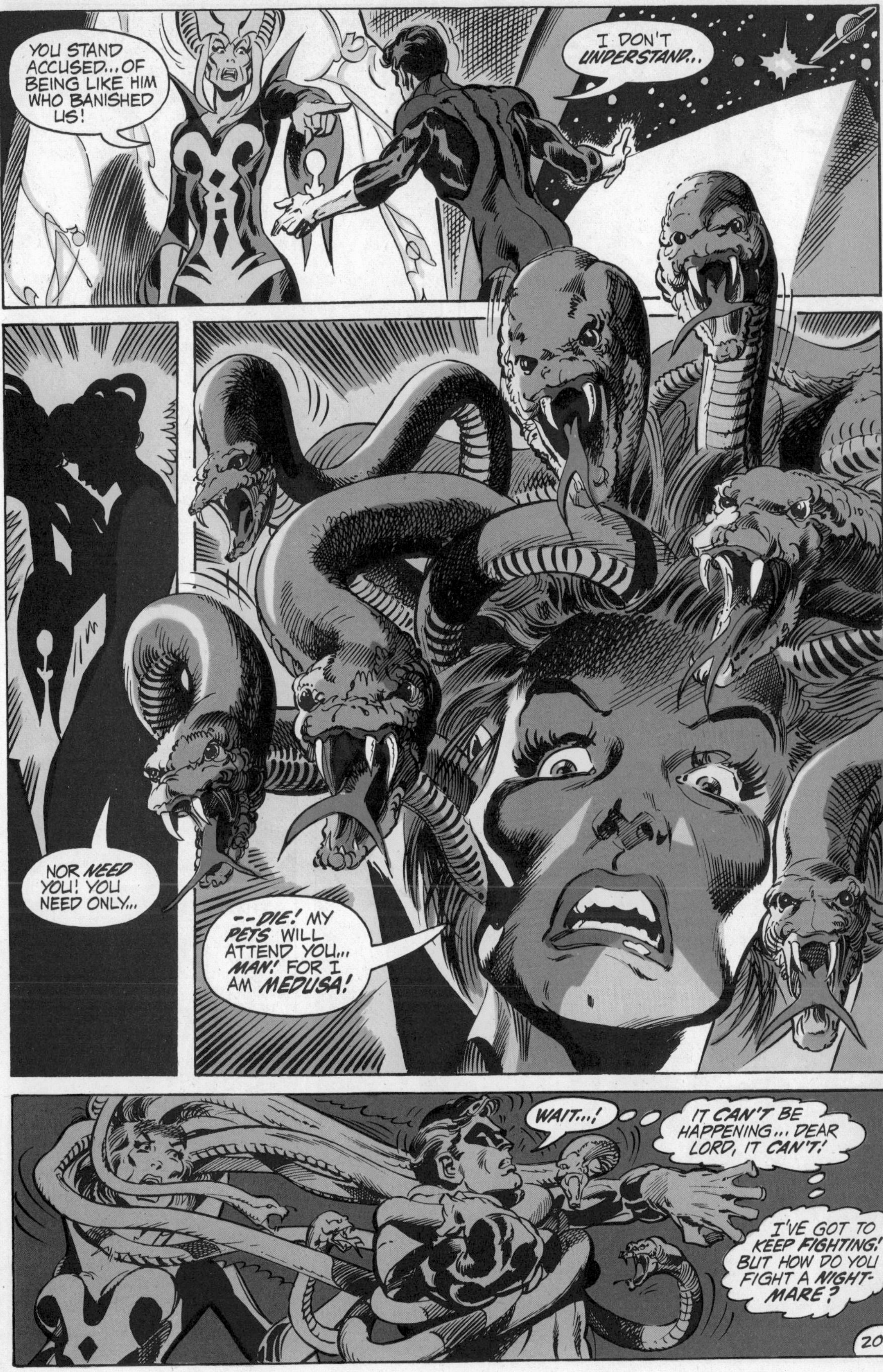
YOU STAND ACCUSED... OF BEING LIKE HIM WHO BANISHED US!
I DON'T UNDERSTAND...
NOR NEED YOU! YOU NEED ONLY...
--DIE! MY PETS WILL ATTEND YOU... MAN! FOR I AM MEDUSA!
WAIT...!
IT CAN'T BE HAPPENING... DEAR LORD, IT CAN'T!
I'VE GOT TO KEEP FIGHTING! BUT HOW DO YOU FIGHT A NIGHT-MARE?
20

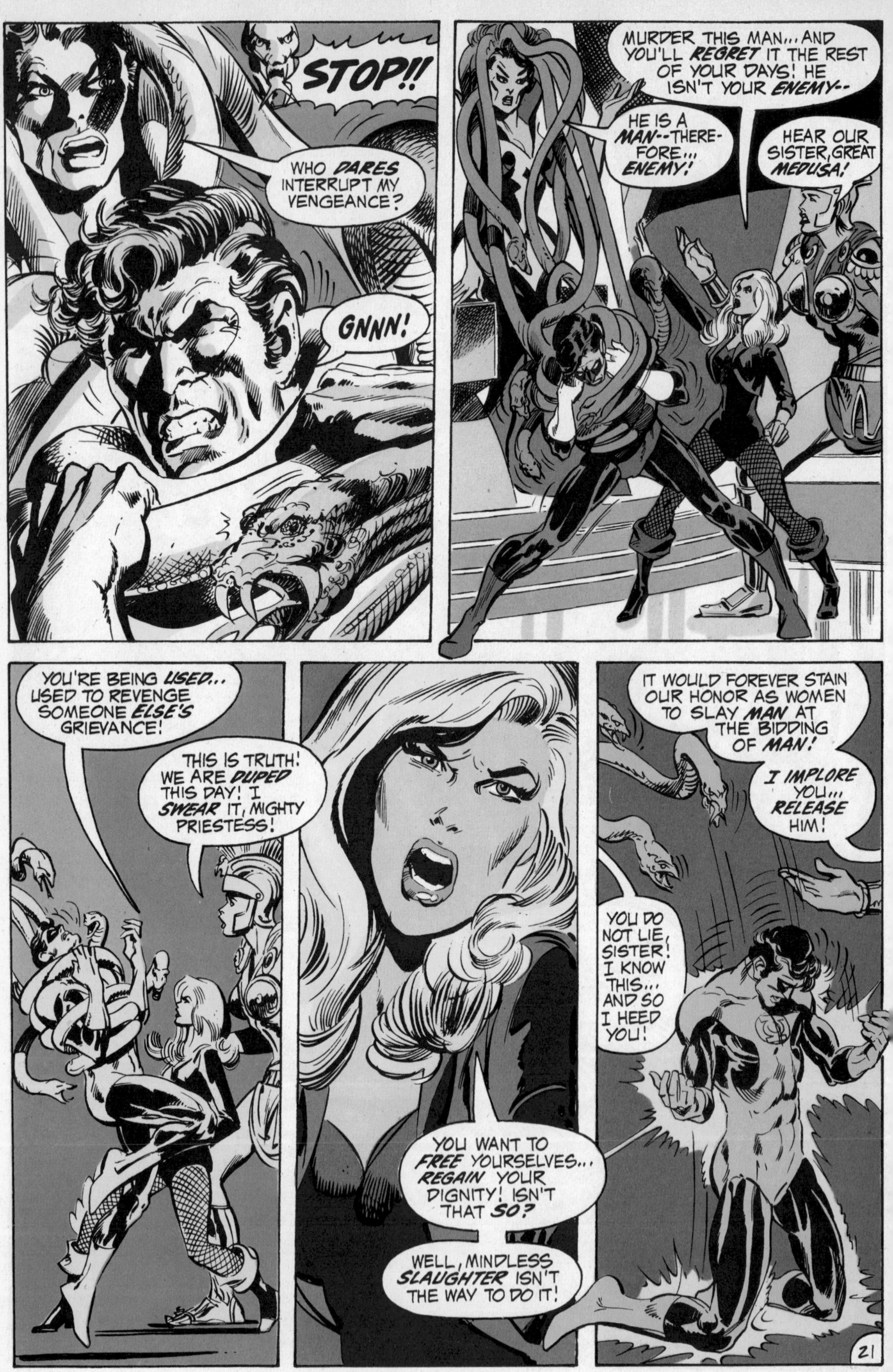
STOP!!
WHO DARES INTERRUPT MY VENGEANCE?
GNNN!
MURDER THIS MAN... AND YOU'LL REGRET IT THE REST OF YOUR DAYS! HE ISN'T YOUR ENEMY--
HE IS A MAN--THEREFORE... ENEMY!
HEAR OUR SISTER, GREAT MEDUSA!
YOU'RE BEING USED... USED TO REVENGE SOMEONE ELSE'S GRIEVANCE!
THIS IS TRUTH! WE ARE DUPED THIS DAY! I SWEAR IT, MIGHTY PRIESTESS!
YOU WANT TO FREE YOURSELVES... REGAIN YOUR DIGNITY! ISN'T THAT SO?
WELL, MINDLESS SLAUGHTER ISN'T THE WAY TO DO IT!
IT WOULD FOREVER STAIN OUR HONOR AS WOMEN TO SLAY MAN AT THE BIDDING OF MAN!
I IMPLORE YOU... RELEASE HIM!
YOU DO NOT LIE, SISTER! I KNOW THIS... AND SO I HEED YOU!
21

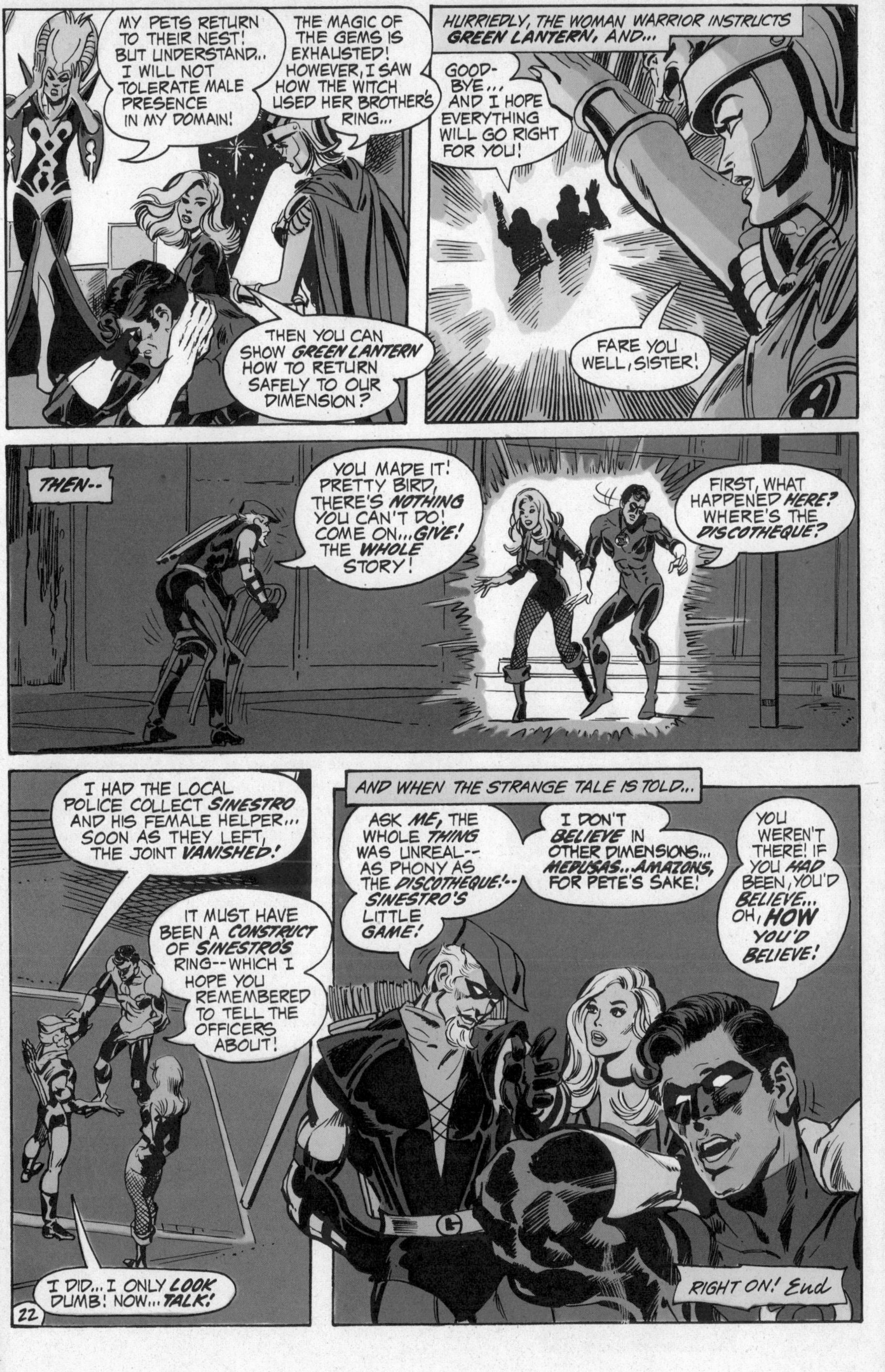
MY PETS RETURN TO THEIR NEST! BUT UNDERSTAND.. I WILL NOT TOLERATE MALE PRESENCE IN MY DOMAIN!
THE MAGIC OF THE GEMS IS EXHAUSTED! HOWEVER, I SAW HOW THE WITCH USED HER BROTHER'S RING...
THEN YOU CAN SHOW GREEN LANTERN HOW TO RETURN SAFELY TO OUR DIMENSION?
HURRIEDLY, THE WOMAN WARRIOR INSTRUCTS GREEN LANTERN, AND...
GOOD-BYE... AND I HOPE EVERYTHING WILL GO RIGHT FOR YOU!
FARE YOU WELL, SISTER!
THEN--
YOU MADE IT! PRETTY BIRD, THERE'S NOTHING YOU CAN'T DO! COME ON...GIVE! THE WHOLE STORY!
FIRST, WHAT HAPPENED HERE? WHERE'S THE DISCOTHEQUE?
I HAD THE LOCAL POLICE COLLECT SINESTRO AND HIS FEMALE HELPER... SOON AS THEY LEFT, THE JOINT VANISHED!
IT MUST HAVE BEEN A CONSTRUCT OF SINESTRO'S RING--WHICH I HOPE YOU REMEMBERED TO TELL THE OFFICERS ABOUT!
I DID... I ONLY LOOK DUMB! NOW... TALK!
22
AND WHEN THE STRANGE TALE IS TOLD...
ASK ME, THE WHOLE THING WAS UNREAL-- AS PHONY AS THE DISCOTHEQUE!-- SINESTRO'S LITTLE GAME!
I DON'T BELIEVE IN OTHER DIMENSIONS... MEDUSAS...AMAZONS, FOR PETE'S SAKE!
YOU WEREN'T THERE! IF YOU HAD BEEN, YOU'D BELIEVE... OH, HOW YOU'D BELIEVE!
RIGHT ON! End

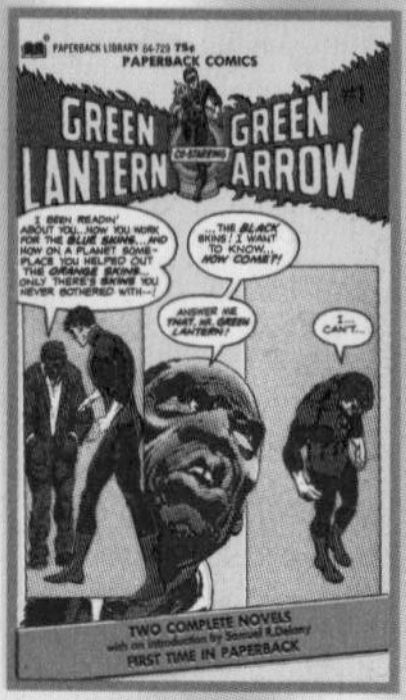
PAPERBACK COMICS
GREEN LANTERN
GREEN ARROW
YOU MUST PAY FOR WHAT THE WHITE MAN DID TO MY PEOPLE!
TWO COMPLETE NOVELS
FIRST TIME IN PAPERBACK

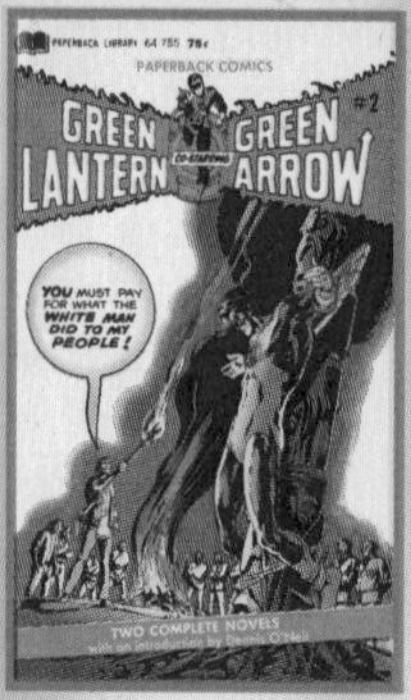
PAPERBACK COMICS
GREEN LANTERN
GREEN ARROW
#2
YOU MUST PAY FOR WHAT THE WHITE MAN DID TO MY PEOPLE!
TWO COMPLETE NOVELS

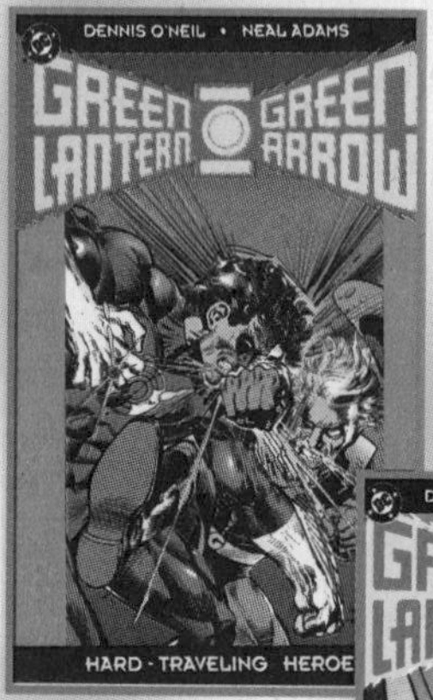
DENNIS O'NEIL • NEAL ADAMS
GREEN LANTERN
GREEN ARROW
HARD-TRAVELING HEROES

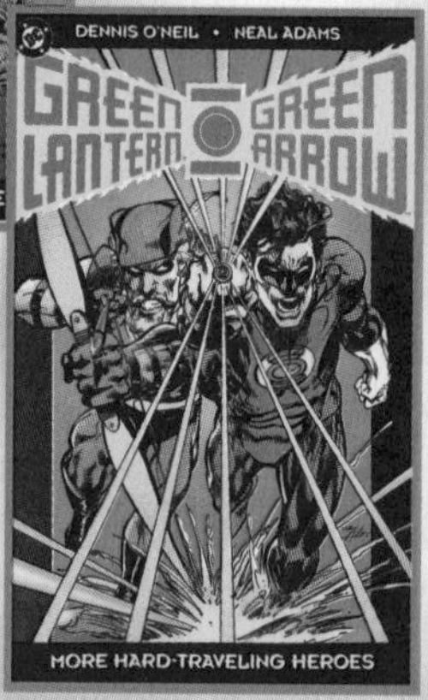
DENNIS O'NEIL • NEAL ADAMS
GREEN LANTERN
GREEN ARROW
MORE HARD-TRAVELING HEROES

Almost immediately, the media picked up on the sudden relevance in comic books. As a result, the Green Lantern/Green Arrow stories were written up frequently, long after the individual issues had sold out.

In what was a rarity in the early 1970s, Warner Books released two volumes collecting the stories in black and white.

After DC Comics helped build a market for trade collections in the wake of BATMAN: THE DARK KNIGHT RETURNS and THE WATCHMEN, these stories were among the most requested. Bowing to demand, the classic tales were collected yet again with new covers by Neal Adams. This is where the now familiar term "Hard-Traveling Heroes" was first coined.

The first story, "No Evil Shall Escape My Sight," has been printed seven times prior to this collection — which, while not a record, certainly speaks to its enduring quality.

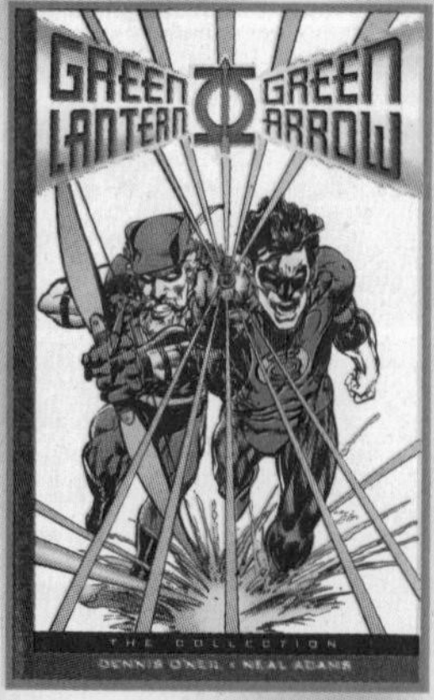
GREEN LANTERN
GREEN ARROW
THE COLLECTION
DENNIS O'NEIL • NEAL ADAMS

And finally, in 2000, DC put them all together in one deluxe slipcased edition which was a sell-out.

NEAL ADAMS

Born on June 6, 1941 in New York, Neal Adams began his career assisting on and occasionally pencilling the *Bat Masterson* syndicated comic strip. At the same time, Adams did advertising illustration, developing a realistic art style that would become his trademark. From there, Neal went on to a brief stint at Archie Comics and to his own newspaper strip, *Ben Casey*, based on the popular television series. Adams joined DC in 1967 and became an overnight sensation by infusing a new visual vitality into longtime characters. Working closely with Carmine Infantino, Adams quickly became DC's preeminent cover artist during this period, contributing radical and dynamic illustrations to virtually the company's entire line. His work on WORLD'S FINEST COMICS, SUPERMAN, THE SPECTRE, GREEN LANTERN and the Deadman strip made him an instant fan favorite. Adams became one of the most talked-about creator/writer/artist/publishers in the medium and continues to influence, directly and indirectly, today's young comics artists.

DAN ADKINS

Born in 1937, Dan Adkins worked as a commercial artist and magazine illustrator before breaking into the comics industry in the late 1960s. Though he is best known for his inking work on such classic comics as BATMAN, GREEN LANTERN, SUPERMAN, *The Avengers* and *Conan the Barbarian*, Adkins is also an accomplished penciller and writer.

FRANK GIACOIA

Born in Italy in 1925, Frank Giacoia came to the United States at the age of seven. Trained in the Chesler and Iger shops during the early 1940s, Giacoia went on to become one of comicdom's most prolific inkers, with a career spanning five decades. His inks have adorned stories of nearly every major comic-book character from the Big Two publishers, including Batman, Superman, the Flash, Captain America and the Fantastic Four. He passed away in 1989.

DICK GIORDANO

Dick Giordano was part of a creative team that helped change the face of comic books in the late 1960s and early 1970s. Along with writer Dennis O'Neil and penciller Neal Adams, Giordano helped bring Batman back to his roots as a dark, brooding "creature of the night," and brought relevance to comics in the pages of GREEN LANTERN/GREEN ARROW. Giordano began his career as an artist for Charlton Comics in 1952 and became the company's editor-in-chief in 1965. In that capacity, he revamped the Charlton line by adding an emphasis on such heroes as the Question, Captain Atom, and the Blue Beetle. In 1967, Giordano came over to DC for a three-year stint as editor, bringing with him many of the talents who would help shape the industry of the day, including Dennis O'Neil, Jim Aparo, and Steve Skeates. Winner of numerous industry awards, Giordano later returned to DC, rising to the position of Vice President-Executive Editor before "retiring" in 1993 to once again pursue a full-time career as penciller and inker.

DENNIS O'NEIL

Dennis O'Neil began his career as a comic-book writer in 1965 at Charlton, where then-editor Dick Giordano assigned him to several features. When Giordano moved to DC, O'Neil soon followed. At DC, O'Neil scripted several series for Giordano and Julius Schwartz, quickly becoming one of the most respected writers in comics. O'Neil earned a reputation for being able to "revamp" such characters as Superman, Green Lantern, Captain Marvel — and the Batman, whom O'Neil (with the help of Neal Adams and Giordano) brought back to his roots as a dark, mysterious, gothic avenger. Besides being the most important Batman writer of the 1970s, O'Neil served as an editor at both Marvel and DC. After a long tenure as group editor of the Batman line of titles, he retired to write full-time. O'Neil, fittingly, wrote a Green Lantern novel for Pocket Books, to be published in 2005.

JULIUS SCHWARTZ

Perhaps more than any other editor, Julie Schwartz helped shape the face of the comic-book medium. Born in New York in 1915, Schwartz was one of the earliest and most vocal fans of the literary genre that became known as "science fiction," in time establishing himself as an agent for Ray Bradbury, Henry Kuttner, Robert Bloch and other giants of the SF and fantasy field. Hired as a DC editor in 1944, Schwartz brought an inventiveness and dedication to the craft of storytelling that soon made him a legend in his own right, a man known for employing only the finest and most talented writers and artists in the field. His true legacy, however, came to flower in the 1950s and early 1960s, at a time when the future of comics was at best dubious. Schwartz — together with John Broome, Robert Kanigher, Gardner Fox, and others — revived and revitalized the all but abandoned super-hero genre, transforming such nearly forgotten heroes as the Flash and Green Lantern into super-stars. Julie passed away on February 8, 2004, leaving behind an amazing legacy.

BERNI WRIGHTSON

Born in 1948, Berni Wrightson is best known as the co-creator of the Swamp Thing. He has disturbed impressionable readers for nearly two decades with his uncanny renderings of imaginary horrors. At present he resides in Los Angeles, providing book covers and movie production art. His most recent efforts include covers for Stephen King's *The Dark Tower* series. In Hollywood, he did designs for Lion's Gates' forthcoming *Ghost Rider* film.